FAIRY TAIL

5

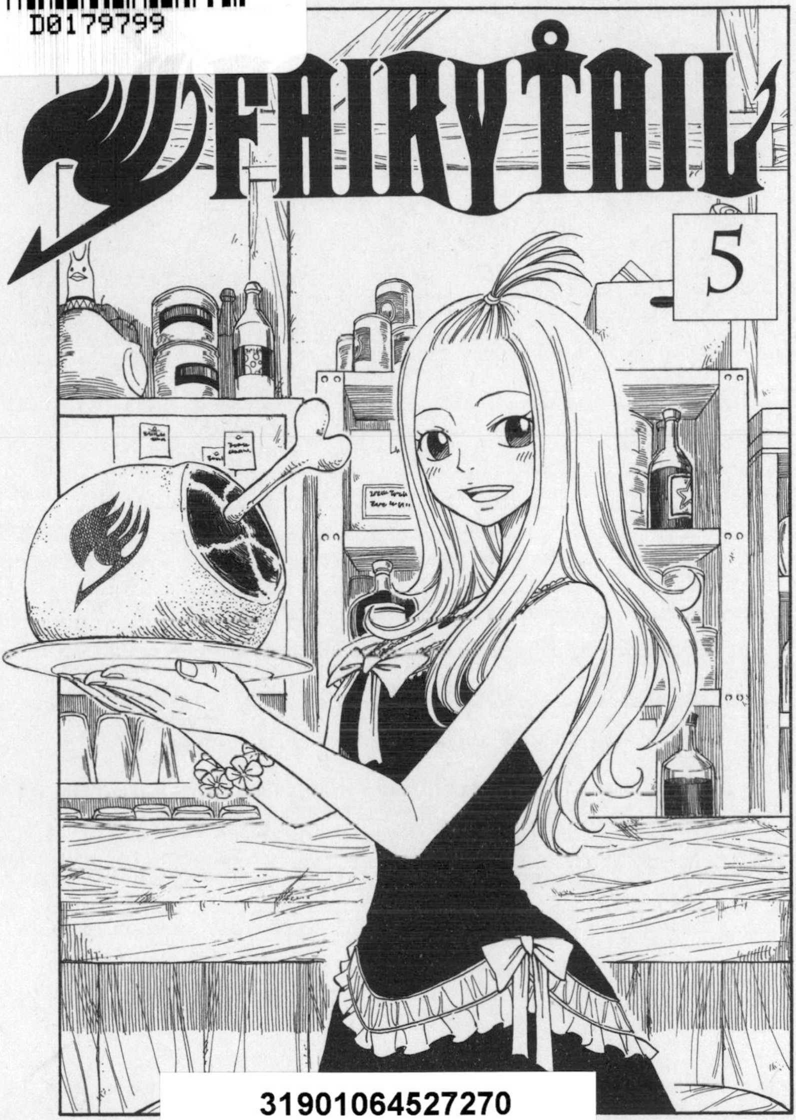

HIRO MASHIMA

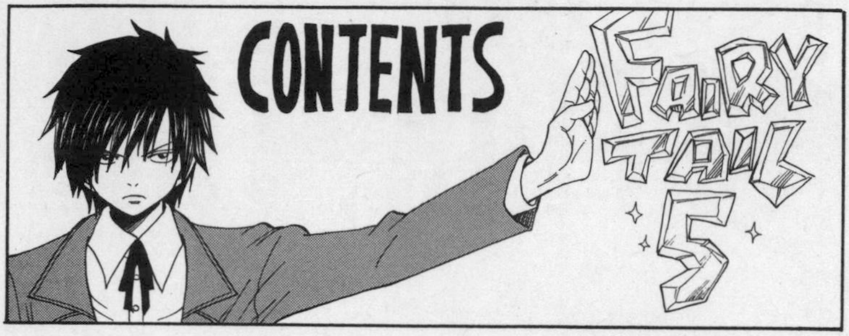
CONTENTS
FAIRY TAIL
5

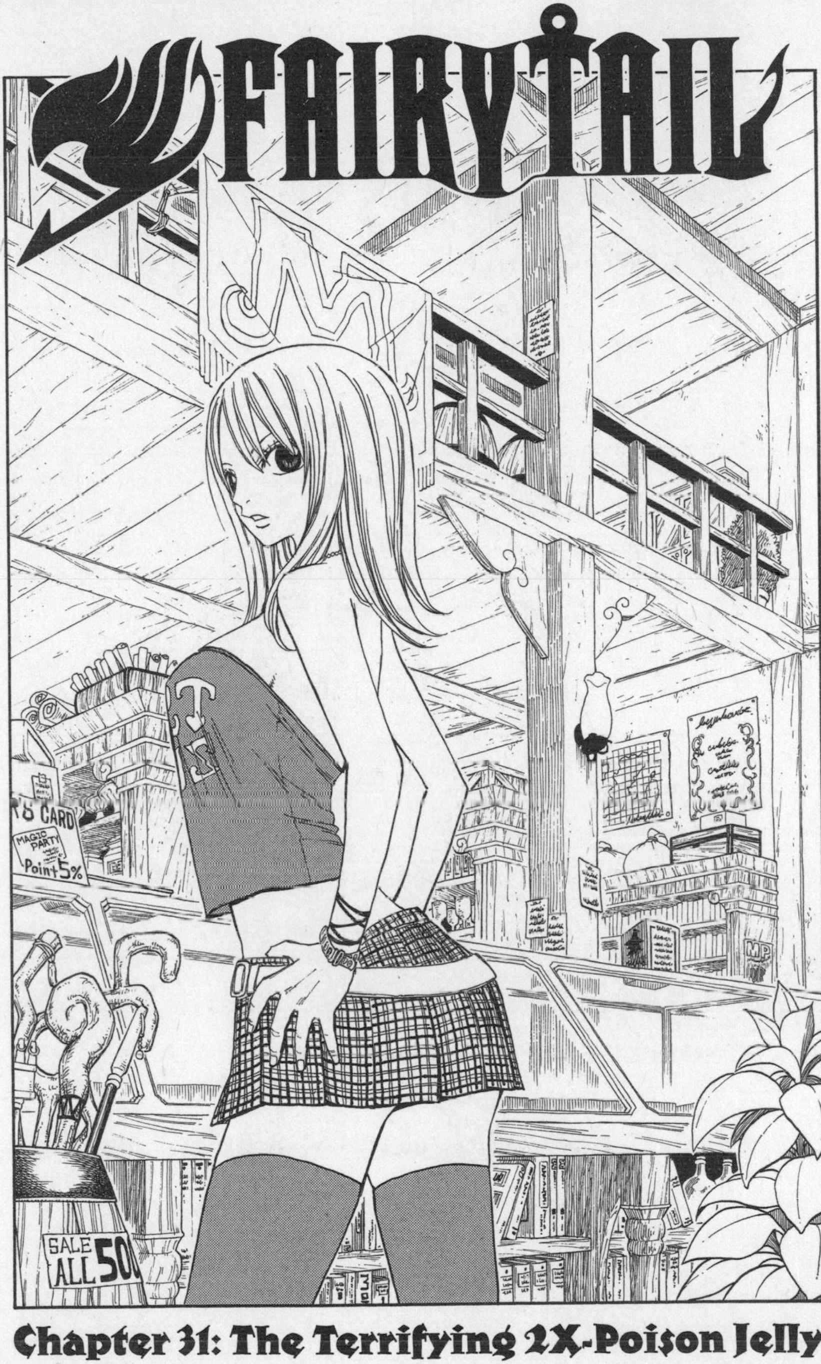
FAIRY TAIL
'S CARD
MAGIC PARTY
Point 5%
SALE
ALL 50
MP

Chapter 31: The Terrifying 2X-Poison Jelly

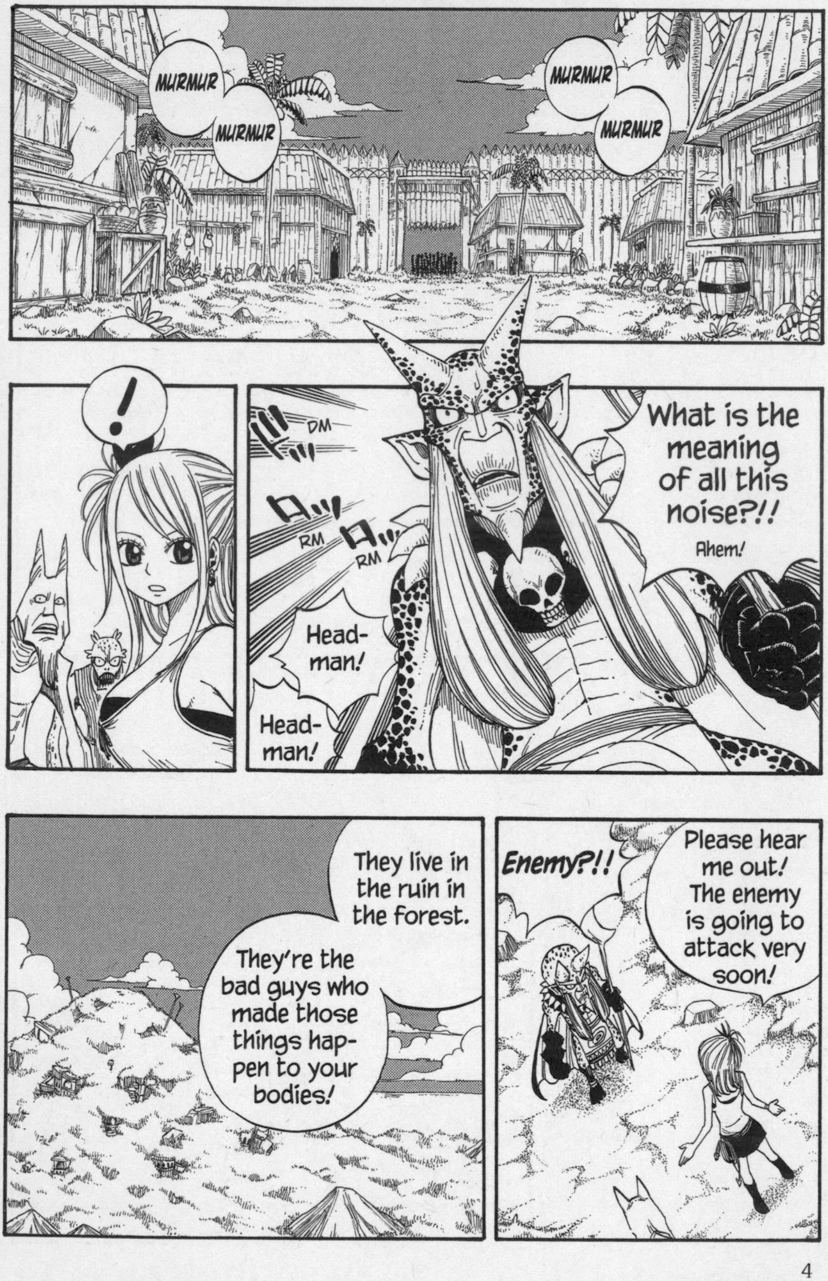
MURMUR
MURMUR
MURMUR
MURMUR
What is the meaning of all this noise?!!
Ahem!
DM
RM
RM
Head-man!
Head-man!
!
Please hear me out! The enemy is going to attack very soon!
Enemy?!!
They live in the ruin in the forest.
They're the bad guys who made those things hap-pen to your bodies!

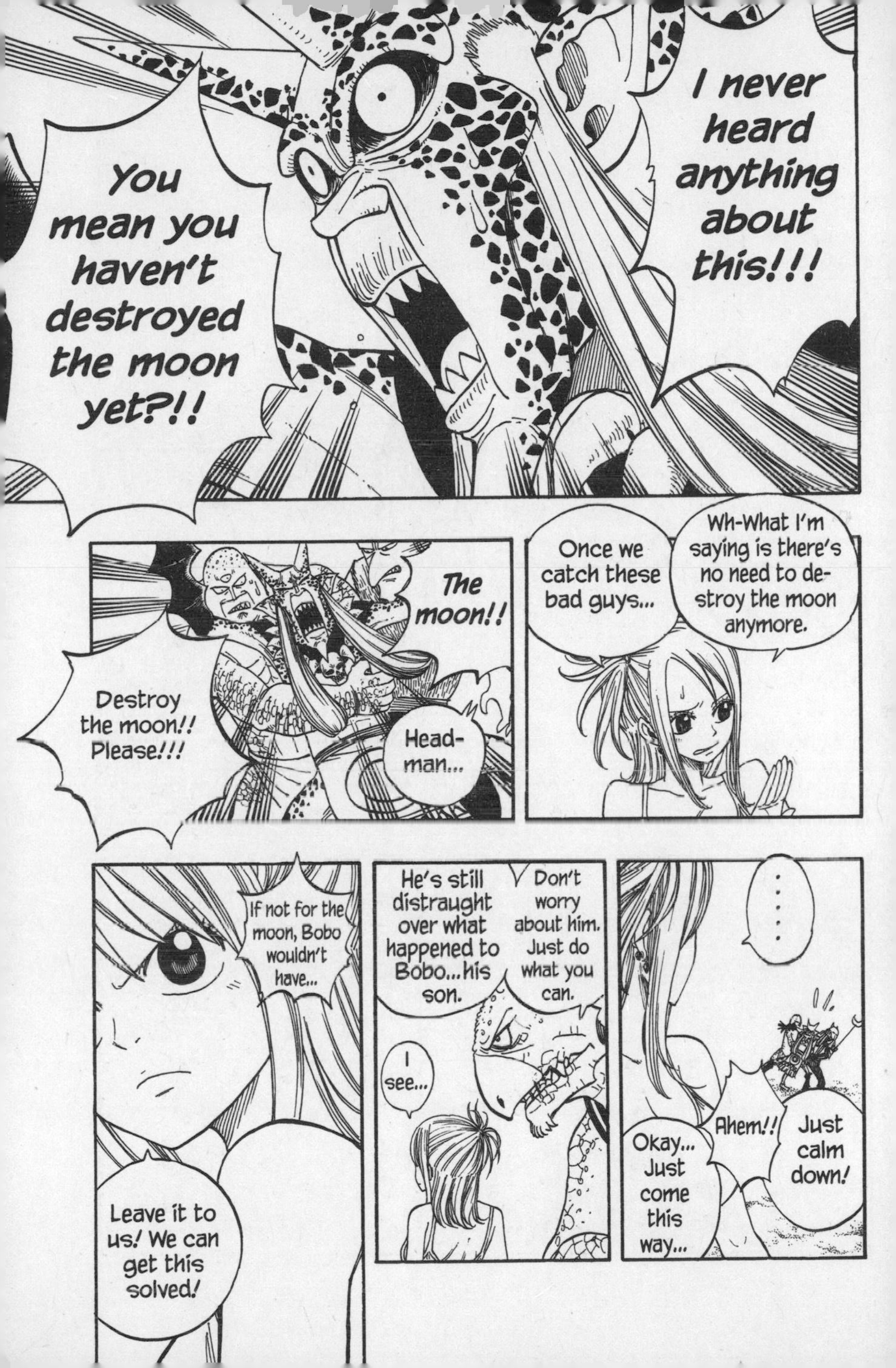
I never heard anything about this!!!
You mean you haven't destroyed the moon yet?!!
Wh-What I'm saying is there's no need to de-stroy the moon anymore.
Once we catch these bad guys...
The moon!!
Head-man...
Destroy the moon!! Please!!!
......
Just calm down!
Ahem!!
Okay... Just come this way...
Don't worry about him. Just do what you can.
He's still distraught over what happened to Bobo...his son.
I see...
If not for the moon, Bobo wouldn't have...
Leave it to us! We can get this solved!

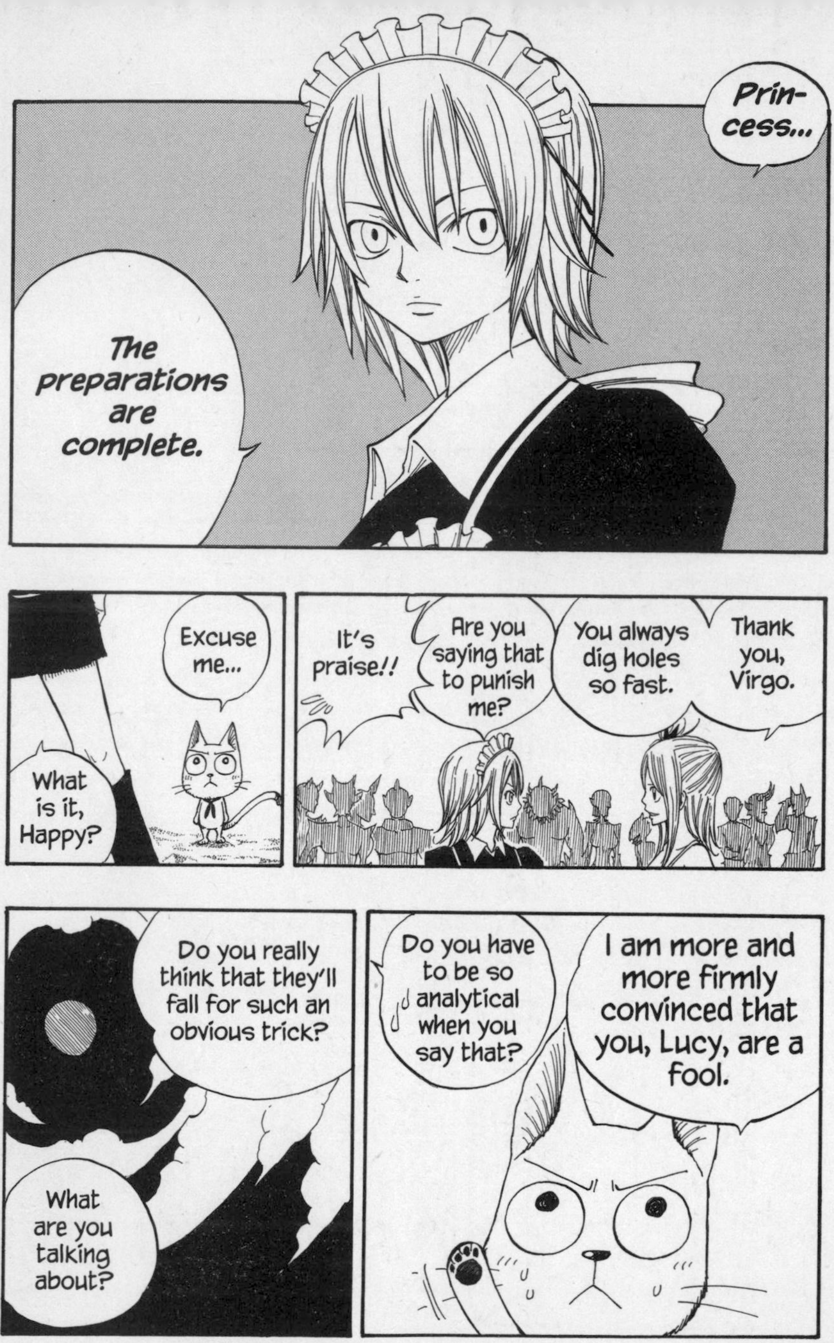
Prin-cess...
The preparations are complete.
Thank you, Virgo.
You always dig holes so fast.
Are you saying that to punish me?
It's praise!!
Excuse me...
What is it, Happy?
I am more and more firmly convinced that you, Lucy, are a fool.
Do you have to be so analytical when you say that?
Do you really think that they'll fall for such an obvious trick?
What are you talking about?

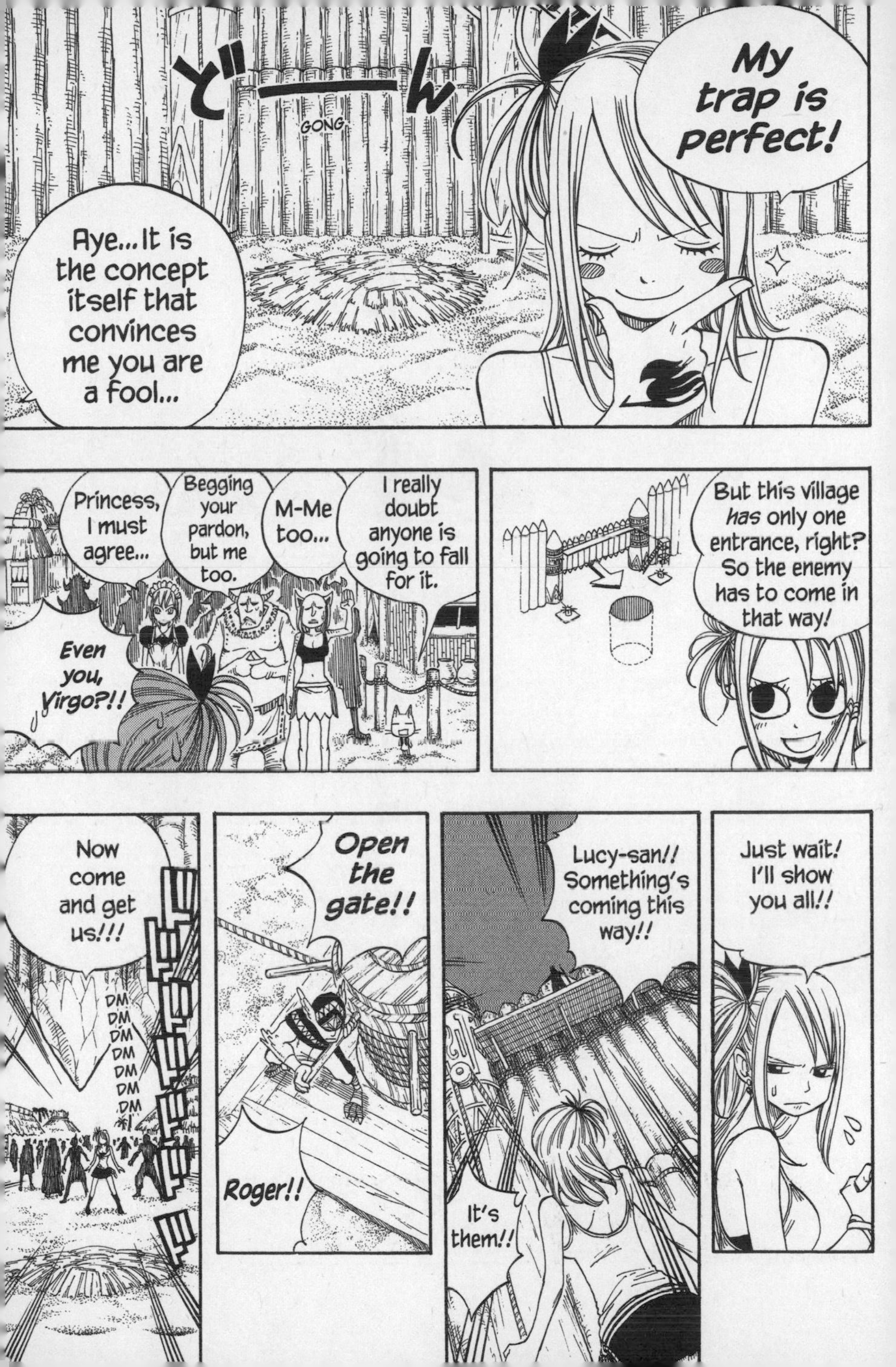
My trap is perfect!
GONG
Aye... It is the concept itself that convinces me you are a fool...
But this village *has* only one entrance, right? So the enemy has to come in that way!
I really doubt anyone is going to fall for it.
M-Me too...
Begging your pardon, but me too.
Princess, I must agree...
Even you, Virgo?!!
Just wait! I'll show you all!!
Lucy-san!! Something's coming this way!!
It's them!!
Open the gate!!
Roger!!
Now come and get us!!!
DM DM DM DM DM DM DM

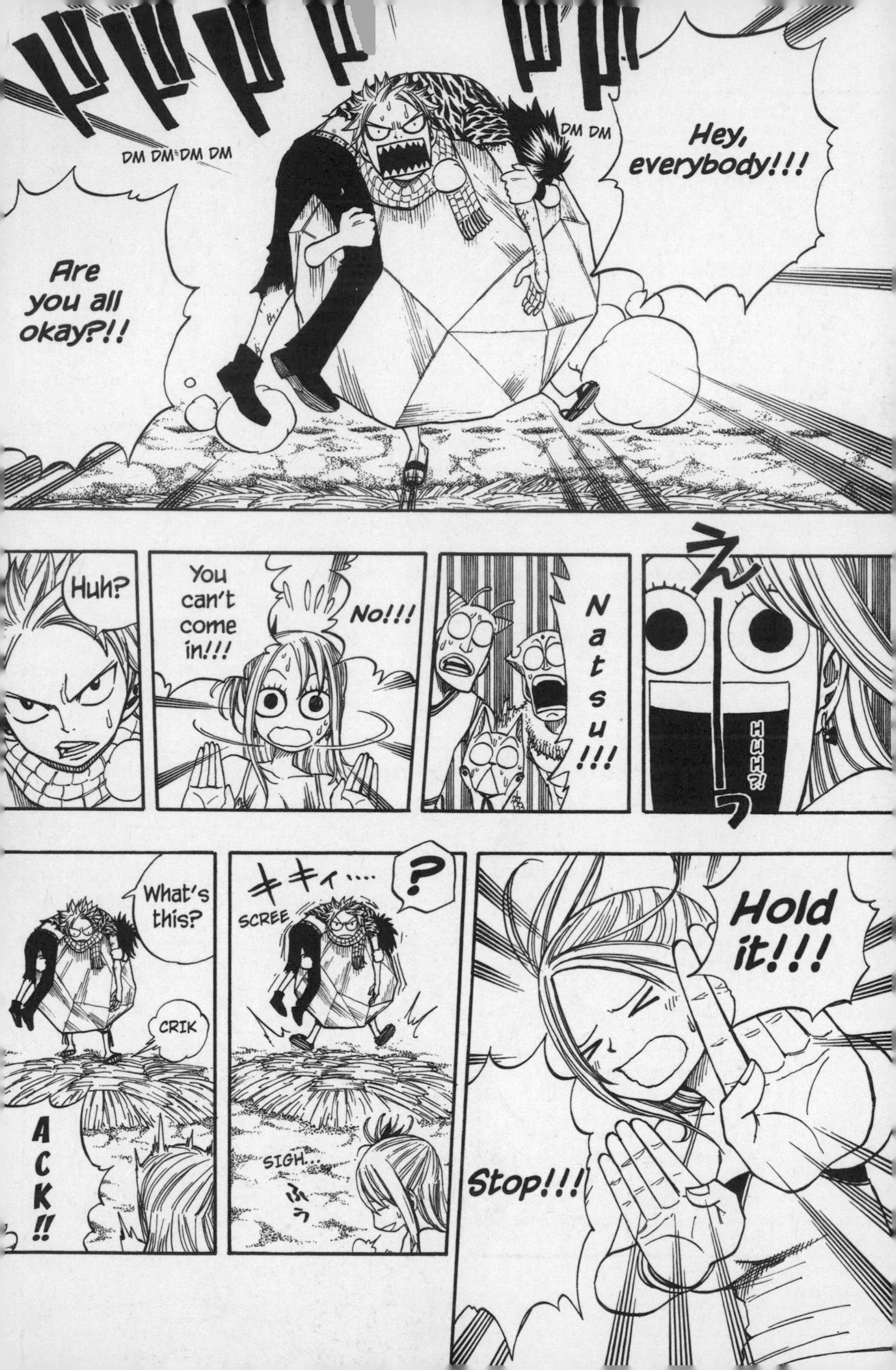
DM DM
Hey, everybody!!!
DM DM DM DM
Are you all okay?!!
えーっ
HUH?!
Natsu!!!
You can't come in!!!
No!!!
Huh?
Hold it!!!
Stop!!!
?
キキィ…
SCREE
SIGH...
ふっ
What's this?
CRIK
ACK!!

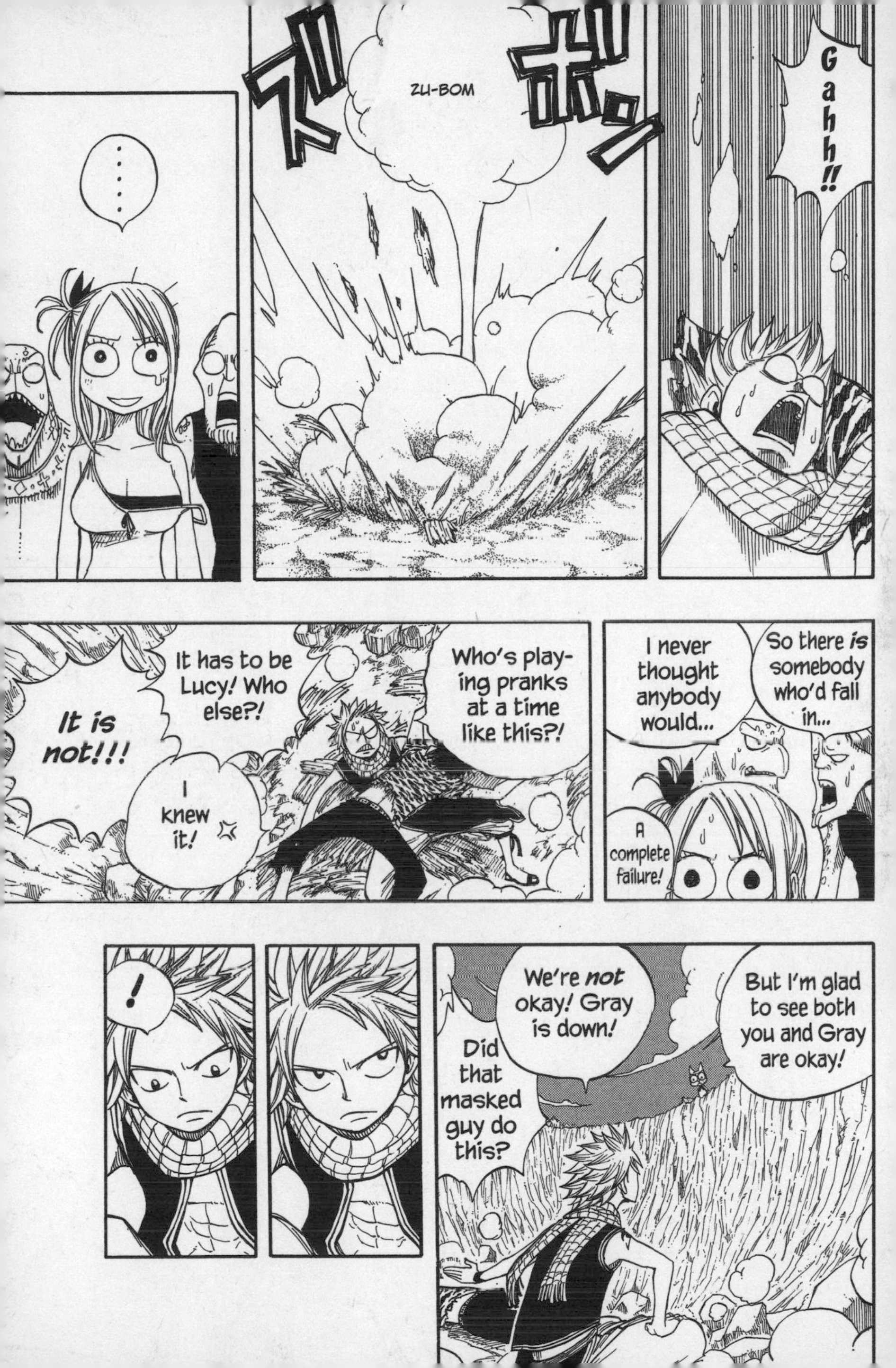
Gahh!!
ZU-BOM
......
So there *is* somebody who'd fall in...
I never thought anybody would...
A complete failure!
Who's play-ing pranks at a time like this?!
It has to be Lucy! Who else?!
It is not!!!
I knew it!
But I'm glad to see both you and Gray are okay!
We're *not* okay! Gray is down!
Did that masked guy do this?
!

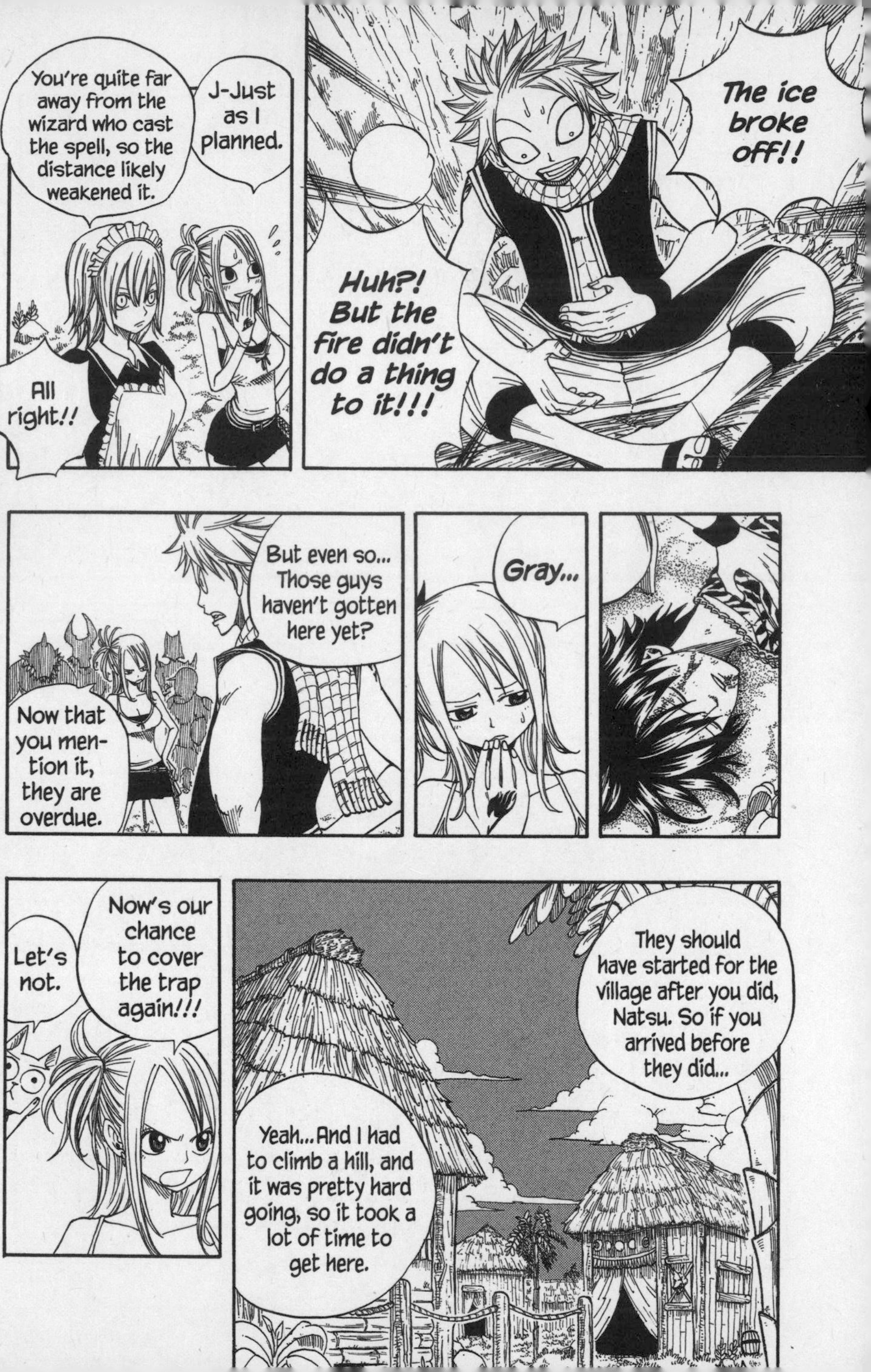
The ice broke off!!
Huh?! But the fire didn't do a thing to it!!!
J-Just as I planned.
You're quite far away from the wizard who cast the spell, so the distance likely weakened it.
All right!!
Gray...
But even so... Those guys haven't gotten here yet?
Now that you mention it, they are overdue.
They should have started for the village after you did, Natsu. So if you arrived before they did...
Yeah...And I had to climb a hill, and it was pretty hard going, so it took a lot of time to get here.
Now's our chance to cover the trap again!!!
Let's not.

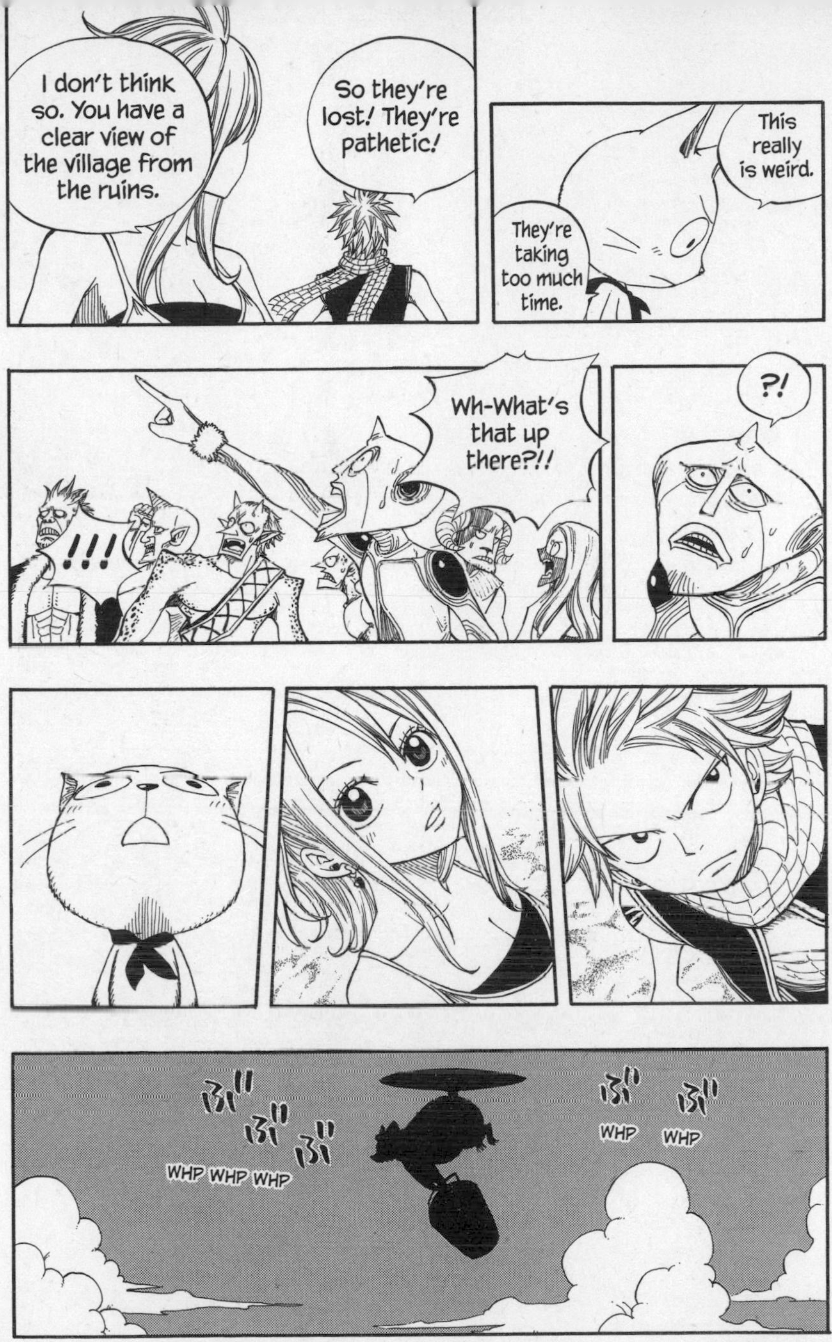
This really is weird.
They're taking too much time.
So they're lost! They're pathetic!
I don't think so. You have a clear view of the village from the ruins.
?!
Wh-What's that up there?!!
!!!
WHP
WHP
WHP WHP WHP

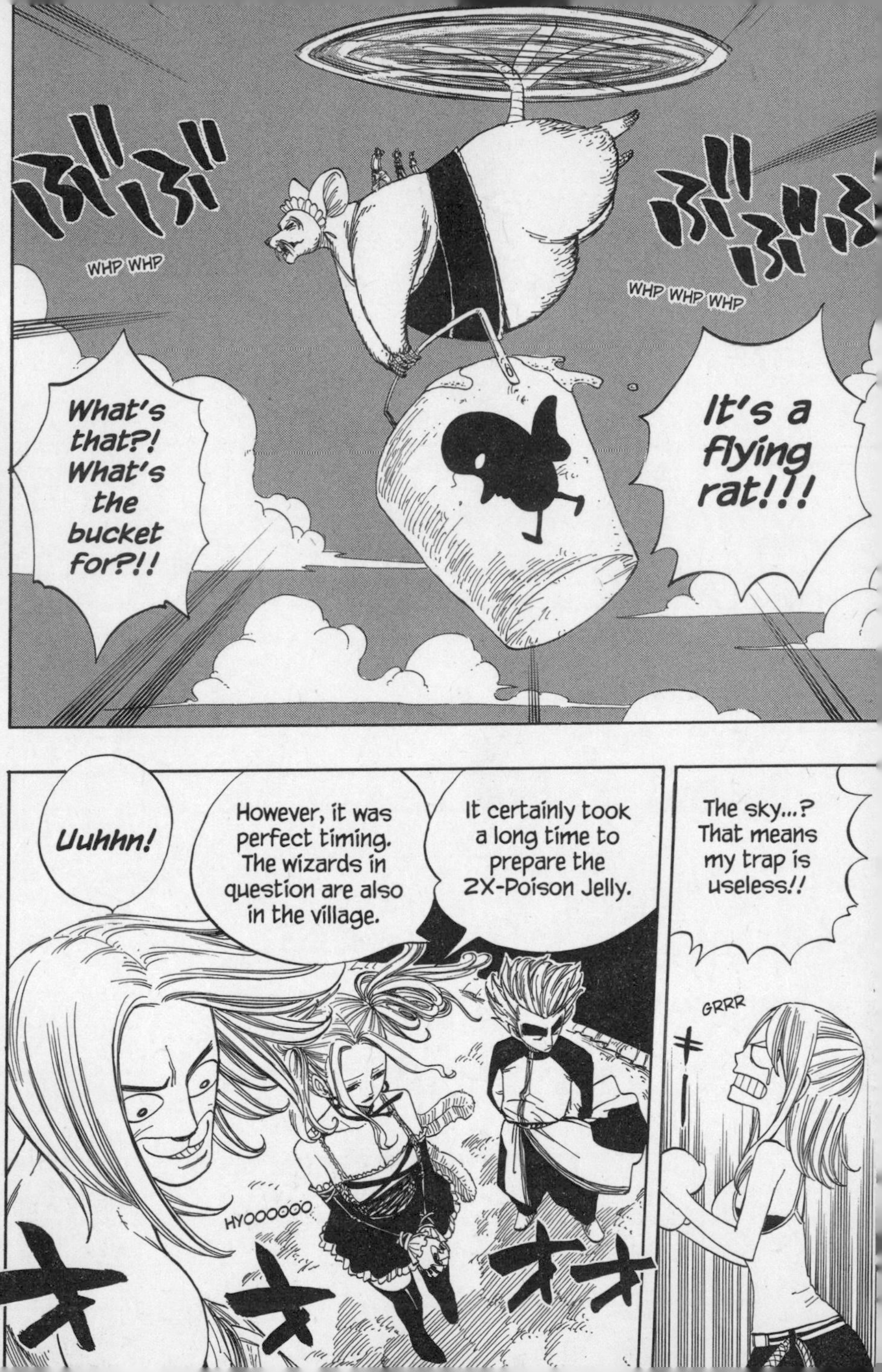
WHP WHP WHP
It's a flying rat!!!
WHP WHP
What's that?! What's the bucket for?!!
The sky...? That means my trap is useless!!
GRRR
It certainly took a long time to prepare the 2X-Poison Jelly.
However, it was perfect timing. The wizards in question are also in the village.
Uuhhn!
HYOOOOOO

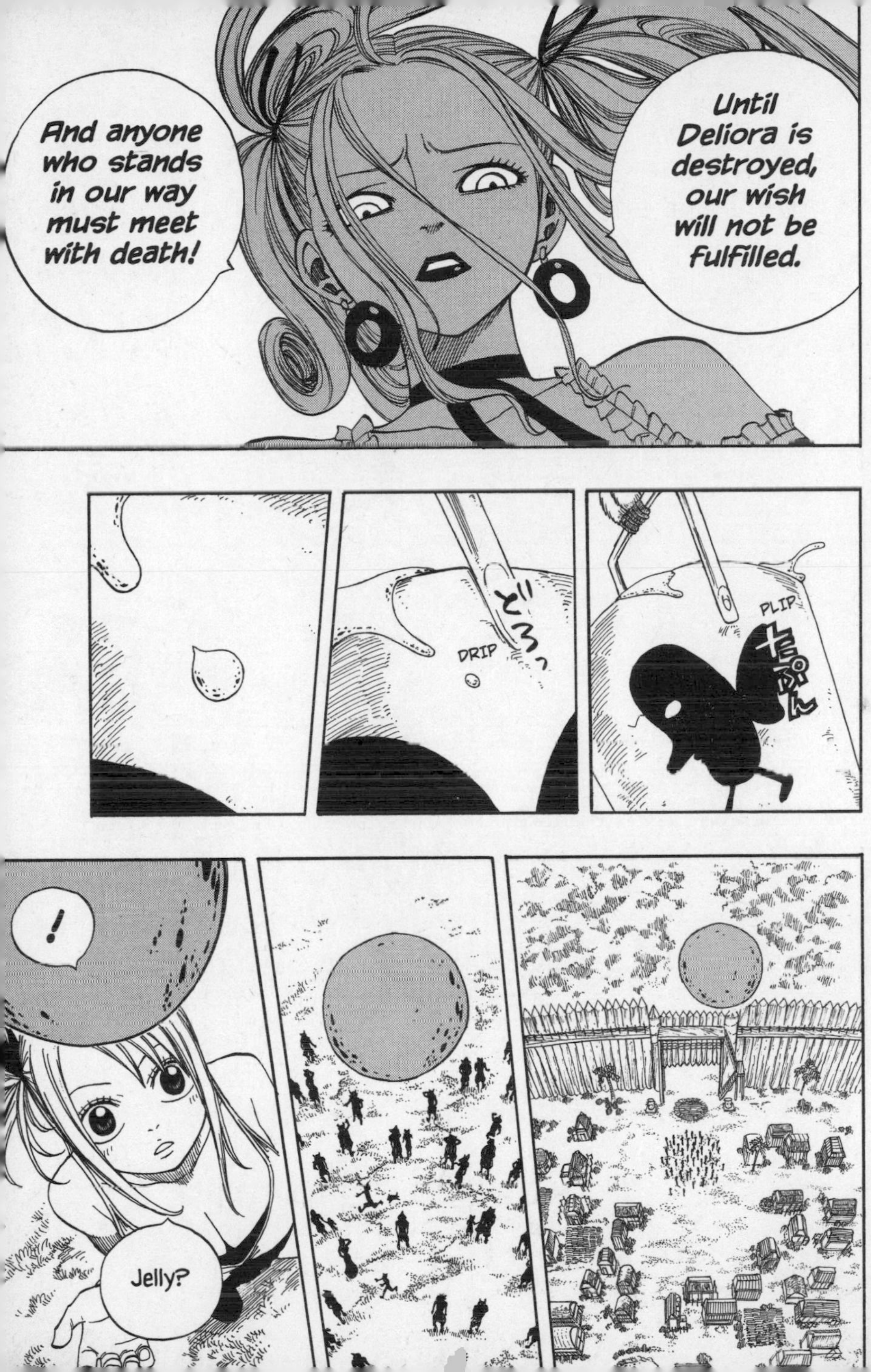

Until Deliora is destroyed, our wish will not be fulfilled.
And anyone who stands in our way must meet with death!
PLIP
どろっ
DRIP
!
Jelly?

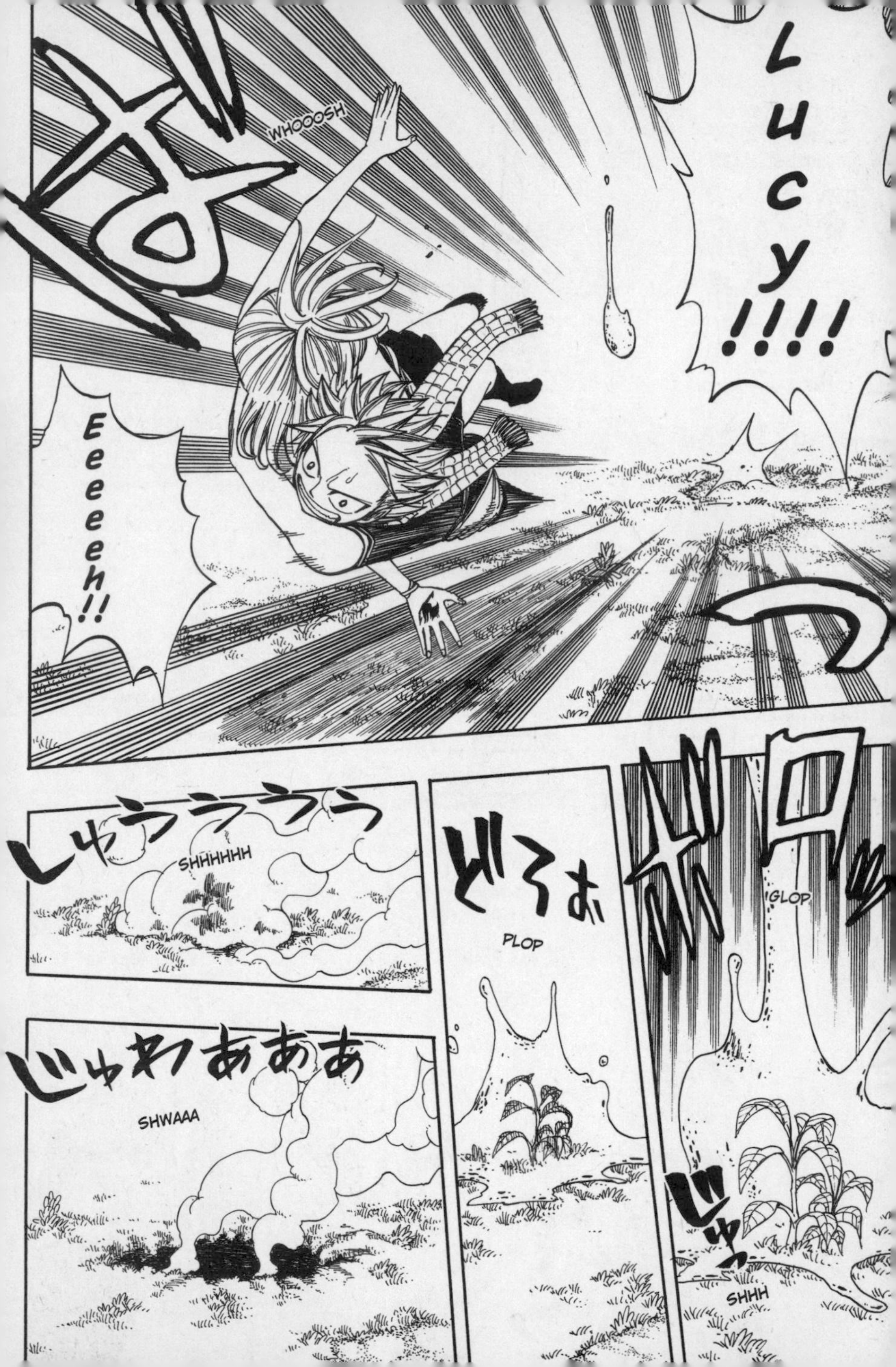

Lucy!!!!
WHOOOSH
Eeeeeeh!!
GLOP
SHHH
PLOP
SHHHHHH
SHWAAA

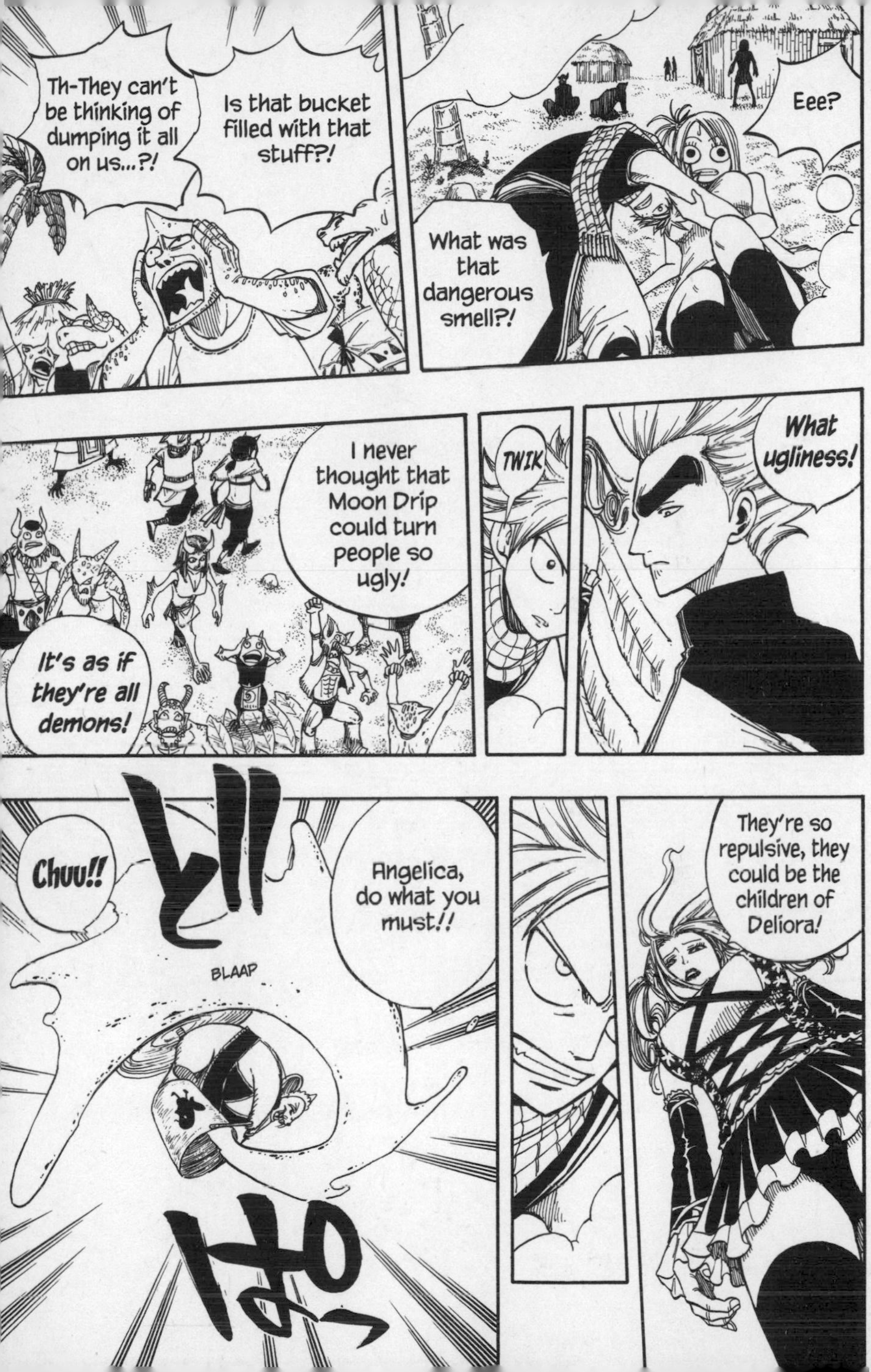
Eee?
What was that dangerous smell?!
Is that bucket filled with that stuff?!
Th-They can't be thinking of dumping it all on us...?!
What ugliness!
TWIK
I never thought that Moon Drip could turn people so ugly!
It's as if they're all demons!
They're so repulsive, they could be the children of Deliora!
Angelica, do what you must!!
Chuu!!
BLAAP

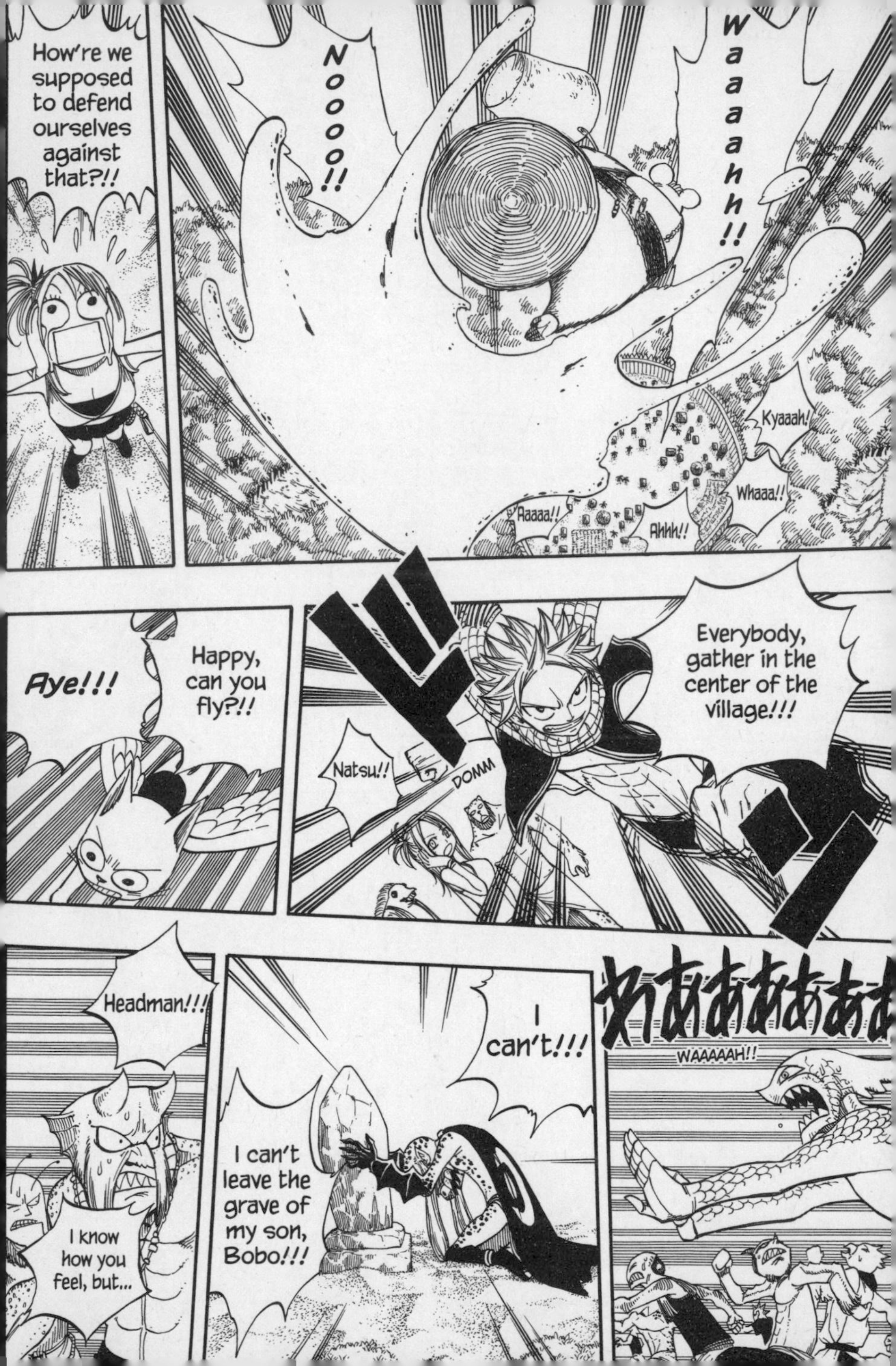

Waaaahh!!
Noooooo!!
Kyaaah!
Whaaa!!
Ahhh!!
Raaaa!!
How're we supposed to defend ourselves against that?!!
Everybody, gather in the center of the village!!!
Natsu!!
DOMM
Happy, can you fly?!!
Aye!!!
わああああああ
WAAAAAH!!
I can't!!!
I can't leave the grave of my son, Bobo!!!
Headman!!!
I know how you feel, but...

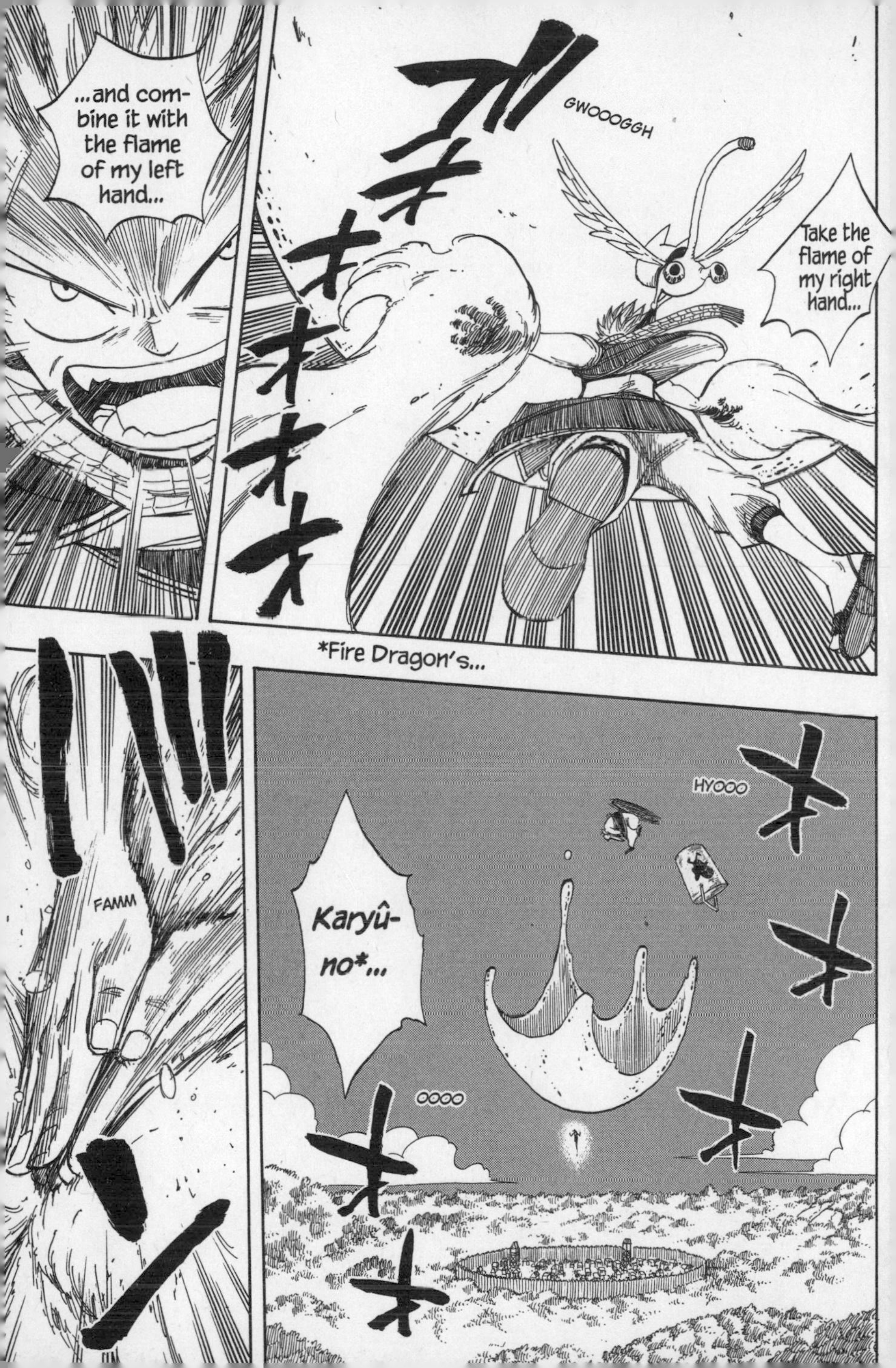
GWOOOGGH
Take the flame of my right hand...
...and combine it with the flame of my left hand...
*Fire Dragon's...
HYOOO
Karyû-no*...
OOOO
FAMM

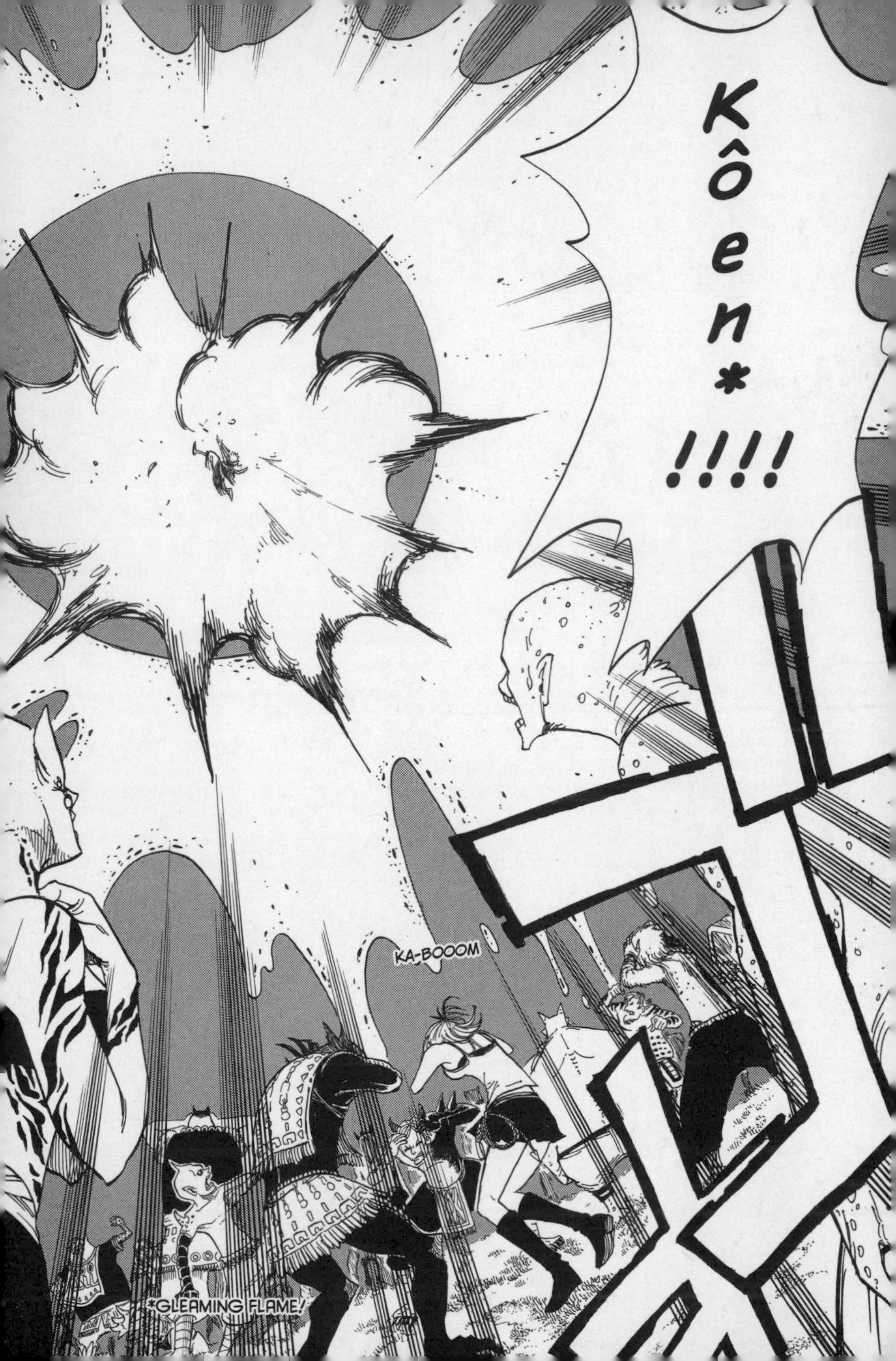
Kôen*!!!!
KA-BOOOM
*GLEAMING FLAME!

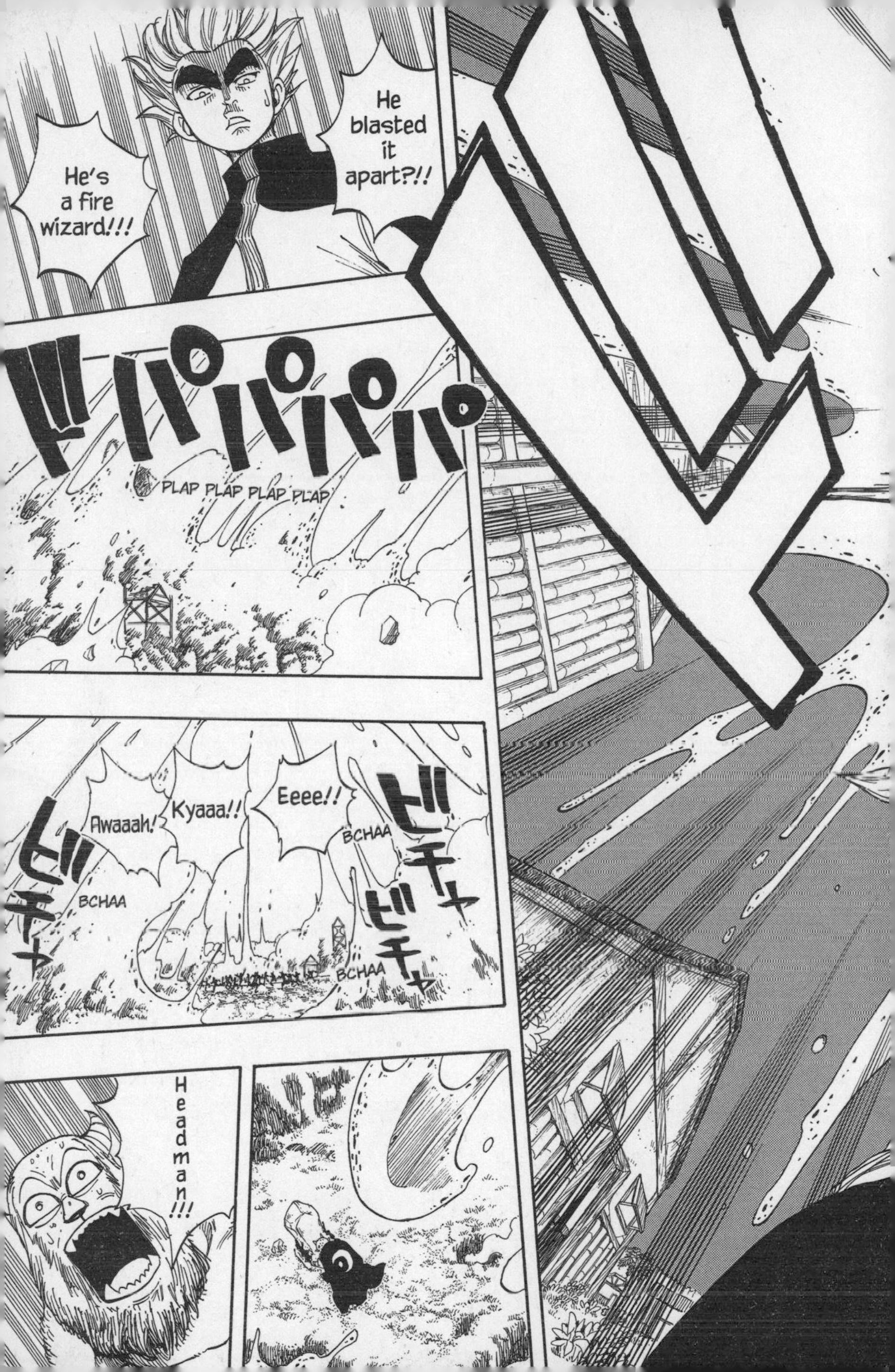
He blasted it apart?!!
He's a fire wizard!!!
ドパパパパ
PLAP PLAP PLAP PLAP
ビチャ
BCHAA
Eeee!!
Kyaaa!!
Awaaah!
ビチャ
BCHAA
ビチャ
BCHAA
Headman!!!

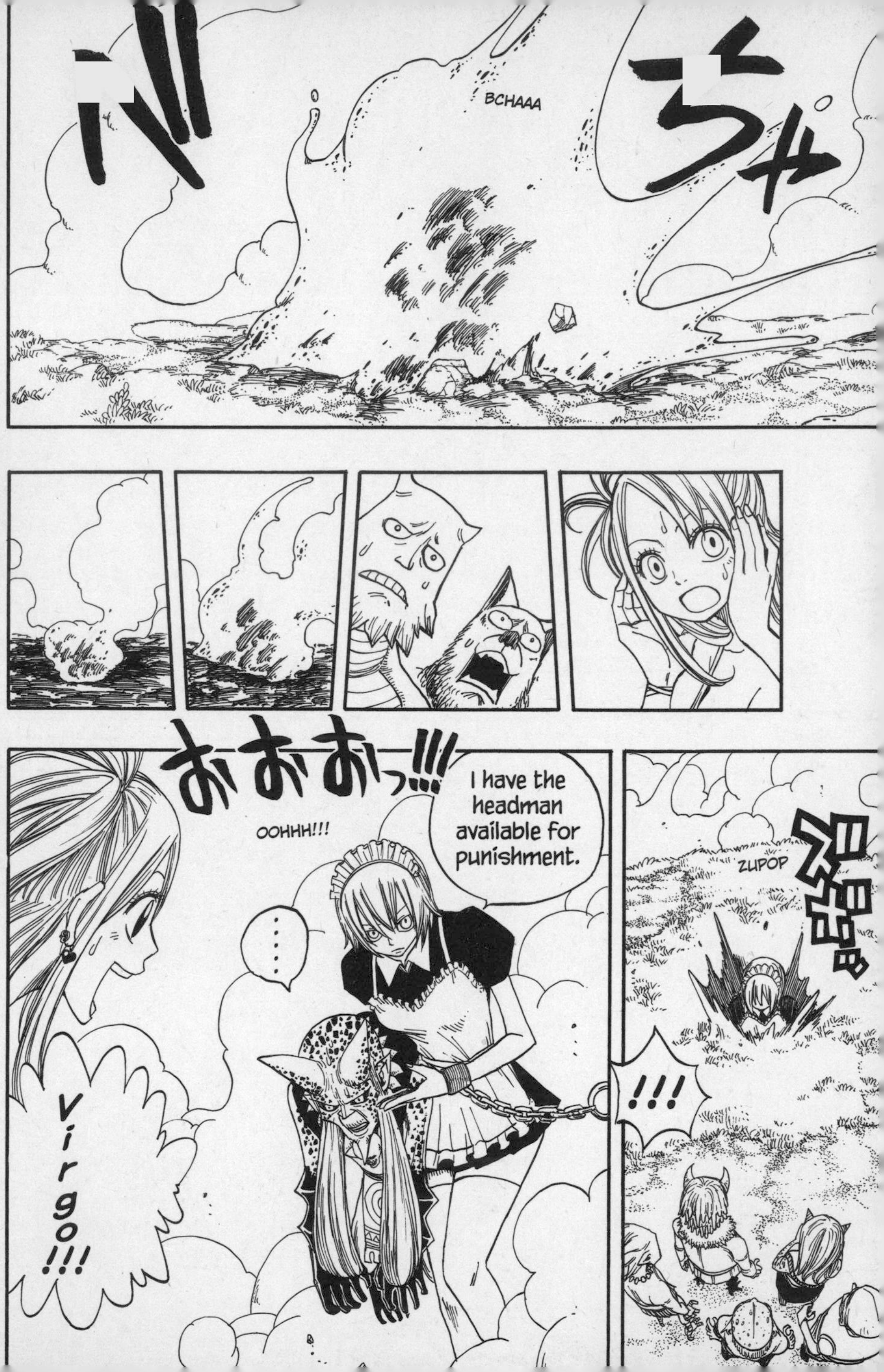
BCHAAA
ZUPOP
!!!
おおおっ!!!
OOHHH!!!
I have the headman available for punishment.
......
Virgo!!!

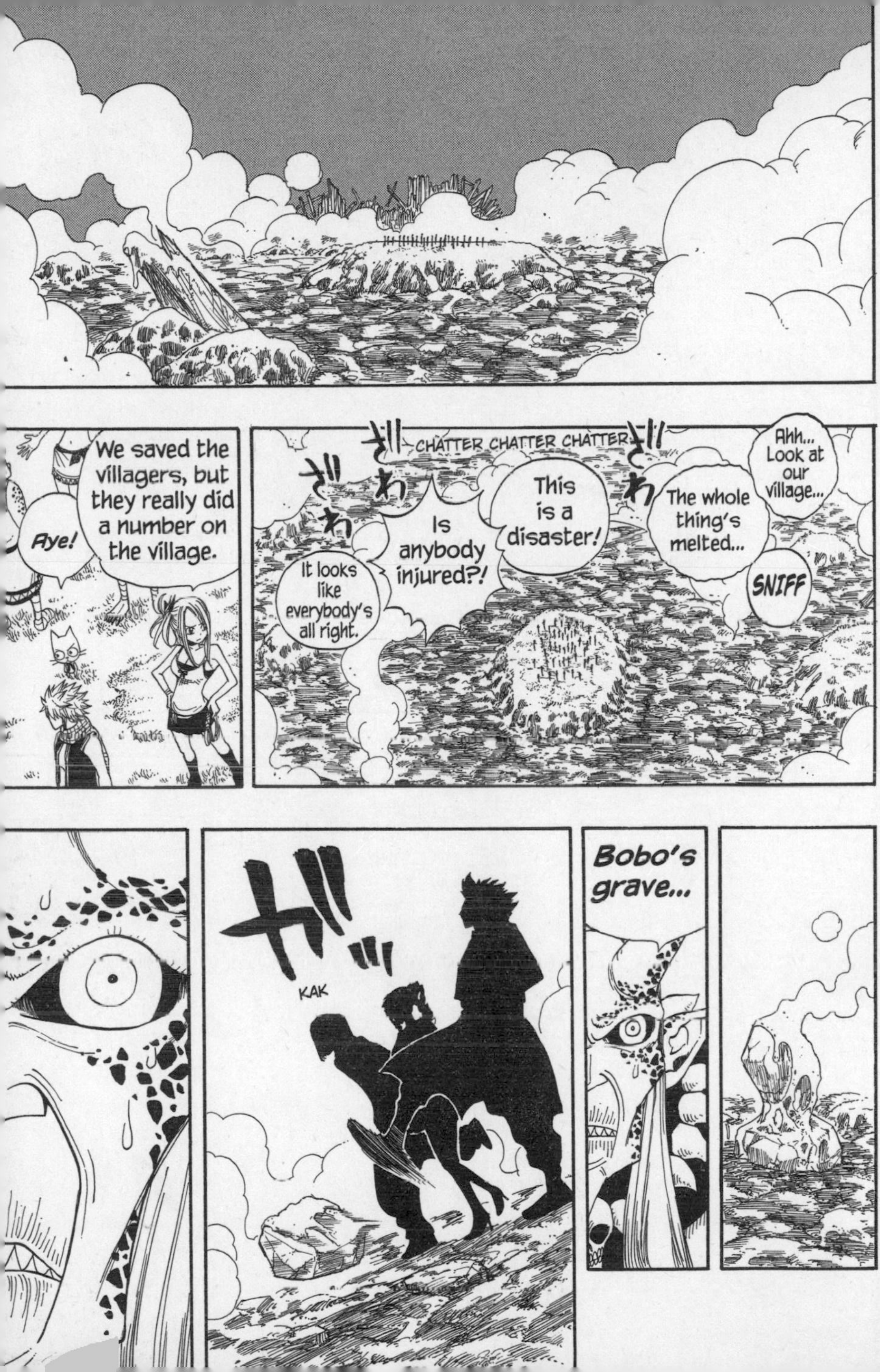

Ahh... Look at our village...
SNIFF
The whole thing's melted...
ざわ
CHATTER CHATTER CHATTER
ざわ
This is a disaster!
Is anybody injured?!
ざわ
It looks like everybody's all right.
We saved the villagers, but they really did a number on the village.
Aye!
Bobo's grave...
ザッ
KAK

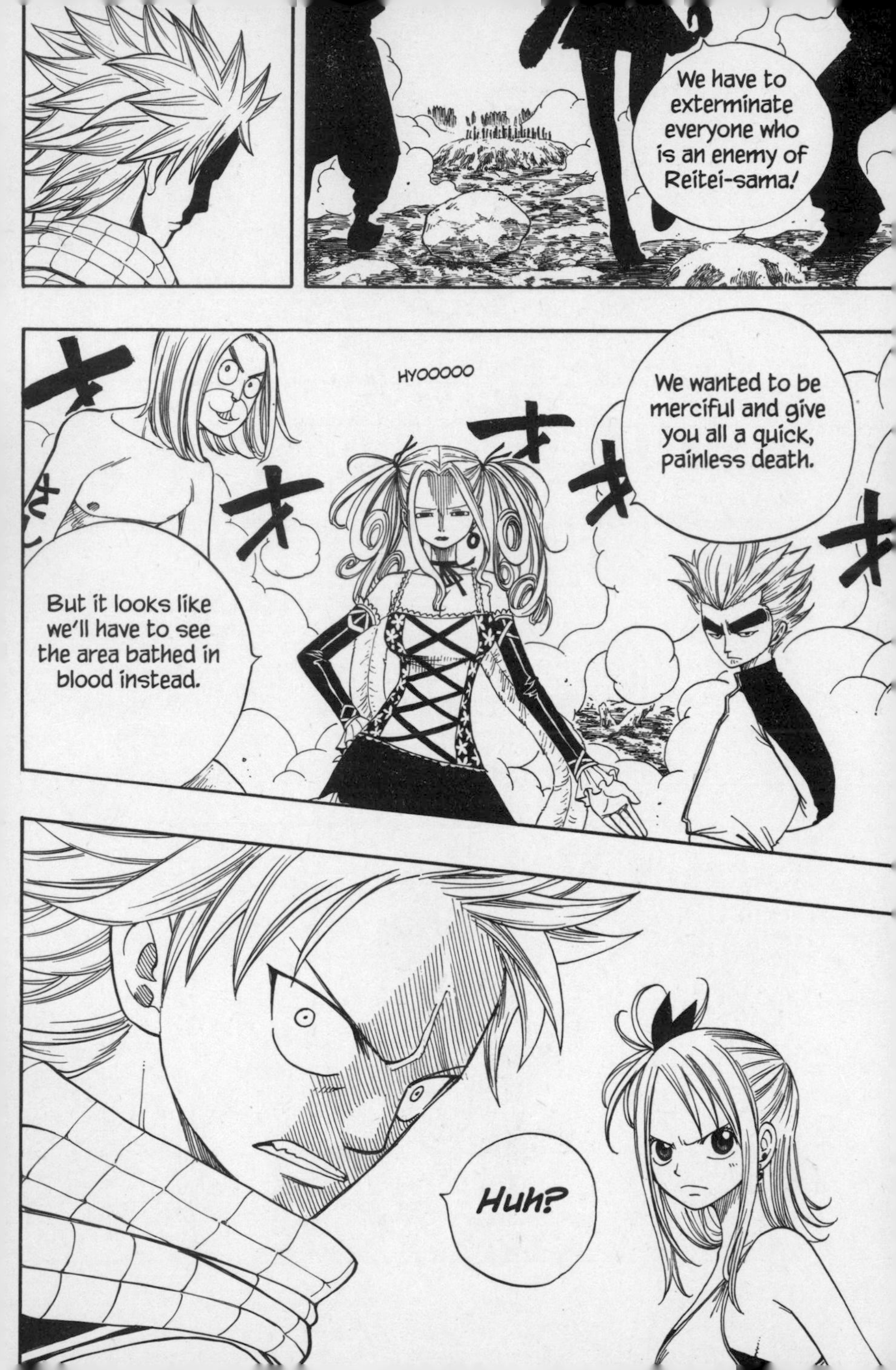
We have to exterminate everyone who is an enemy of Reitei-sama!
We wanted to be merciful and give you all a quick, painless death.
HYOOOOO
But it looks like we'll have to see the area bathed in blood instead.
Huh?

FAIRY TAIL

Chapter 32: Natsu vs. Wave-Motion Yûka

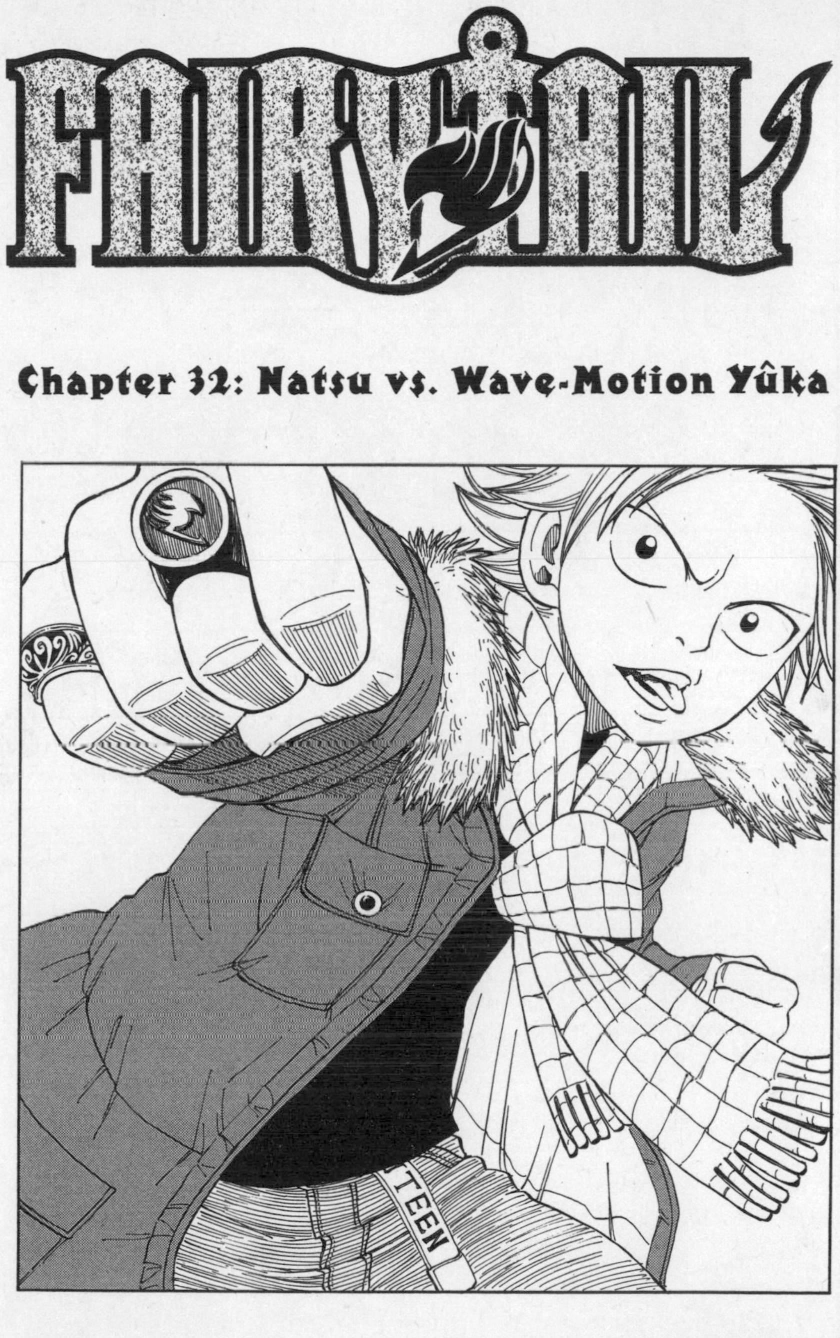

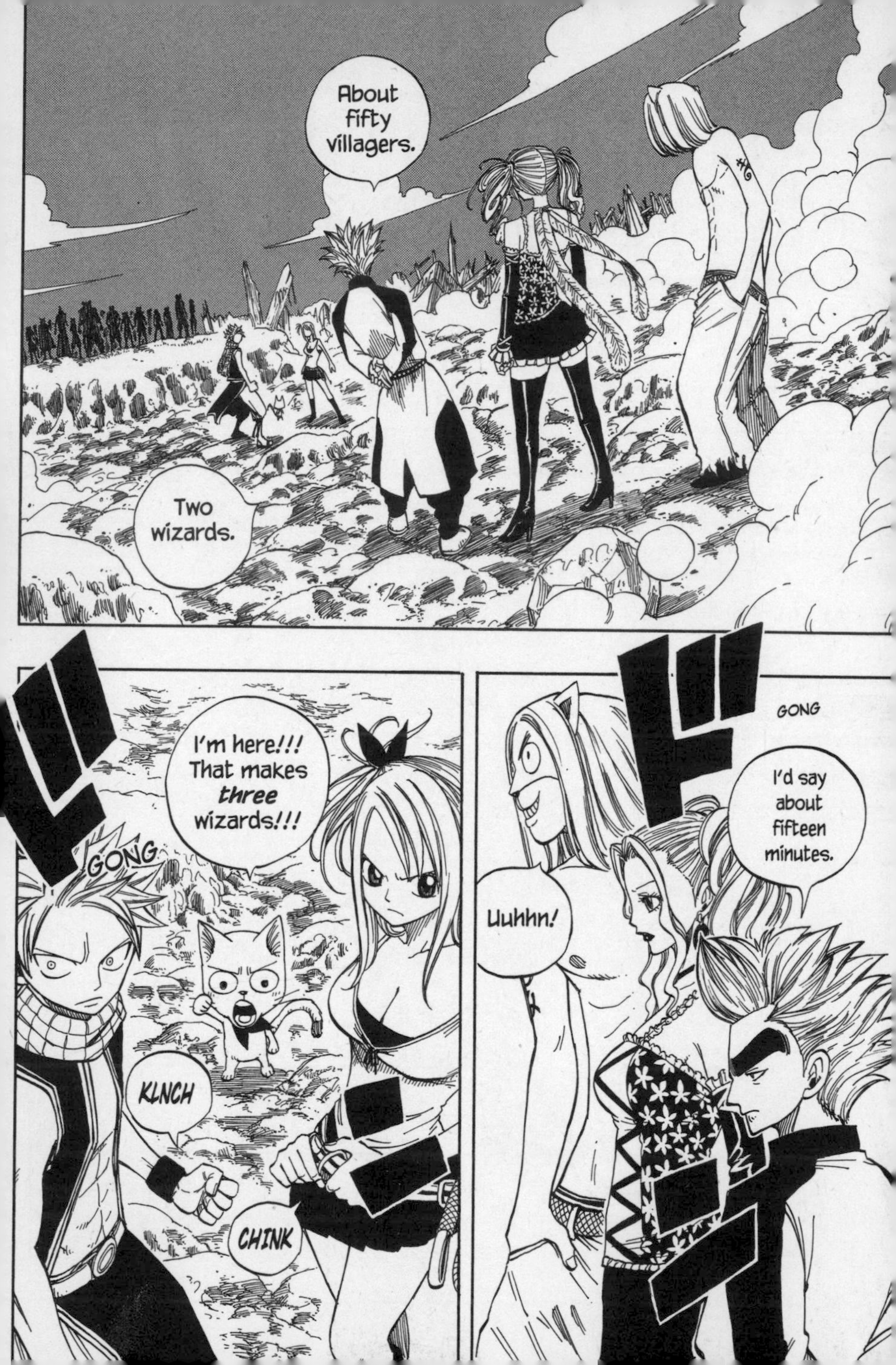
About fifty villagers.
Two wizards.
GONG
I'd say about fifteen minutes.
Uuhhn!
I'm here!!! That makes *three* wizards!!!
GONG
KLNCH
CHINK

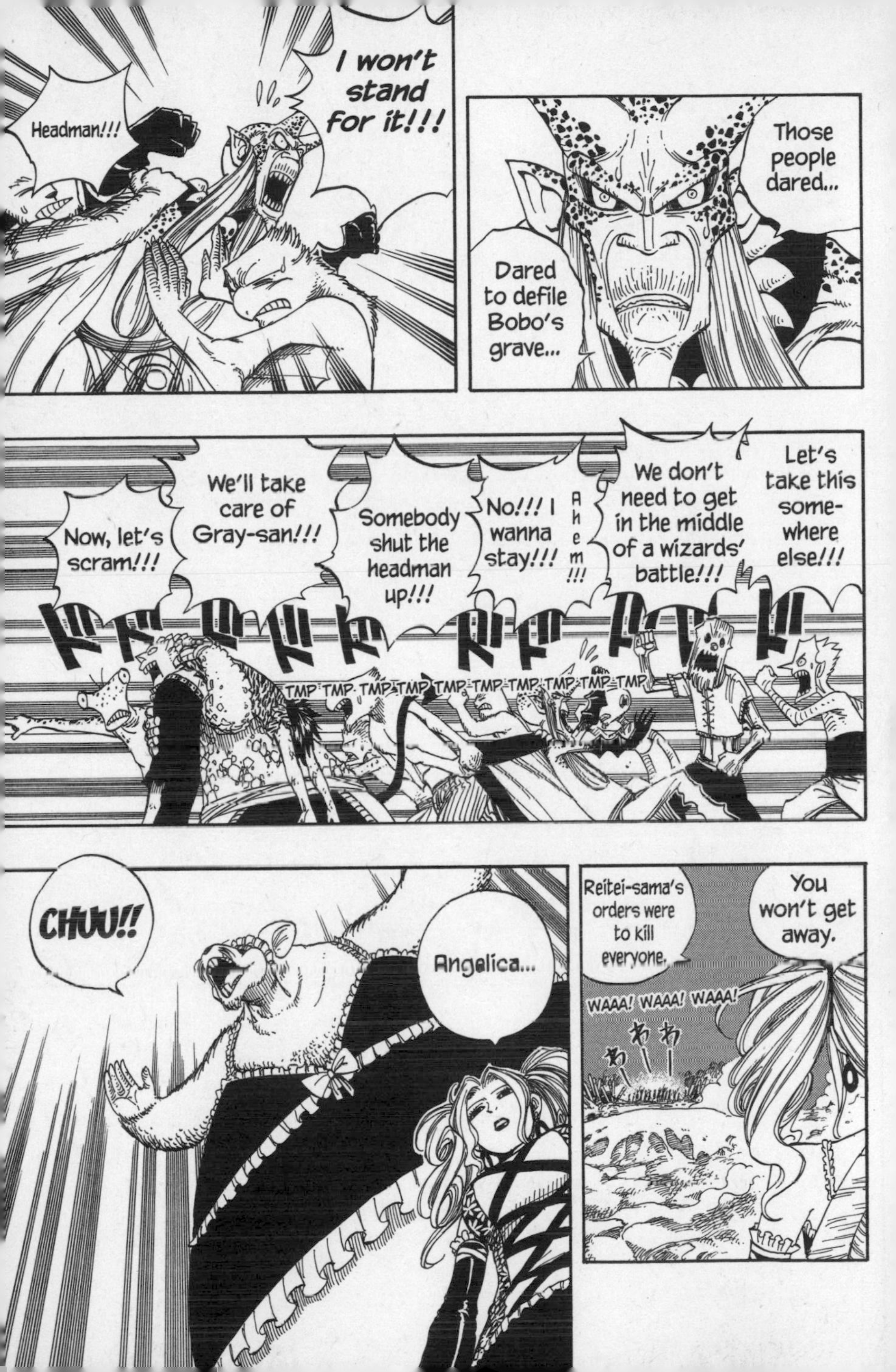
Those people dared...
Dared to defile Bobo's grave...
I won't stand for it!!!
Headman!!!
Let's take this some-where else!!!
We don't need to get in the middle of a wizards' battle!!!
Ahem!!!
No!!! I wanna stay!!!
Somebody shut the headman up!!!
We'll take care of Gray-san!!!
Now, let's scram!!!
TMP TMP TMP TMP TMP TMP TMP TMP TMP TMP
You won't get away.
Reitei-sama's orders were to kill everyone.
WAAA! WAAA! WAAA!
わ わ わ
Angelica...
CHUU!!

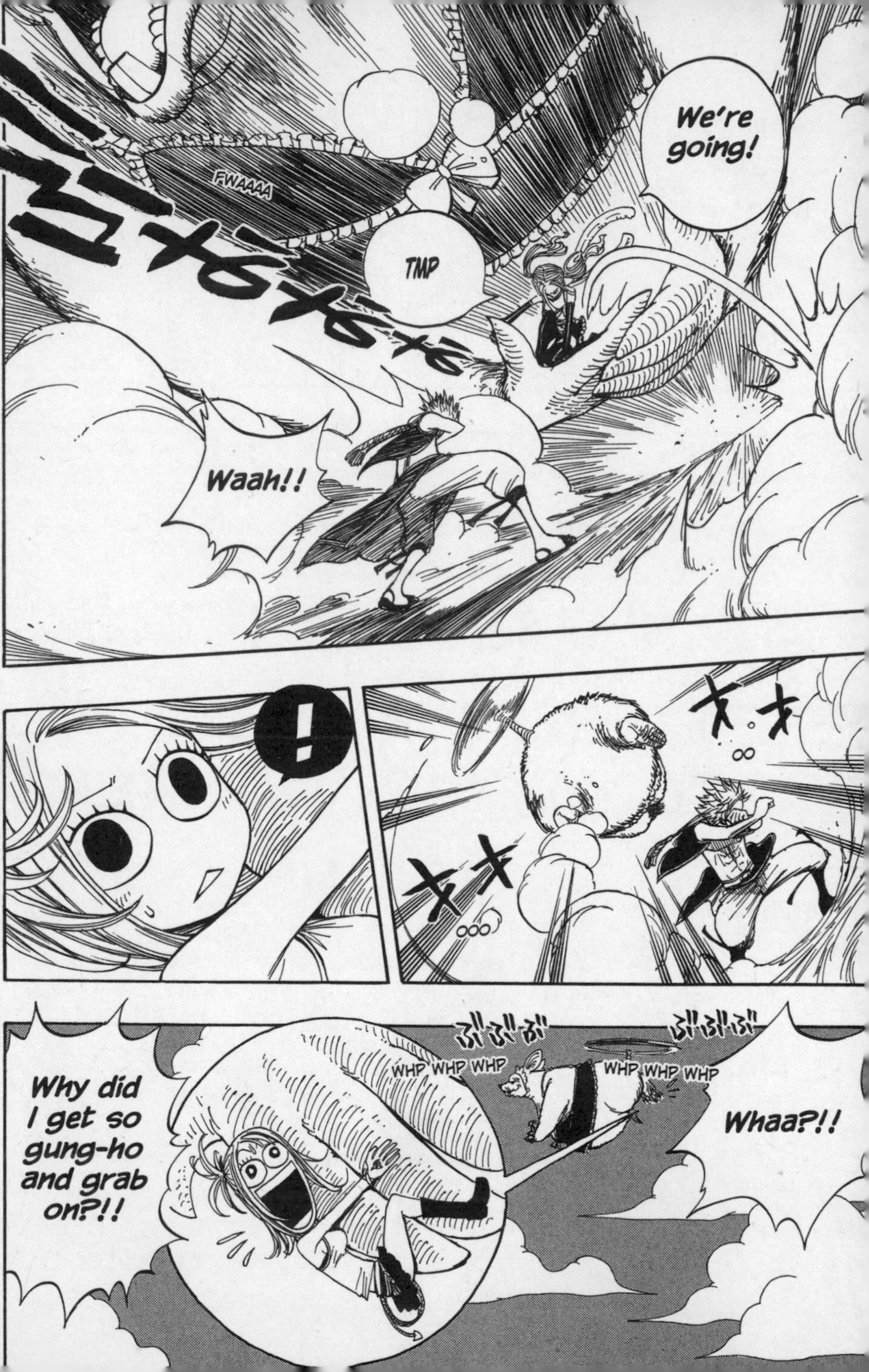
We're going!
TMP
FWAAAA
Waah!!
!
Whaa?!!
WHP WHP WHP
WHP WHP WHP
Why did I get so gung-ho and grab on?!!

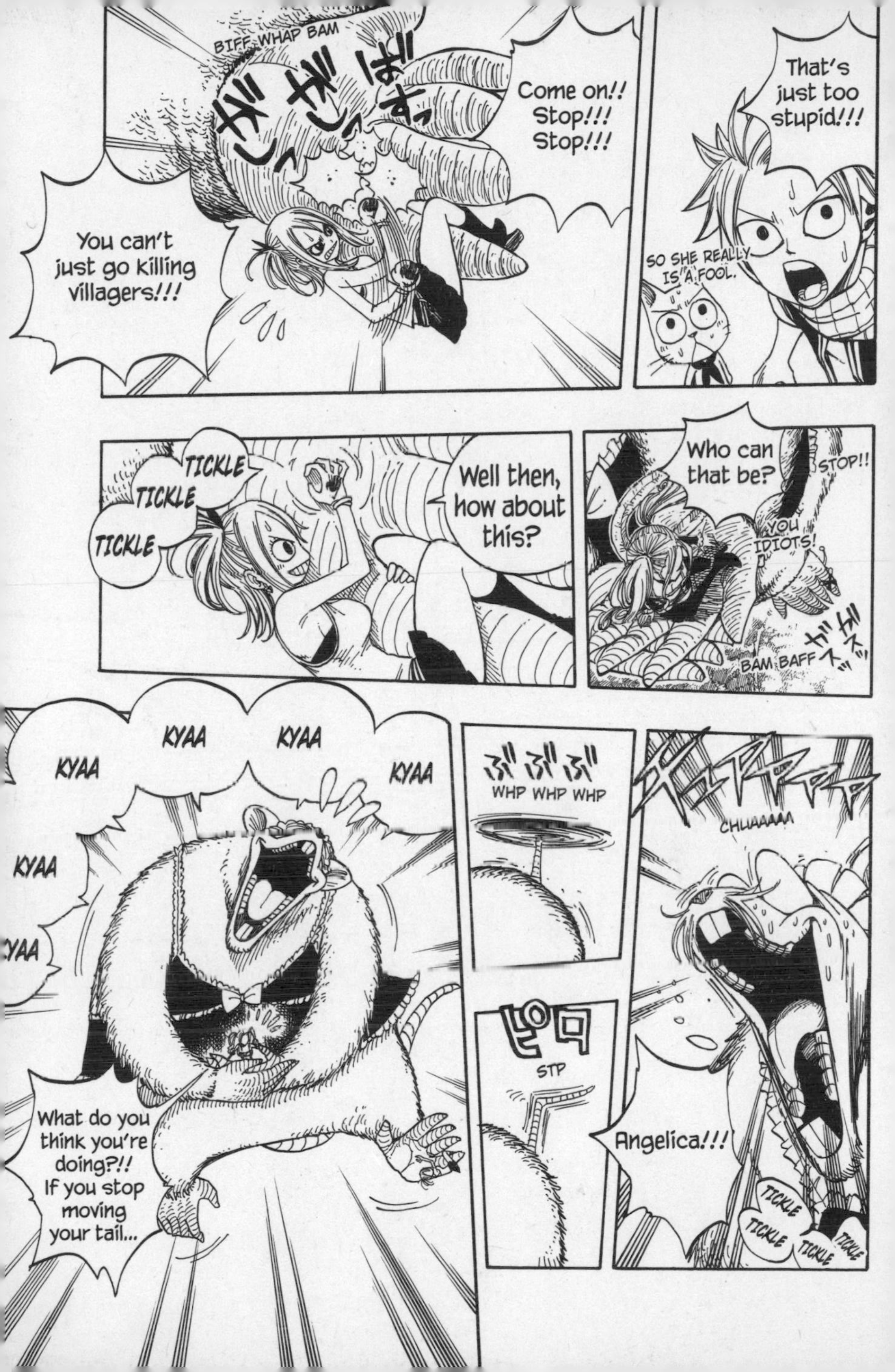

That's just too stupid!!!
SO SHE REALLY IS A FOOL.
BIFF WHAP BAM
Come on!! Stop!!! Stop!!!
You can't just go killing villagers!!!
Who can that be?
STOP!!
YOU IDIOTS!
BAM BAFF
Well then, how about this?
TICKLE
TICKLE
TICKLE
CHUAAAAA
Angelica!!!
TICKLE
TICKLE
TICKLE
TICKLE
ぶぶぶ
WHP WHP WHP
STP
KYAA
KYAA
KYAA
KYAA
KYAA
KYAA
What do you think you're doing?!! If you stop moving your tail...

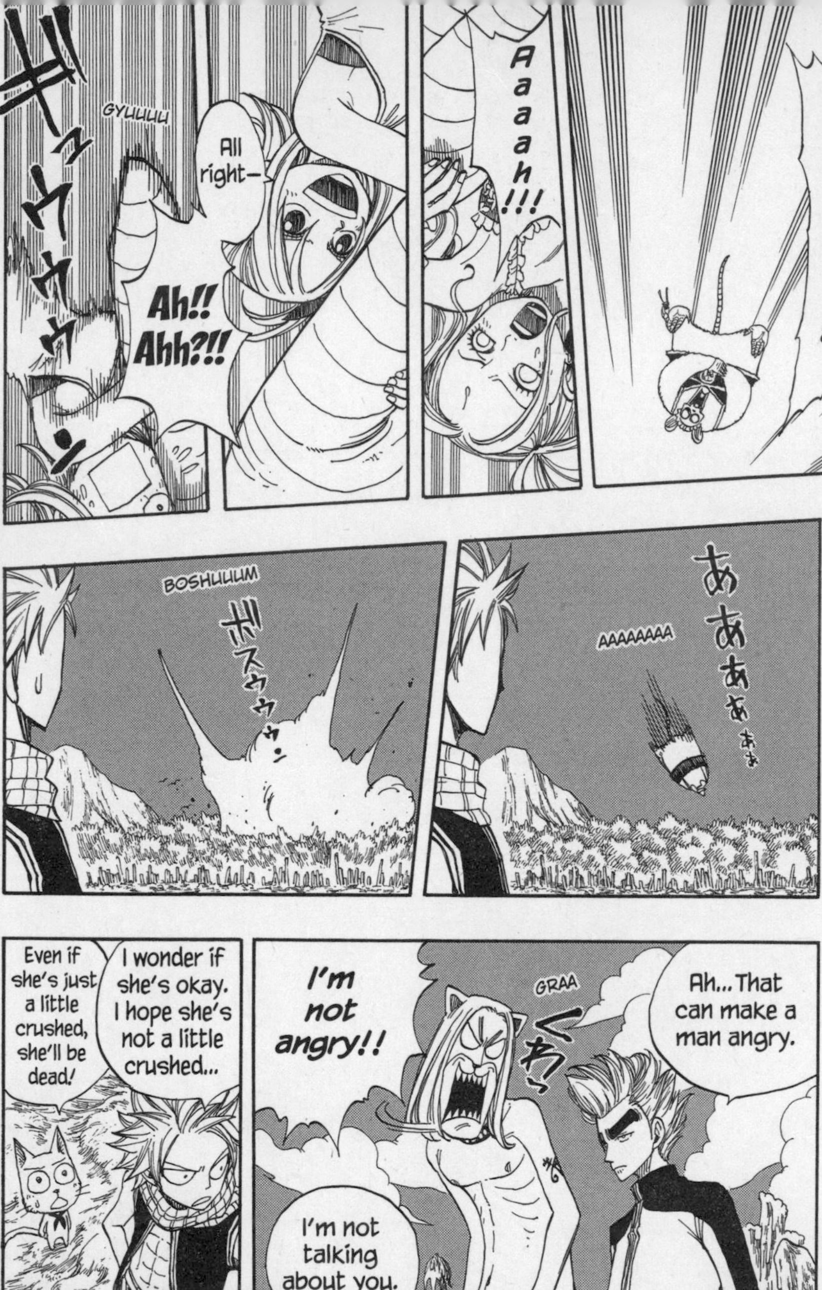
Chuuuuu!!!
Aaaaah!!!
All right—
Ah!! Ahh?!!
ギュウウウン
GYUUUU
ああああ
AAAAAAAA
ボスウウウン
BOSHUUUM
Ah... That can make a man angry.
くわっ
GRAA
I'm not angry!!
I'm not talking about you.
I wonder if she's okay. I hope she's not a little crushed...
Even if she's just a little crushed, she'll be dead!

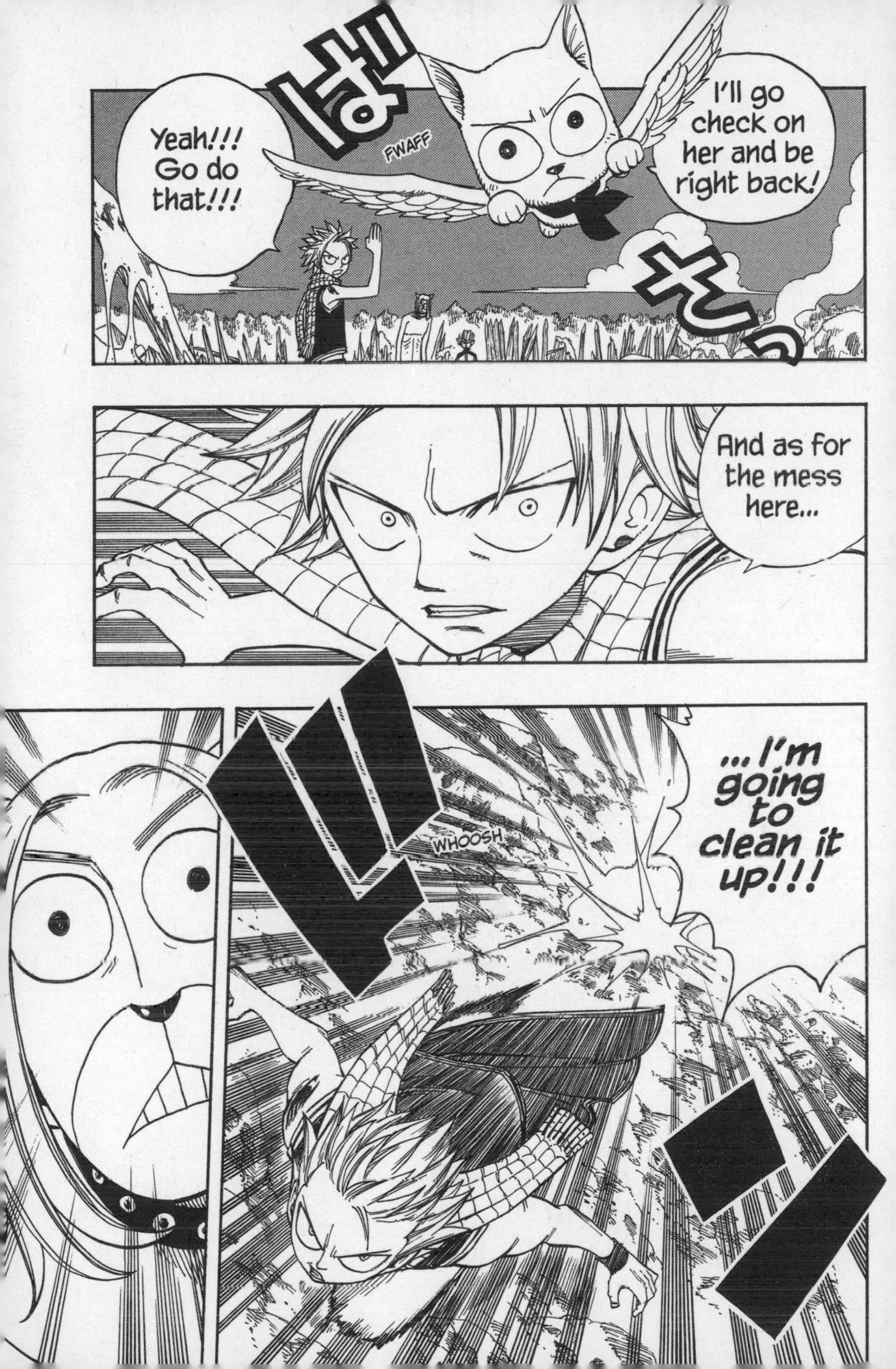
I'll go check on her and be right back!
FWAFF
Yeah!!! Go do that!!!
And as for the mess here...
...I'm going to clean it up!!!
WHOOSH

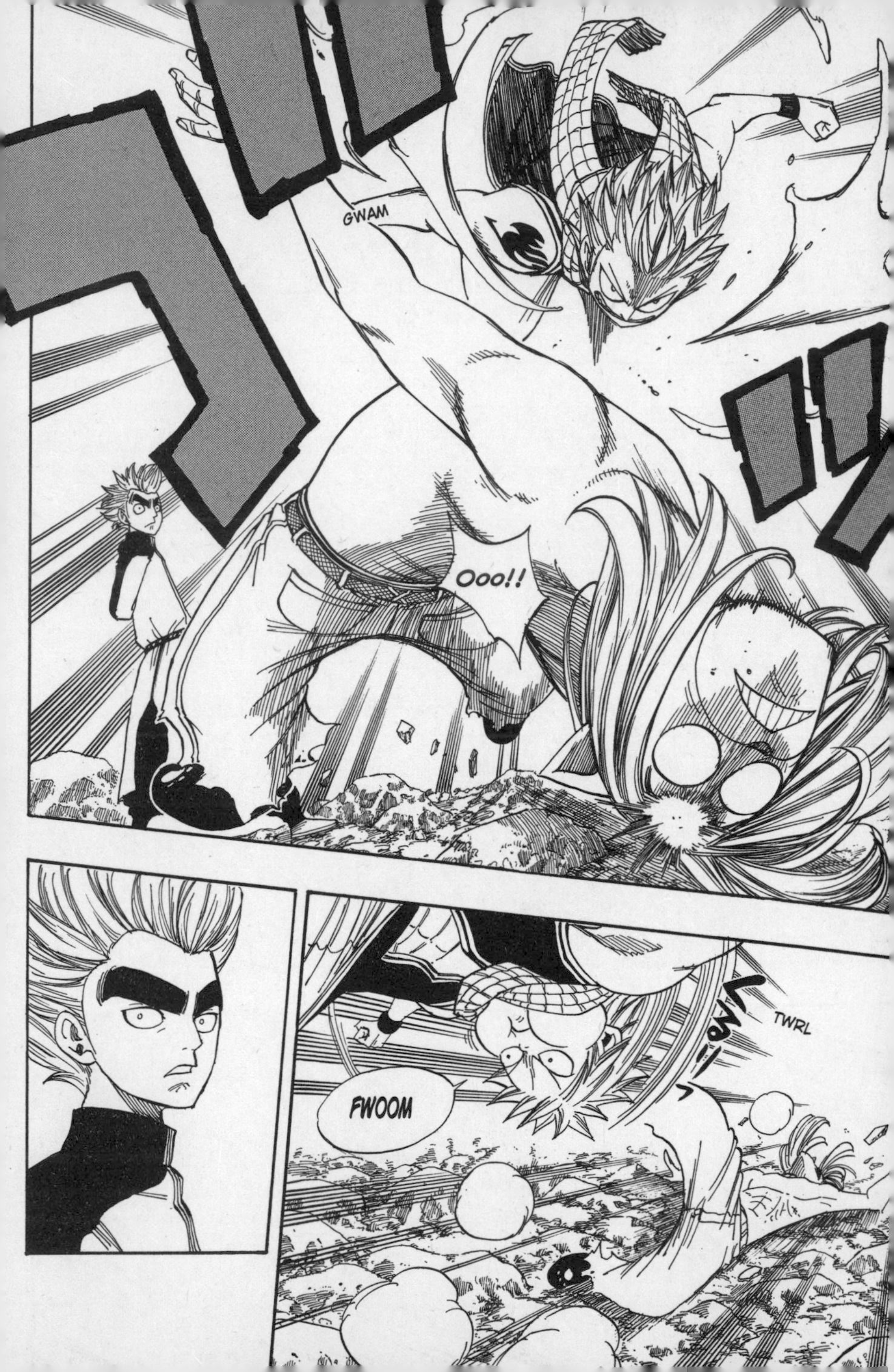
GWAM
Ooo!!
TWRL
FWOOM

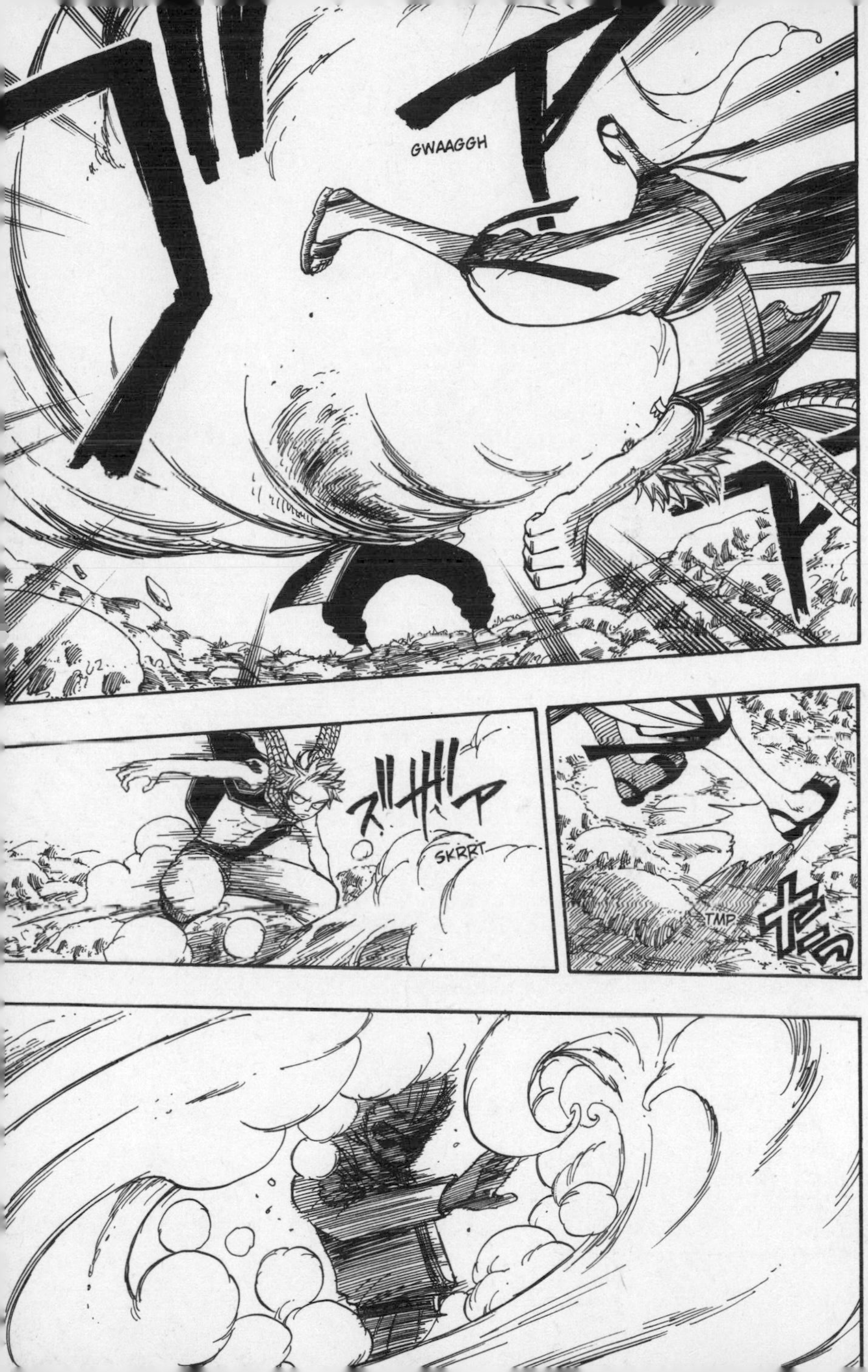
GWAAGGH
TMP
SKRRT

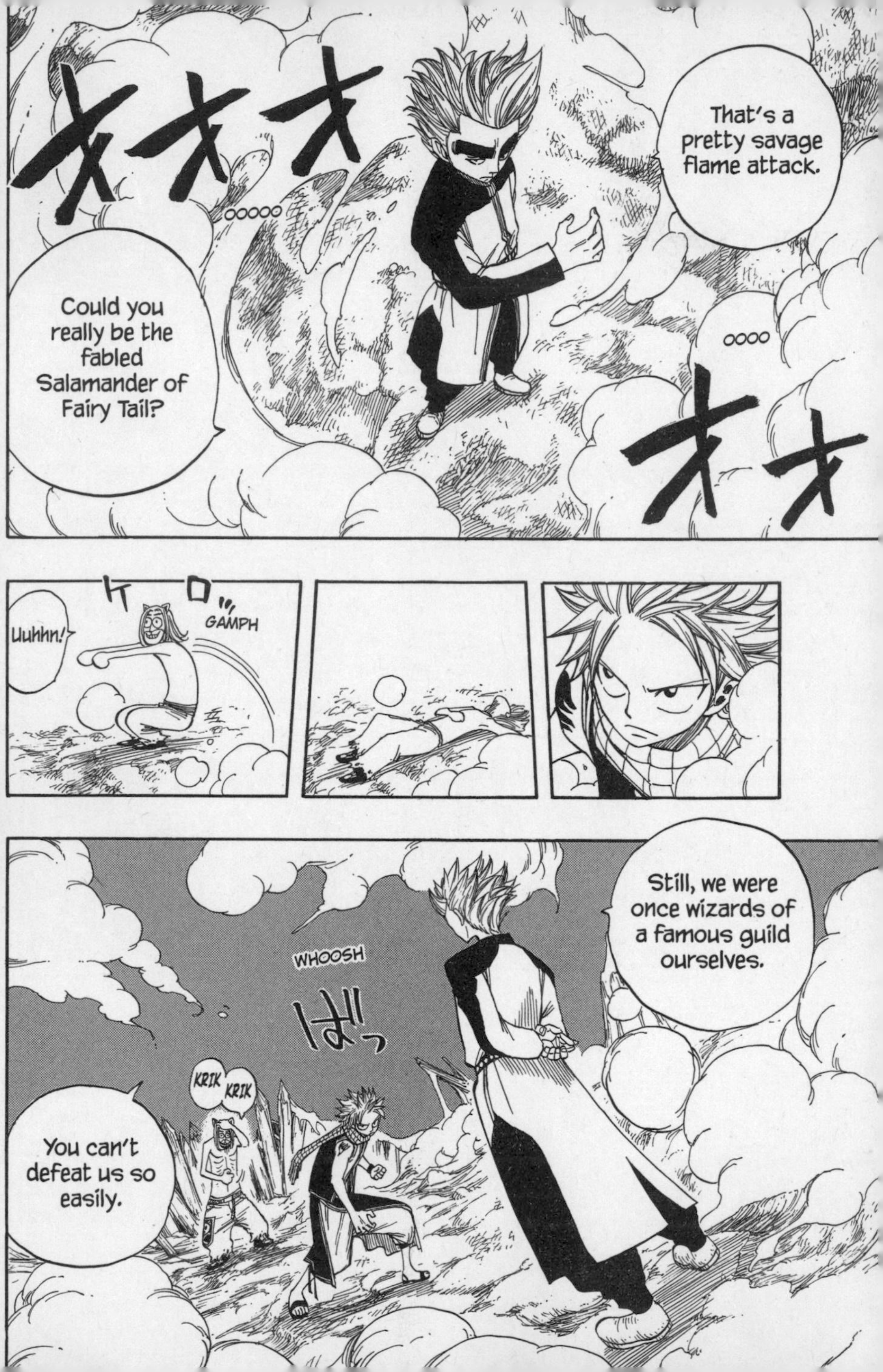
That's a pretty savage flame attack.
オオオ
OOOOO
OOOO
オオ
Could you really be the fabled Salamander of Fairy Tail?
ケロ
GAMPH
Uuhhn!
Still, we were once wizards of a famous guild ourselves.
WHOOSH
ばっ
KRIK
KRIK
You can't defeat us so easily.

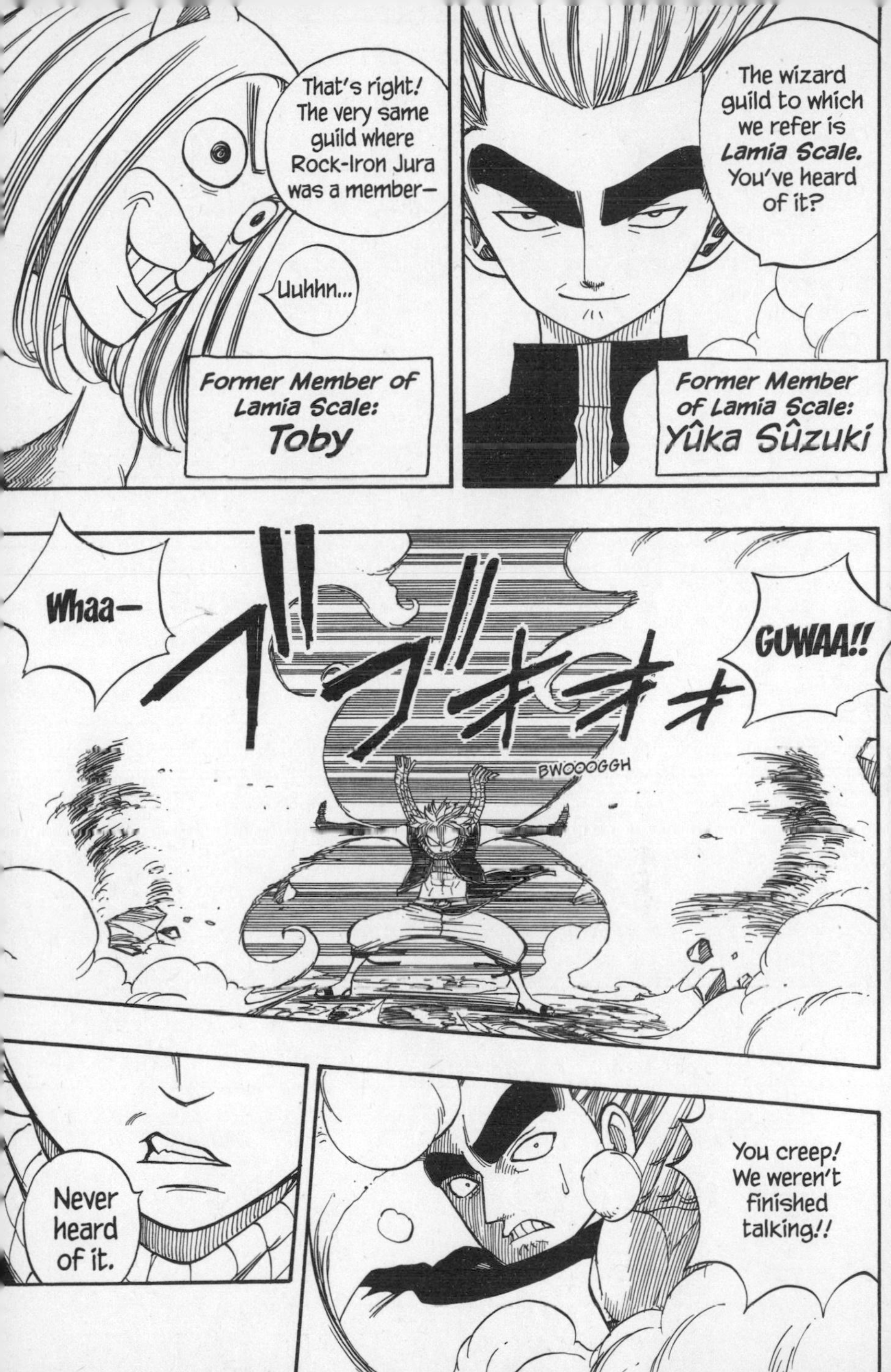
The wizard guild to which we refer is *Lamia Scale.* You've heard of it?
Former Member of Lamia Scale: Yûka Sûzuki
That's right! The very same guild where Rock-Iron Jura was a member–
Uuhhn...
Former Member of Lamia Scale: Toby
GUWAA!!
Whaa–
BWOOOGGH
You creep! We weren't finished talking!!
Never heard of it.

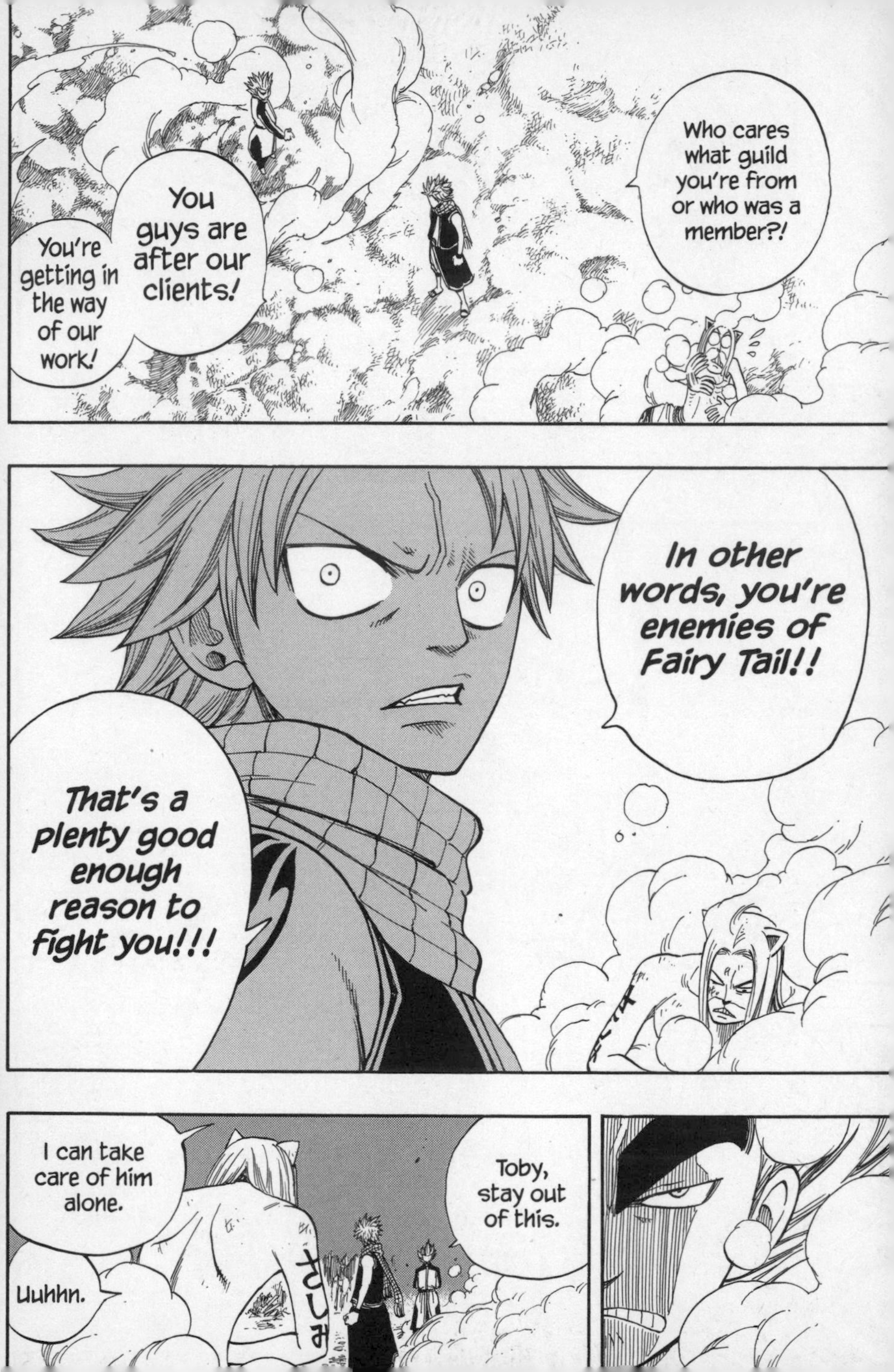
Who cares what guild you're from or who was a member?!
You guys are after our clients!
You're getting in the way of our work!
In other words, you're enemies of Fairy Tail!!
That's a plenty good enough reason to fight you!!!
Toby, stay out of this.
I can take care of him alone.
Uuhhn.

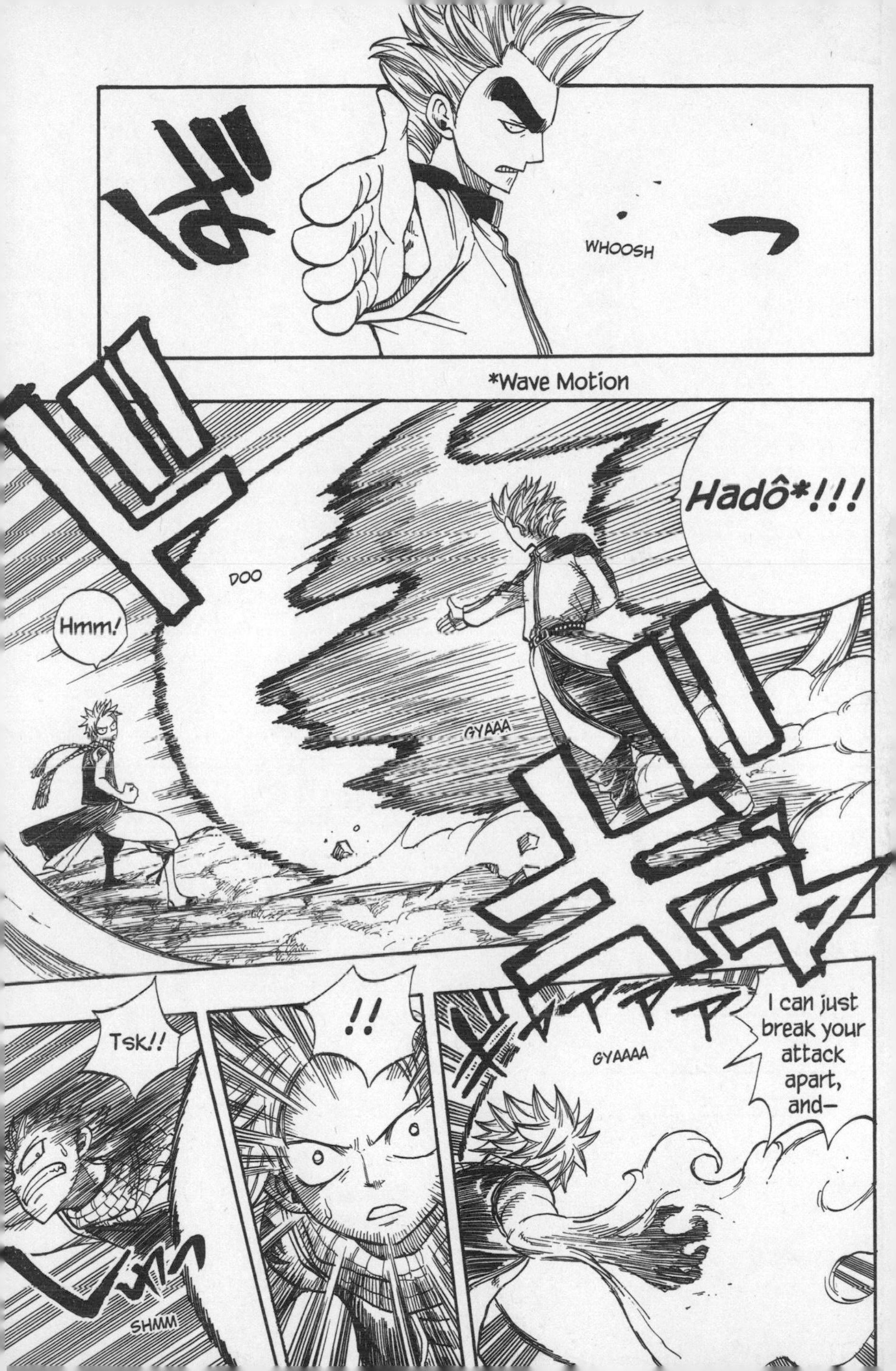
WHOOSH
*Wave Motion
Hadô*!!!
DOO
GYAAA
Hmm!
I can just break your attack apart, and—
GYAAAA
!!
Tsk!!
SHMM

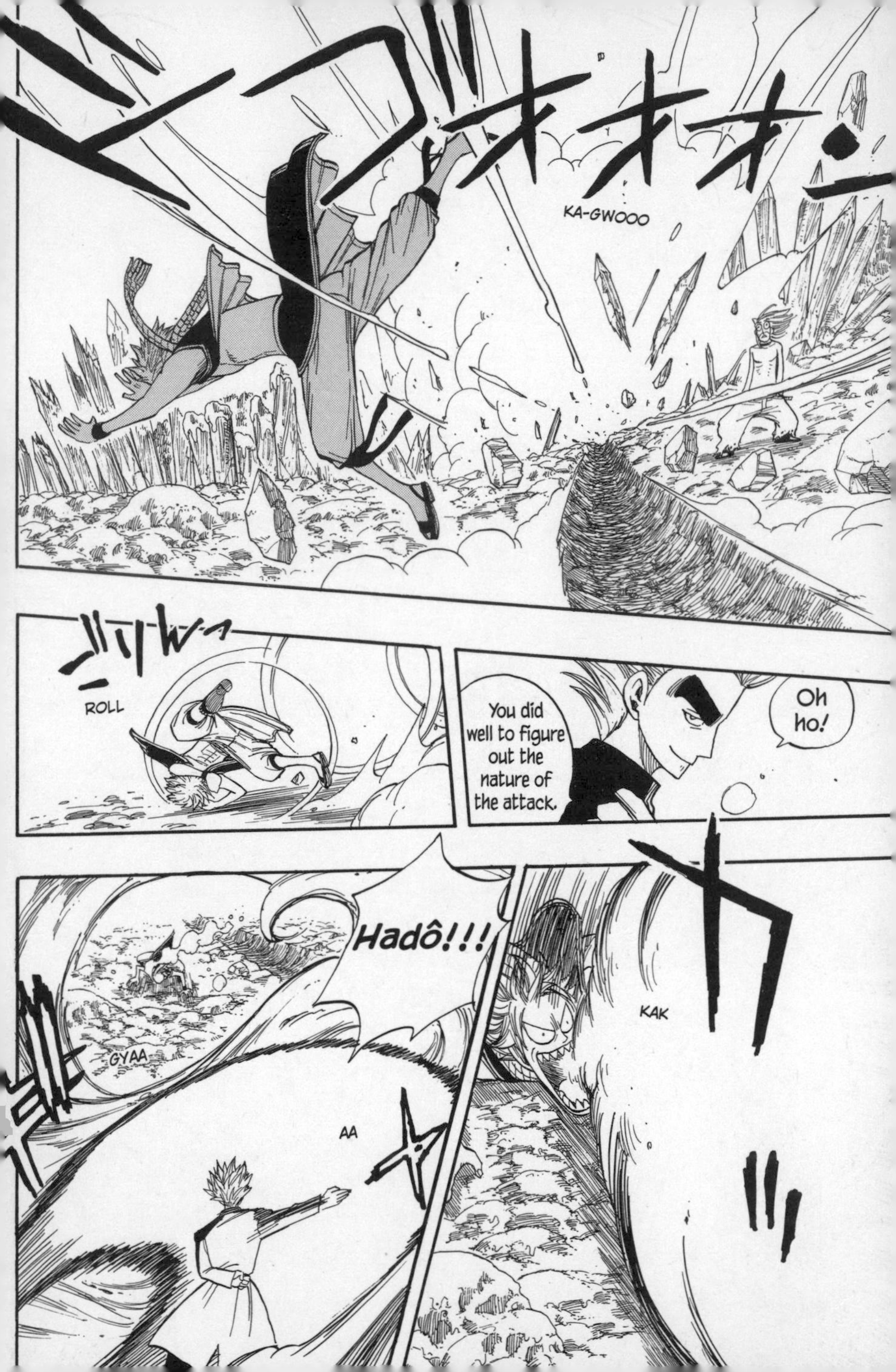
KA-GWOOO
Oh ho!
You did well to figure out the nature of the attack.
ROLL
KAK
Hadô!!!
GYAA
AA

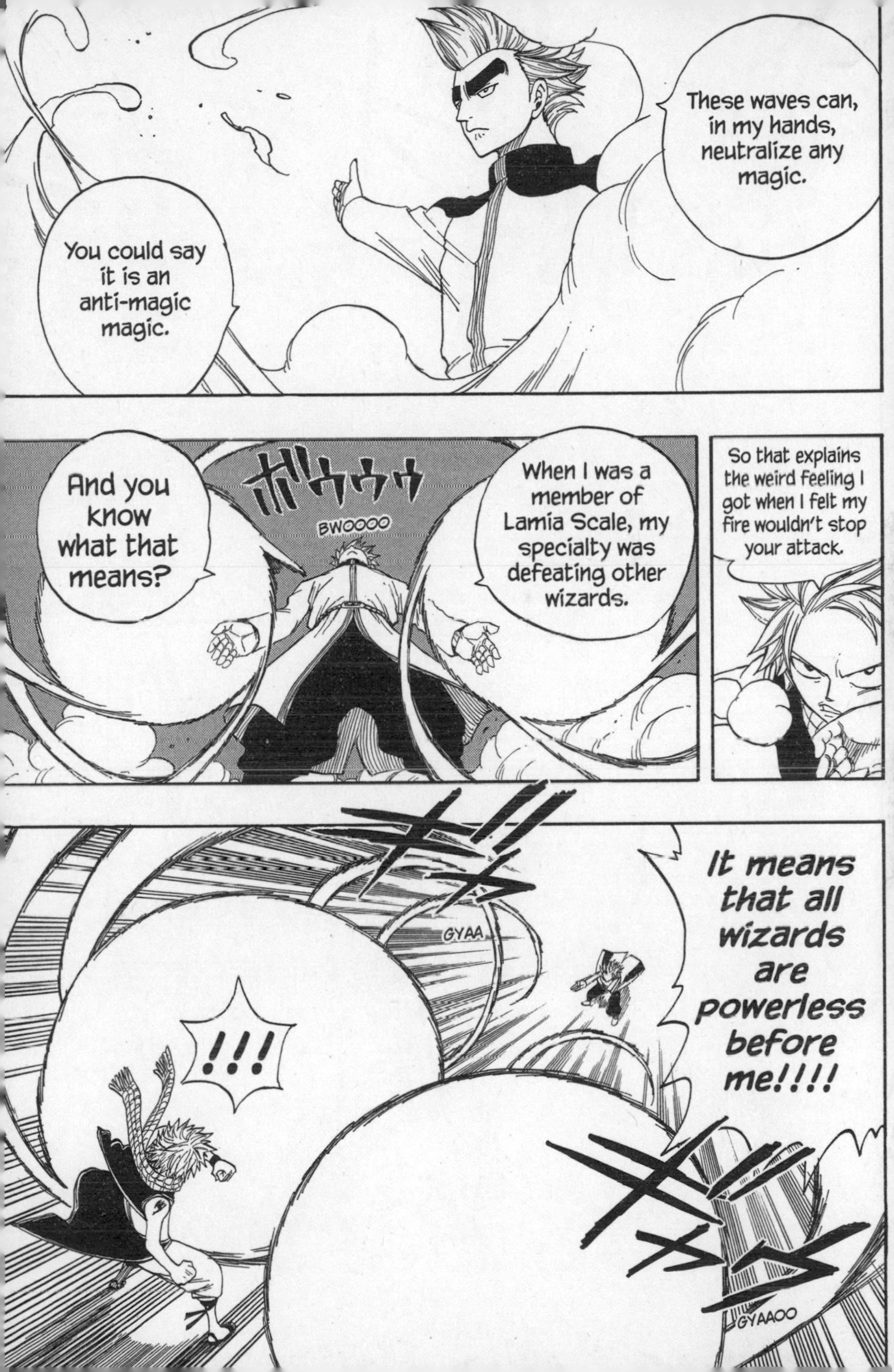
These waves can, in my hands, neutralize any magic.
You could say it is an anti-magic magic.
So that explains the weird feeling I got when I felt my fire wouldn't stop your attack.
When I was a member of Lamia Scale, my specialty was defeating other wizards.
ボウウウ
BWOOOO
And you know what that means?
It means that all wizards are powerless before me!!!!
GYAA
!!!
GYAAOO

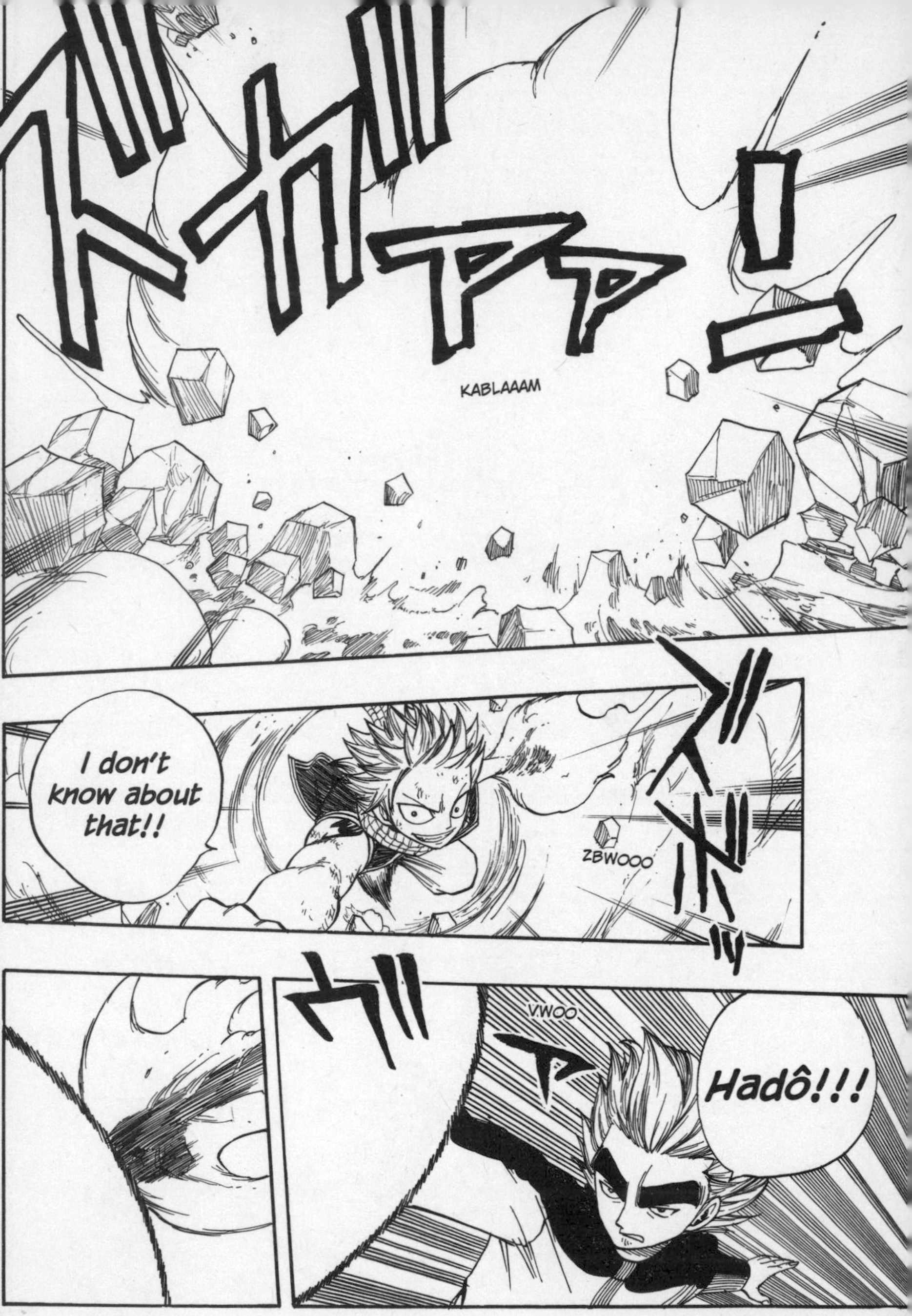
KABLAAAM
ZBWOOO
I don't know about that!!
V.WOO
Hadô!!!

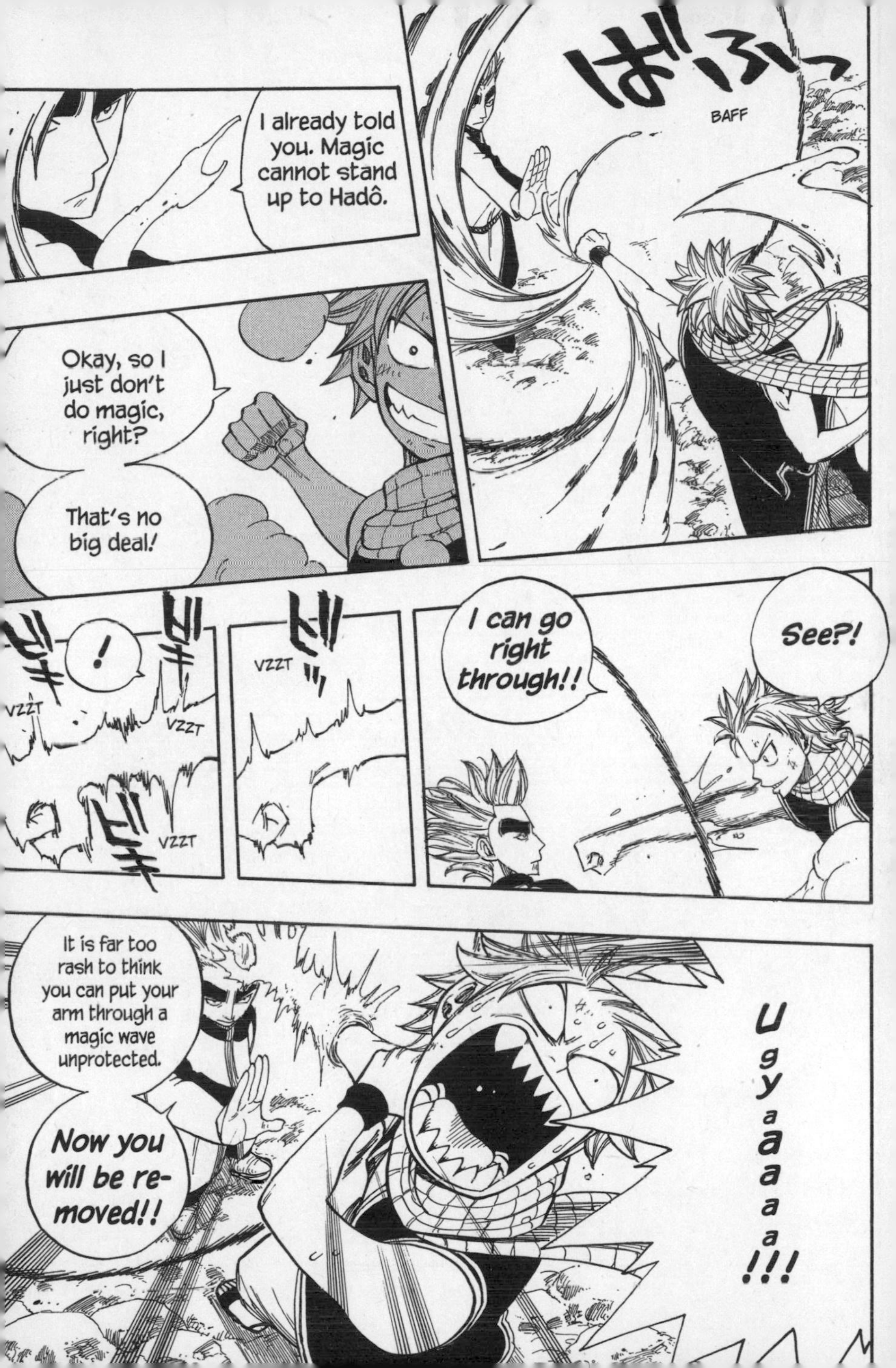

ばふっ
BAFF
I already told you. Magic cannot stand up to Hadô.
Okay, so I just don't do magic, right?
That's no big deal!
See?!
I can go right through!!
VZZT
!
VZZT
VZZT
VZZT
Ugyaaaaa!!!
It is far too rash to think you can put your arm through a magic wave unprotected.
Now you will be re-moved!!

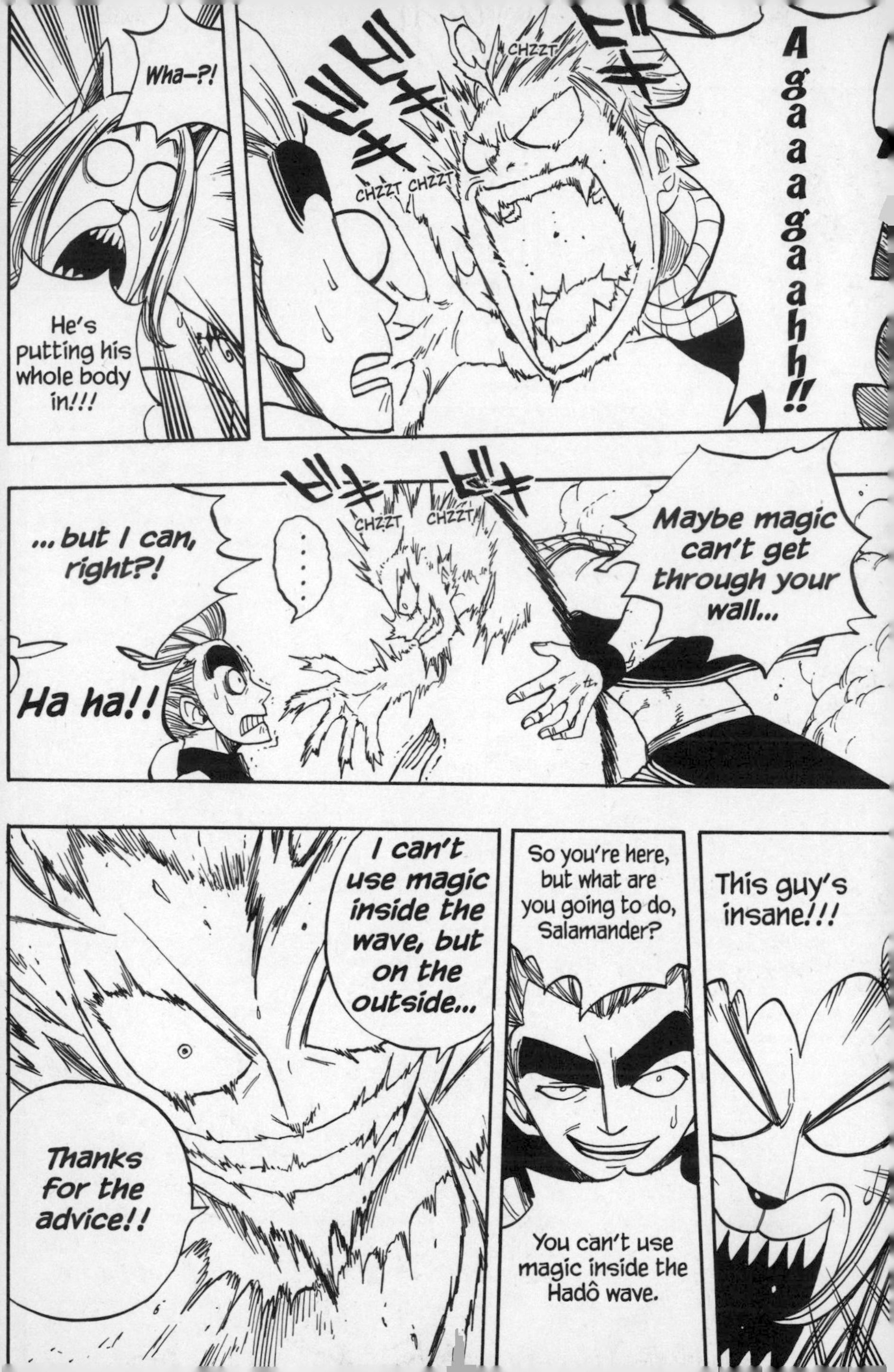
Agaaagaahh!!
CHZZT
CHZZT CHZZT
Wha-?!
He's putting his whole body in!!!
Maybe magic can't get through your wall...
CHZZT
CHZZT
...
...but I can, right?!
Ha ha!!
This guy's insane!!!
So you're here, but what are you going to do, Salamander?
You can't use magic inside the Hadô wave.
I can't use magic inside the wave, but on the outside...
Thanks for the advice!!

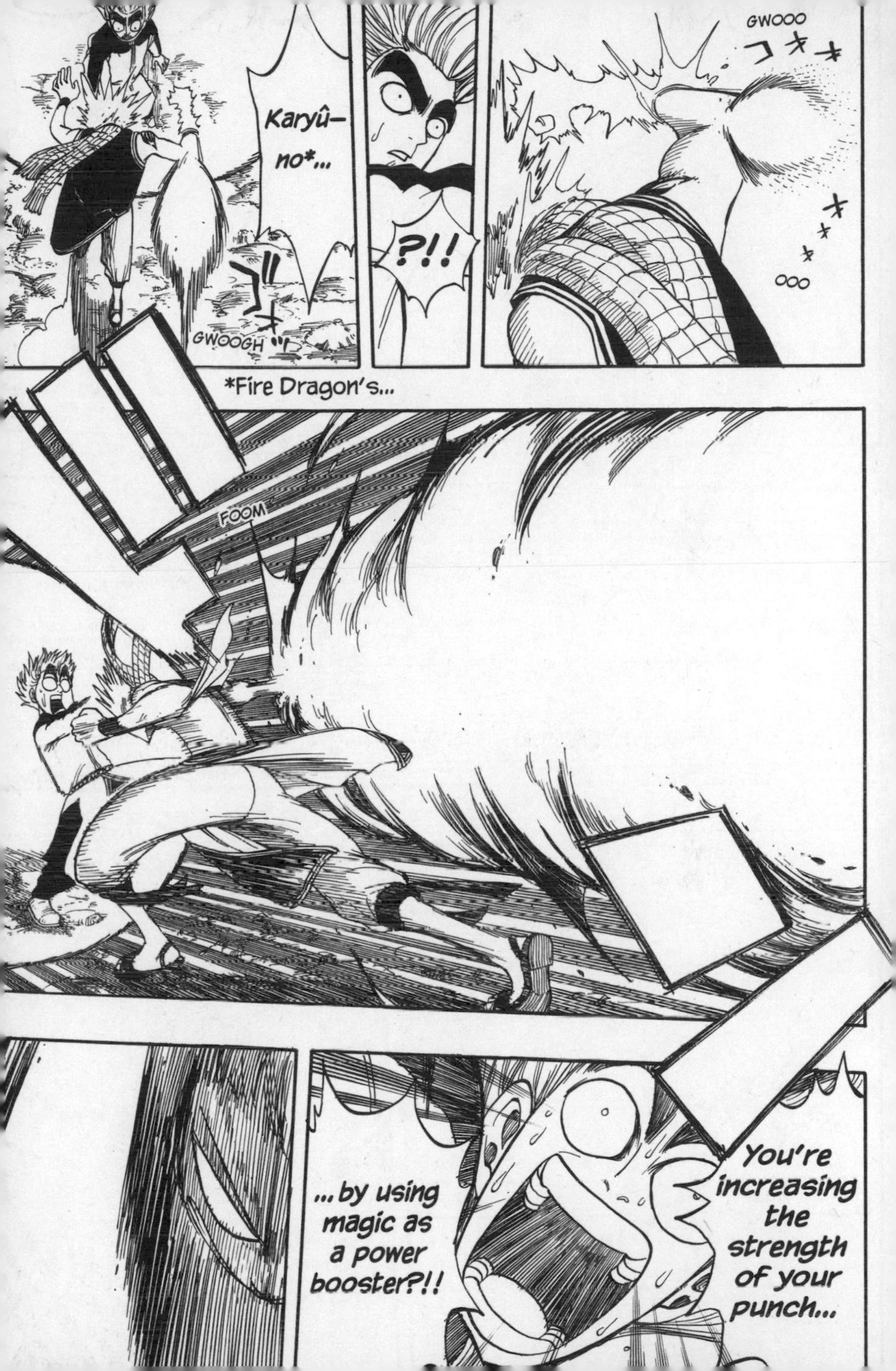
GWOOO
?!!
Karyû-no*...
GWOOGH
*Fire Dragon's...
FOOM
You're increasing the strength of your punch...
...by using magic as a power booster?!!

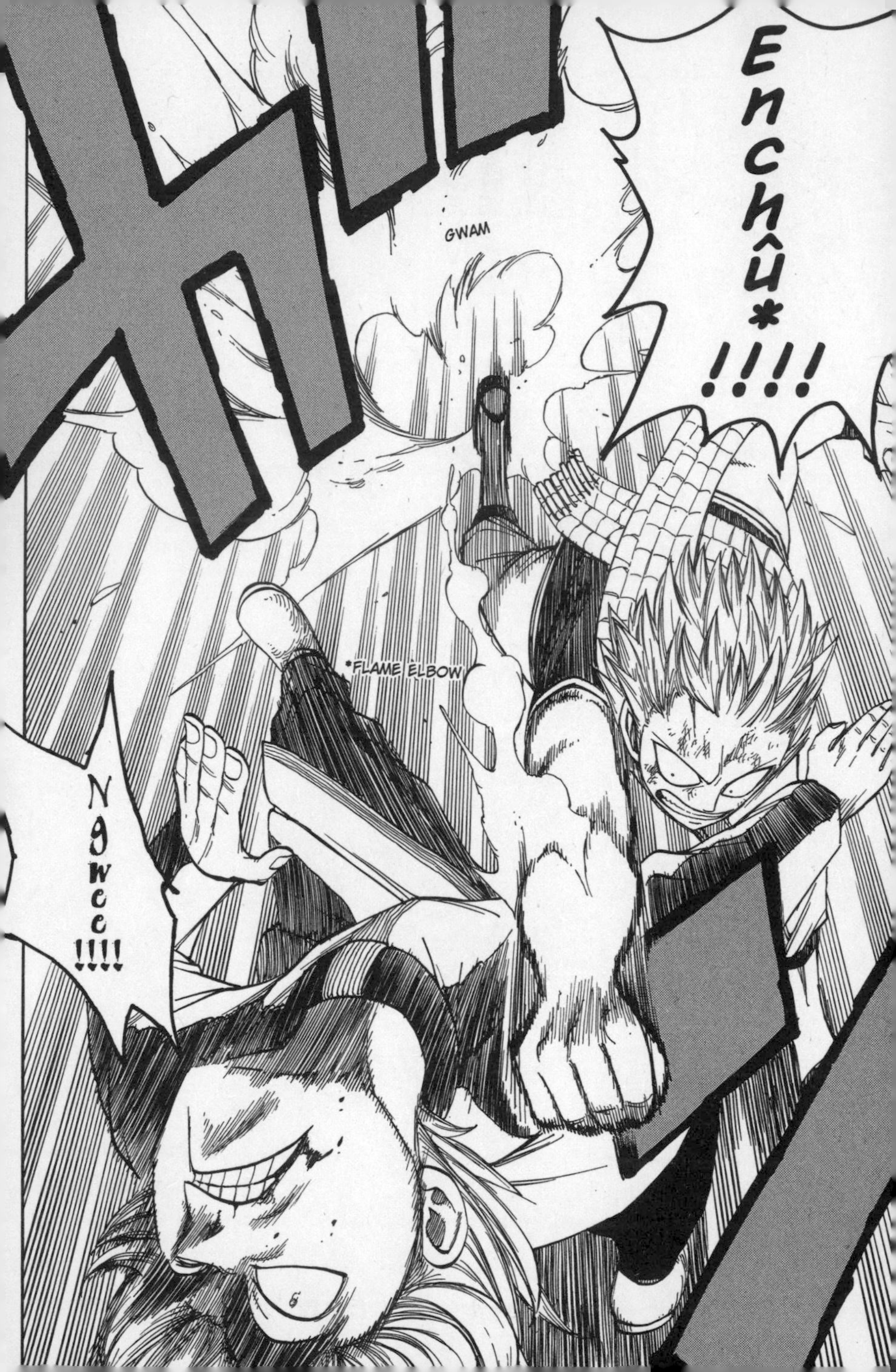
Enchû*!!!!
GWAM
Ngwee!!!!
*FLAME ELBOW

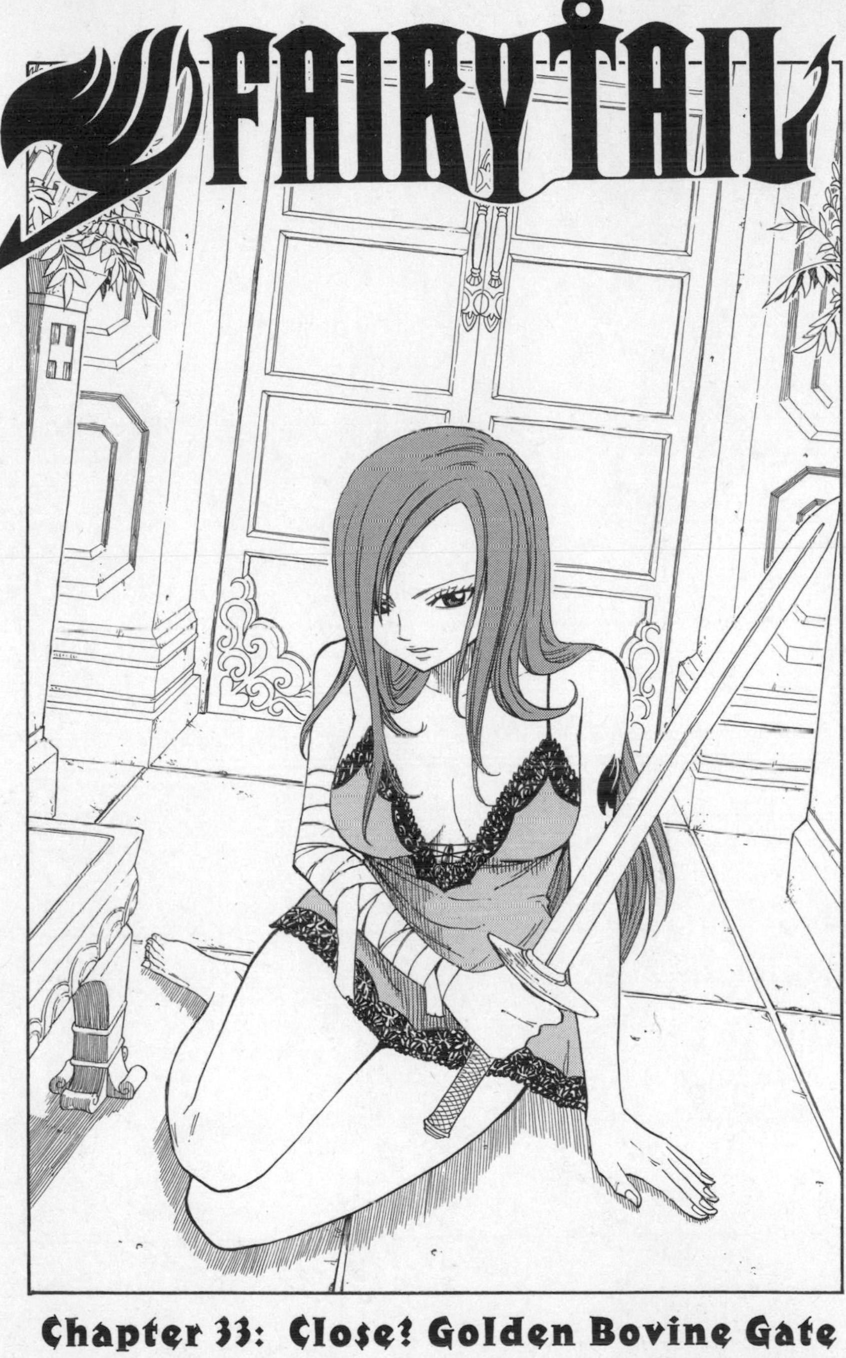
FAIRY TAIL

Chapter 33: Close! Golden Bovine Gate

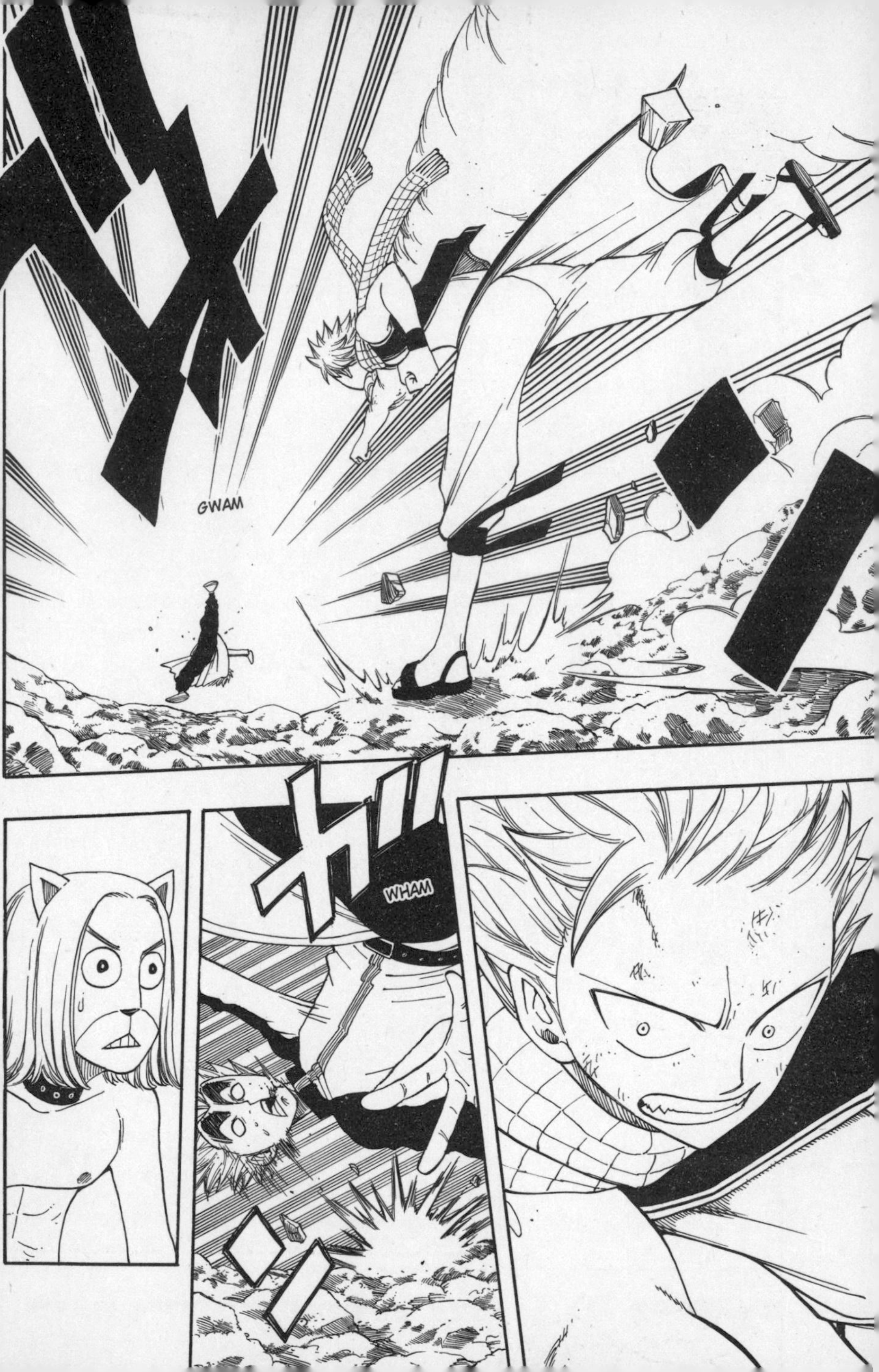
GWAM
WHAM

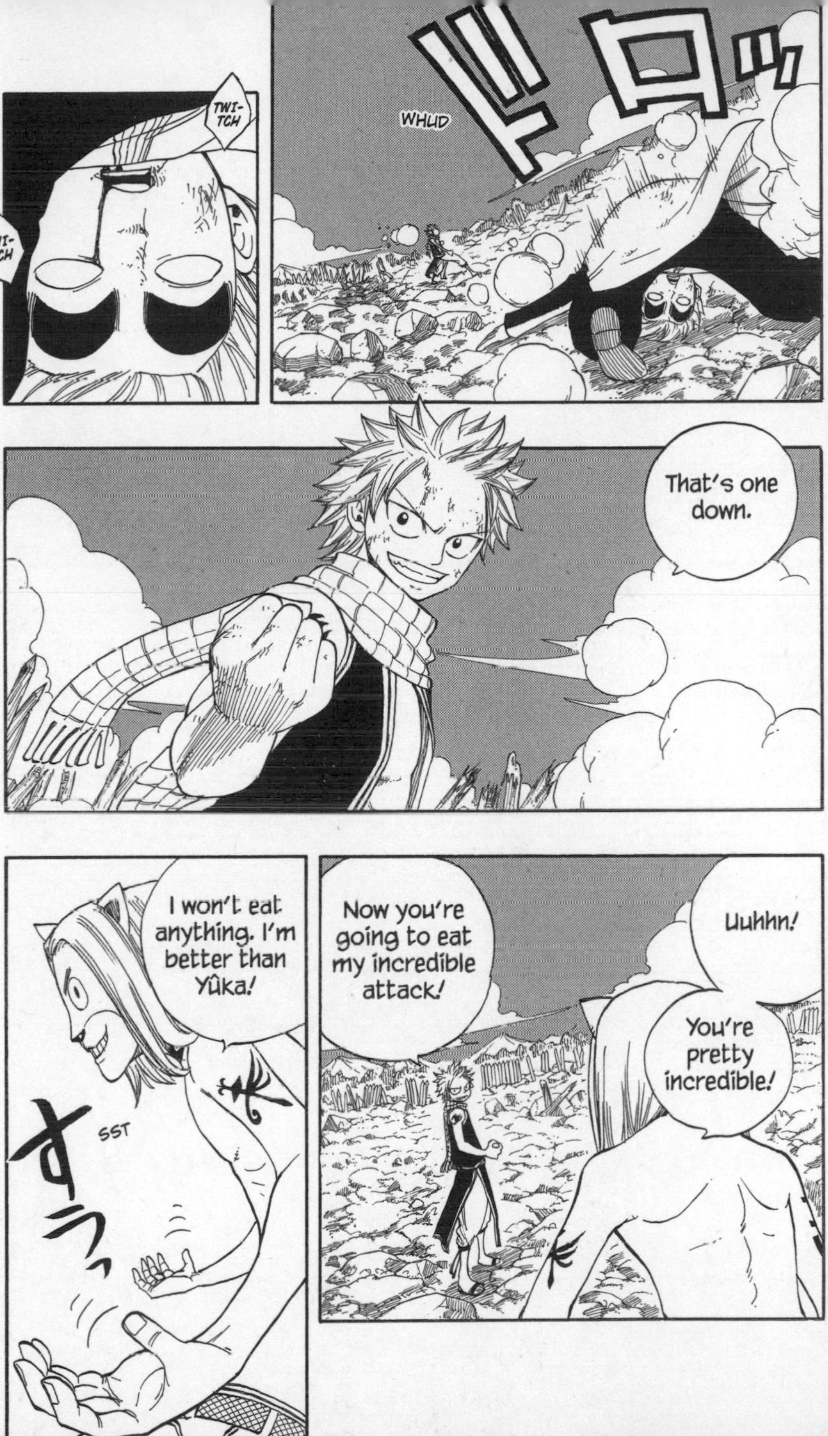
WHUD
TWI-TCH
TWI-TCH
That's one down.
Uuhhn!
You're pretty incredible!
Now you're going to eat my incredible attack!
I won't eat anything. I'm better than Yûka!
SST

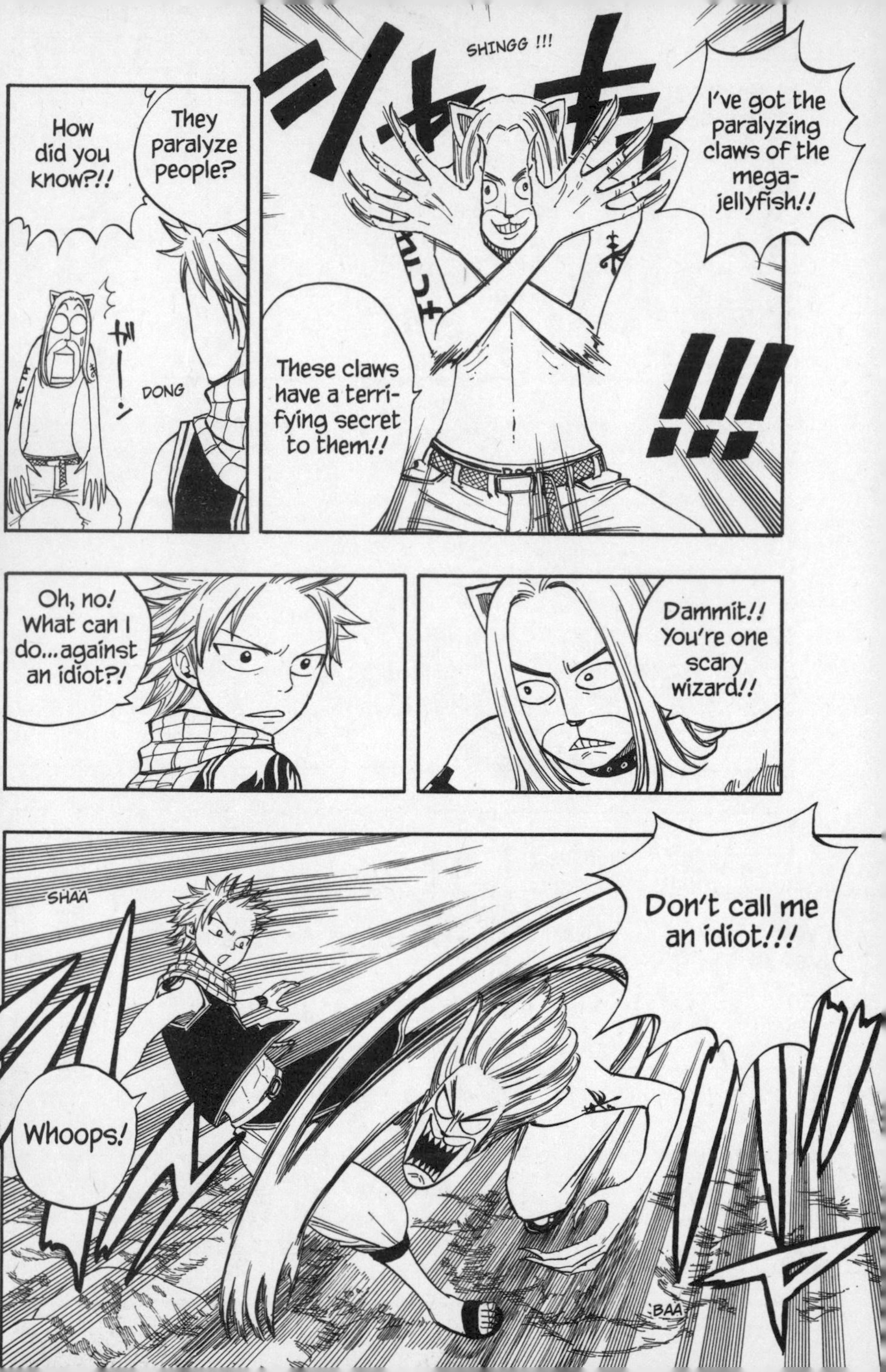
SHINGG !!!
I've got the paralyzing claws of the mega-jellyfish!!
These claws have a terrifying secret to them!!
They paralyze people?
How did you know?!!
DONG
Dammit!! You're one scary wizard!!
Oh, no! What can I do...against an idiot?!
Don't call me an idiot!!!
SHAA
Whoops!
BAA

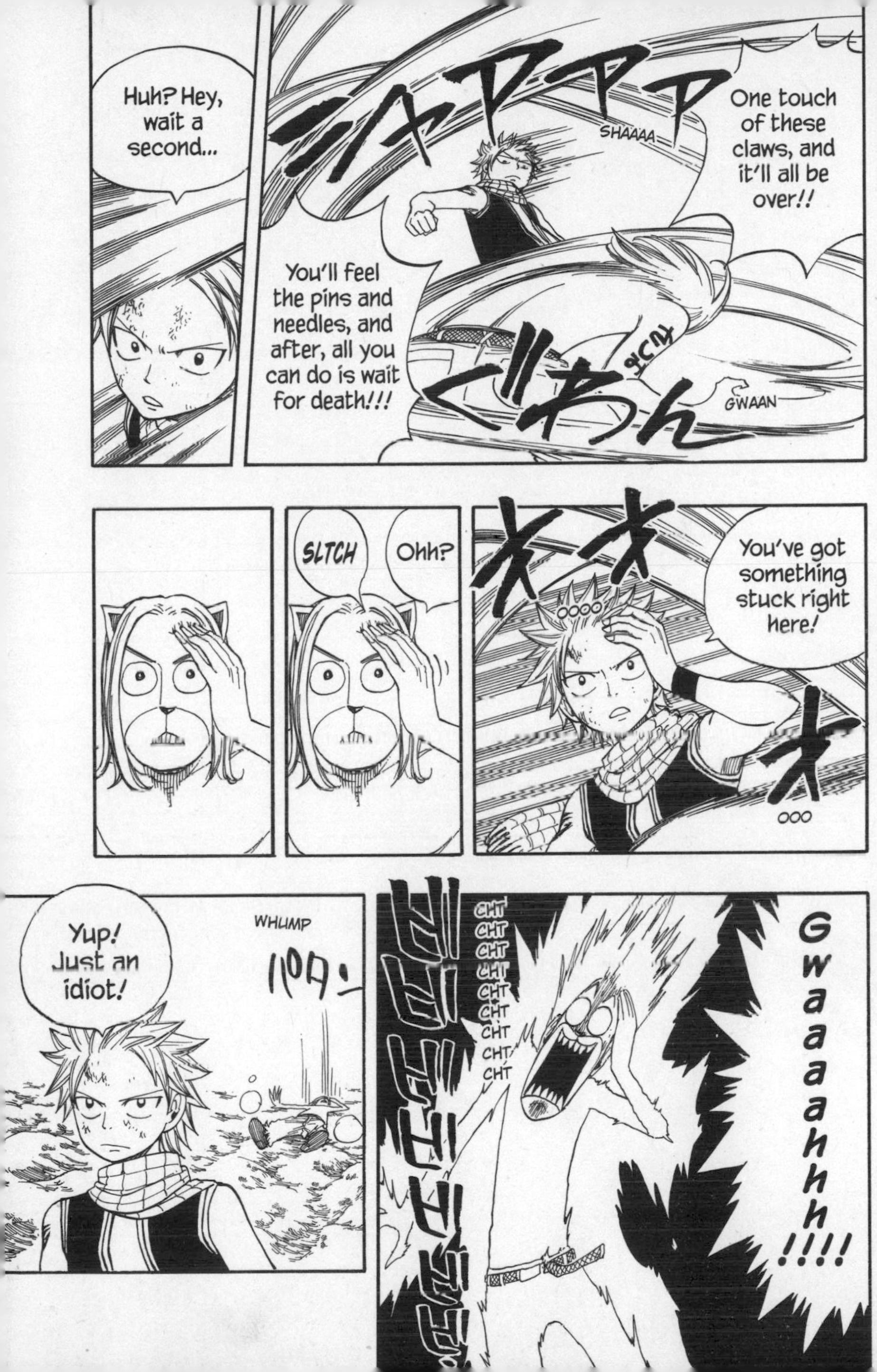

One touch of these claws, and it'll all be over!!
SHAAAA
You'll feel the pins and needles, and after, all you can do is wait for death!!!
GWAAN
Huh? Hey, wait a second...
You've got something stuck right here!
OOO
Ohh?
SLTCH
Gwaaaaahhh!!!!
CHT CHT CHT CHT CHT CHT CHT CHT CHT
Yup! Just an idiot!
WHUMP

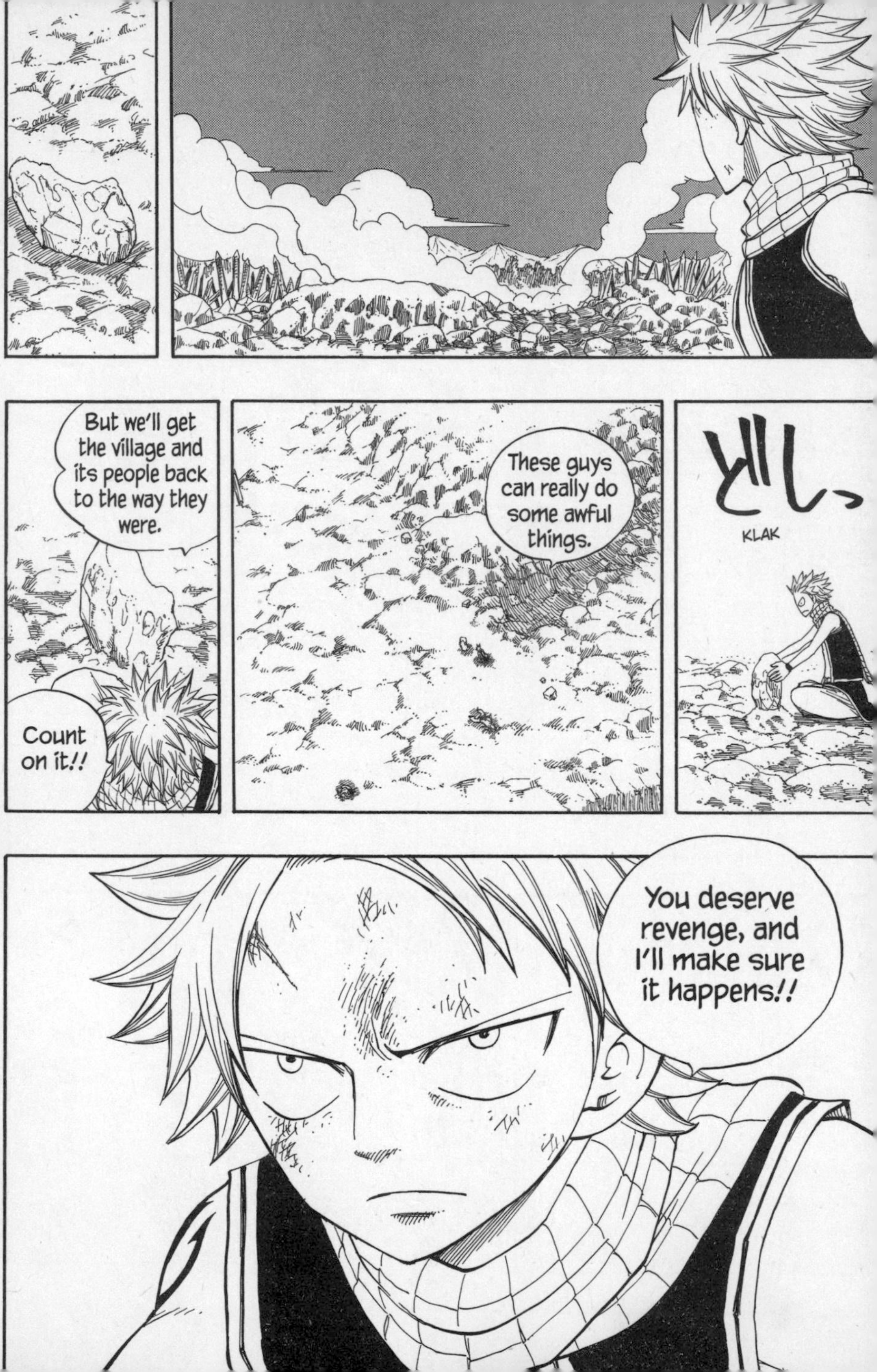
どしっ
KLAK
These guys can really do some awful things.
But we'll get the village and its people back to the way they were.
Count on it!!
You deserve revenge, and I'll make sure it happens!!

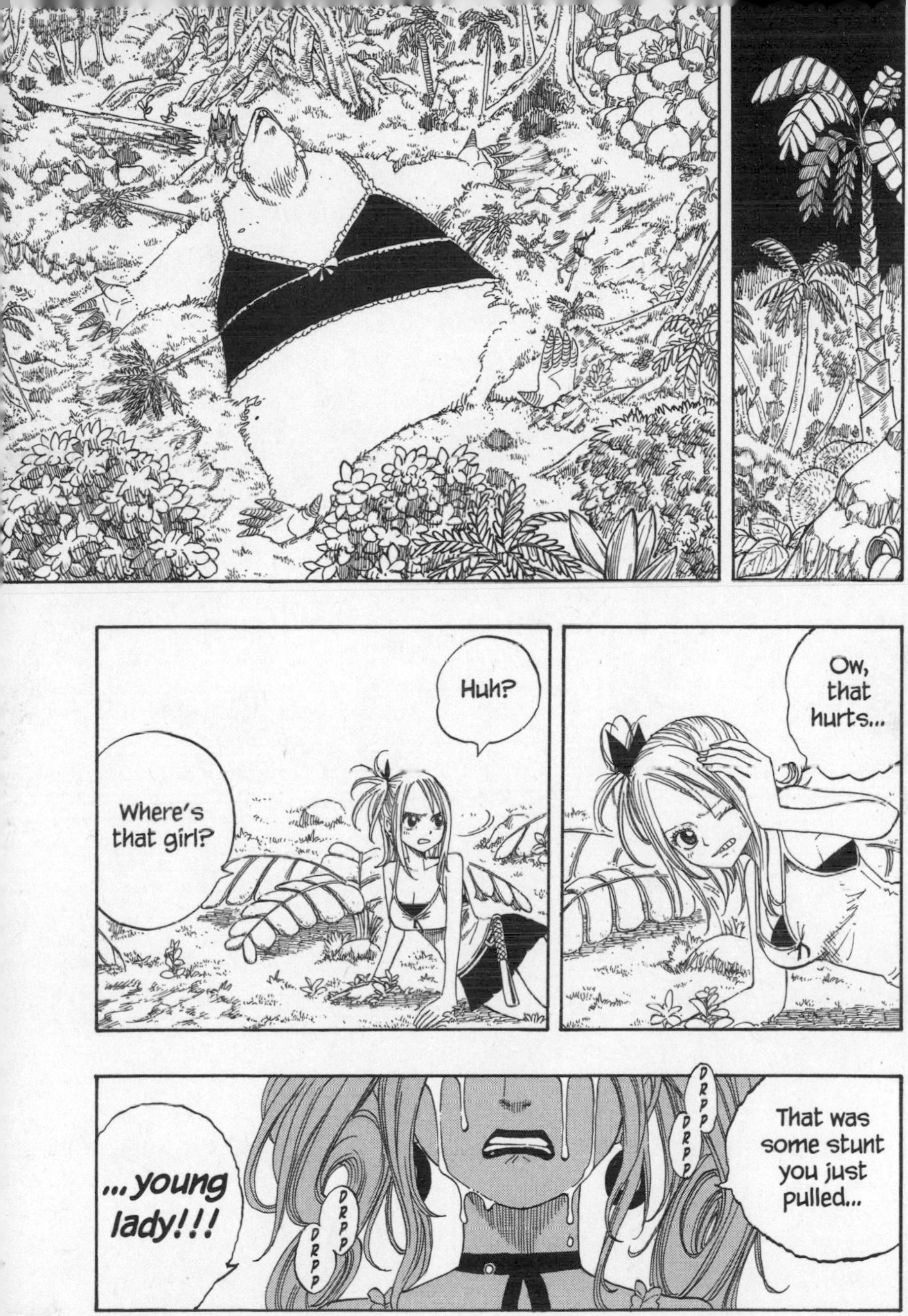

Ow, that hurts...
Huh?
Where's that girl?
That was some stunt you just pulled...
DRPP DRPP
DRPP DRPP
...young lady!!!

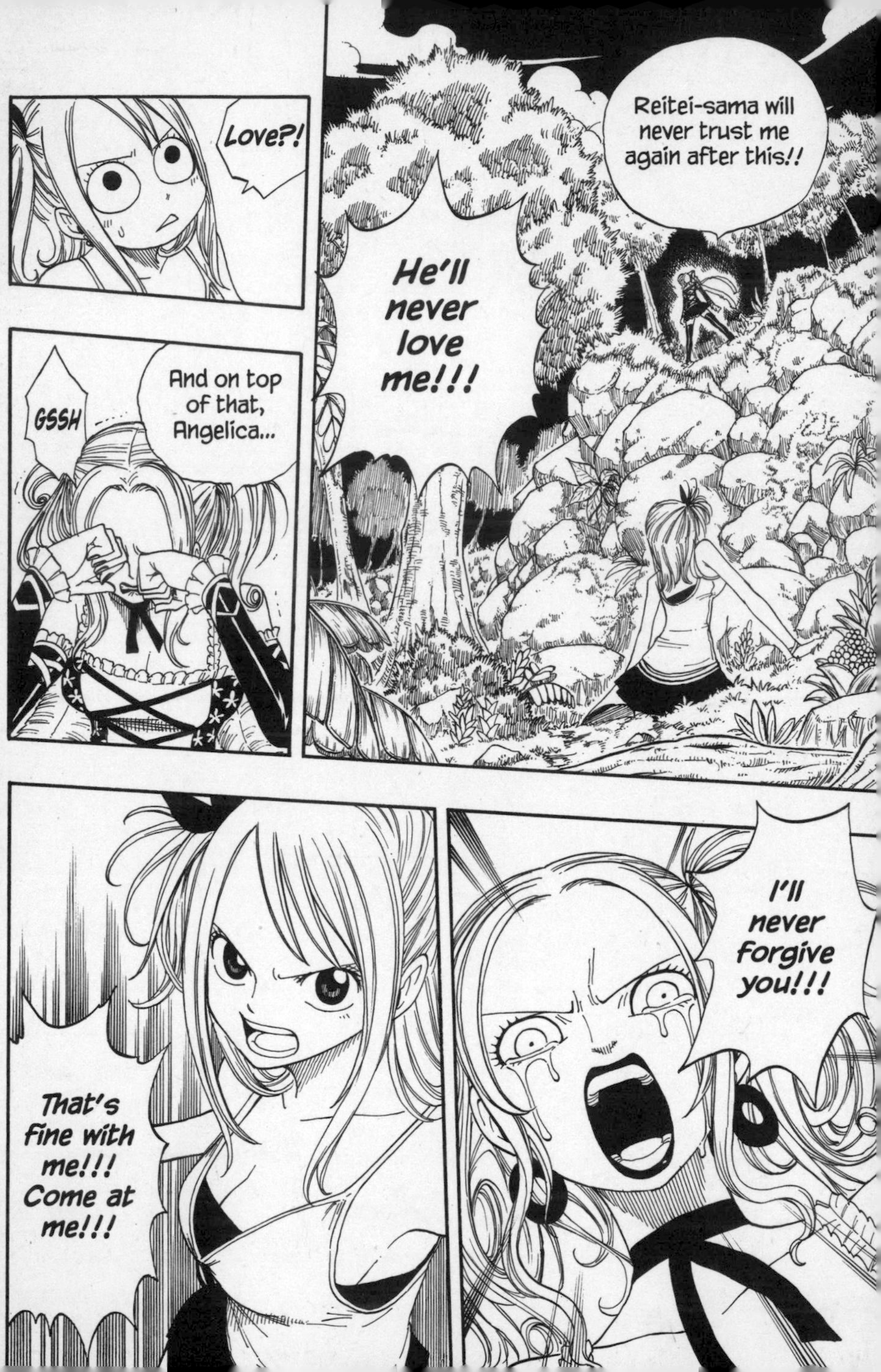
Reitei-sama will never trust me again after this!!
He'll never love me!!!
Love?!
And on top of that, Angelica...
GSSH
I'll never forgive you!!!
That's fine with me!!! Come at me!!!

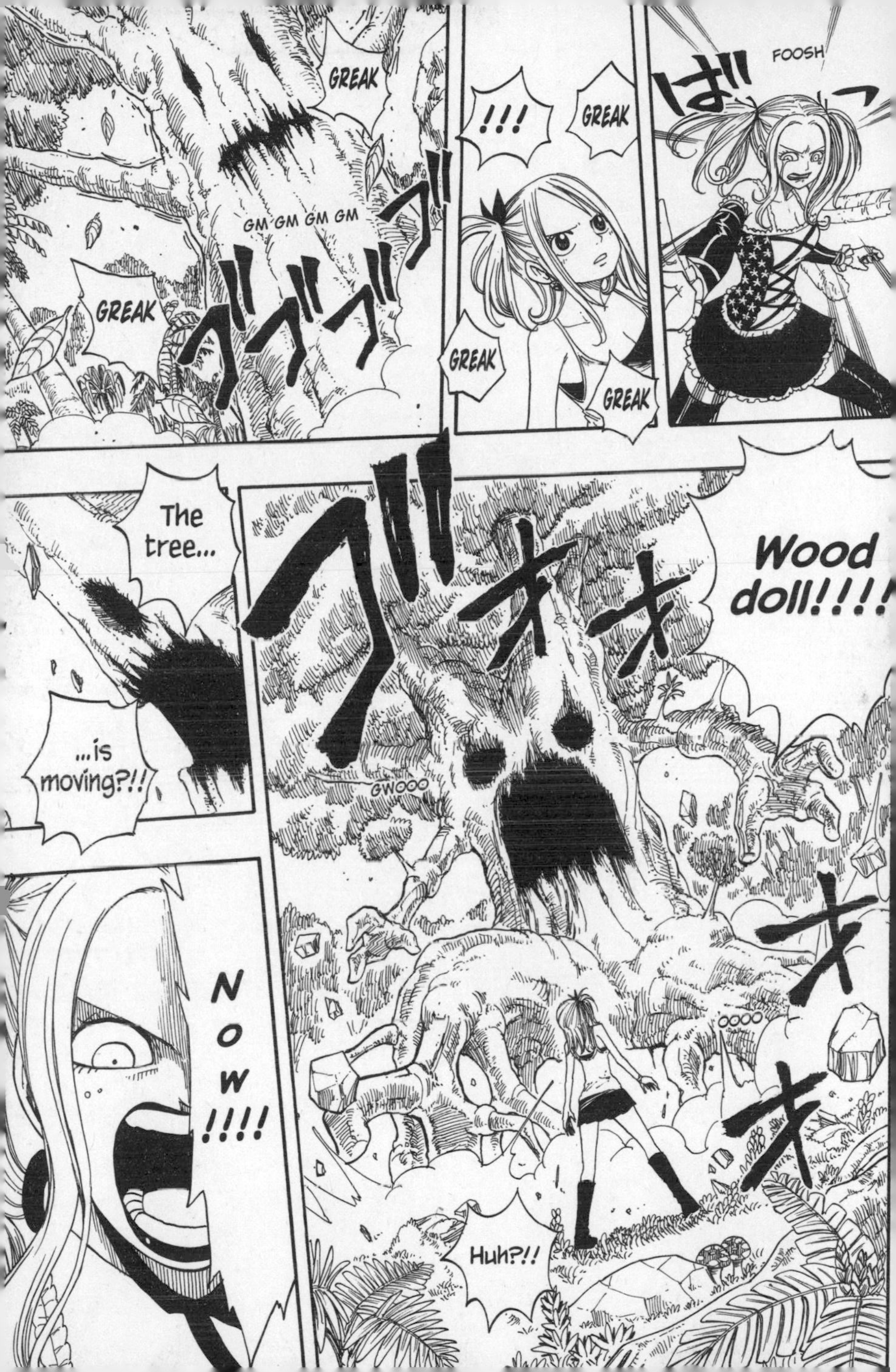
FOOSH
!!!
GREAK
GREAK
GREAK
GREAK
GM GM GM GM
GREAK
Wood doll!!!!
GWOOO
OOOO
Huh?!!
The tree...
...is moving?!!
NOW!!!!

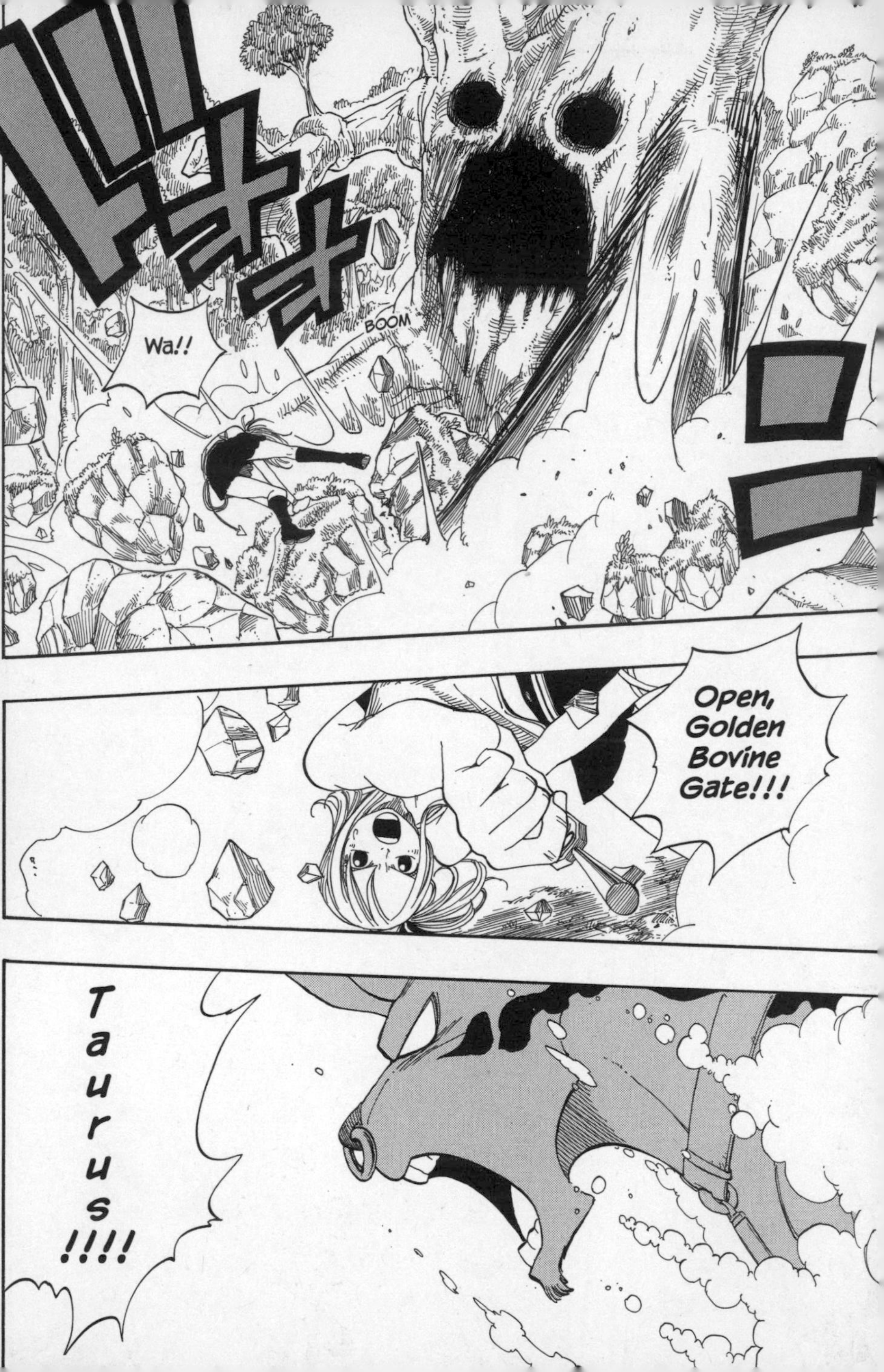
BOOM
Wa!!
Open, Golden Bovine Gate!!!
Taurus!!!!

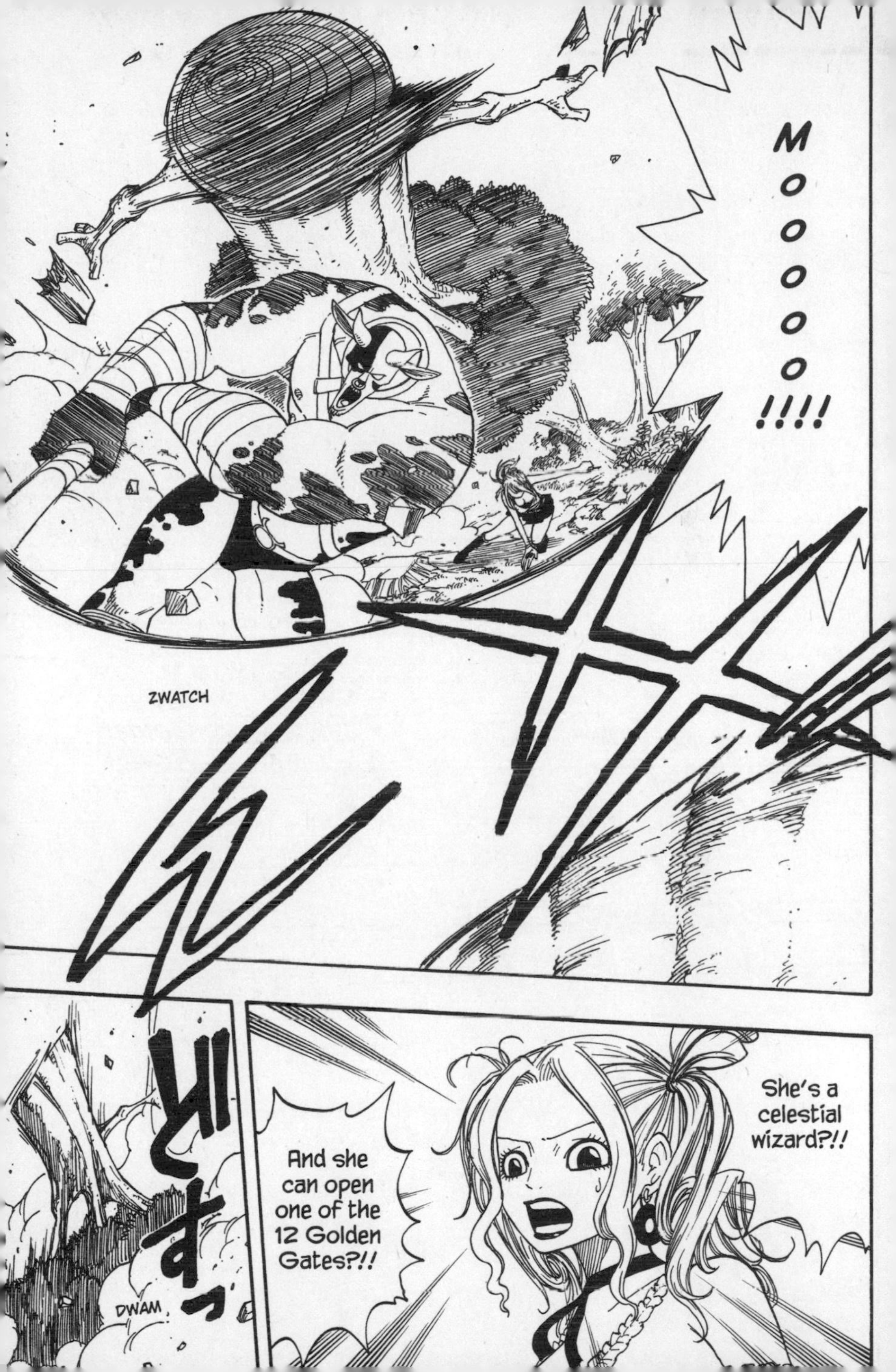
MOOOOO!!!!
ZWATCH
She's a celestial wizard?!!
And she can open one of the 12 Golden Gates?!!
どすっ
DWAM

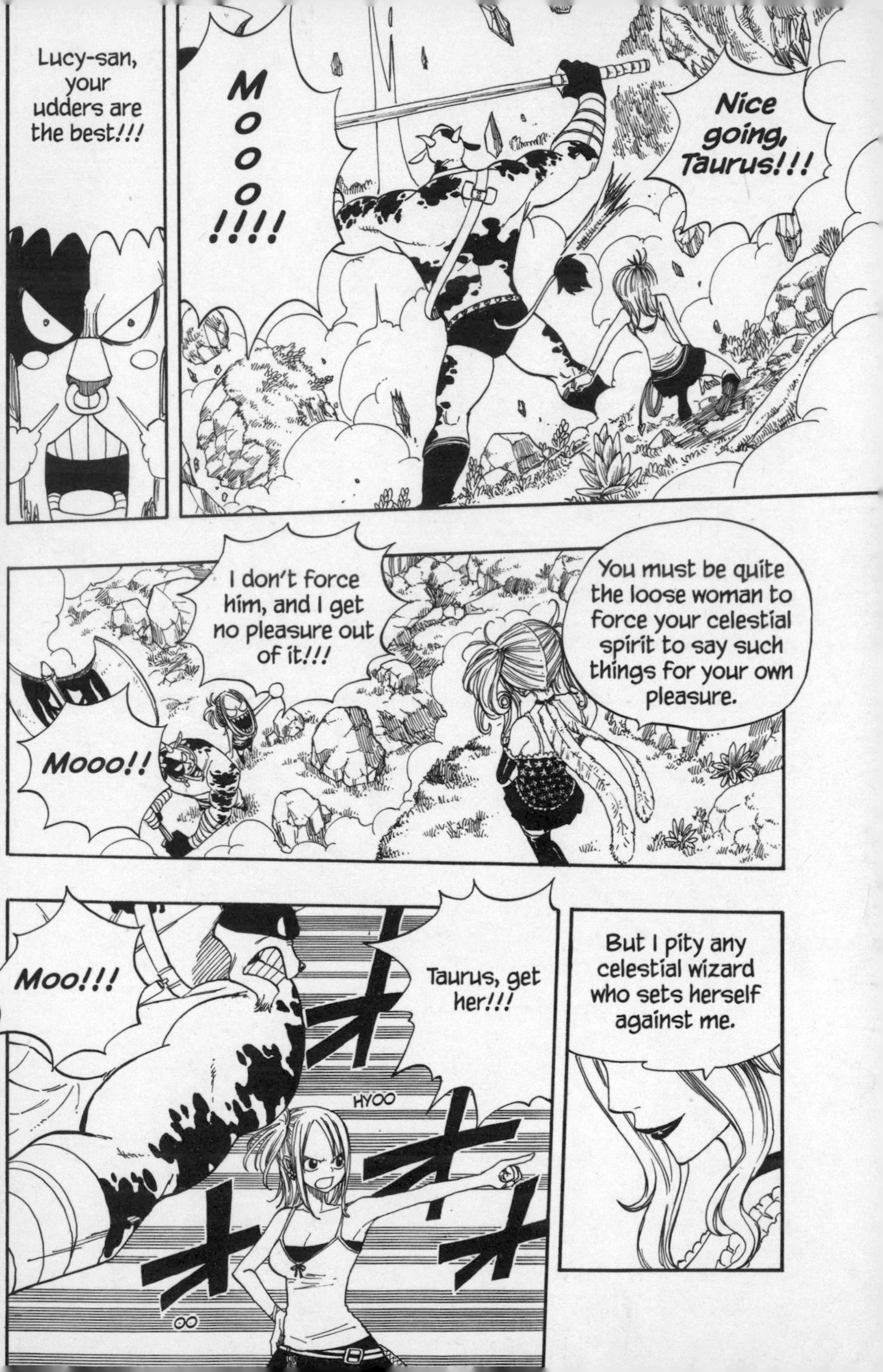
Nice going, Taurus!!!
Moooo!!!!
Lucy-san, your udders are the best!!!
You must be quite the loose woman to force your celestial spirit to say such things for your own pleasure.
I don't force him, and I get no pleasure out of it!!!
Mooo!!
But I pity any celestial wizard who sets herself against me.
Taurus, get her!!!
Moo!!!
HYOO

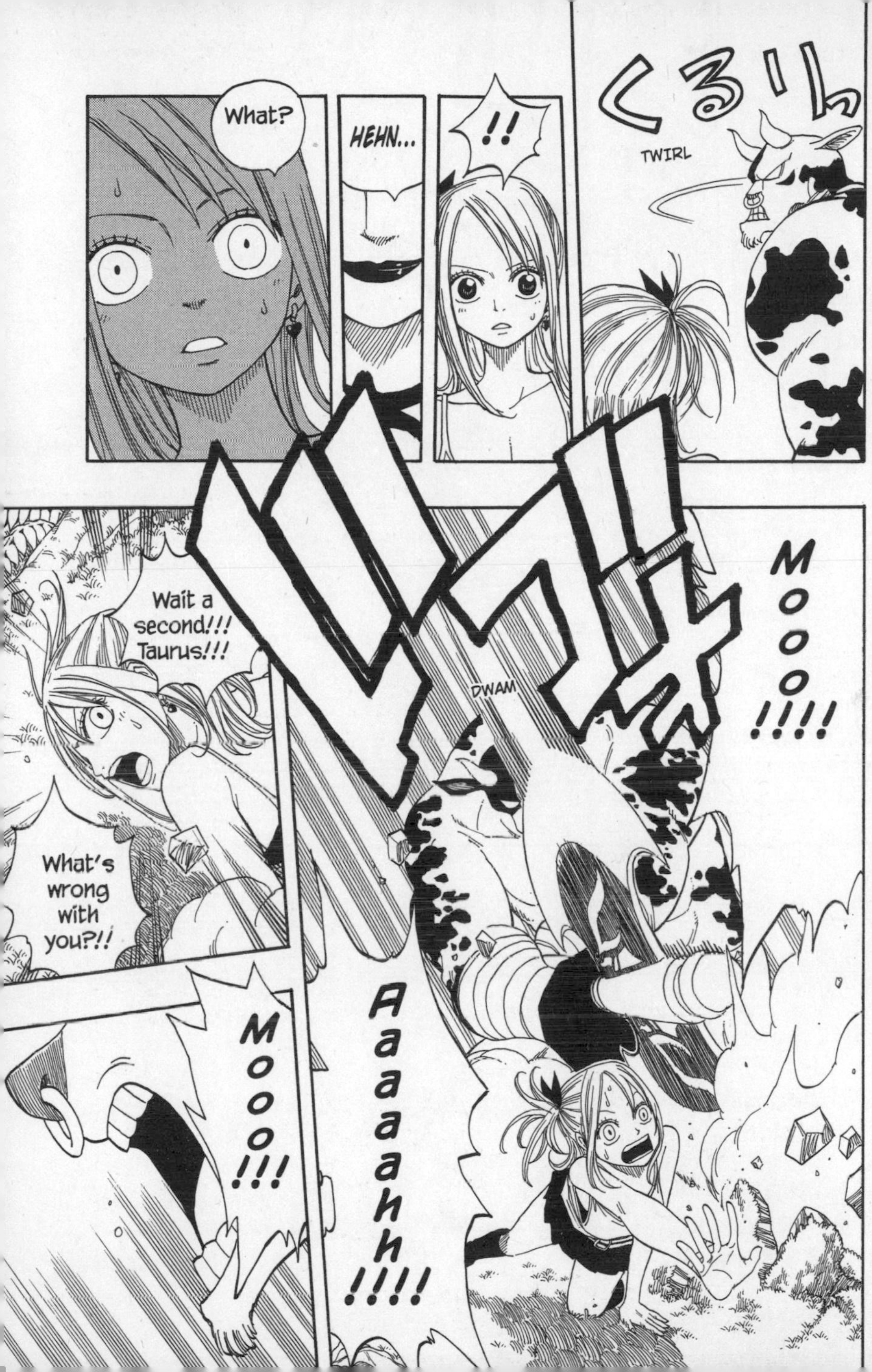
くるりん
TWIRL
!!
HEHN...
What?
MOOOO!!!!
DWAM
Wait a second!!! Taurus!!!
What's wrong with you?!!
Aaaaahh!!!!
Mooo!!!

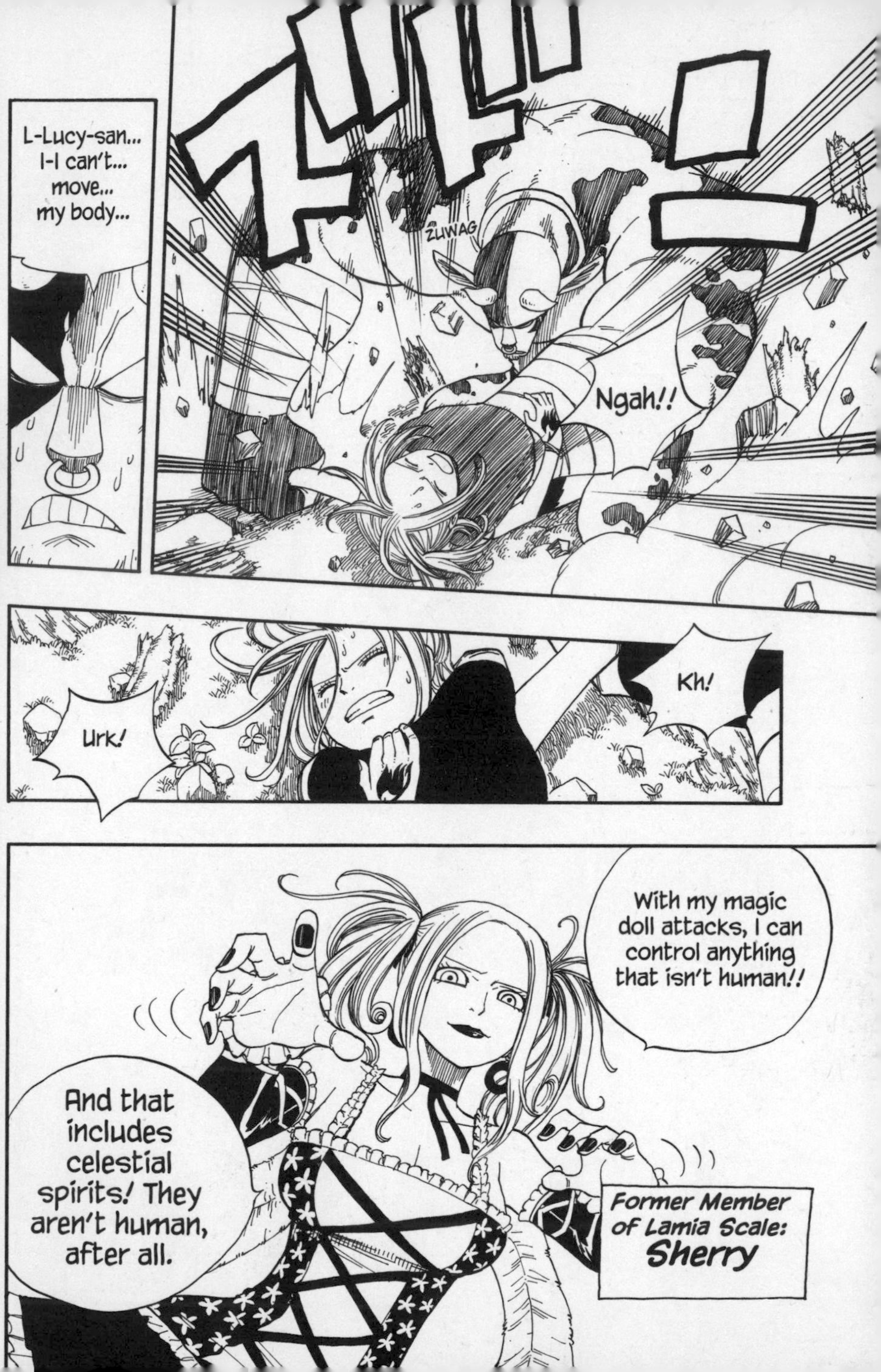
ZUWAG
Ngah!!
L-Lucy-san... I-I can't... move... my body...
Kh!
Urk!
With my magic doll attacks, I can control anything that isn't human!!
And that includes celestial spirits! They aren't human, after all.
Former Member of Lamia Scale: Sherry

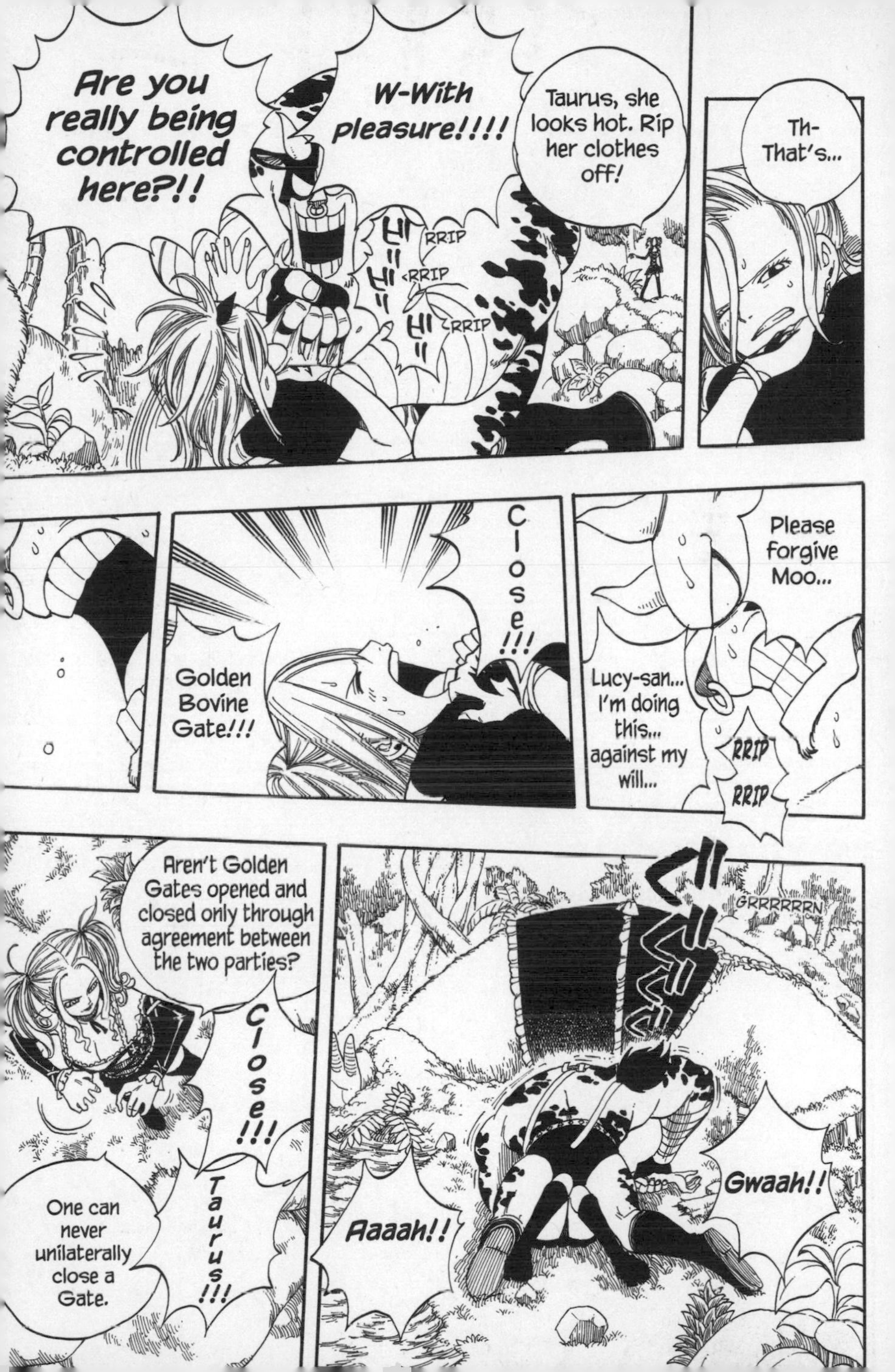
Th- That's...
Taurus, she looks hot. Rip her clothes off!
W-With pleasure!!!!
RRIP
RRIP
RRIP
Are you really being controlled here?!!
Please forgive Moo...
Lucy-san... I'm doing this... against my will...
RRIP
RRIP
Close!!!
Golden Bovine Gate!!!
GRRRRRRN
Gwaah!!
Aaaah!!
Aren't Golden Gates opened and closed only through agreement between the two parties?
Close!!!
Taurus!!!
One can never unilaterally close a Gate.

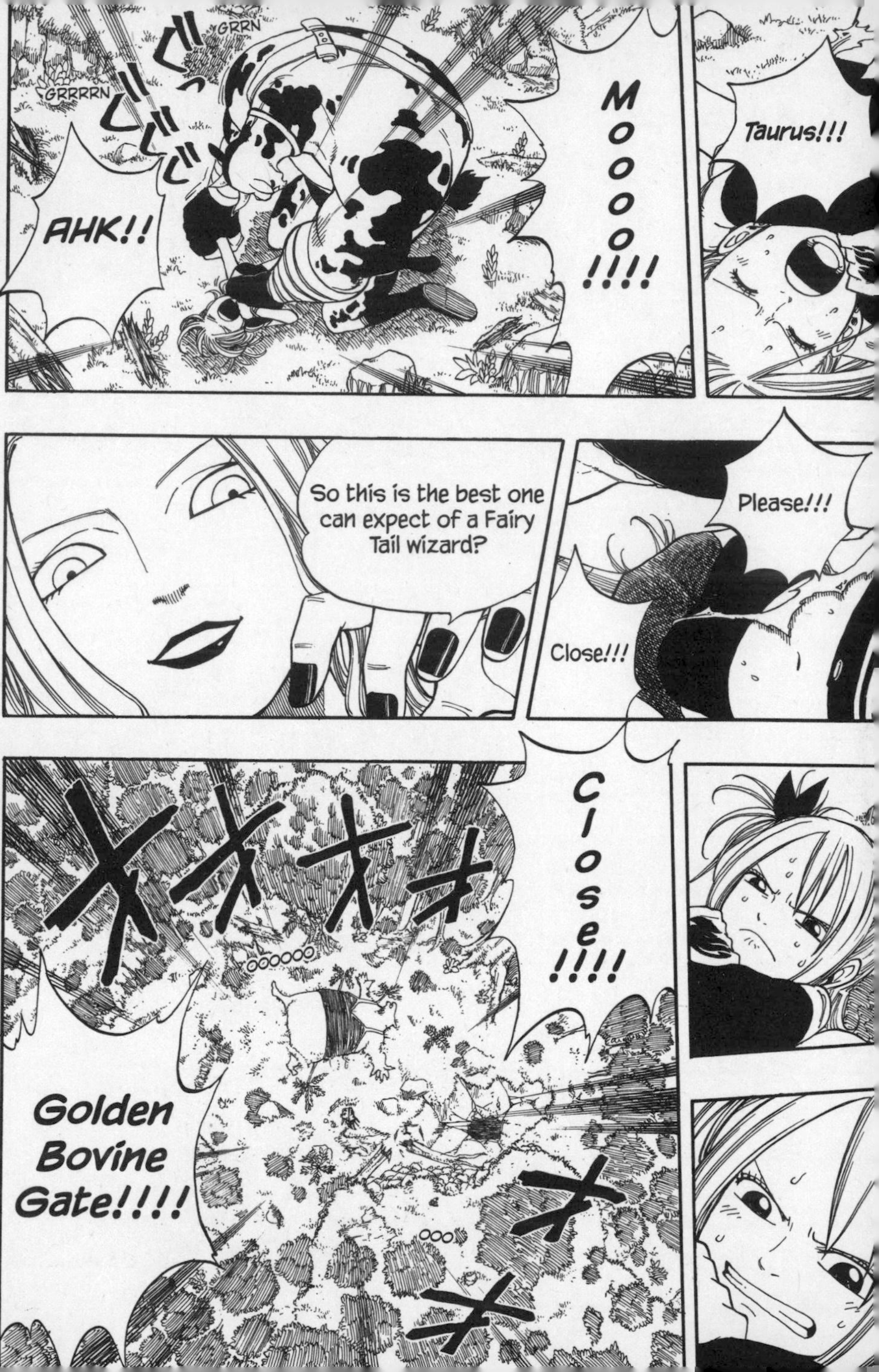
Taurus!!!
GRRN
GRRRRN
Moooo!!!!
AHK!!
Please!!!
Close!!!
So this is the best one can expect of a Fairy Tail wizard?
Close!!!!
oooooo
Golden Bovine Gate!!!!
ooo

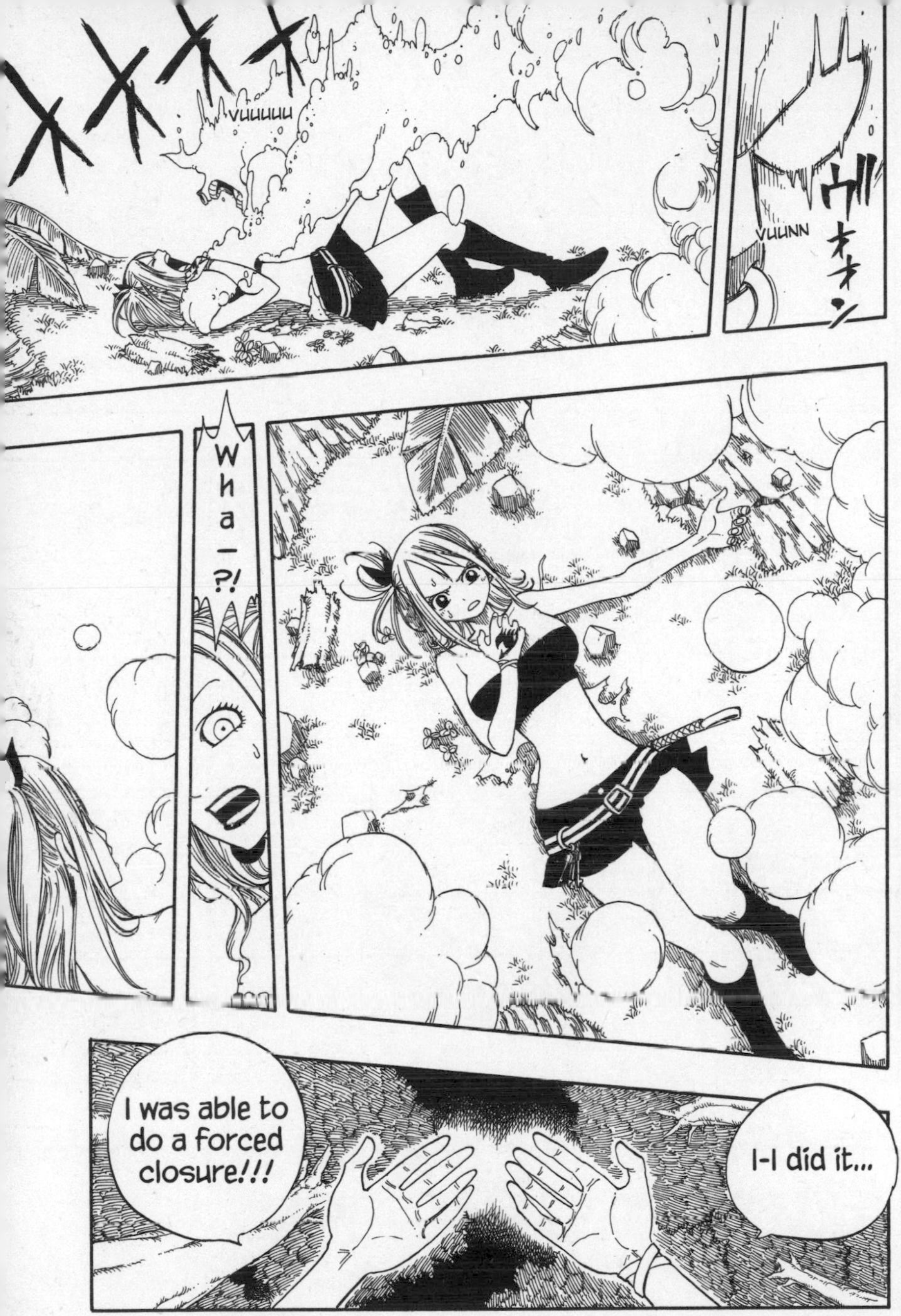
ヴォォン
VUUNN
VUUUUU
Wha—?!
I-I did it...
I was able to do a forced closure!!!

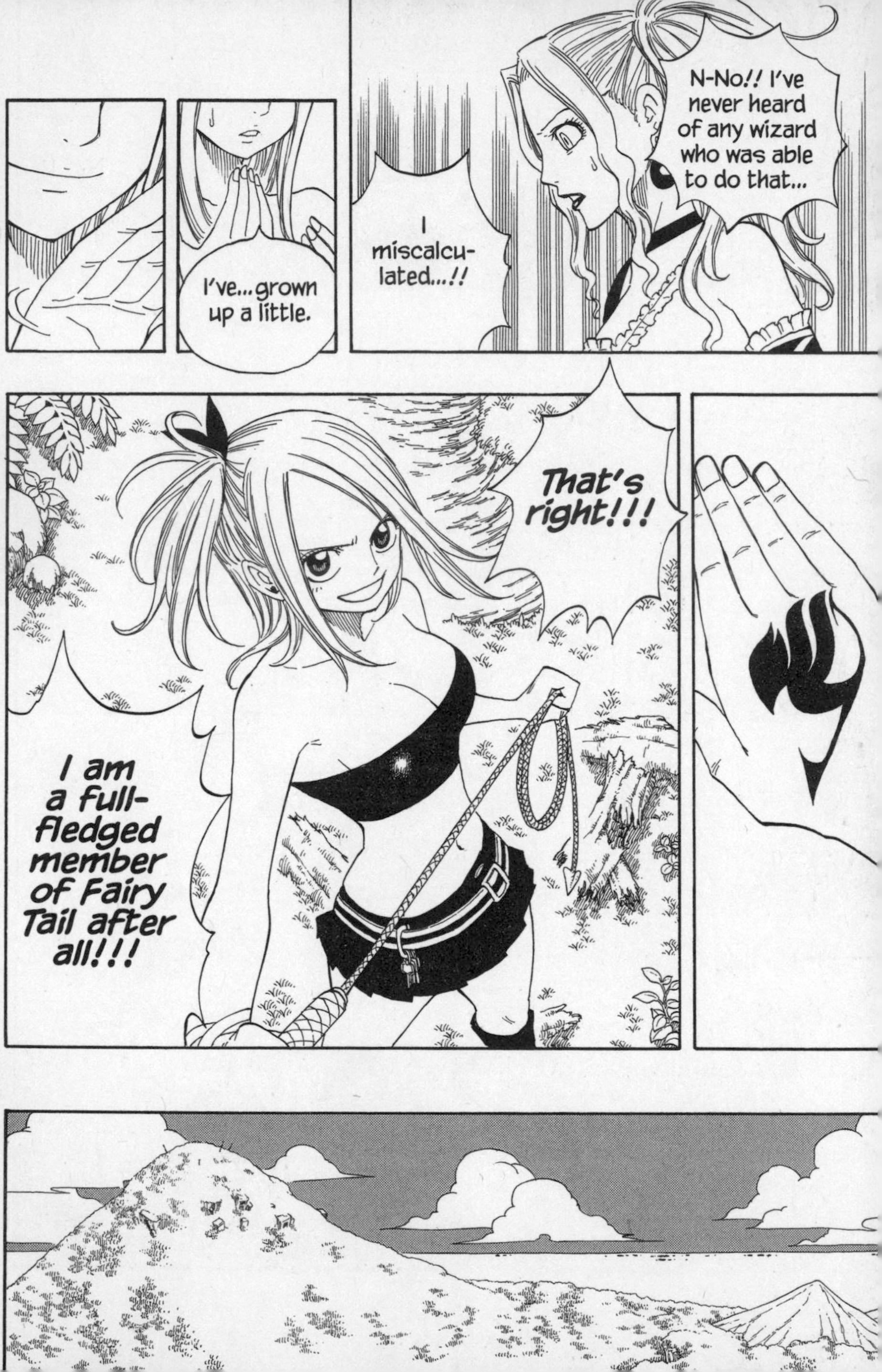
N-No!! I've never heard of any wizard who was able to do that...
I miscalcu-lated...!!
I've...grown up a little.
That's right!!!
I am a full-fledged member of Fairy Tail after all!!!

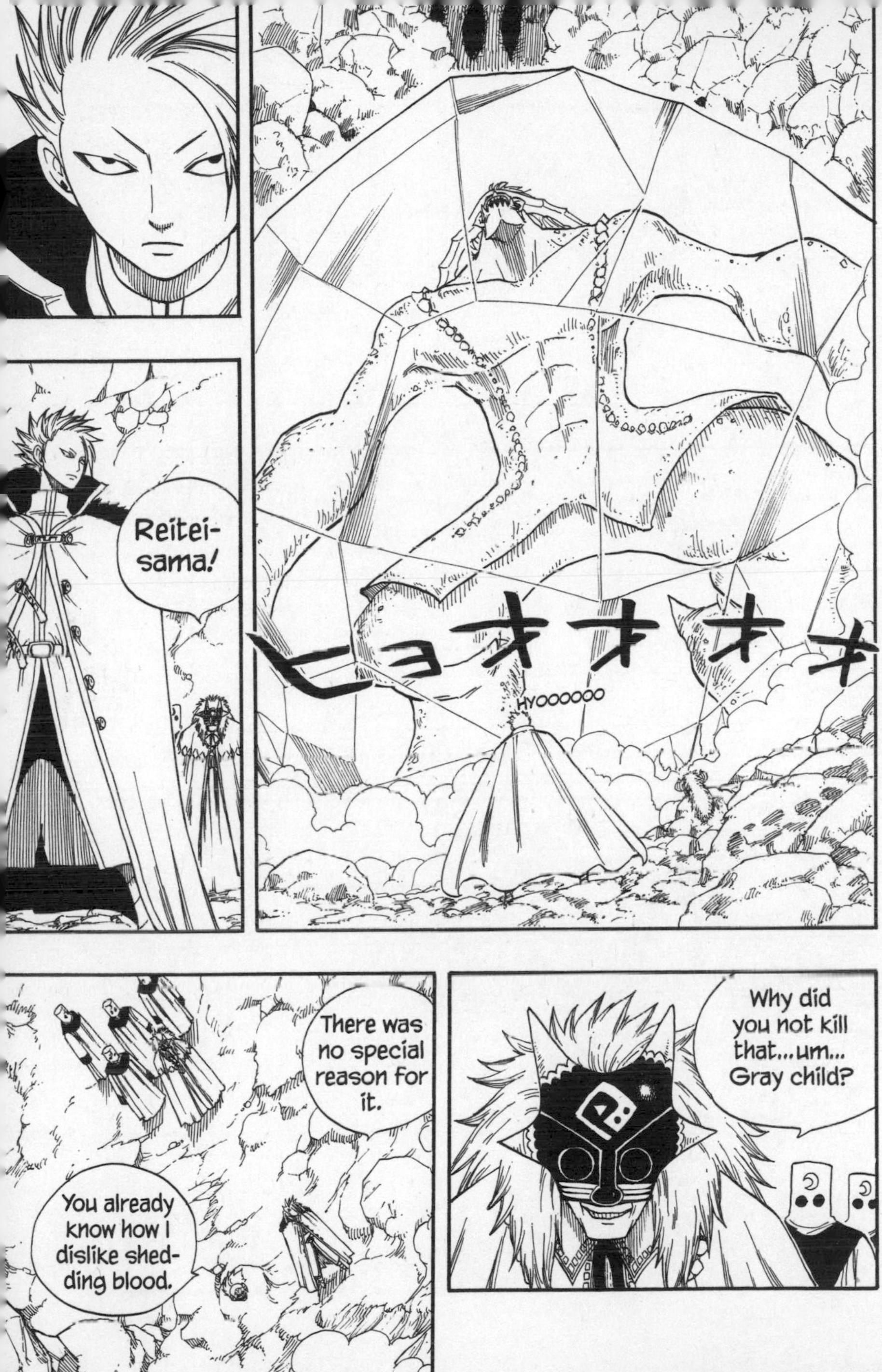
ヒョオオオオ
HYOOOOOO
Reitei-sama!
Why did you not kill that...um... Gray child?
There was no special reason for it.
You already know how I dislike shedding blood.

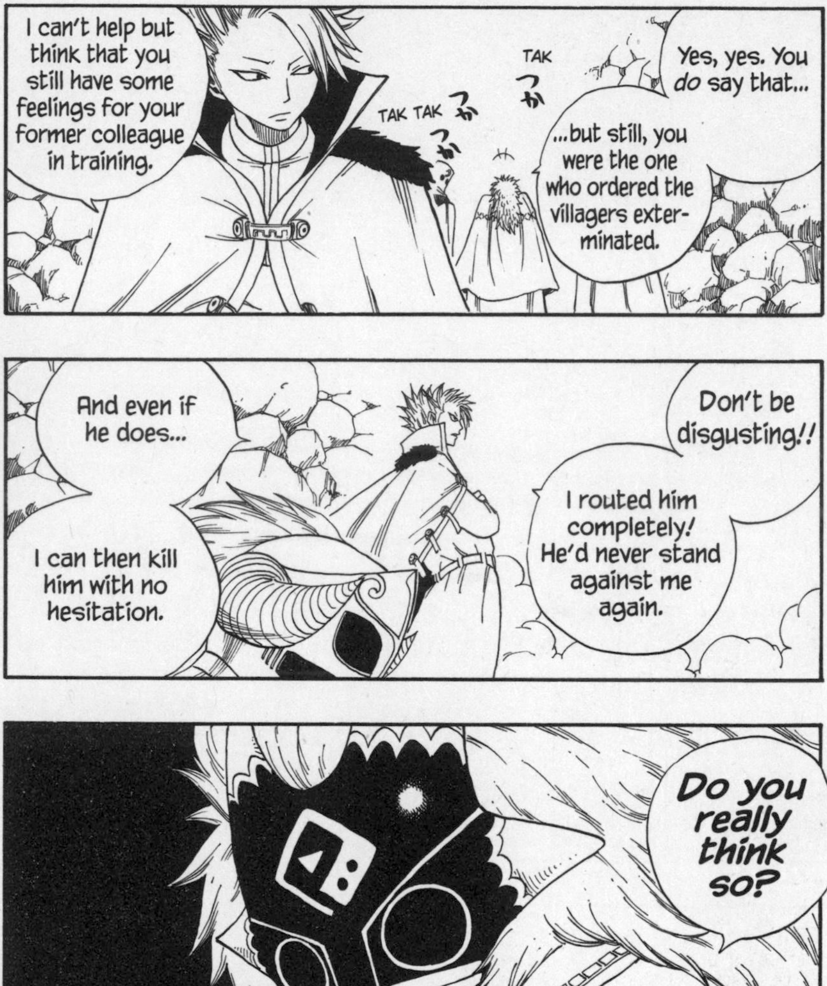
Yes, yes. You *do* say that...
TAK
TAK TAK
...but still, you were the one who ordered the villagers exter-minated.
I can't help but think that you still have some feelings for your former colleague in training.
Don't be disgusting!!
I routed him completely! He'd never stand against me again.
And even if he does...
I can then kill him with no hesitation.
Do you really think so?

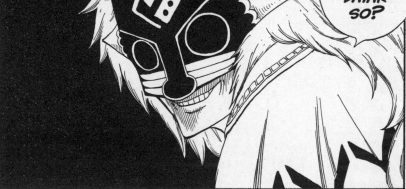

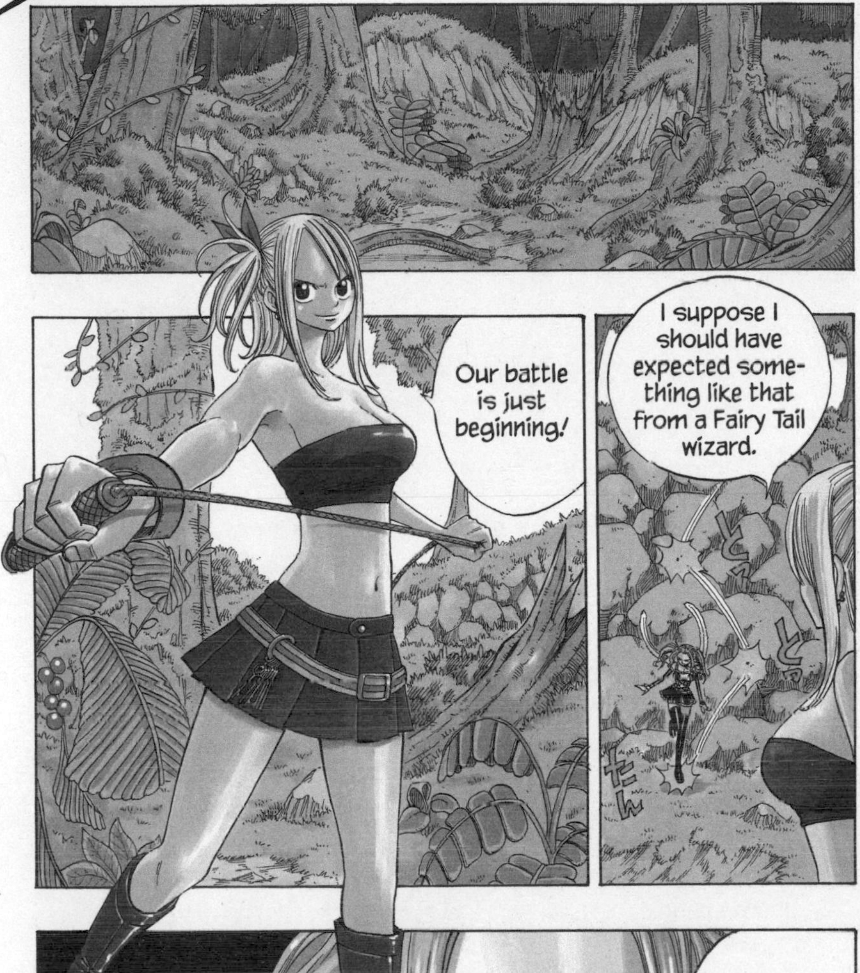
I suppose I should have expected some-thing like that from a Fairy Tail wizard.
Our battle is just beginning!
But be sure not to forget...
Your celestial spirits have no effect on me.

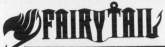

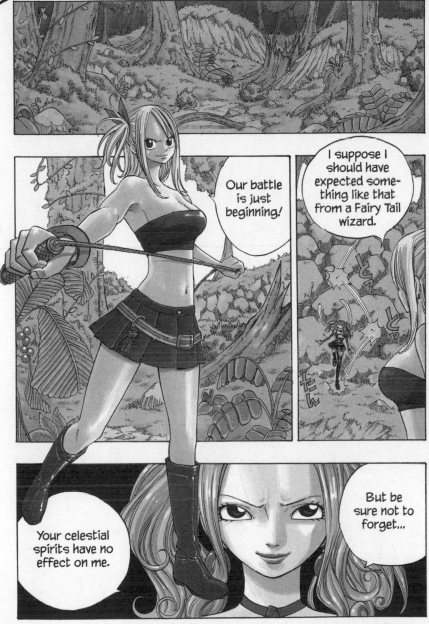

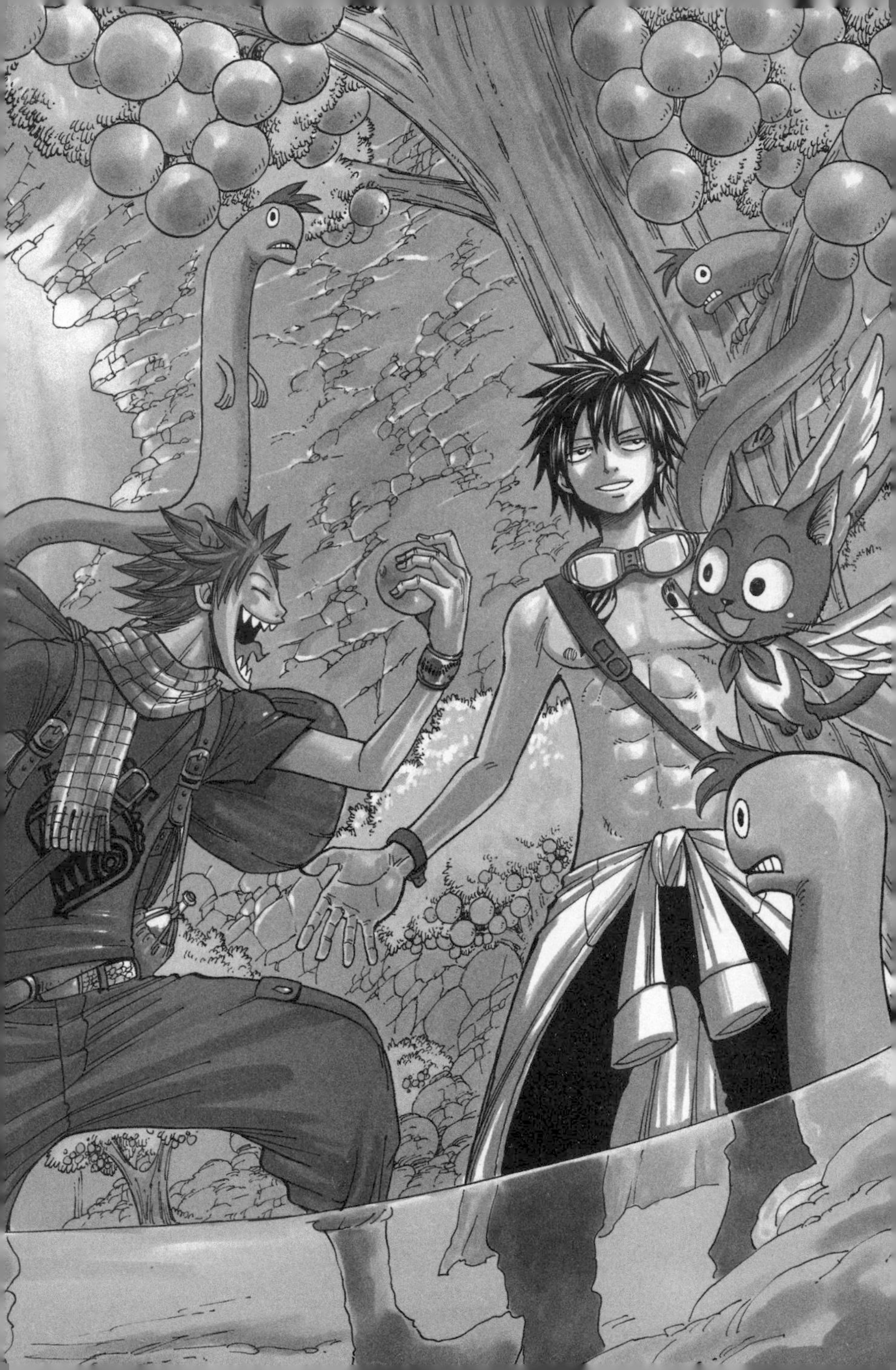

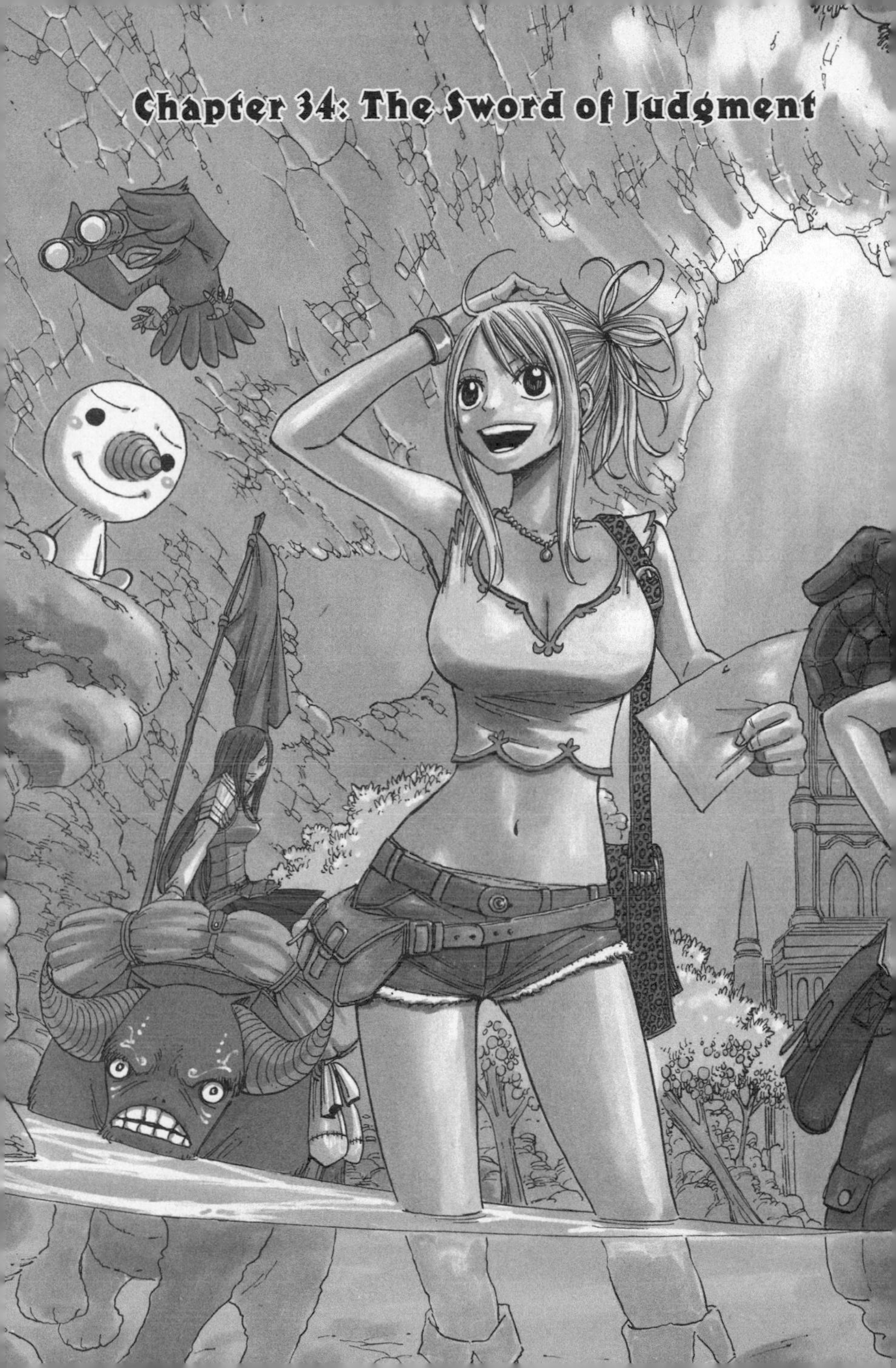
Chapter 34: The Sword of Judgment

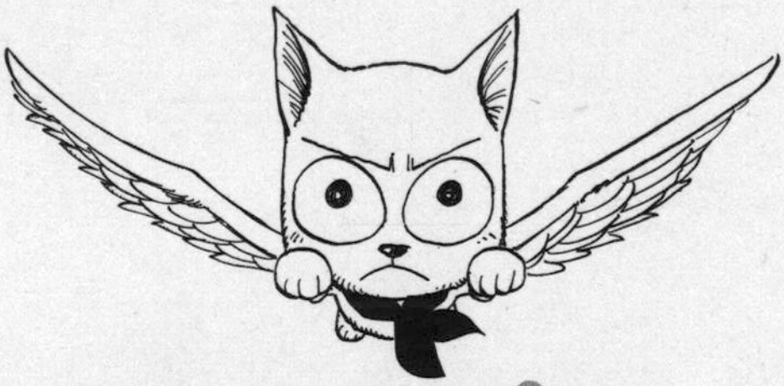

FAIRY TAIL

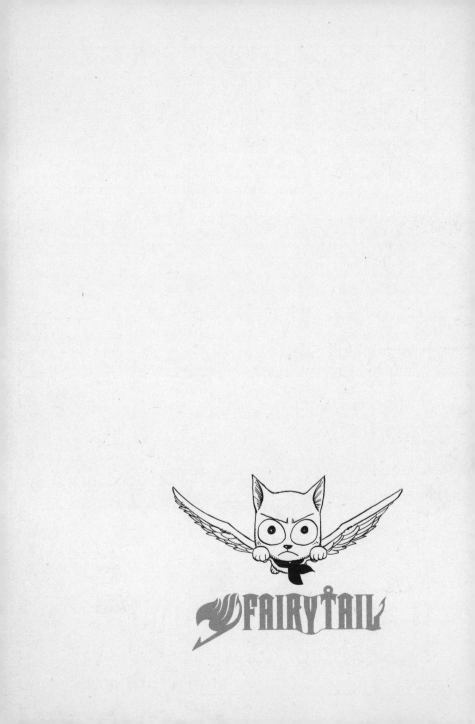

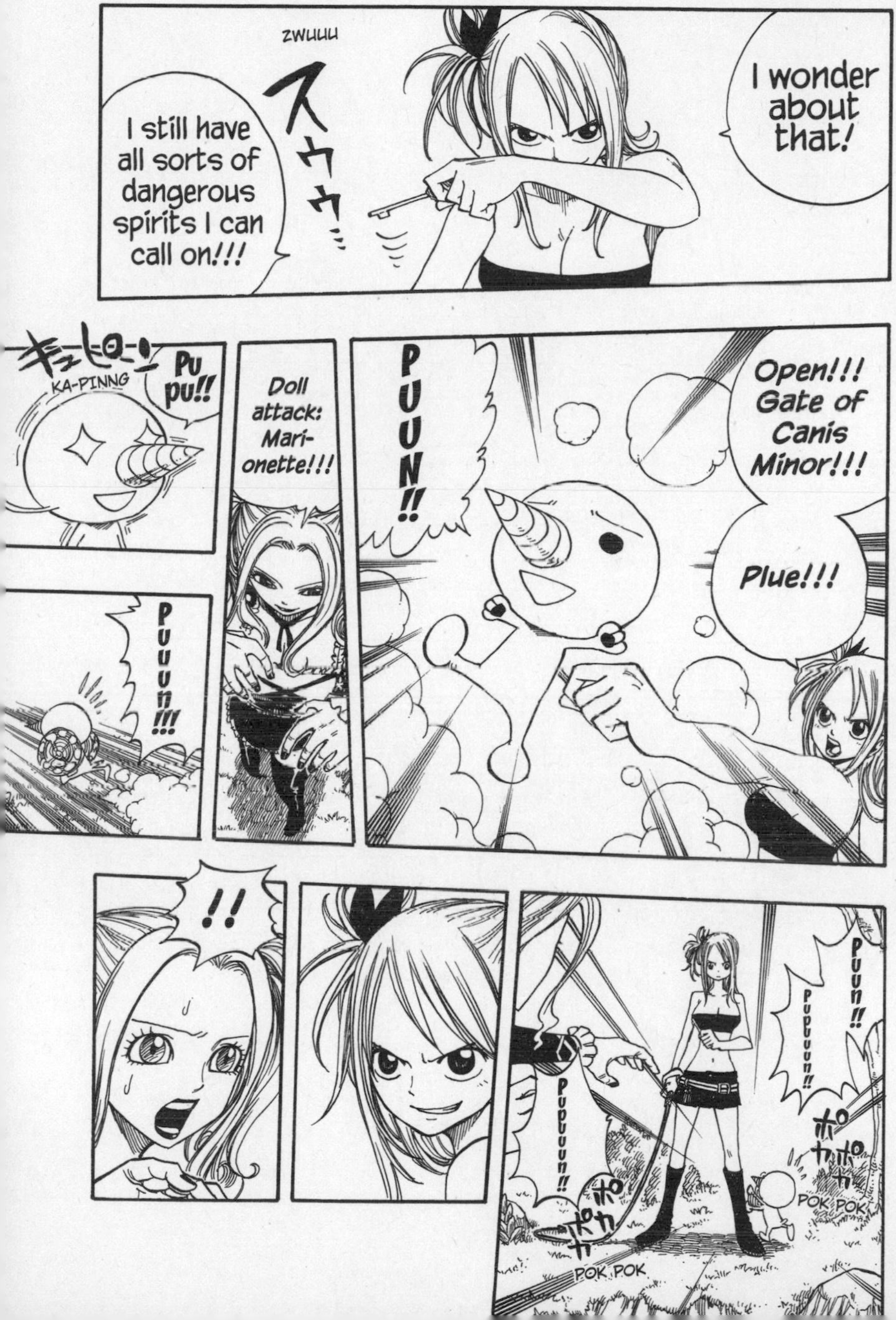
I wonder about that!
ZWUUU
I still have all sorts of dangerous spirits I can call on!!!
Open!!! Gate of Canis Minor!!!
Plue!!!
PUUUN!!
Doll attack: Mari-onette!!!
KA-PINNG
Pu pu!!
Puuuun!!!
Puuun!!
Pupuuun!!
POK POK
Pupuuun!!
POK POK
!!

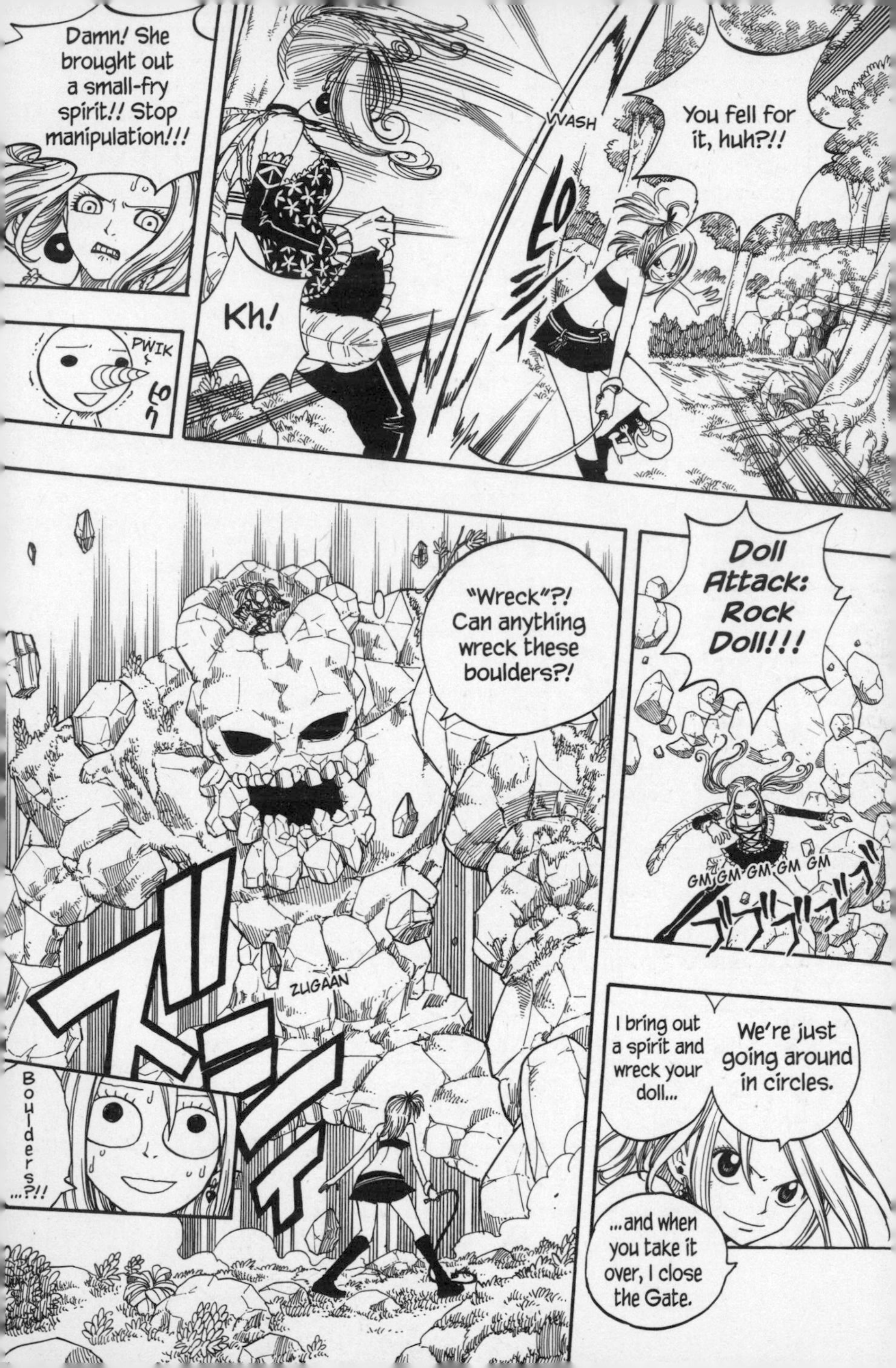
VVASH
You fell for it, huh?!!
Kh!
Damn! She brought out a small-fry spirit!! Stop manipulation!!!
PWIK
Doll Attack: Rock Doll!!!
GM GM GM GM GM
We're just going around in circles.
I bring out a spirit and wreck your doll...
...and when you take it over, I close the Gate.
"Wreck"?! Can anything wreck these boulders?!
ZUGAAN
Boulders...?!!

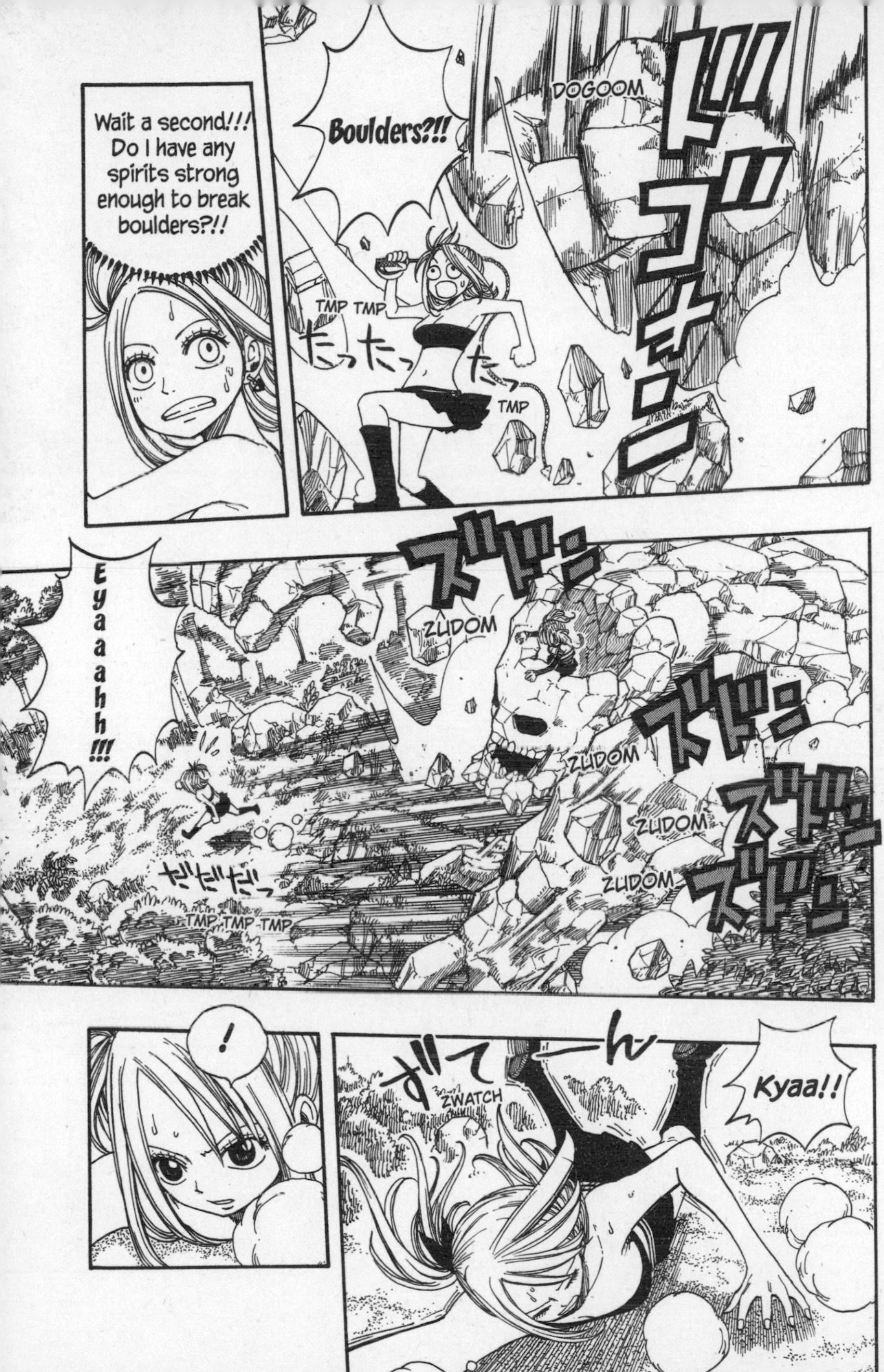
DOGOOM
Boulders?!!
TMP TMP
TMP
Wait a second!!! Do I have any spirits strong enough to break boulders?!!
ZUDOM
ZUDOM
ZUDOM
ZUDOM
Eyaaaahh!!!
TMP TMP TMP
Kyaa!!
ZWATCH
!

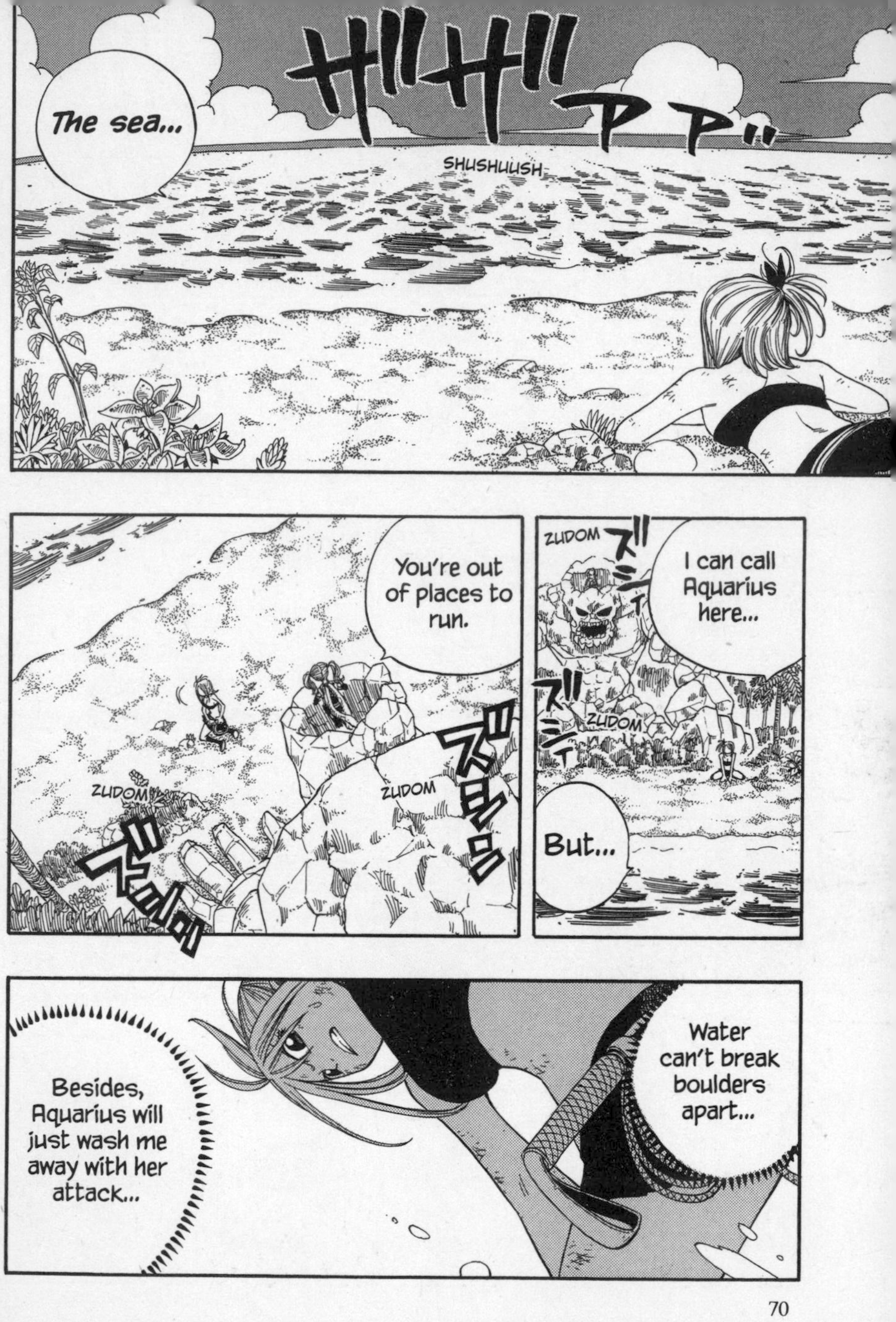
The sea...
SHUSHUUSH
ZUDOM
I can call Aquarius here...
ZUDOM
But...
You're out of places to run.
ZUDOM
ZUDOM
Water can't break boulders apart...
Besides, Aquarius will just wash me away with her attack...

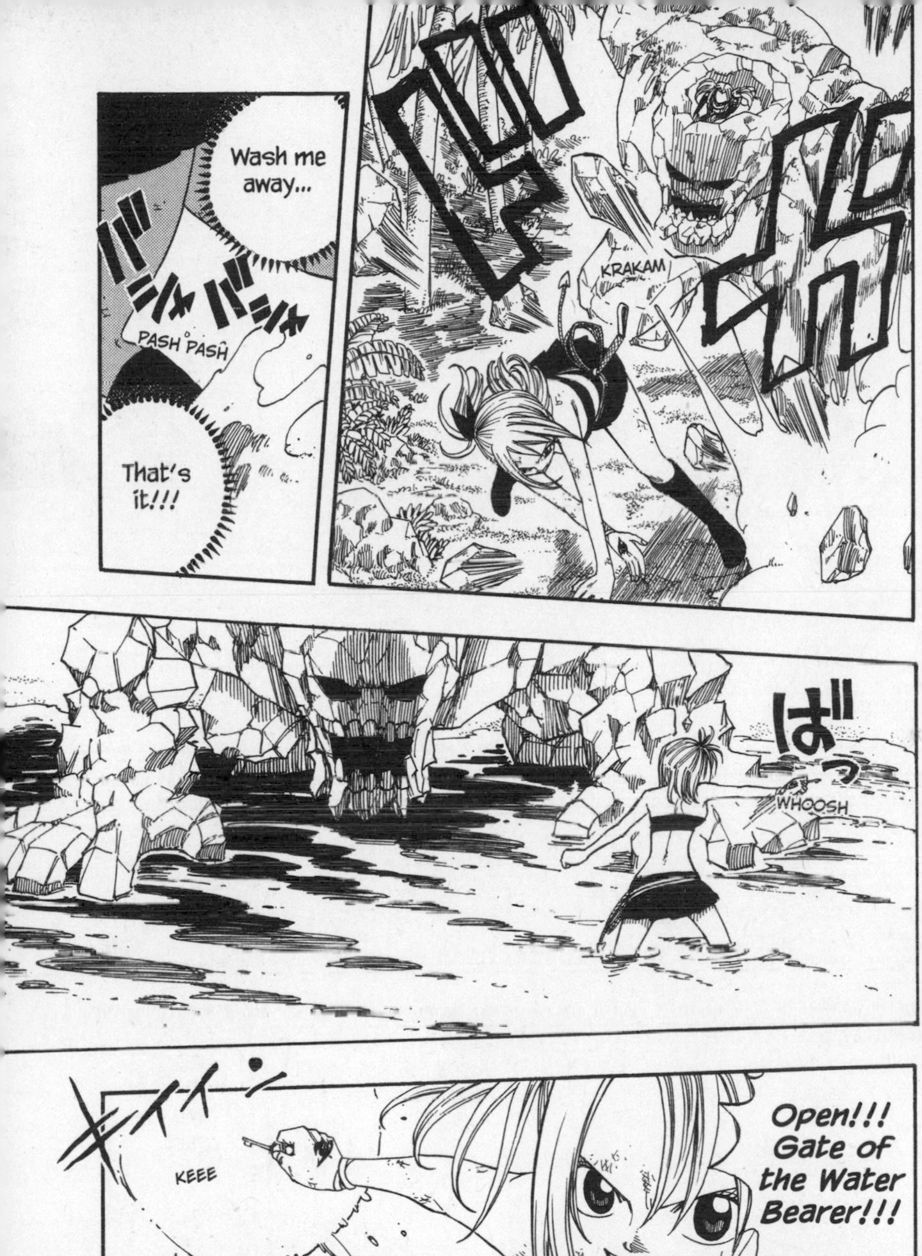
KRAKAM
Wash me away...
バシャ バシャ
PASH PASH
That's it!!!
ばっ
WHOOSH
Open!!! Gate of the Water Bearer!!!
KEEE

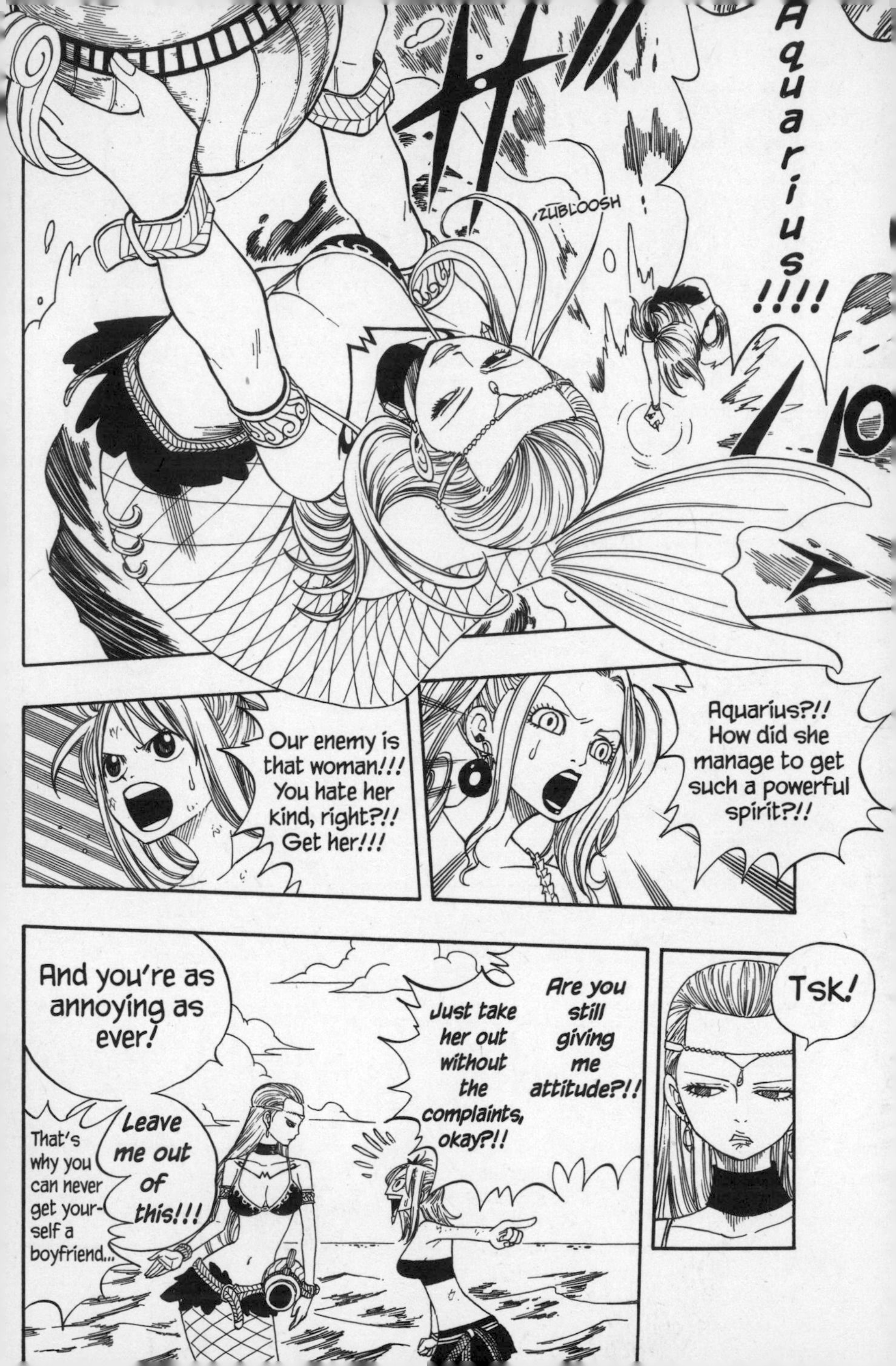
Aquarius!!!!
ZUBLOOSH
Aquarius?!! How did she manage to get such a powerful spirit?!!
Our enemy is that woman!!! You hate her kind, right?!! Get her!!!
Tsk!
Are you still giving me attitude?!!
Just take her out without the complaints, okay?!!
And you're as annoying as ever!
Leave me out of this!!!
That's why you can never get your-self a boyfriend...

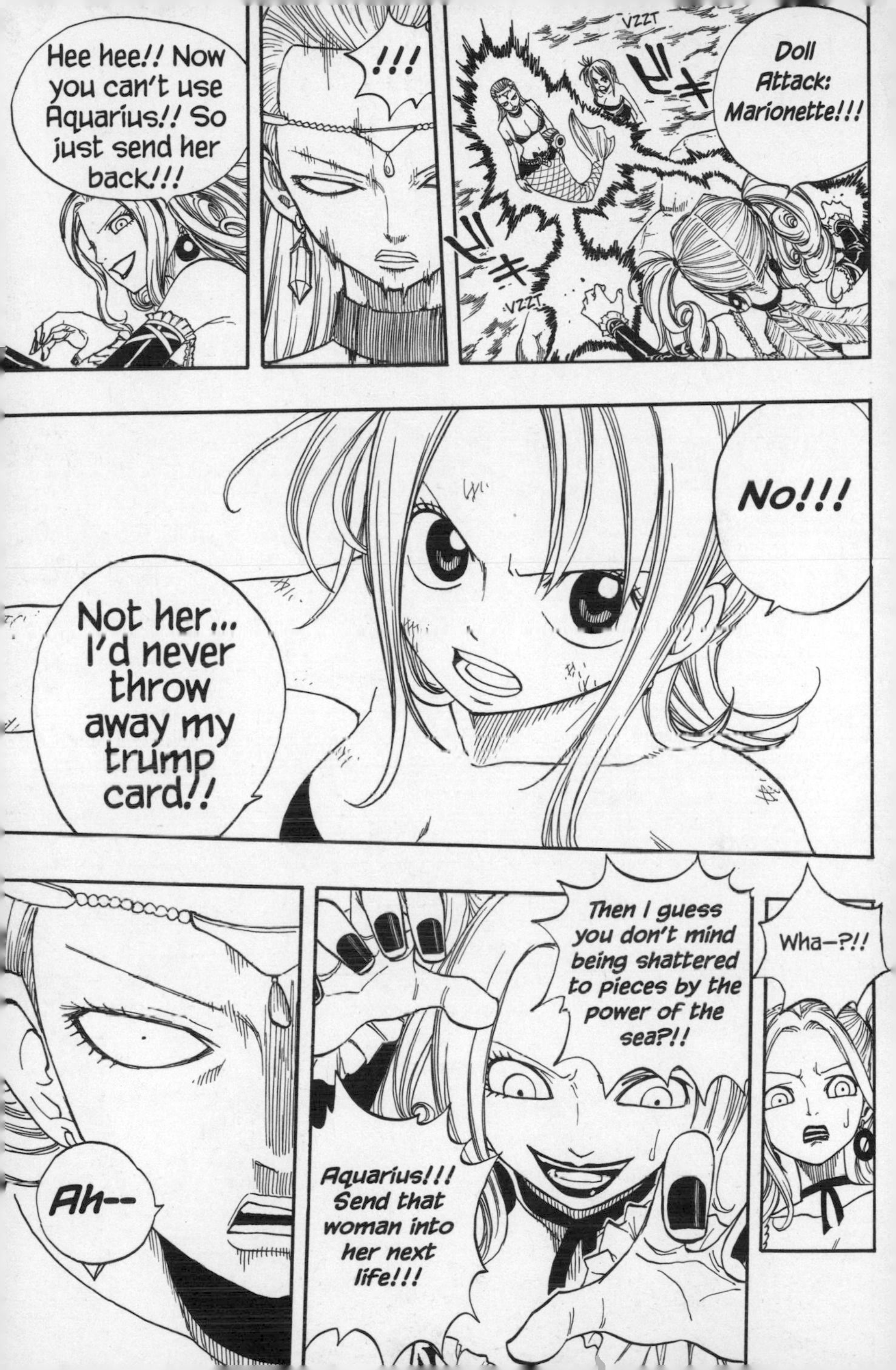
VZZT
Doll Attack: Marionette!!!
VZZT
!!!
Hee hee!! Now you can't use Aquarius!! So just send her back!!!
No!!!
Not her... I'd never throw away my trump card!!
Wha–?!!
Then I guess you don't mind being shattered to pieces by the power of the sea?!!
Aquarius!!! Send that woman into her next life!!!
Ah--

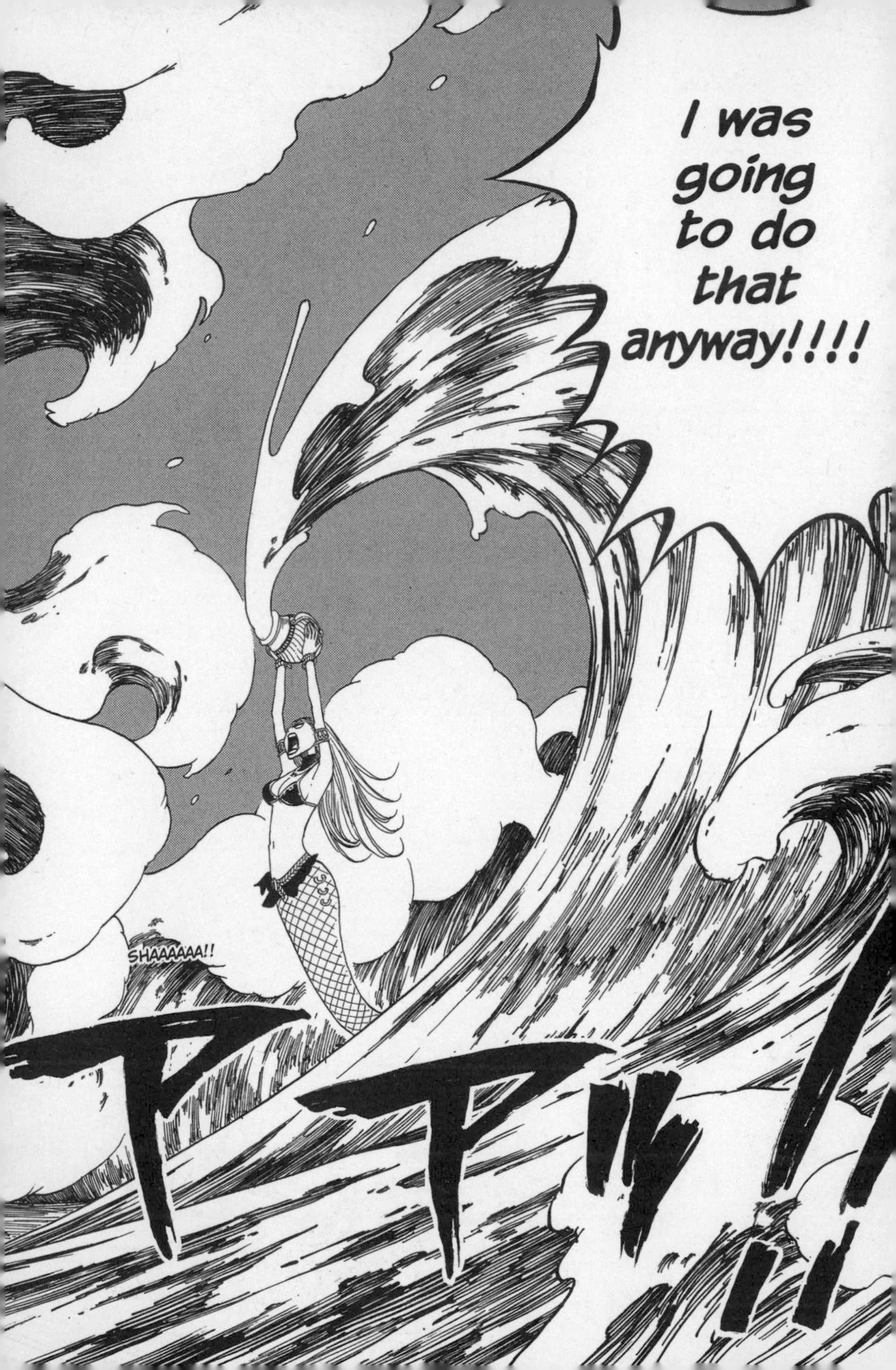
I was going to do that anyway!!!!
SHAAAAAA!!

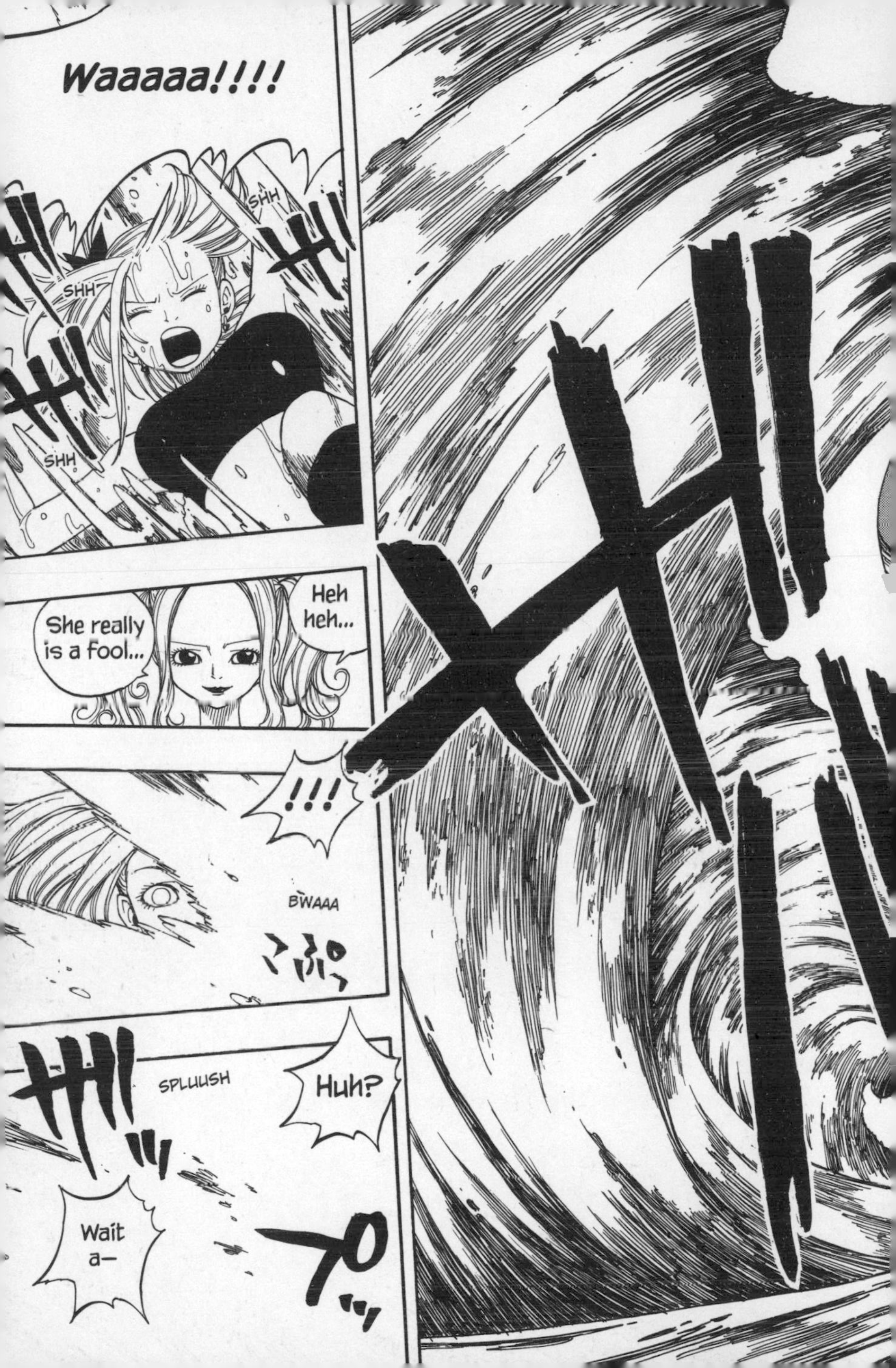
Waaaaa!!!!
SHH
SHH
SHH
Heh heh...
She really is a fool...
!!!
BWAAA
Huh?
SPLUUSH
Wait a—

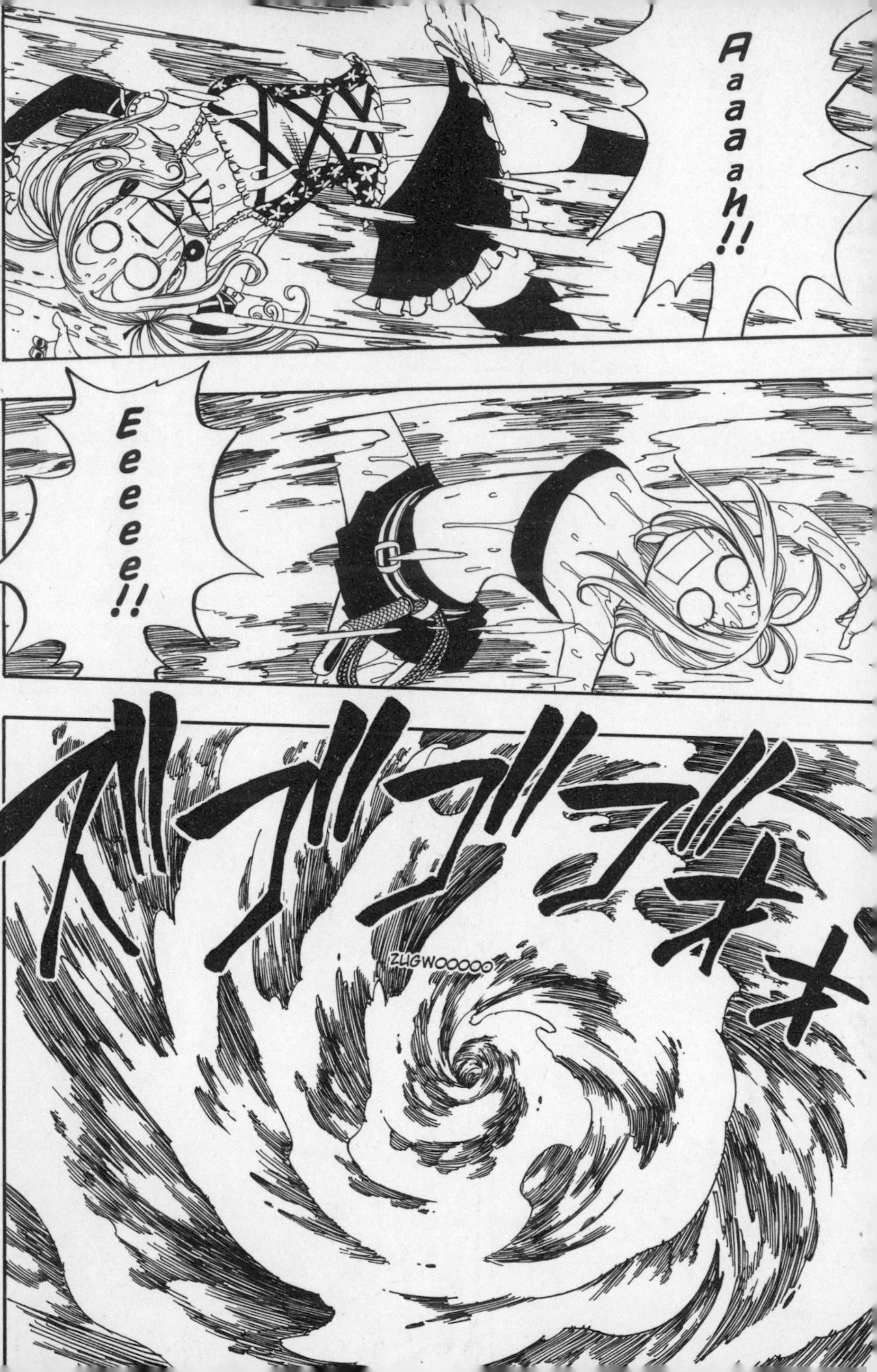
Aaaaah!!
Eeeee!!
ZUGWOOOOOO

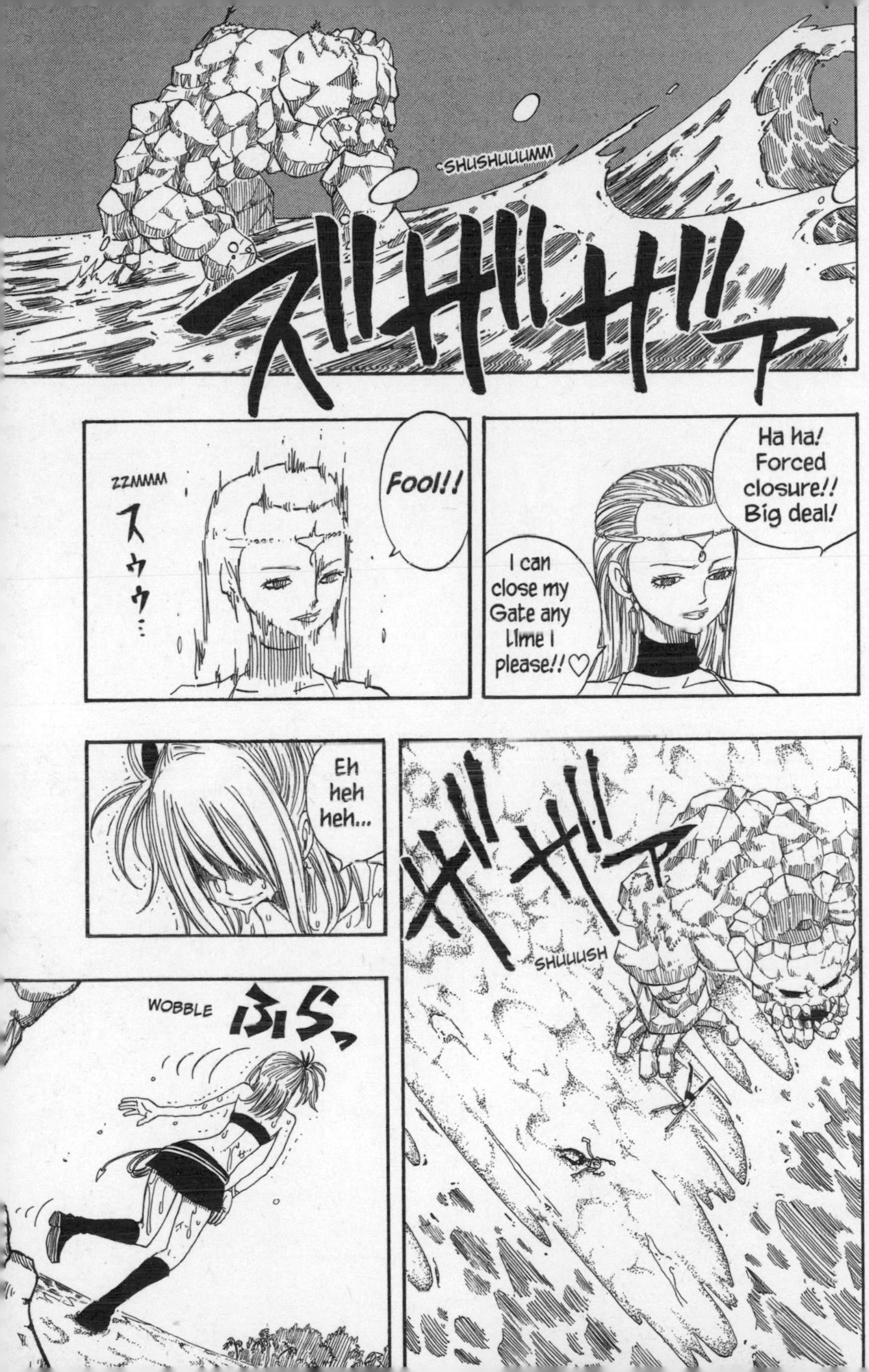
SHUSHUUUMM
ズザザァ
Ha ha! Forced closure!! Big deal!
I can close my Gate any time I please!! ♡
Fool!!
ZZMMM
スウゥ
ザザァ
SHUUUSH
Eh heh heh...
WOBBLE
ふらっ

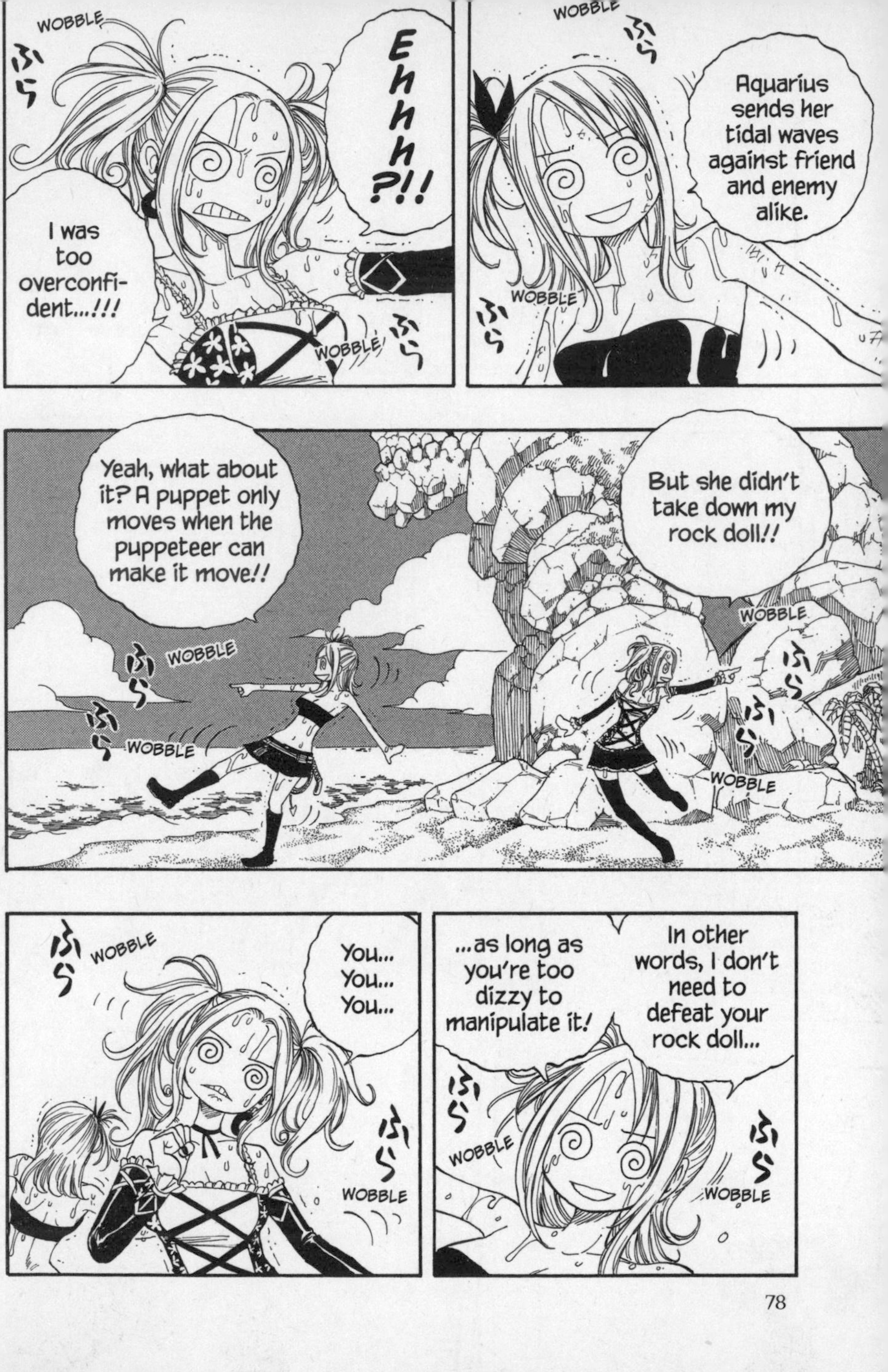
WOBBLE
ふら
Aquarius sends her tidal waves against friend and enemy alike.
WOBBLE
ふら
WOBBLE
ふら
Ehhh?!!
I was too overconfi-dent...!!!
WOBBLE
ふら
But she didn't take down my rock doll!!
WOBBLE
ふら
ふら
WOBBLE
Yeah, what about it? A puppet only moves when the puppeteer can make it move!!
ふら
WOBBLE
ふら
WOBBLE
In other words, I don't need to defeat your rock doll...
...as long as you're too dizzy to manipulate it!
ふら
WOBBLE
ふら
WOBBLE
ふら
WOBBLE
You... You... You...
ふら
WOBBLE

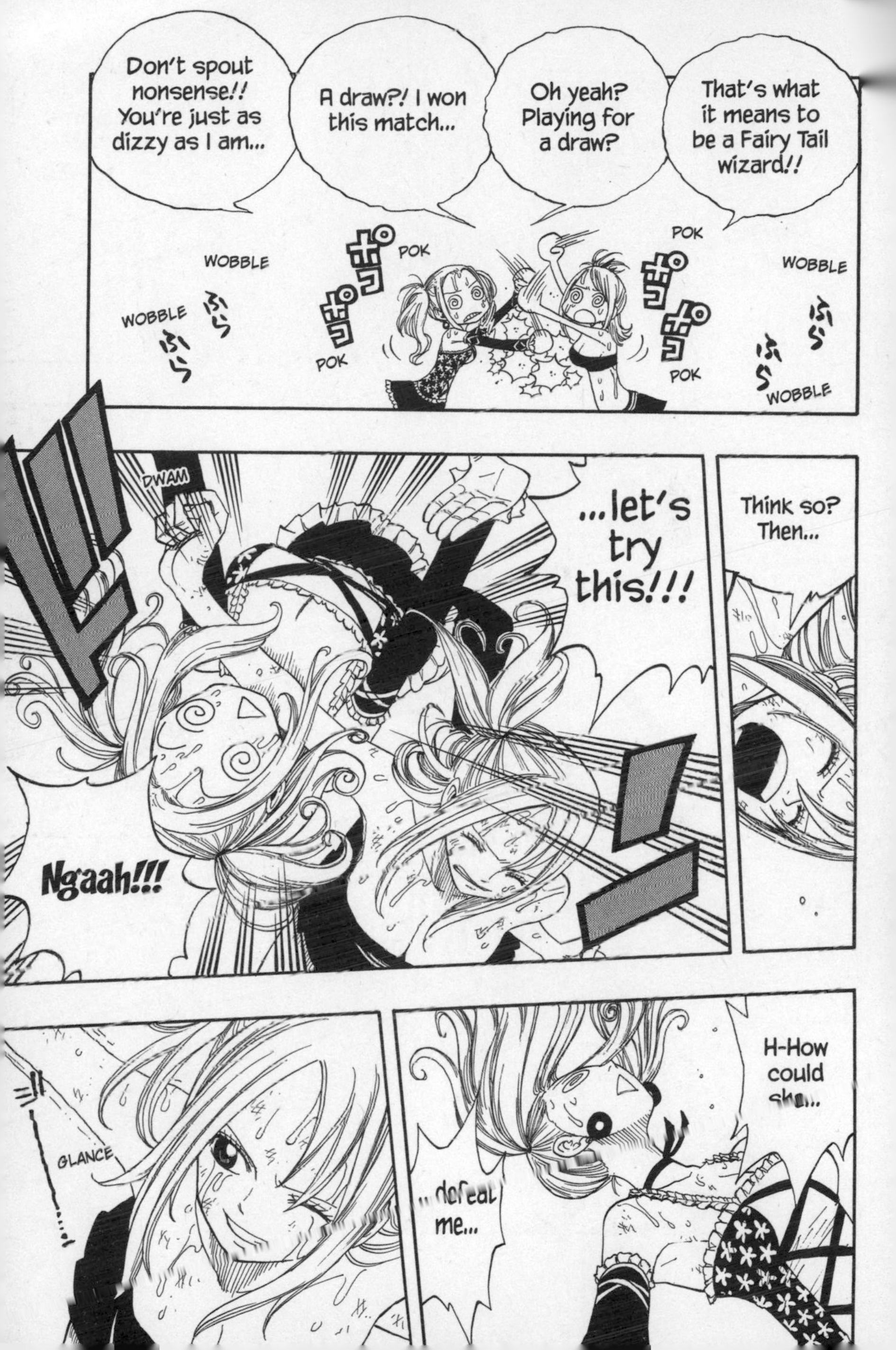

That's what it means to be a Fairy Tail wizard!!
Oh yeah? Playing for a draw?
A draw?! I won this match...
Don't spout nonsense!! You're just as dizzy as I am...
WOBBLE
WOBBLE
POK
POK
POK
POK
WOBBLE
WOBBLE
Think so? Then...
...let's try this!!!
DWAM
Ngaah!!!
H-How could she...
...defeat me...
GLANCE

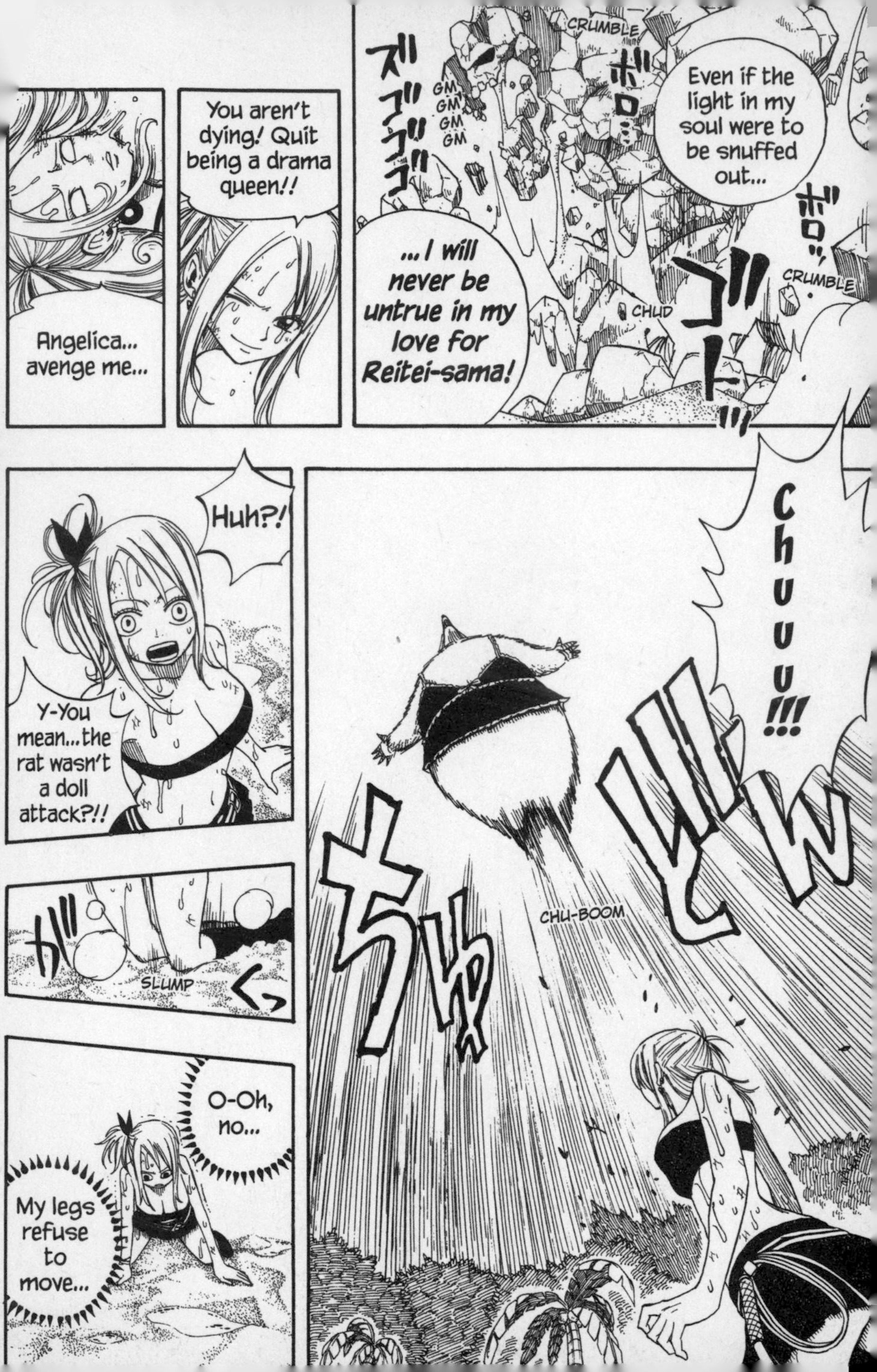
CRUMBLE
Even if the light in my soul were to be snuffed out...
GM GM GM GM
CRUMBLE
...I will never be untrue in my love for Reitei-sama!
CHUD
You aren't dying! Quit being a drama queen!!
Angelica... avenge me...
Chuuuuu!!!
CHU-BOOM
Huh?!
Y-You mean...the rat wasn't a doll attack?!!
SLUMP
O-Oh, no...
My legs refuse to move...

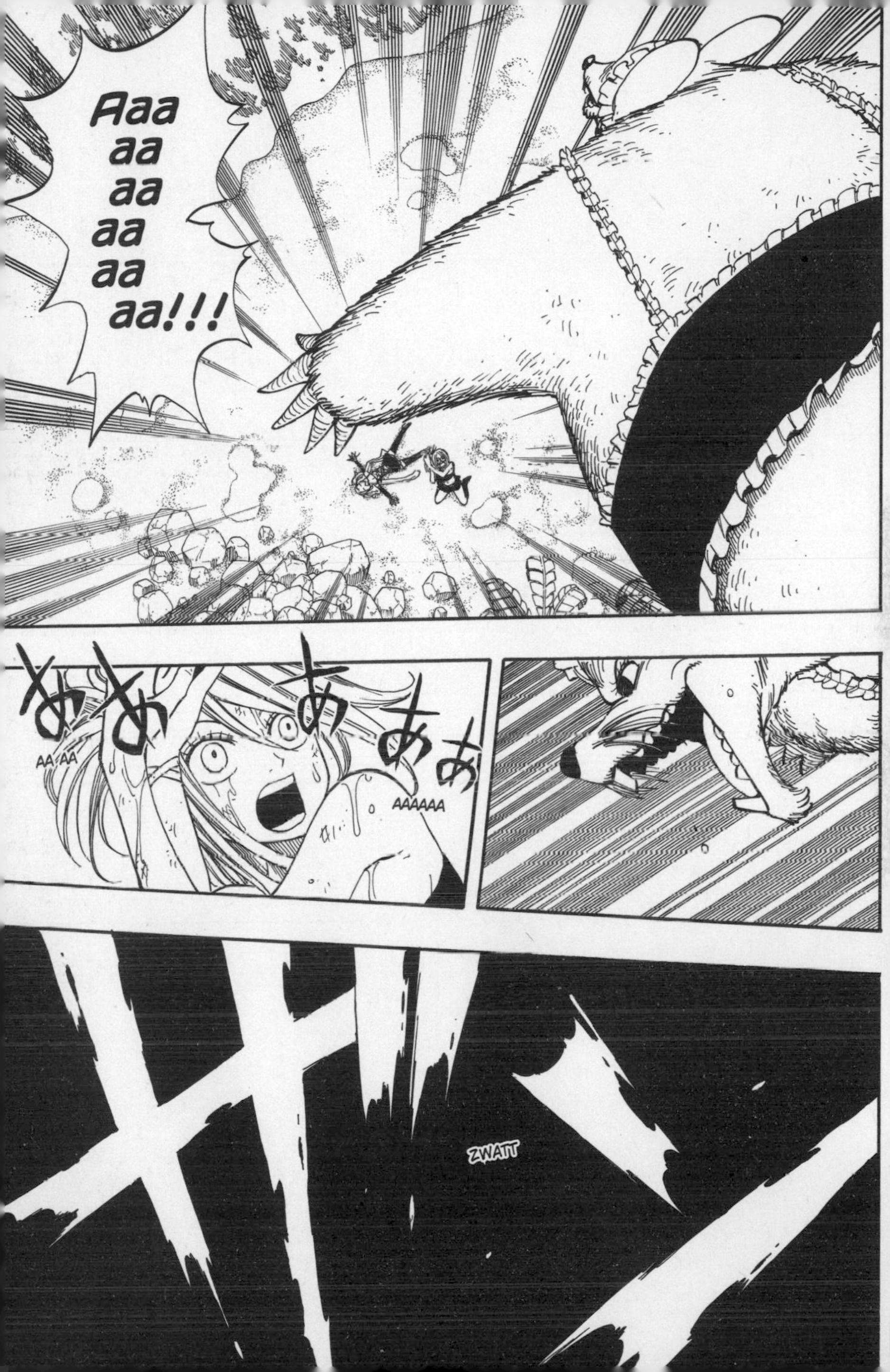
Aaa aa aa aa aa aa!!!
ああああああ
AA AA
AAAAAA
ZWATT

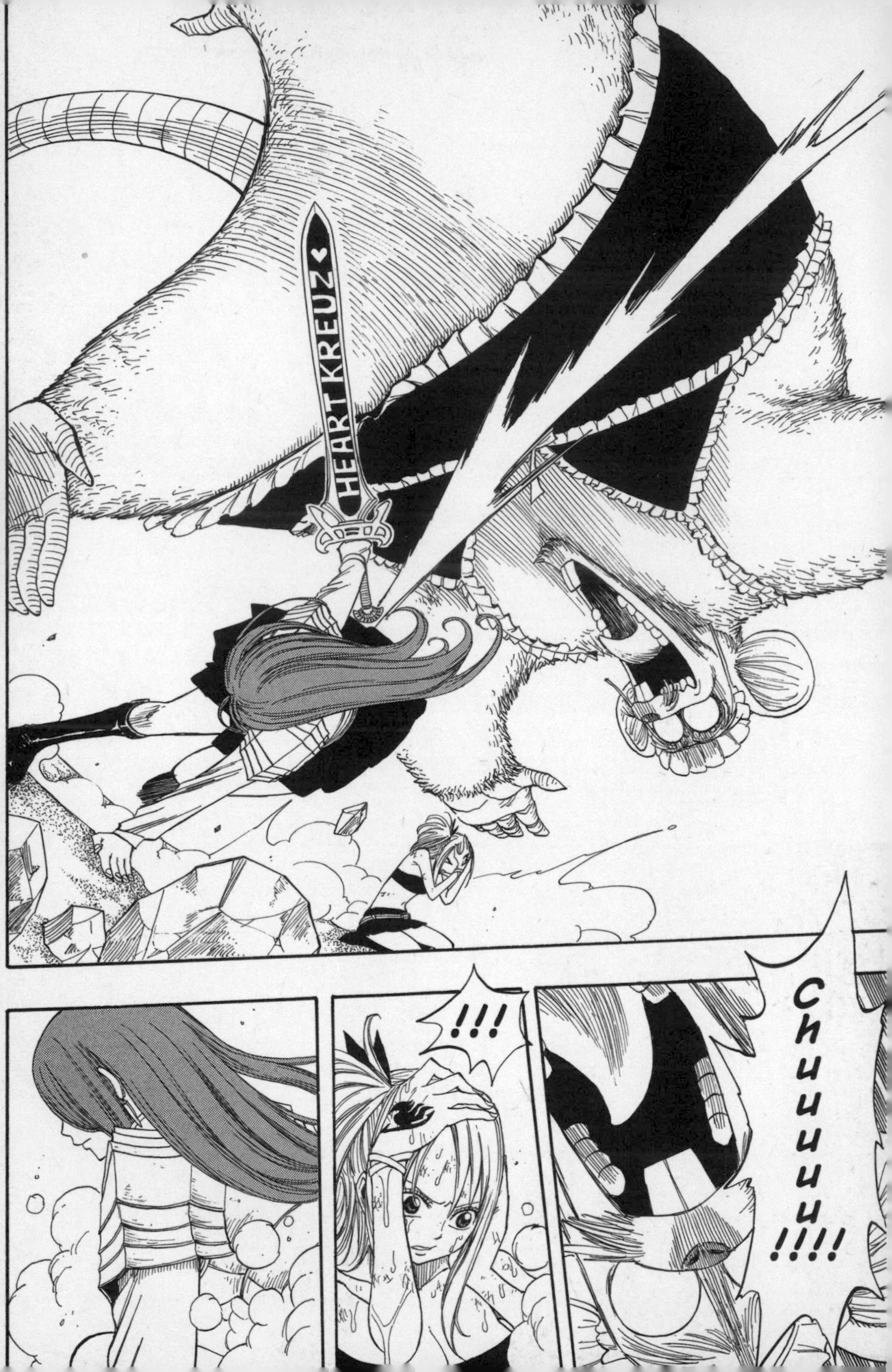
HEART KREUZ♥
Chuuuuu!!!!
!!!

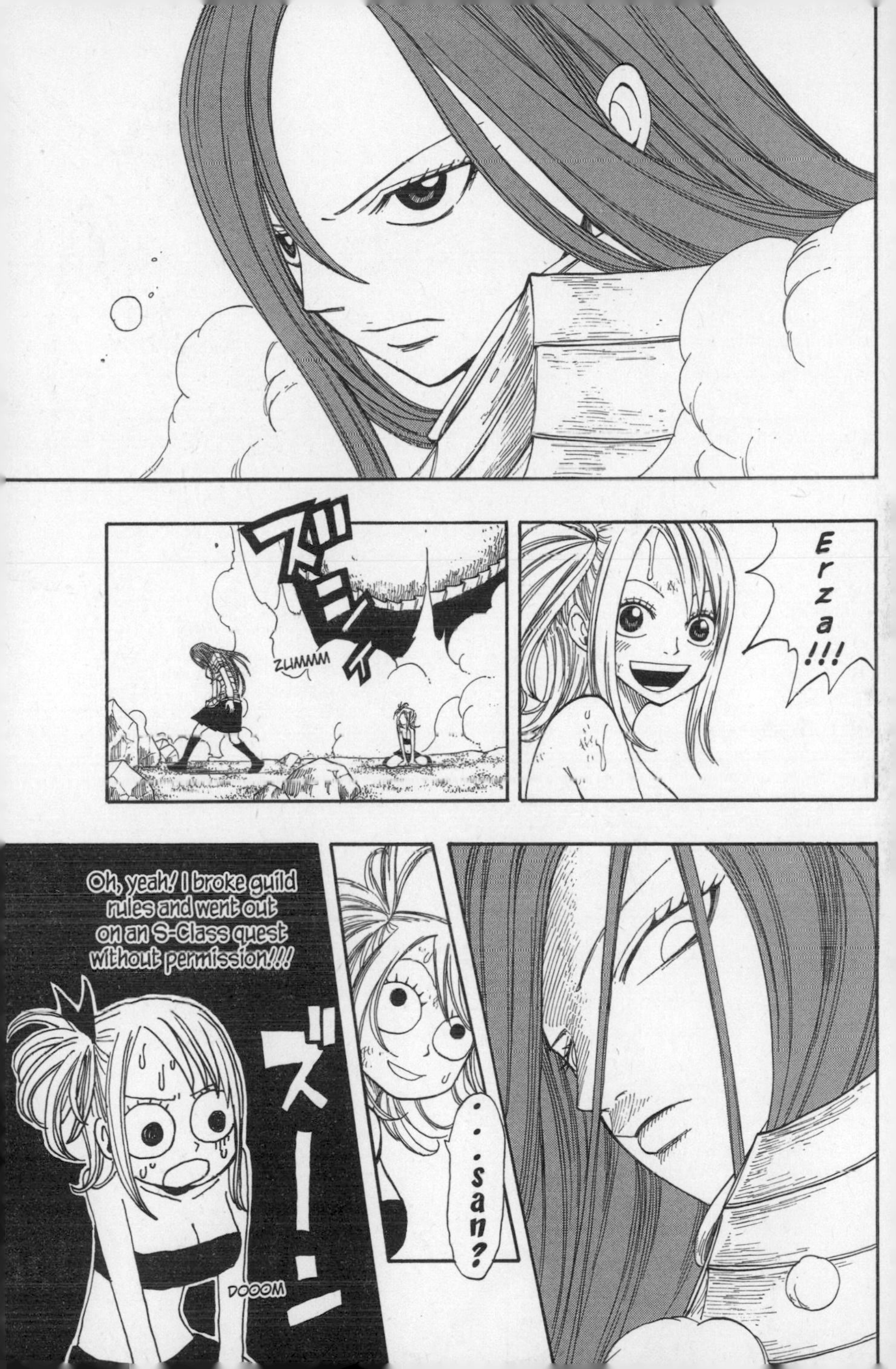
Erza!!!
ZUMMMM
...san?
Oh, yeah! I broke guild rules and went out on an S-Class quest without permission!!!
ズーン
DOOOM

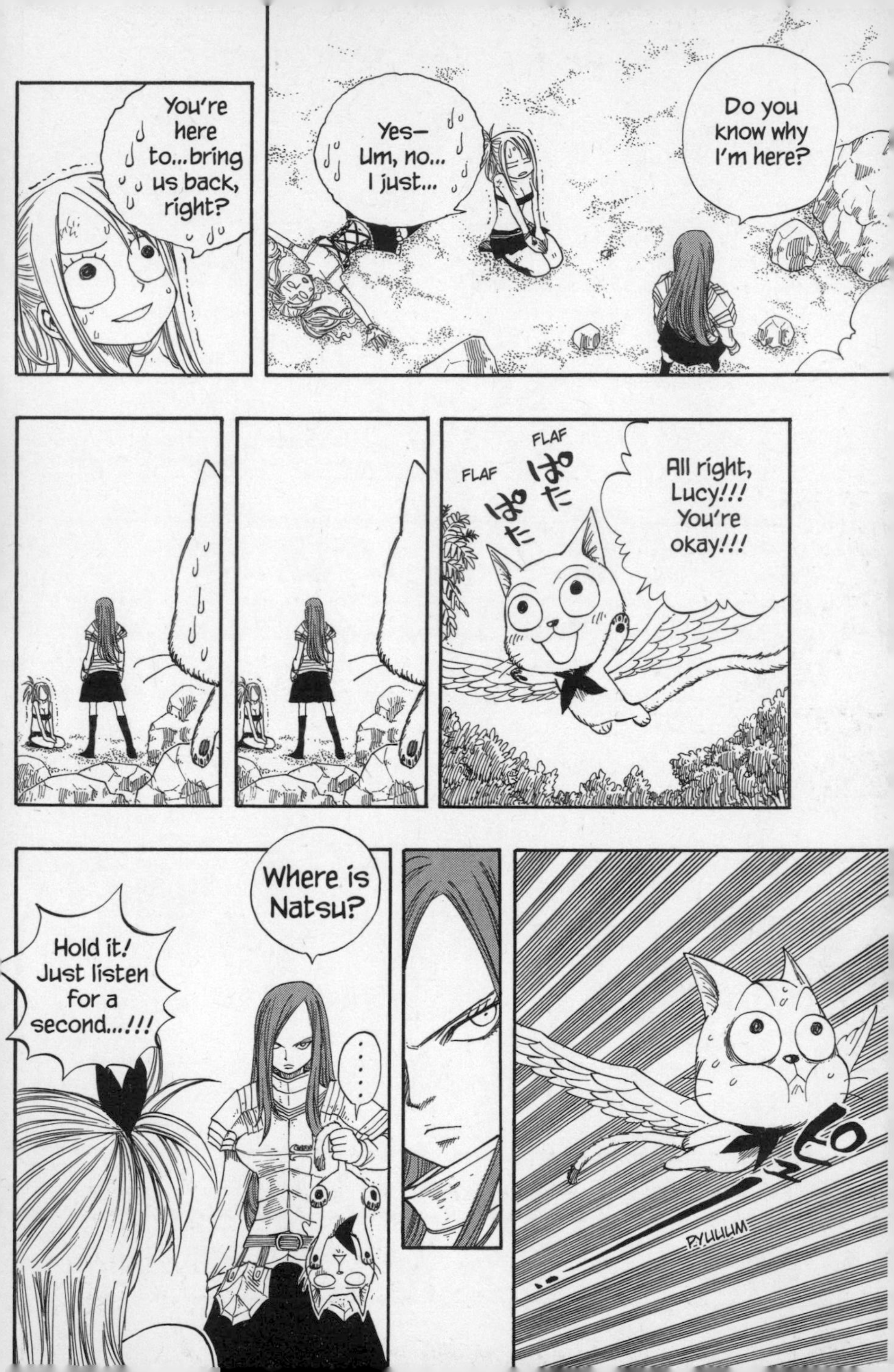
Do you know why I'm here?
Yes— Um, no... I just...
You're here to...bring us back, right?
All right, Lucy!!! You're okay!!!
FLAF
ぱた
FLAF
ぱた
PYUUUM
Where is Natsu?
Hold it! Just listen for a second...!!!
......

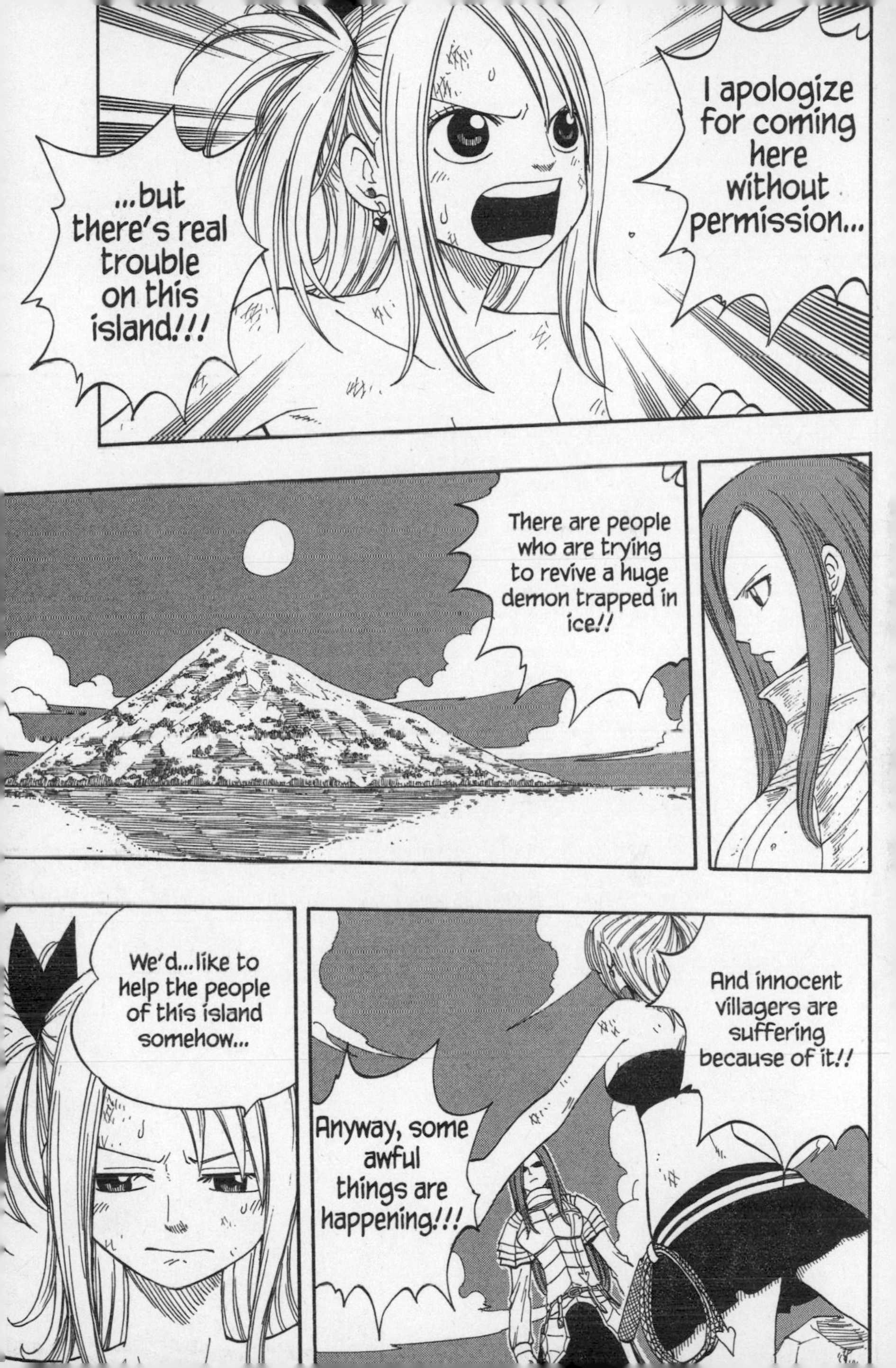
I apologize for coming here without permission...
...but there's real trouble on this island!!!
There are people who are trying to revive a huge demon trapped in ice!!
And innocent villagers are suffering because of it!!
Anyway, some awful things are happening!!!
We'd...like to help the people of this island somehow...

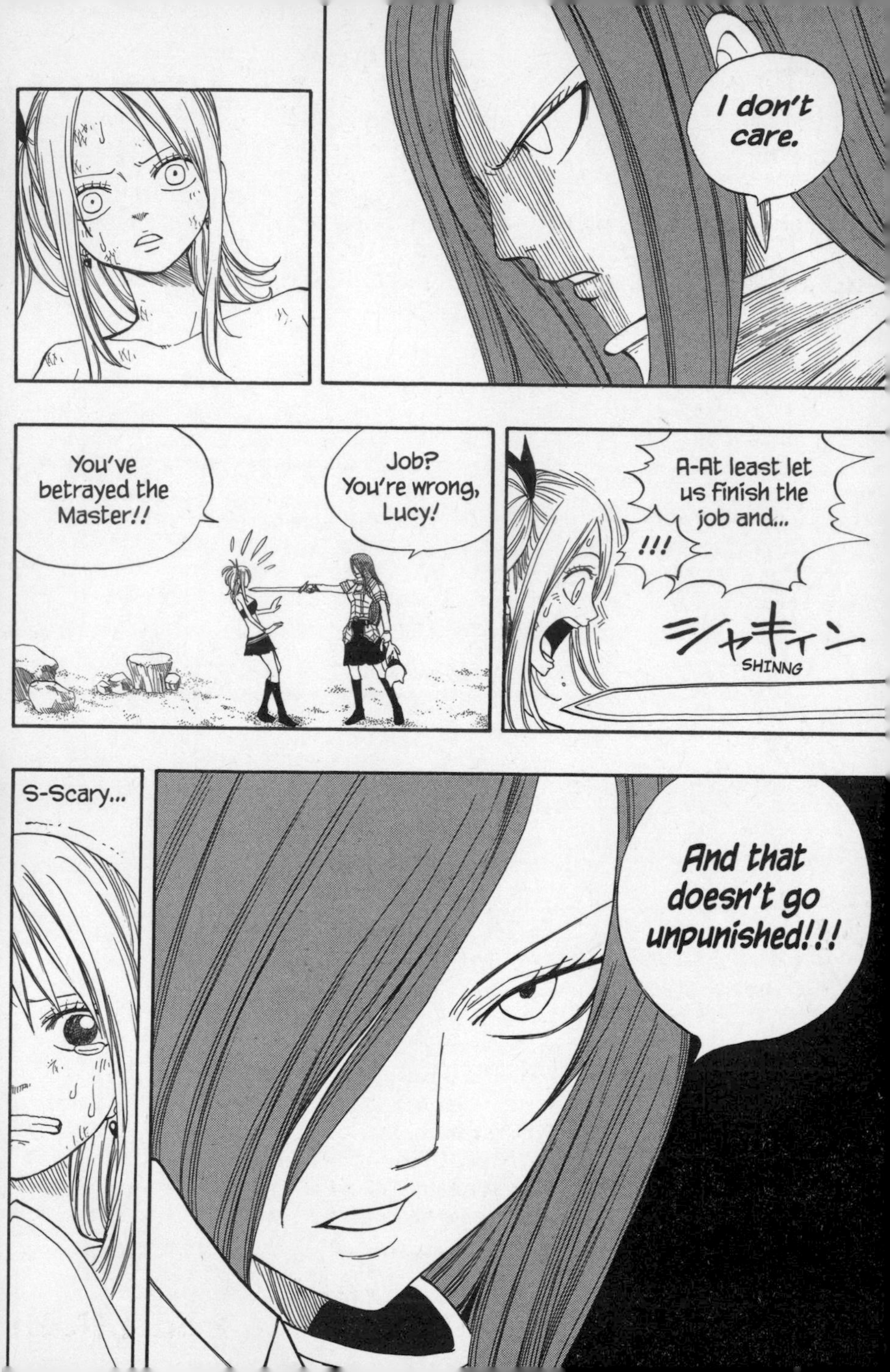
I don't care.
A-At least let us finish the job and...
!!!
シャキィン
SHINNG
Job? You're wrong, Lucy!
You've betrayed the Master!!
And that doesn't go unpunished!!!
S-Scary...

FAIRY TAIL

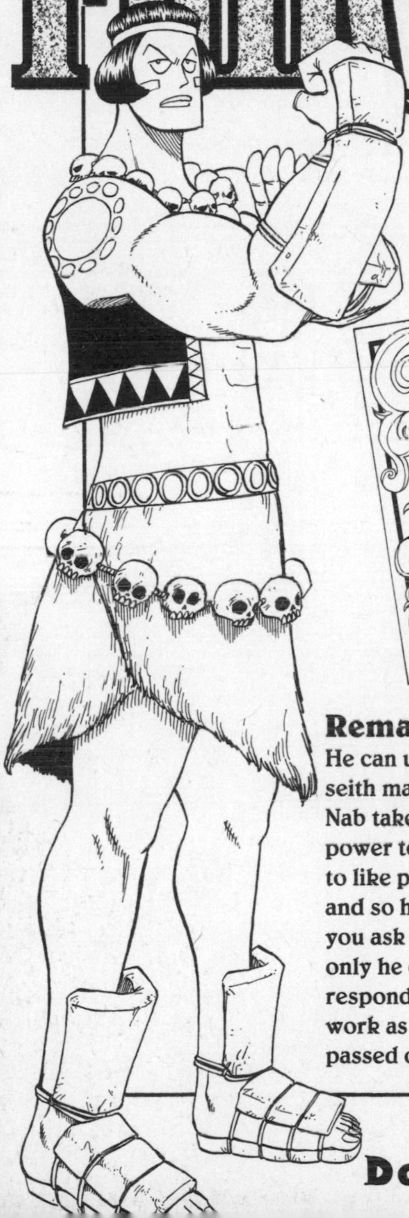

FAIRY TAIL

Name: Nab Lasaro Age: 20 yrs.

Magic: Seith Magic: Animal Possession

Likes: Horror Novels Dislikes: Celery

WIZARD GUILD X633

Remarks

He can use a type of spiritual possession magic called seith magic. There are all types of seith magic, but Nab takes animal spirits into his body and uses their power to fight. But for some reason, he really seems to like procrastinating in front of the request board, and so he is hardly ever seen going out on a job. If you ask him, he'll say that he's looking for work that only he can do. That led to an incident where Mirajane responded by saying, "If that's the case, why don't you work as a Fairy Tail waiter?" At that, a look of defeat passed over his face.

Chapter 35: Do Whatever You Like!!

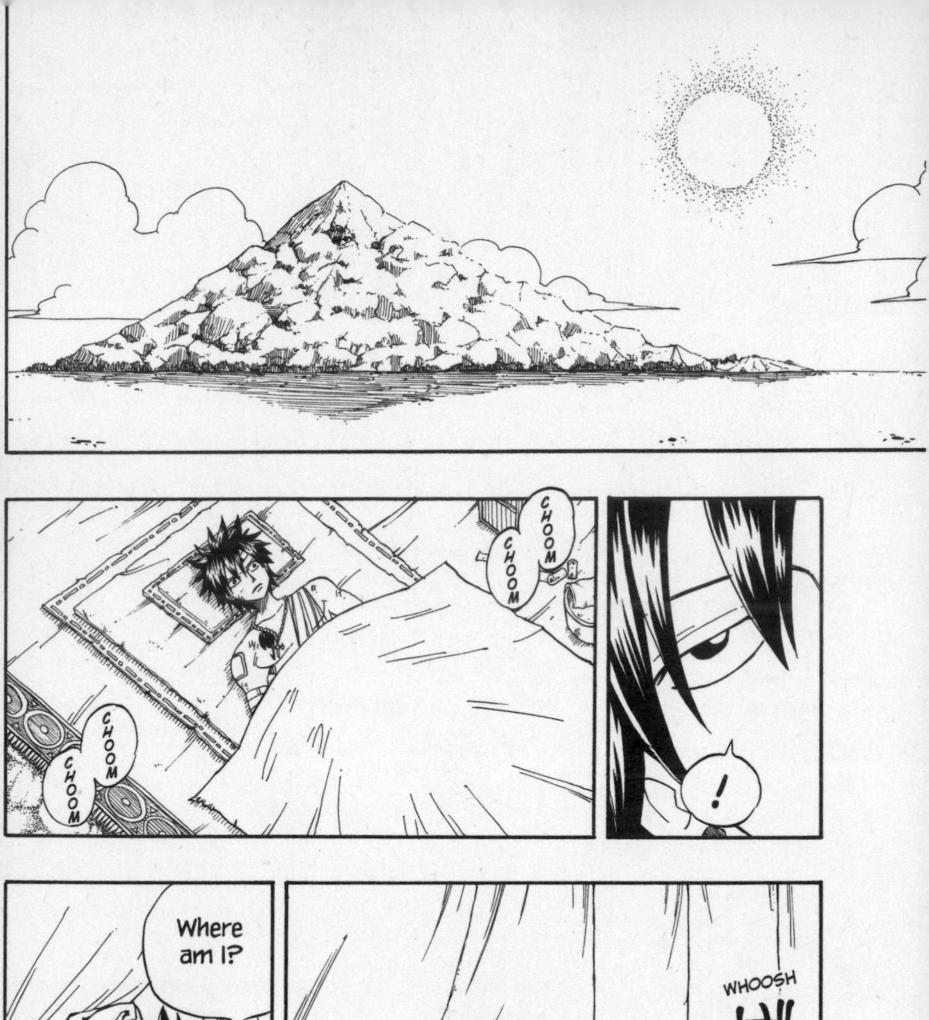
!
CHOOM CHOOM
CHOOM CHOOM
WHOOSH
ばっ
Where am I?

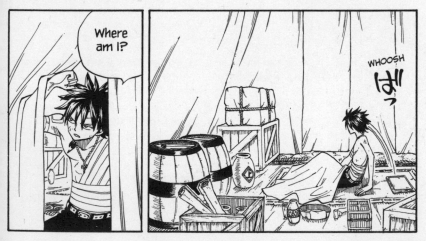

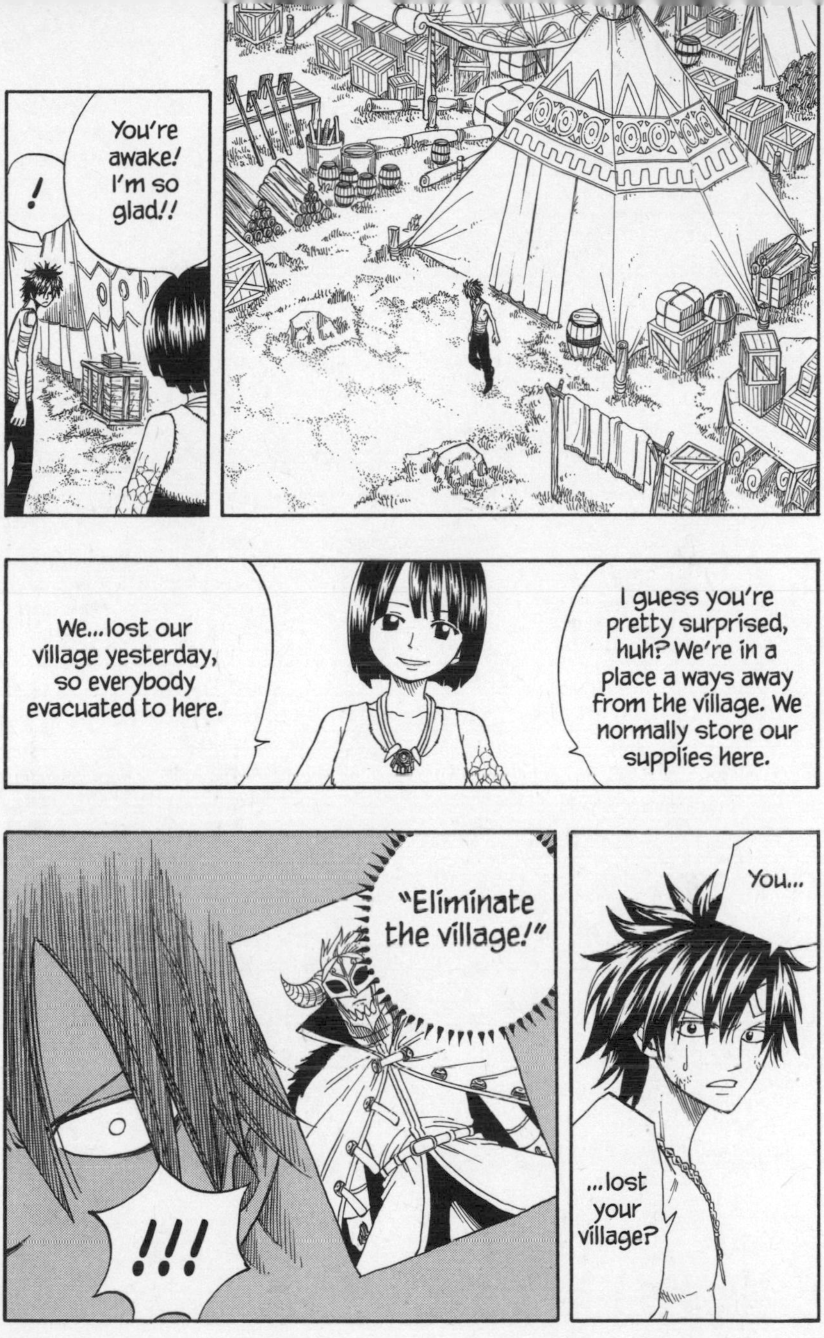
You're awake! I'm so glad!!
!
I guess you're pretty surprised, huh? We're in a place a ways away from the village. We normally store our supplies here.
We...lost our village yesterday, so everybody evacuated to here.
You...
...lost your village?
"Eliminate the village!"
!!!

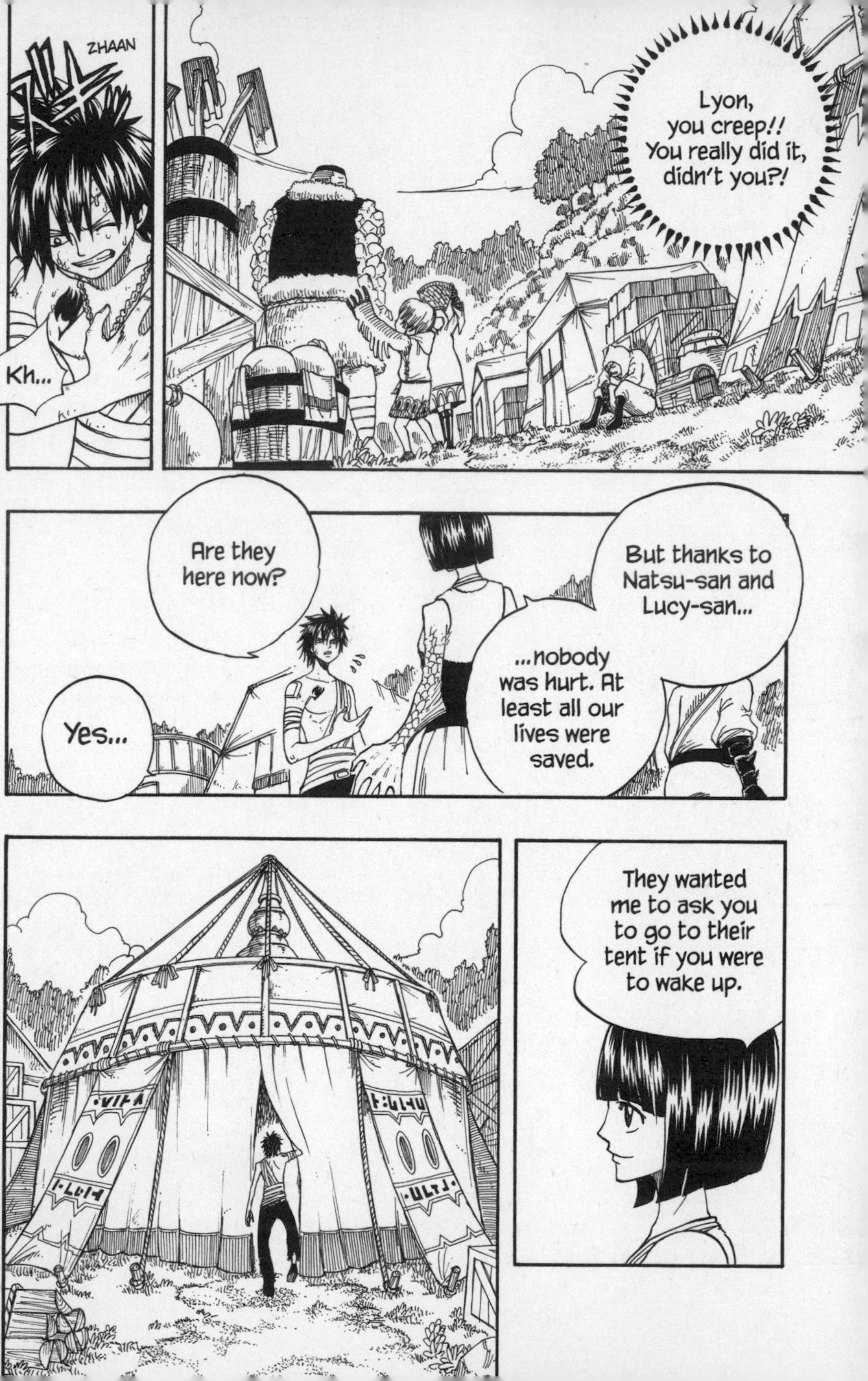
Lyon, you creep!! You really did it, didn't you?!
ZHAAN
Kh...
But thanks to Natsu-san and Lucy-san...
...nobody was hurt. At least all our lives were saved.
Are they here now?
Yes...
They wanted me to ask you to go to their tent if you were to wake up.

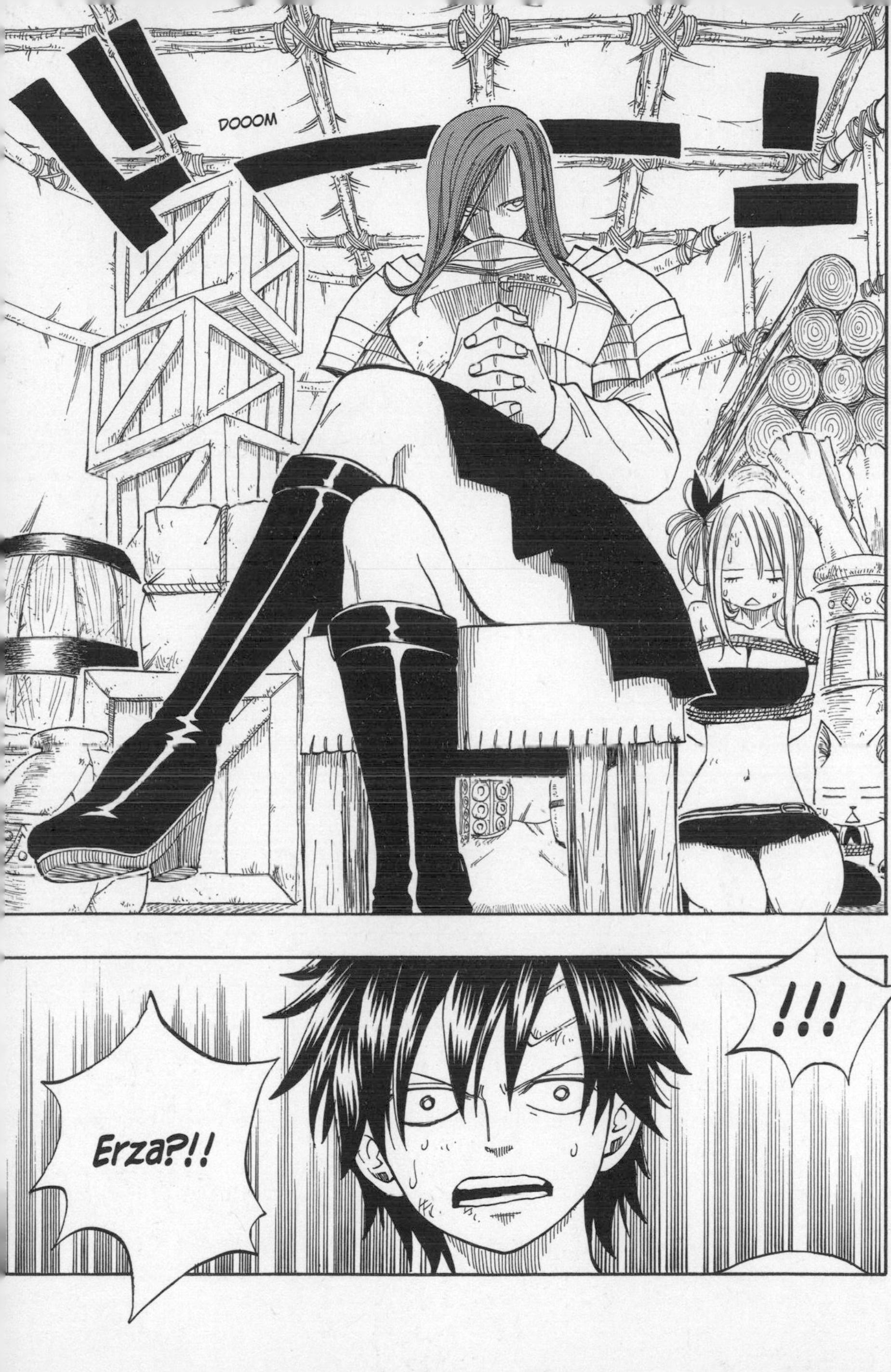
DOOOM
HEART KREUZ
!!!
Erza?!!

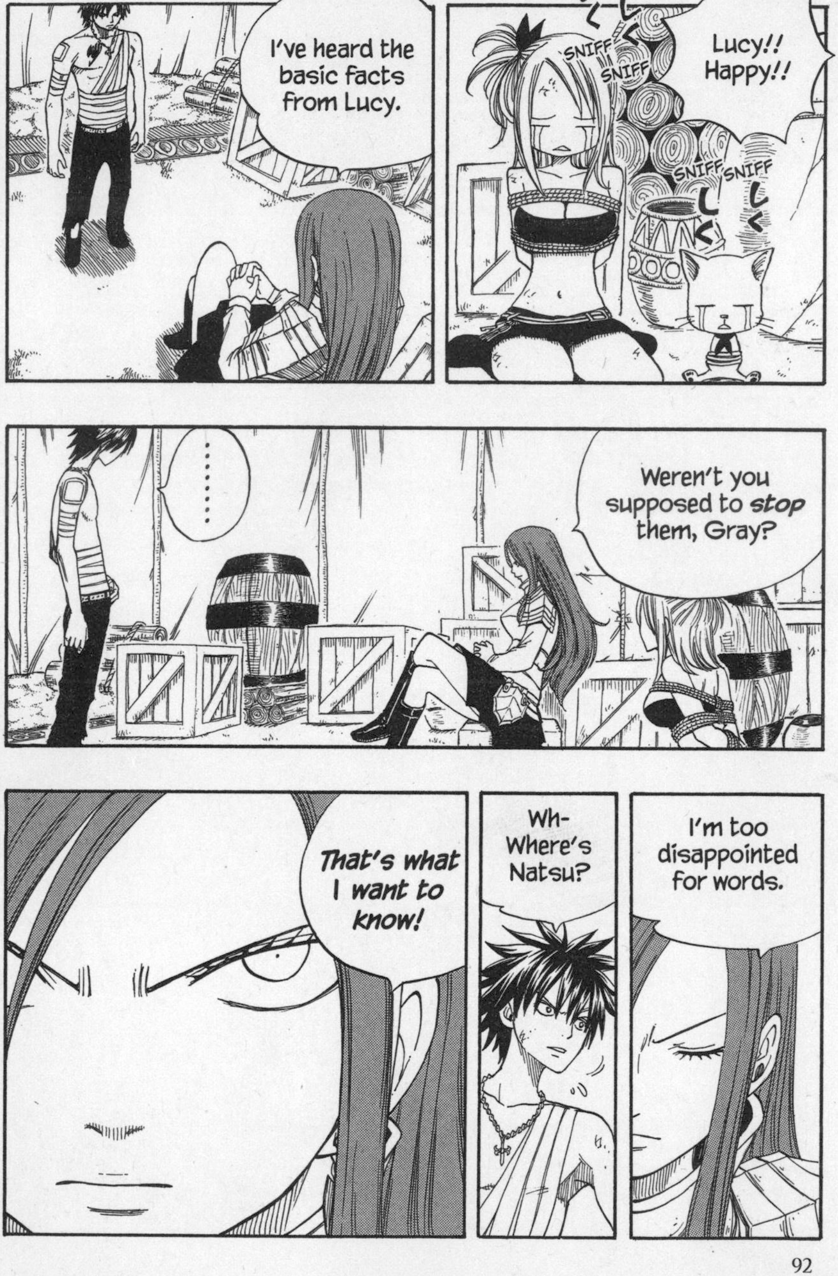
Lucy!! Happy!!
SNIFF SNIFF
SNIFF SNIFF
I've heard the basic facts from Lucy.
Weren't you supposed to *stop* them, Gray?
......
I'm too disappointed for words.
Wh- Where's Natsu?
That's what I want to know!

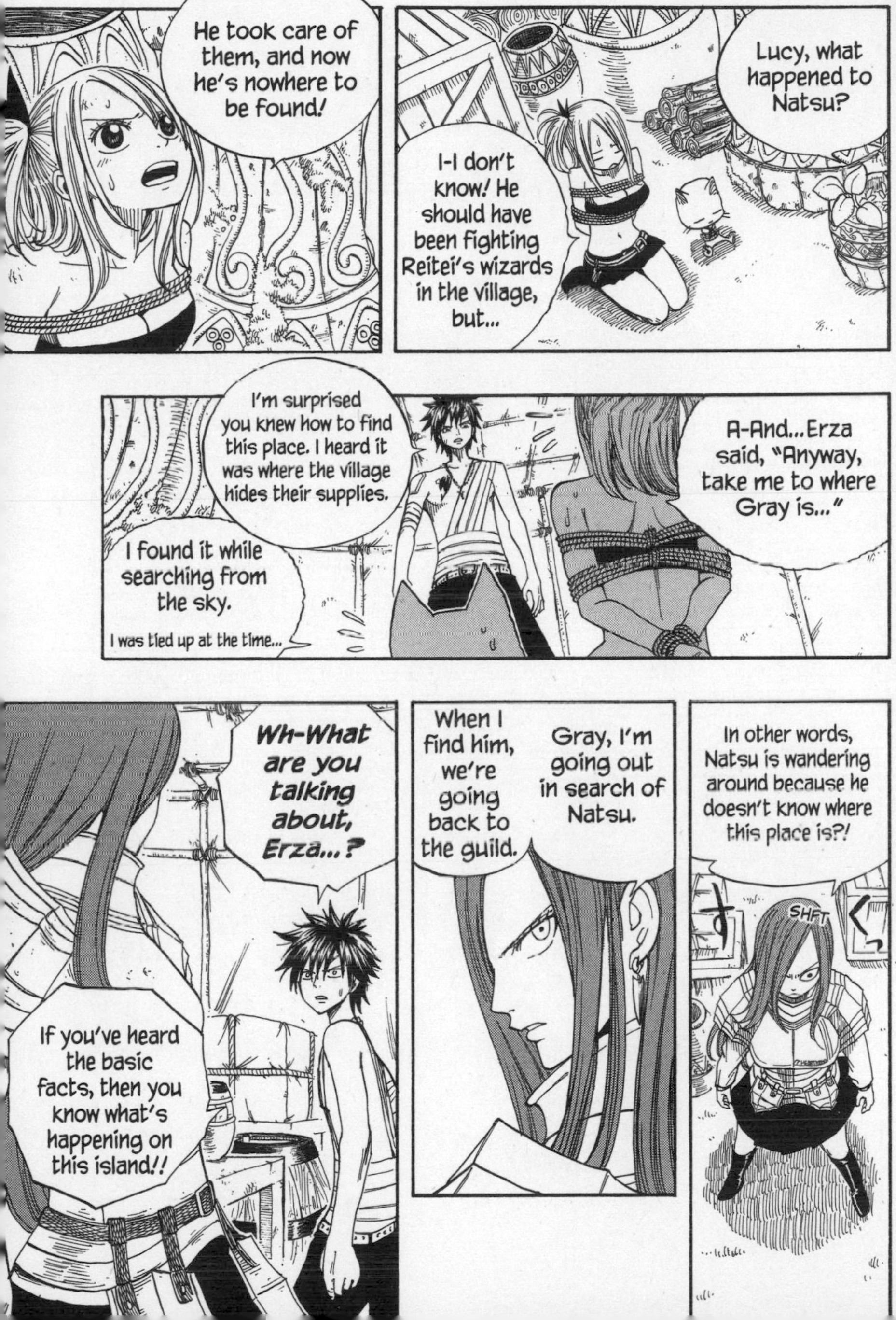
Lucy, what happened to Natsu?
I-I don't know! He should have been fighting Reitei's wizards in the village, but...
He took care of them, and now he's nowhere to be found!
A-And...Erza said, "Anyway, take me to where Gray is..."
I'm surprised you knew how to find this place. I heard it was where the village hides their supplies.
I found it while searching from the sky.
I was tied up at the time...
In other words, Natsu is wandering around because he doesn't know where this place is?!
SHFT
Gray, I'm going out in search of Natsu.
When I find him, we're going back to the guild.
Wh-What are you talking about, Erza...?
If you've heard the basic facts, then you know what's happening on this island!!

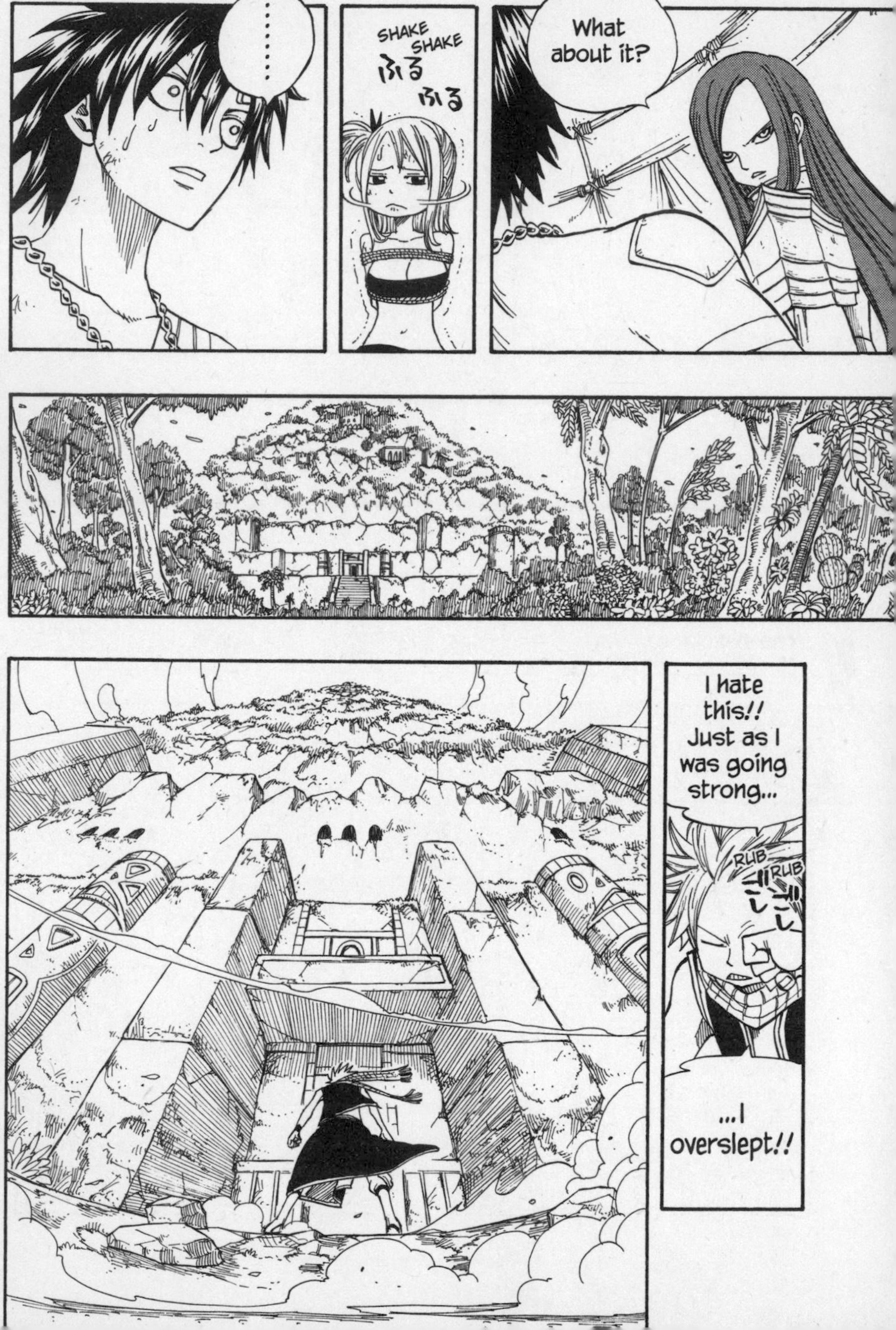
What about it?
SHAKE SHAKE
ふる ふる
......
I hate this!! Just as I was going strong...
RUB RUB
ごし ごし
...I overslept!!

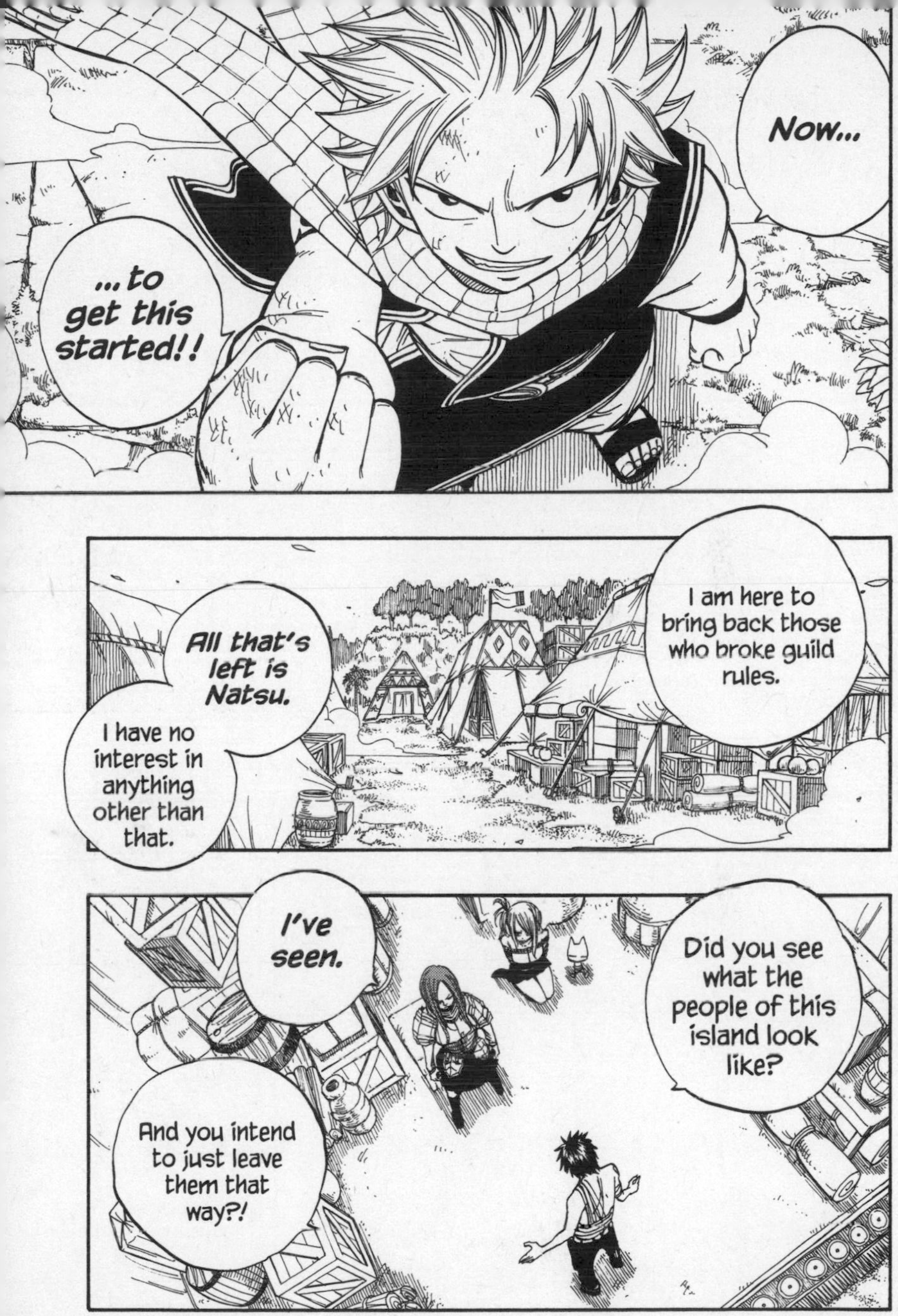
Now...
...to get this started!!
I am here to bring back those who broke guild rules.
All that's left is Natsu.
I have no interest in anything other than that.
Did you see what the people of this island look like?
I've seen.
And you intend to just leave them that way?!

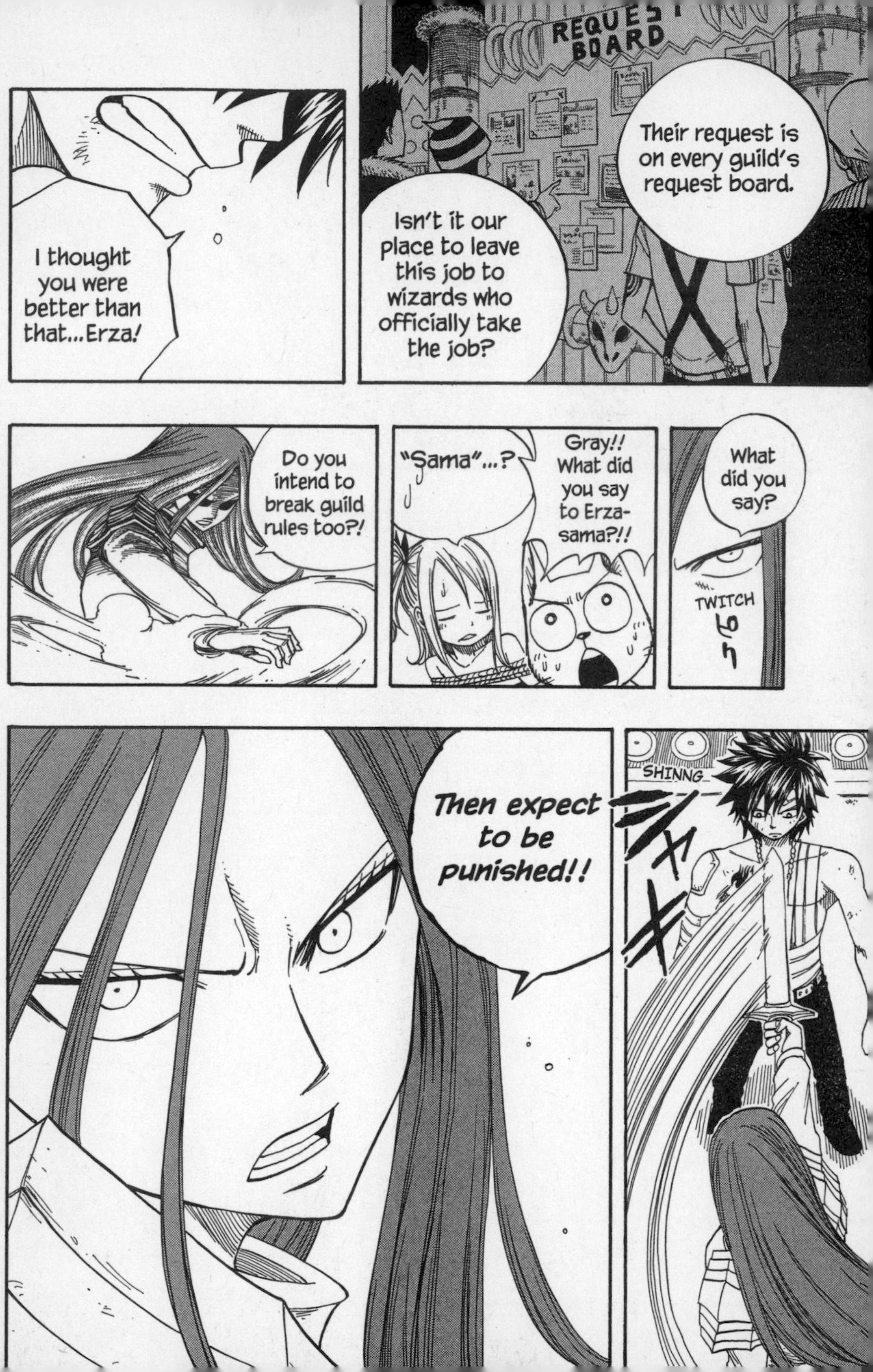
REQUEST BOARD
Their request is on every guild's request board.
Isn't it our place to leave this job to wizards who officially take the job?
I thought you were better than that...Erza!
What did you say?
TWITCH
Gray!! What did you say to Erza-sama?!!
"Sama"...?
Do you intend to break guild rules too?!
SHINNG
Then expect to be punished!!

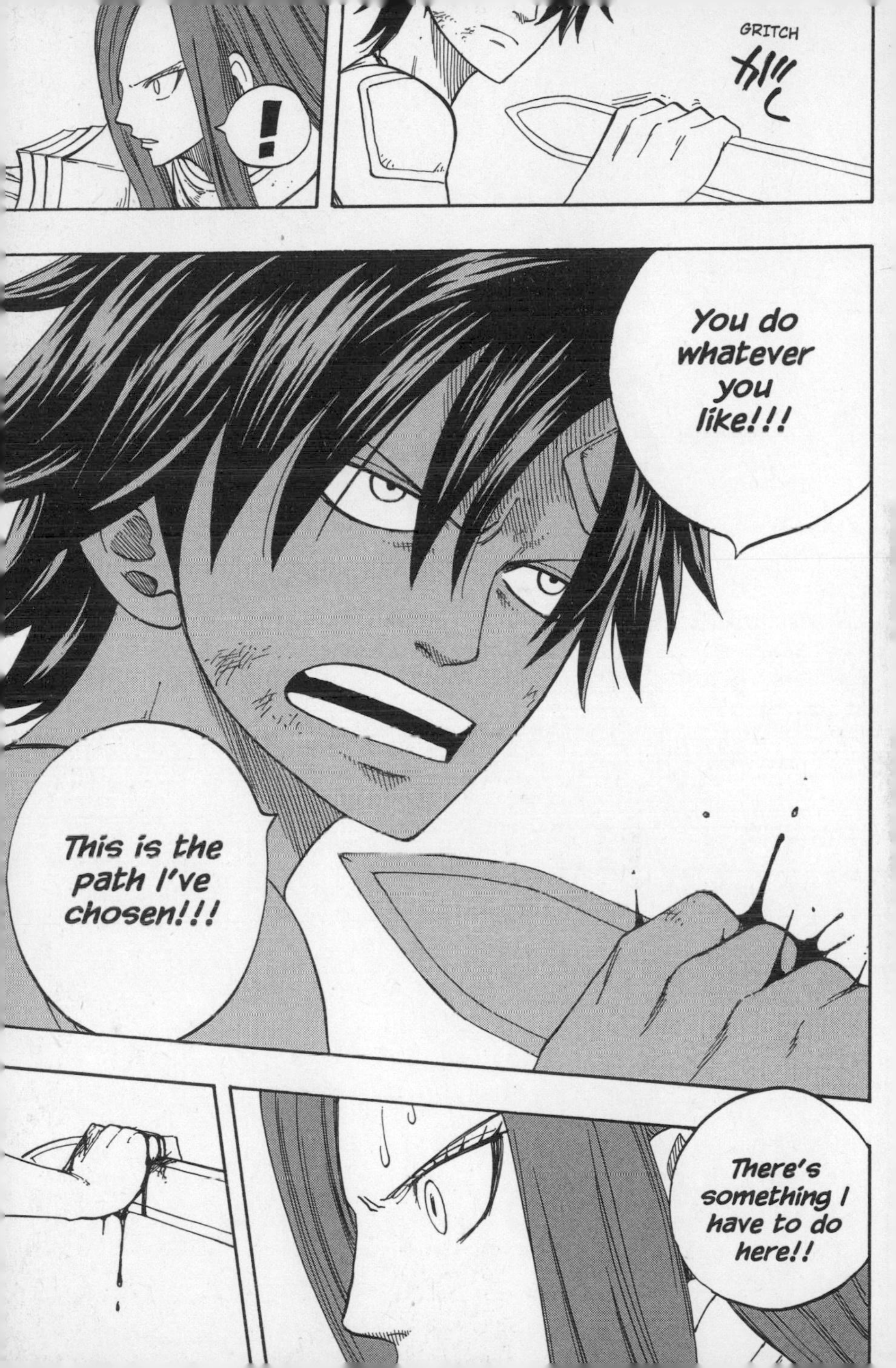
GRITCH
!
You do whatever you like!!!
This is the path I've chosen!!!
There's something I have to do here!!

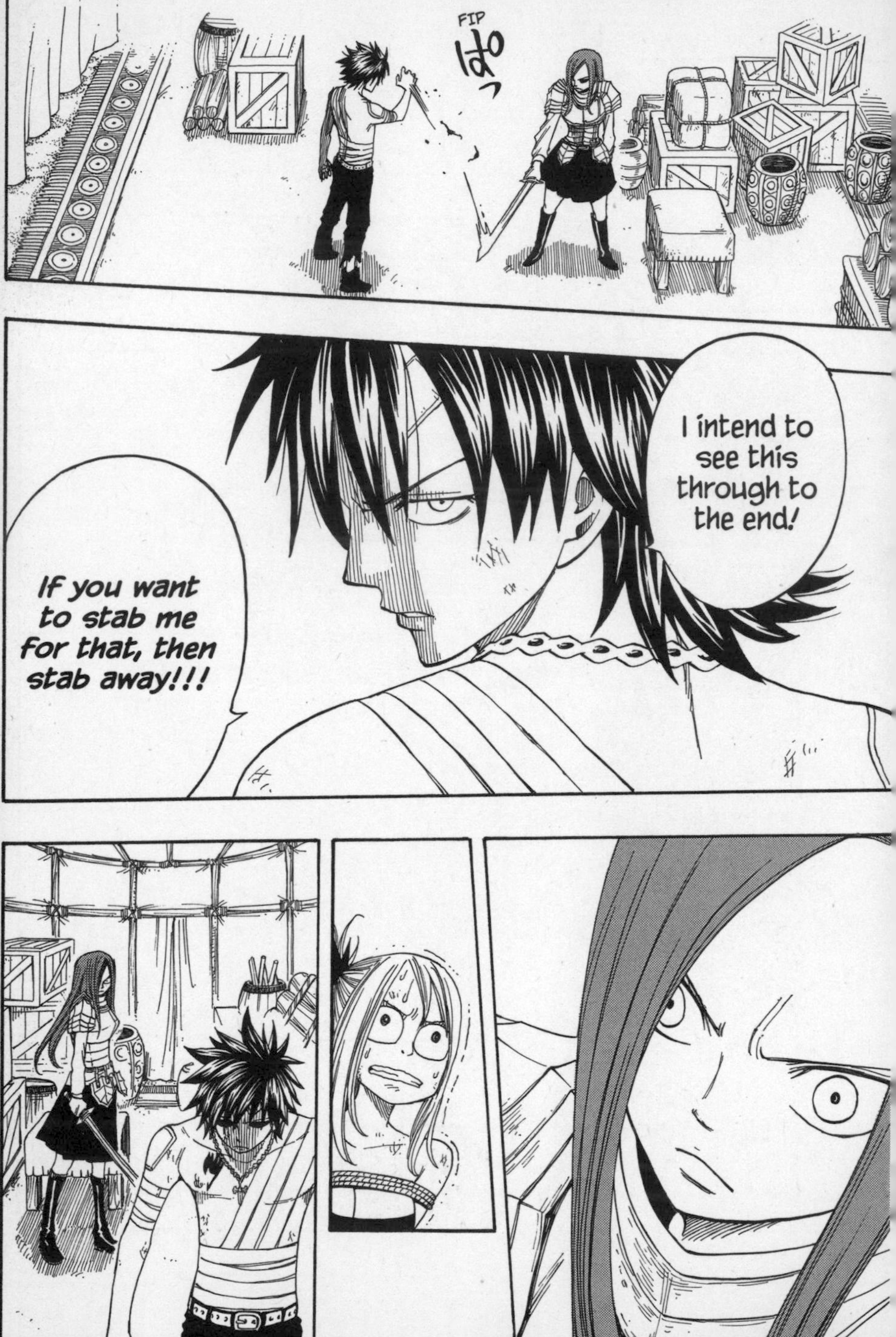
FIP
ぱっ
I intend to see this through to the end!
If you want to stab me for that, then stab away!!!

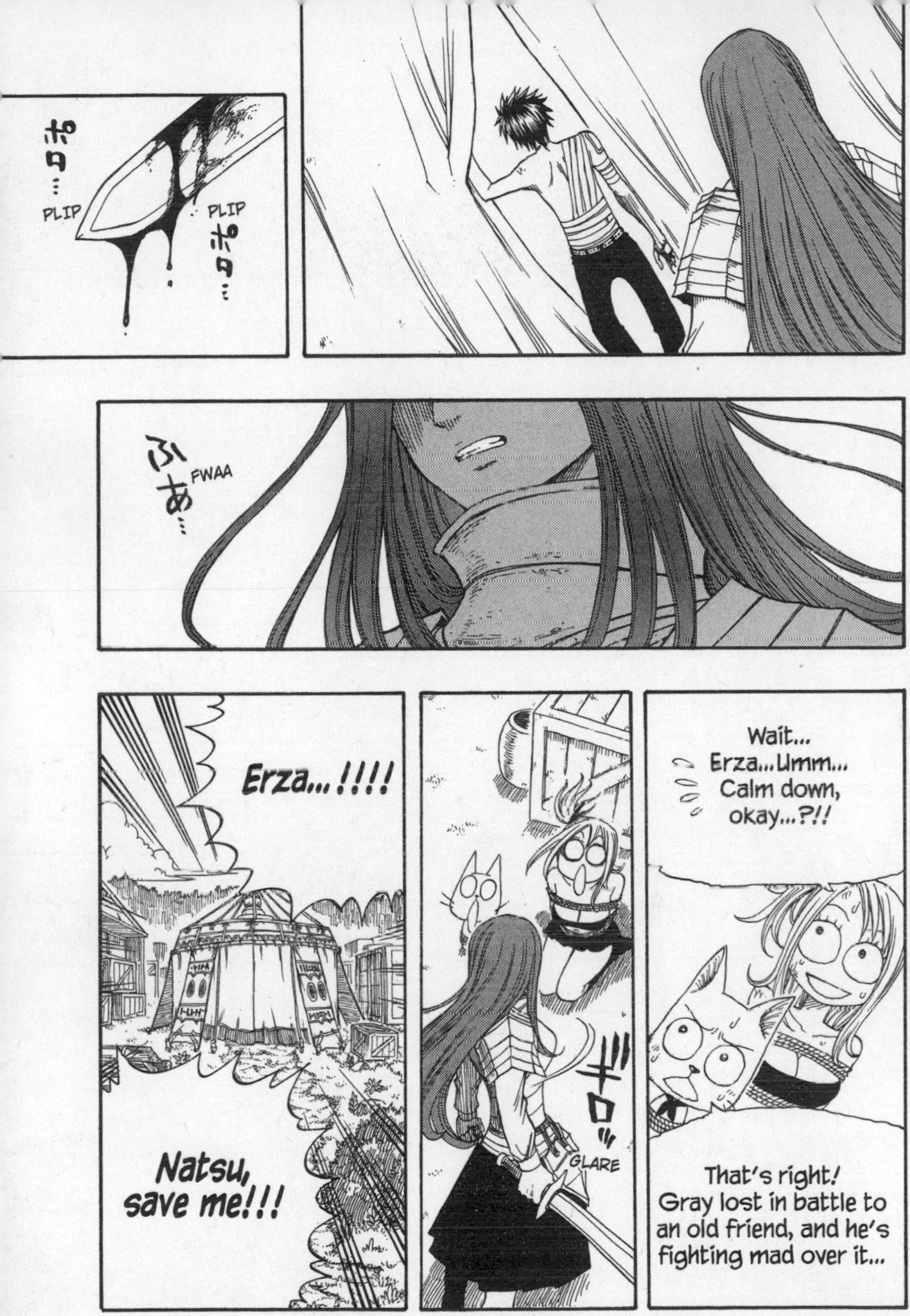
PLIP
ポタ…
PLIP
ポタ…
FWAA
ふあ…
Wait... Erza...Umm... Calm down, okay...?!!
That's right! Gray lost in battle to an old friend, and he's fighting mad over it...
ギロッ
GLARE
Erza...!!!!
Natsu, save me!!!

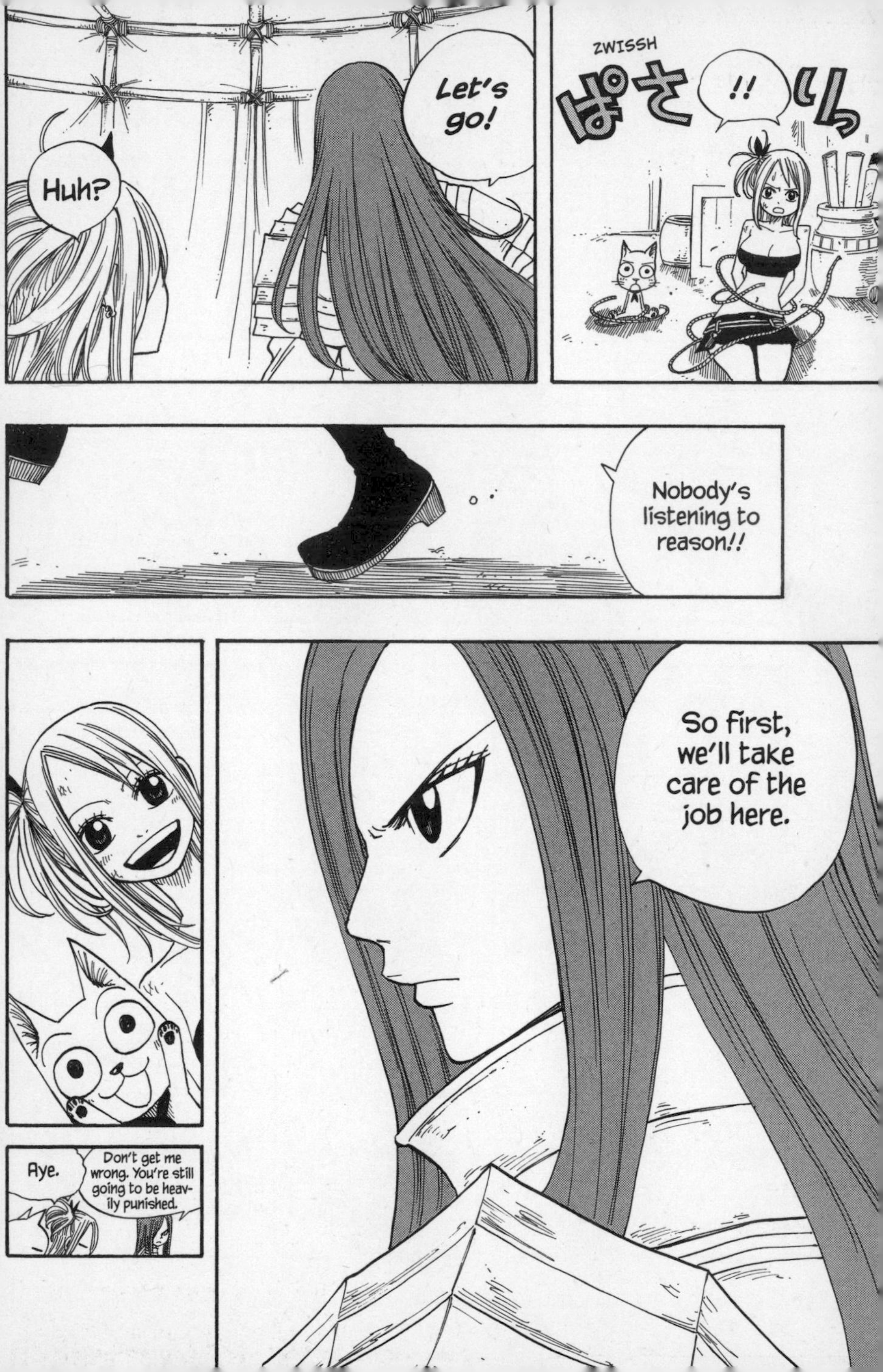
ZWISSH
!!
Let's go!
Huh?
Nobody's listening to reason!!
So first, we'll take care of the job here.
Don't get me wrong. You're still going to be heavily punished.
Aye.

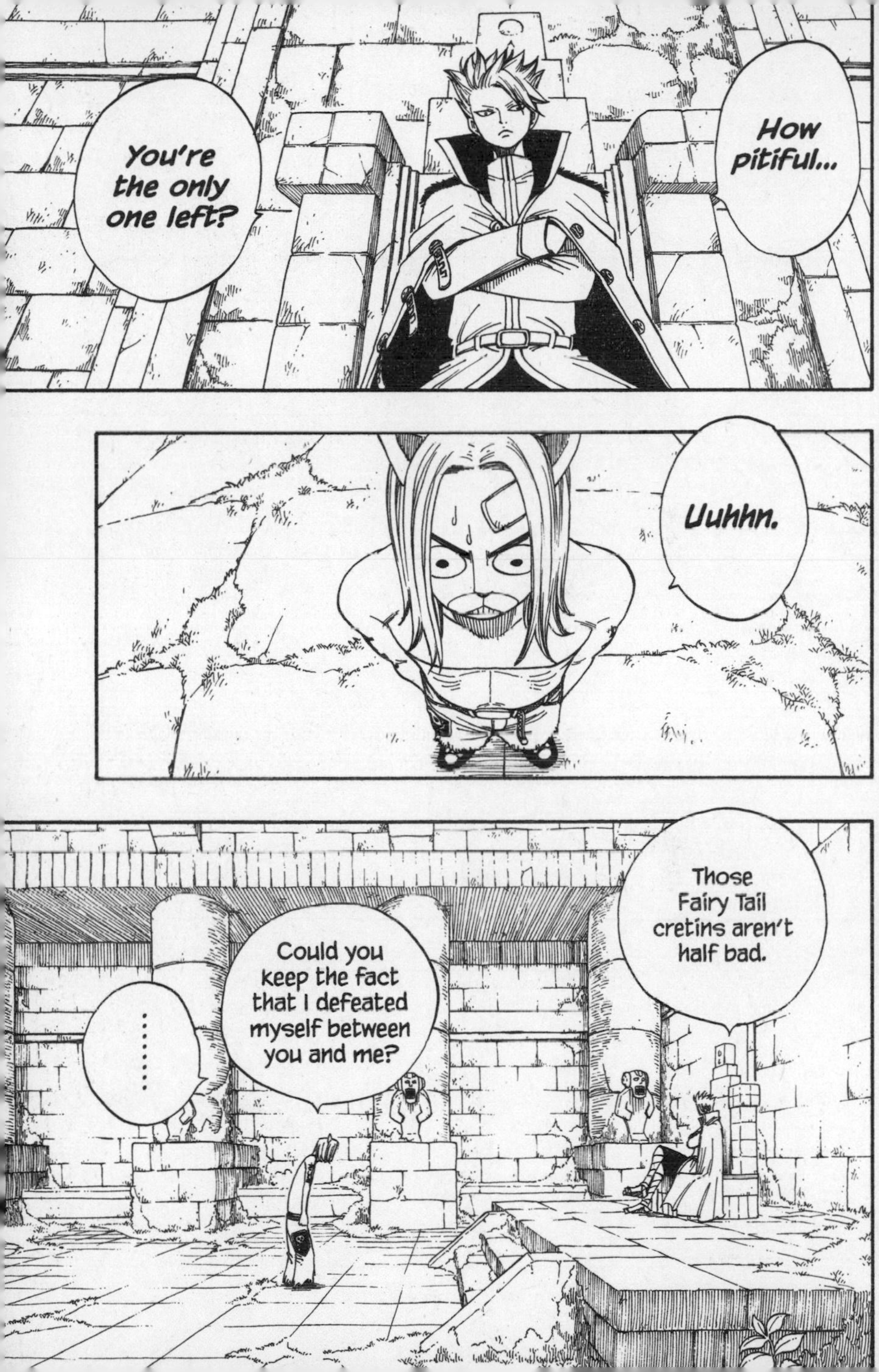
How pitiful...
You're the only one left?
Uuhhn.
Those Fairy Tail cretins aren't half bad.
Could you keep the fact that I defeated myself between you and me?
......

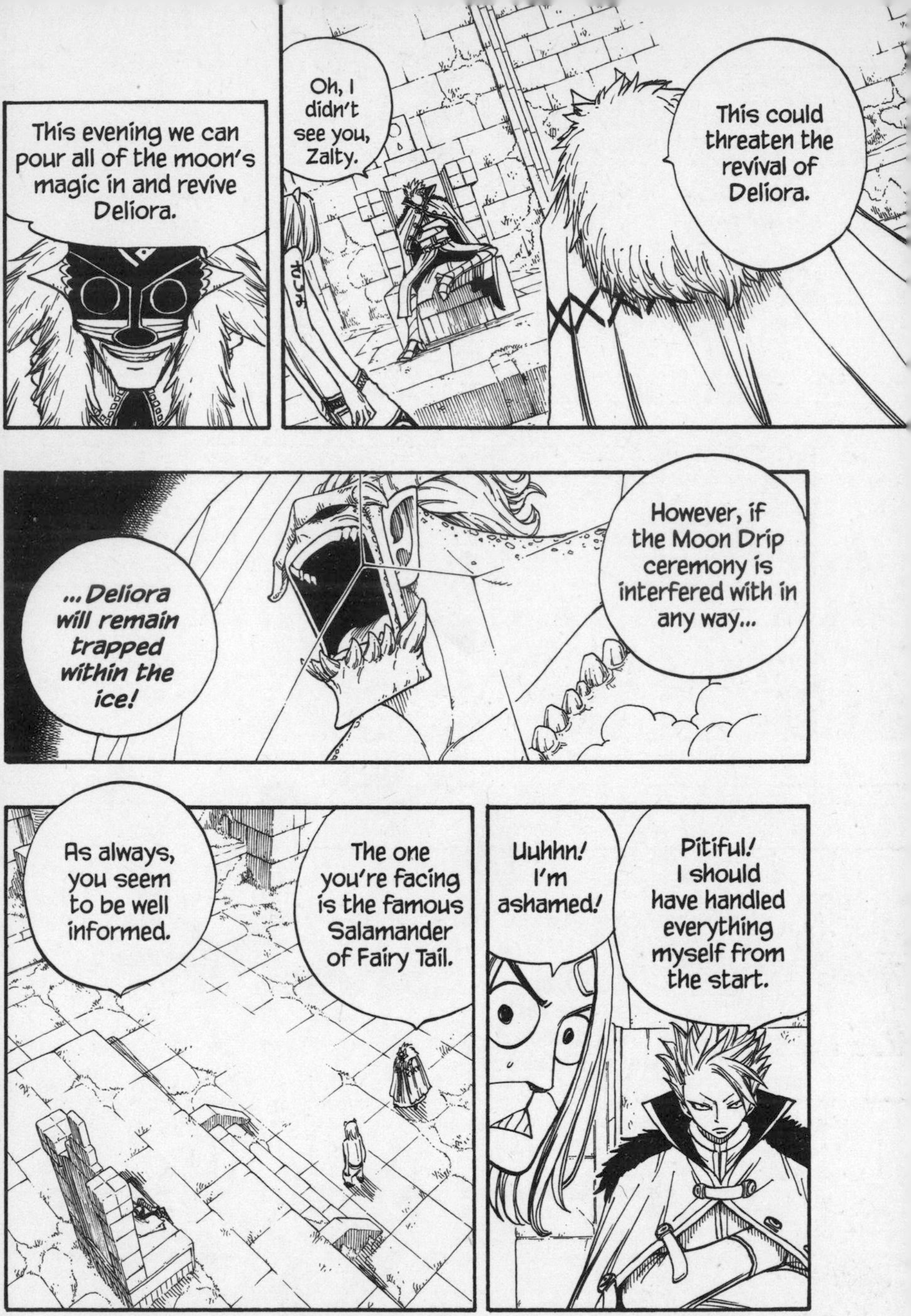
This could threaten the revival of Deliora.
Oh, I didn't see you, Zalty.
This evening we can pour all of the moon's magic in and revive Deliora.
However, if the Moon Drip ceremony is interfered with in any way...
...Deliora will remain trapped within the ice!
Pitiful! I should have handled everything myself from the start.
Uuhhn! I'm ashamed!
The one you're facing is the famous Salamander of Fairy Tail.
As always, you seem to be well informed.

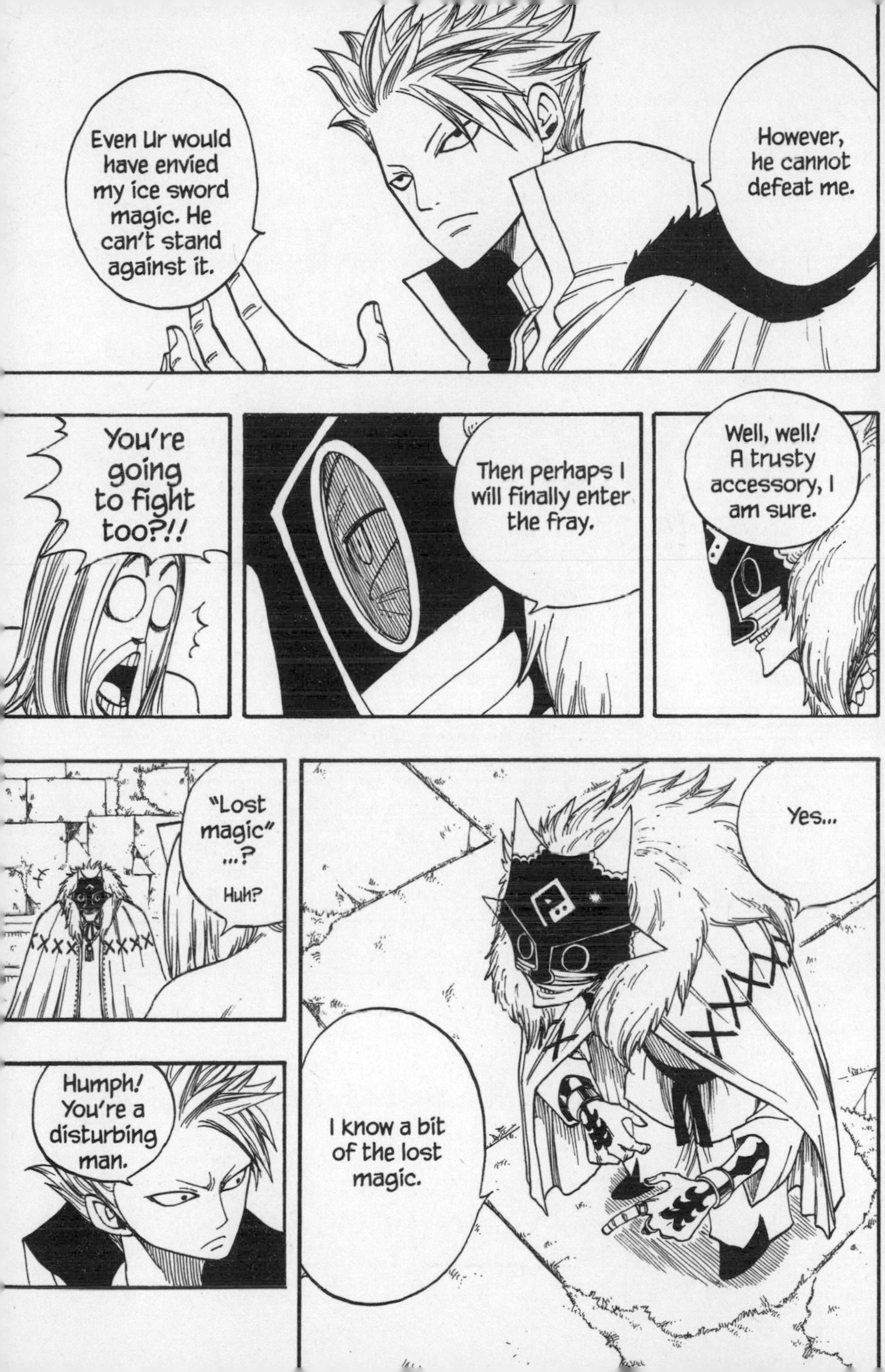
Even Ur would have envied my ice sword magic. He can't stand against it.
However, he cannot defeat me.
Well, well! A trusty accessory, I am sure.
Then perhaps I will finally enter the fray.
You're going to fight too?!!
Yes...
I know a bit of the lost magic.
"Lost magic" ...?
Huh?
Humph! You're a disturbing man.

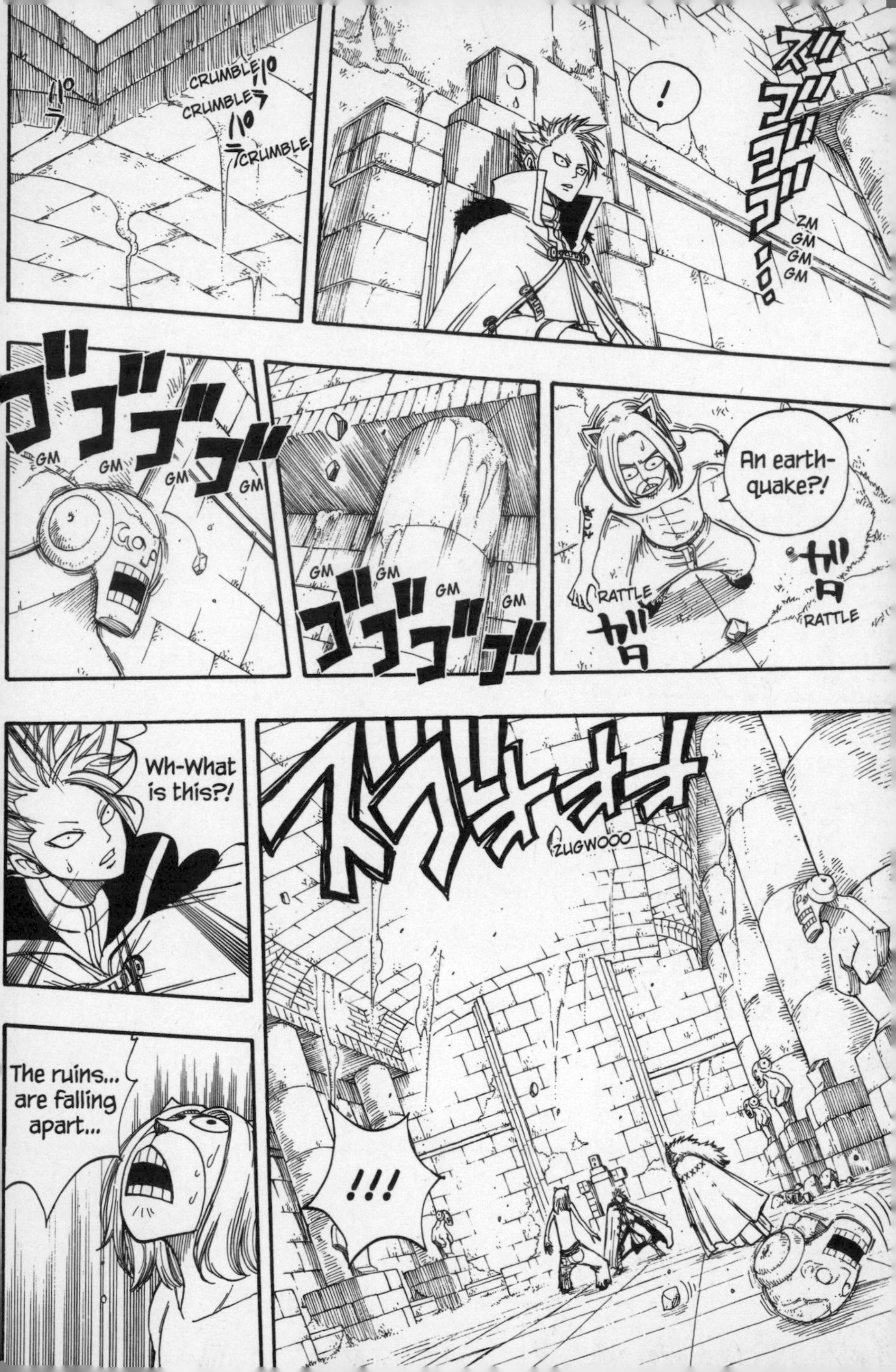
!
ZM GM GM GM
CRUMBLE CRUMBLE CRUMBLE
An earth-quake?!
RATTLE RATTLE
GM GM GM GM
GM GM GM GM
ZUGWOOO
!!!
Wh-What is this?!
The ruins... are falling apart...

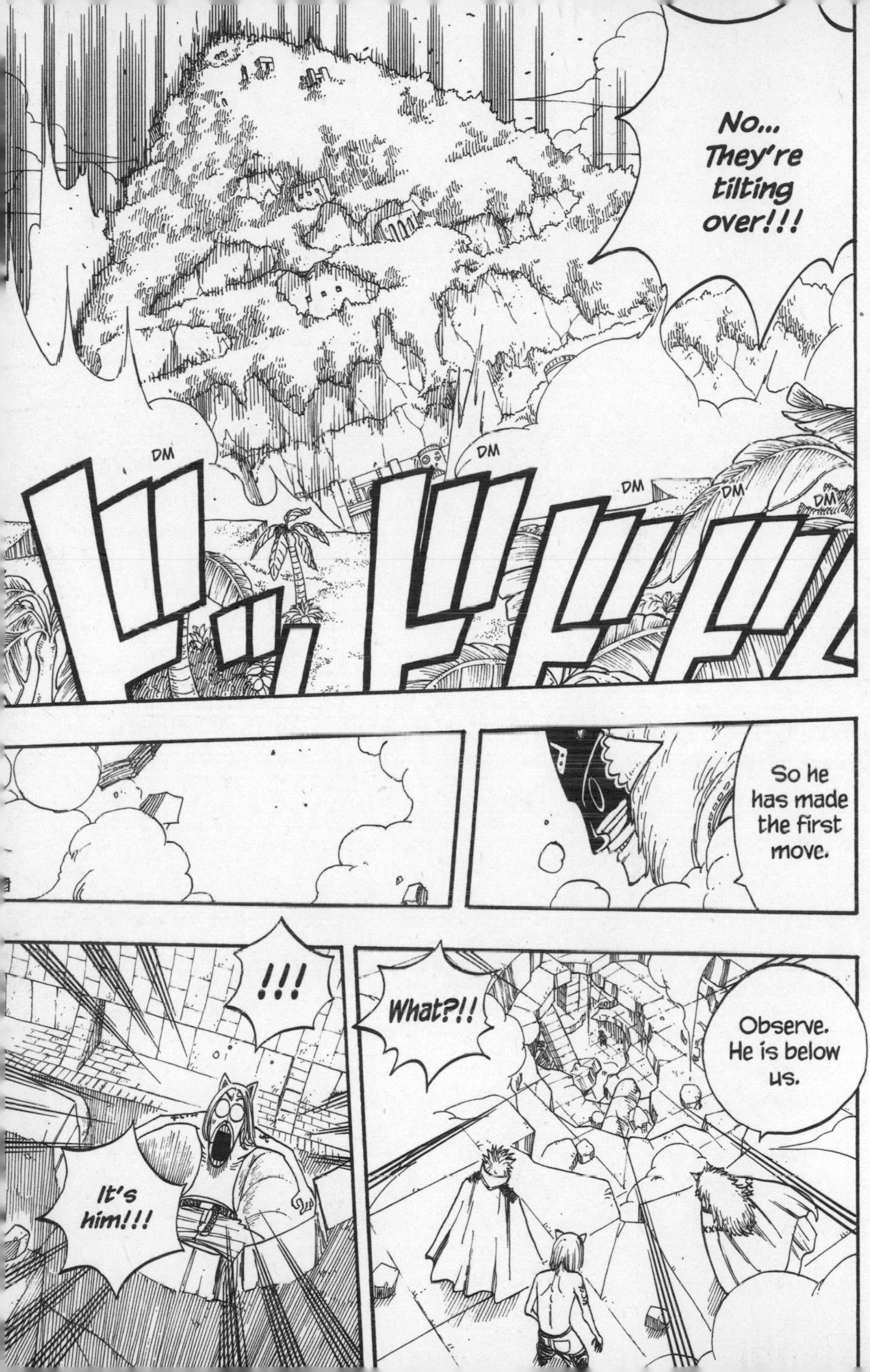

No... They're tilting over!!!
DM
DM
DM
DM
DM
So he has made the first move.
Observe. He is below us.
What?!!
!!!
It's him!!!

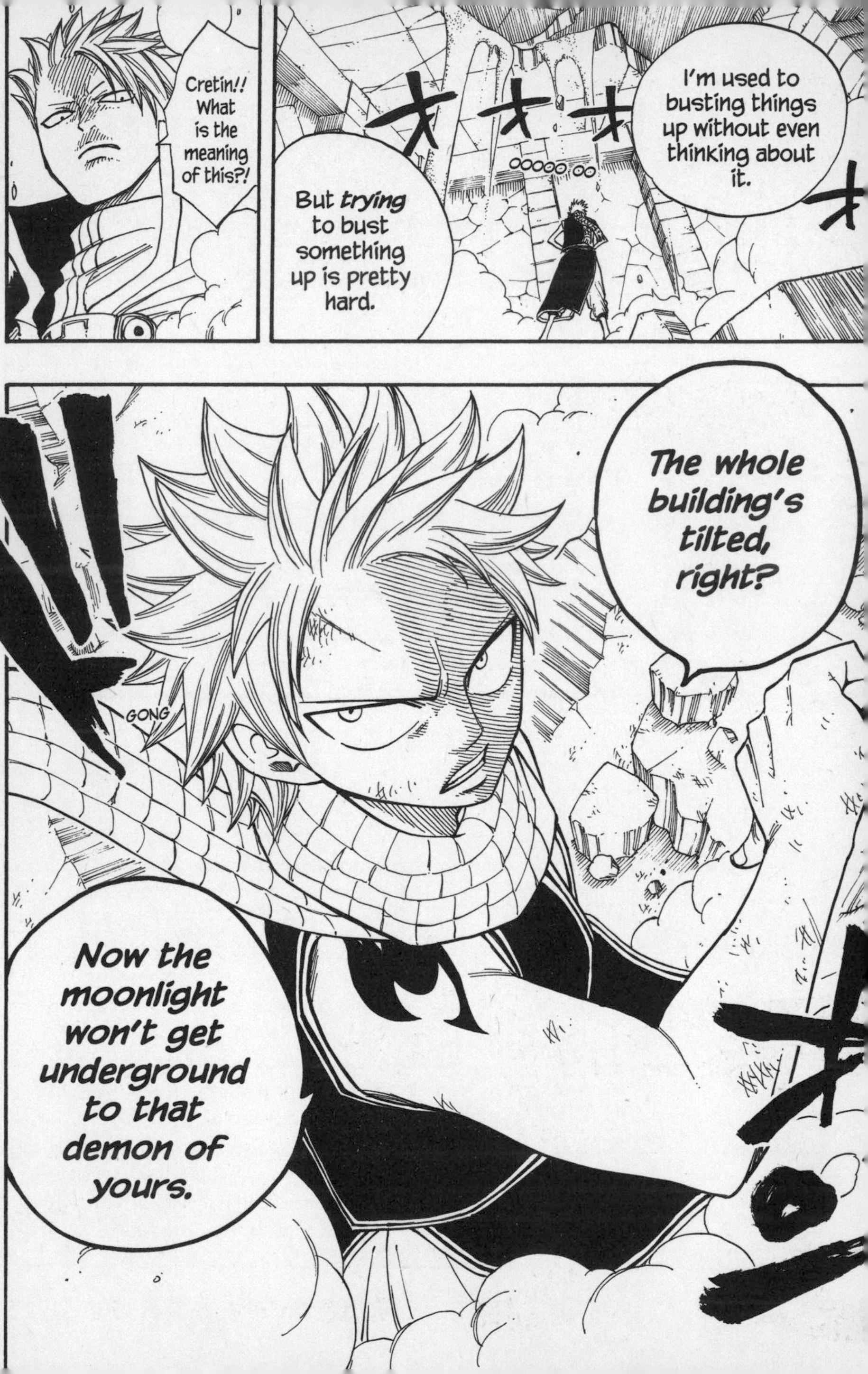
I'm used to busting things up without even thinking about it.
But *trying* to bust something up is pretty hard.
Cretin!! What is the meaning of this?!
The whole building's tilted, right?
GONG
Now the moonlight won't get underground to that demon of yours.

FAIRY TAIL

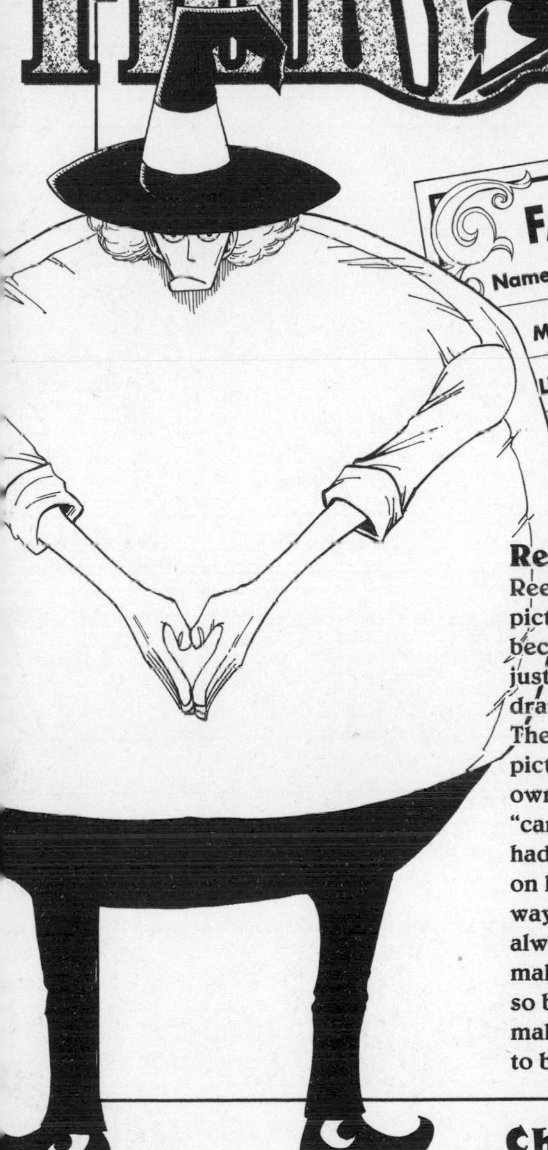

FAIRY TAIL

Name: Reedus Jonah

Age: 27 yrs.

Magic: Pict Magic

Likes: Drawings

Dislikes: Carrots

WIZARD GUILD X633

Remarks

Reedus uses pict magic, in which pictures that he draws move and become weapons. But one can't just draw anywhere and have the drawings move by pict magic. The only "canvas" on which a pict wizard can work is one's own body, and to increase his "canvas" size, rumor has it that he had the master cast giant magic on him. That is why he looks the way he does. The latest light pens always seem to be delayed by the maker, and Reedus wanted them so badly he went directly to the maker's factory. But was not able to buy any of the new pens.

Chapter 36: Ur

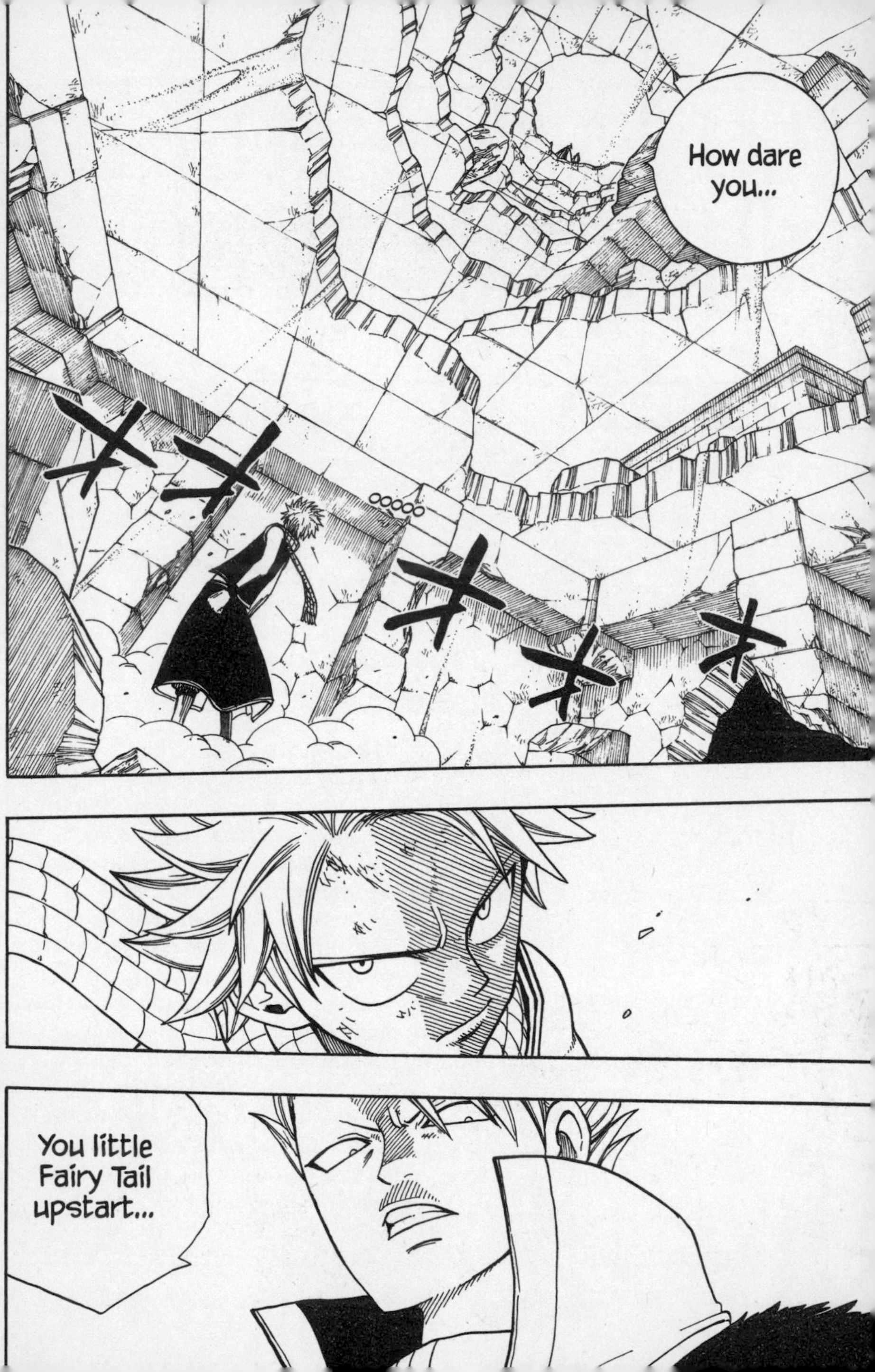
How dare you...
You little Fairy Tail upstart...

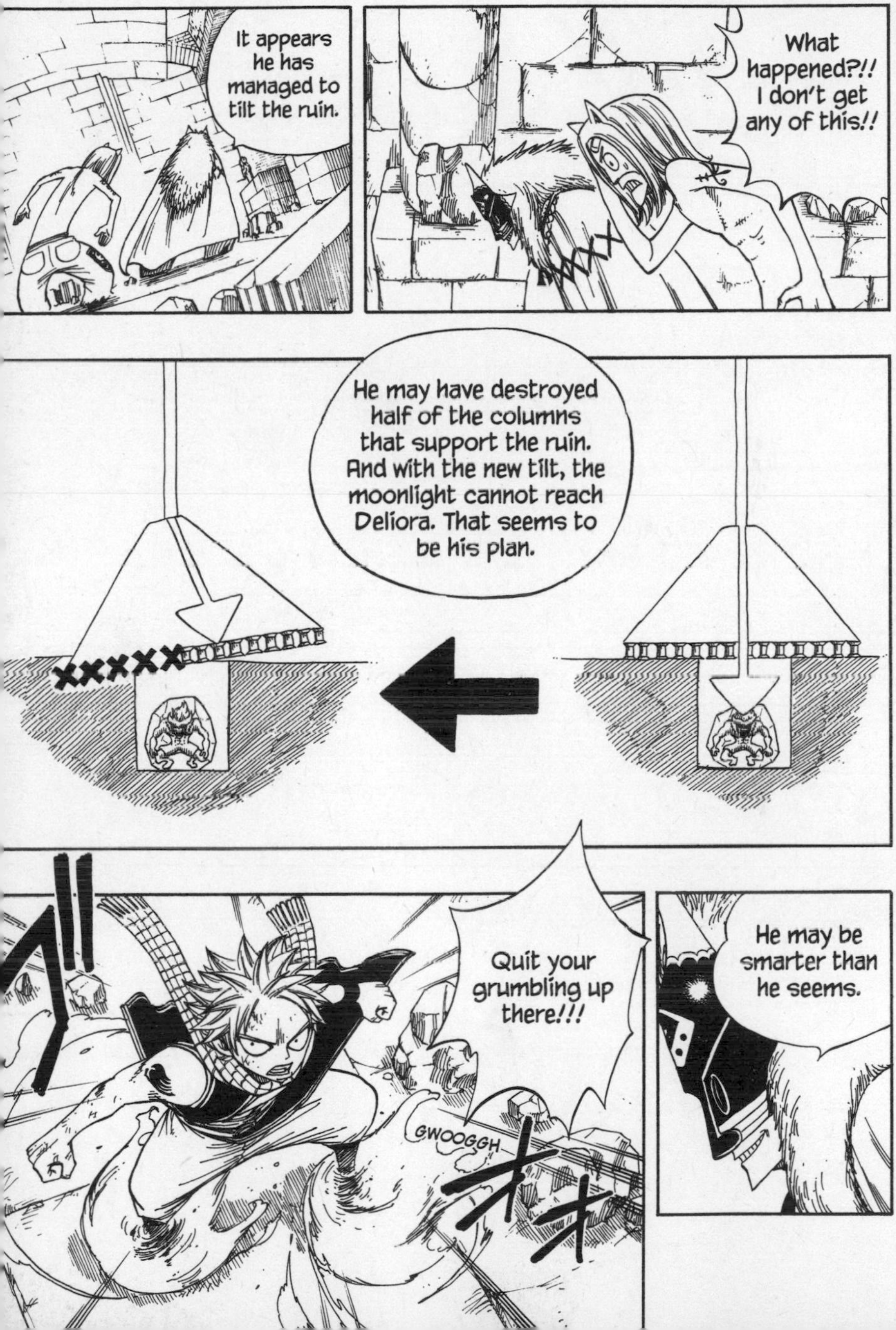
What happened?!! I don't get any of this!!
It appears he has managed to tilt the ruin.
He may have destroyed half of the columns that support the ruin. And with the new tilt, the moonlight cannot reach Deliora. That seems to be his plan.
He may be smarter than he seems.
Quit your grumbling up there!!!
GWOOGGH

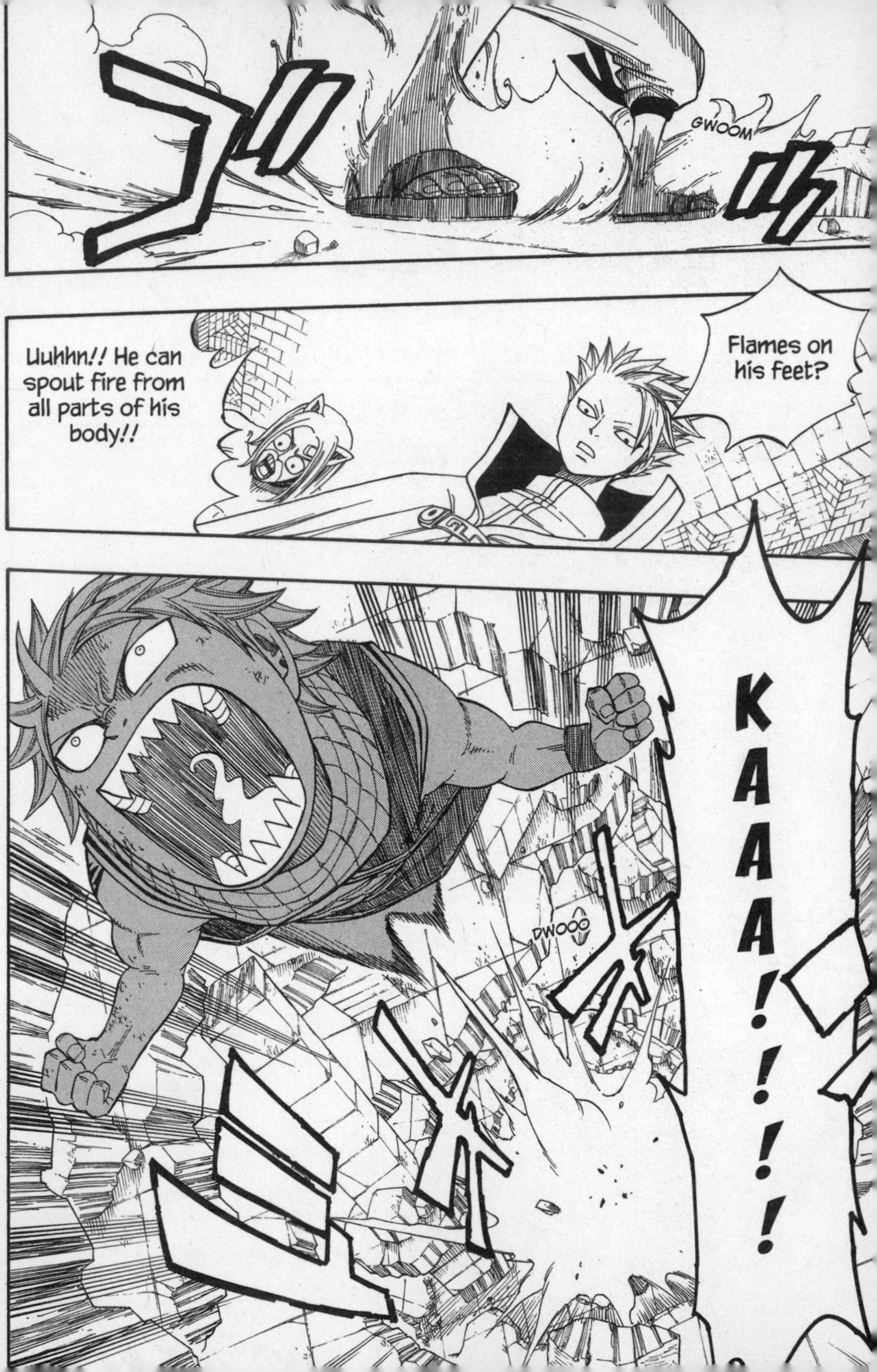
GWOOM
Flames on his feet?
Uuhhn!! He can spout fire from all parts of his body!!
KAAA!!!!!
DWOOO

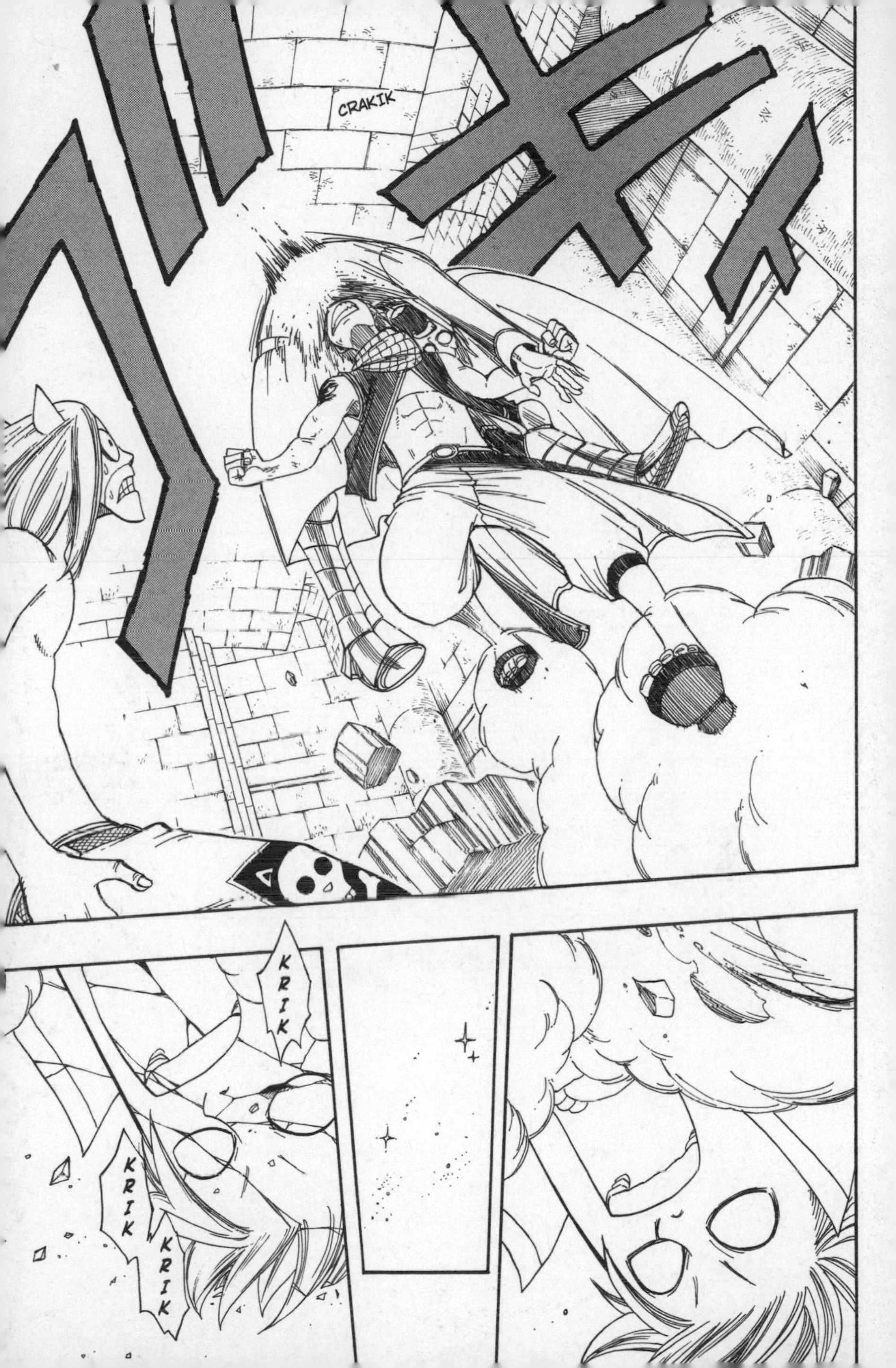
CRAKIK
KRIK KRIK
KRIK
KRIK

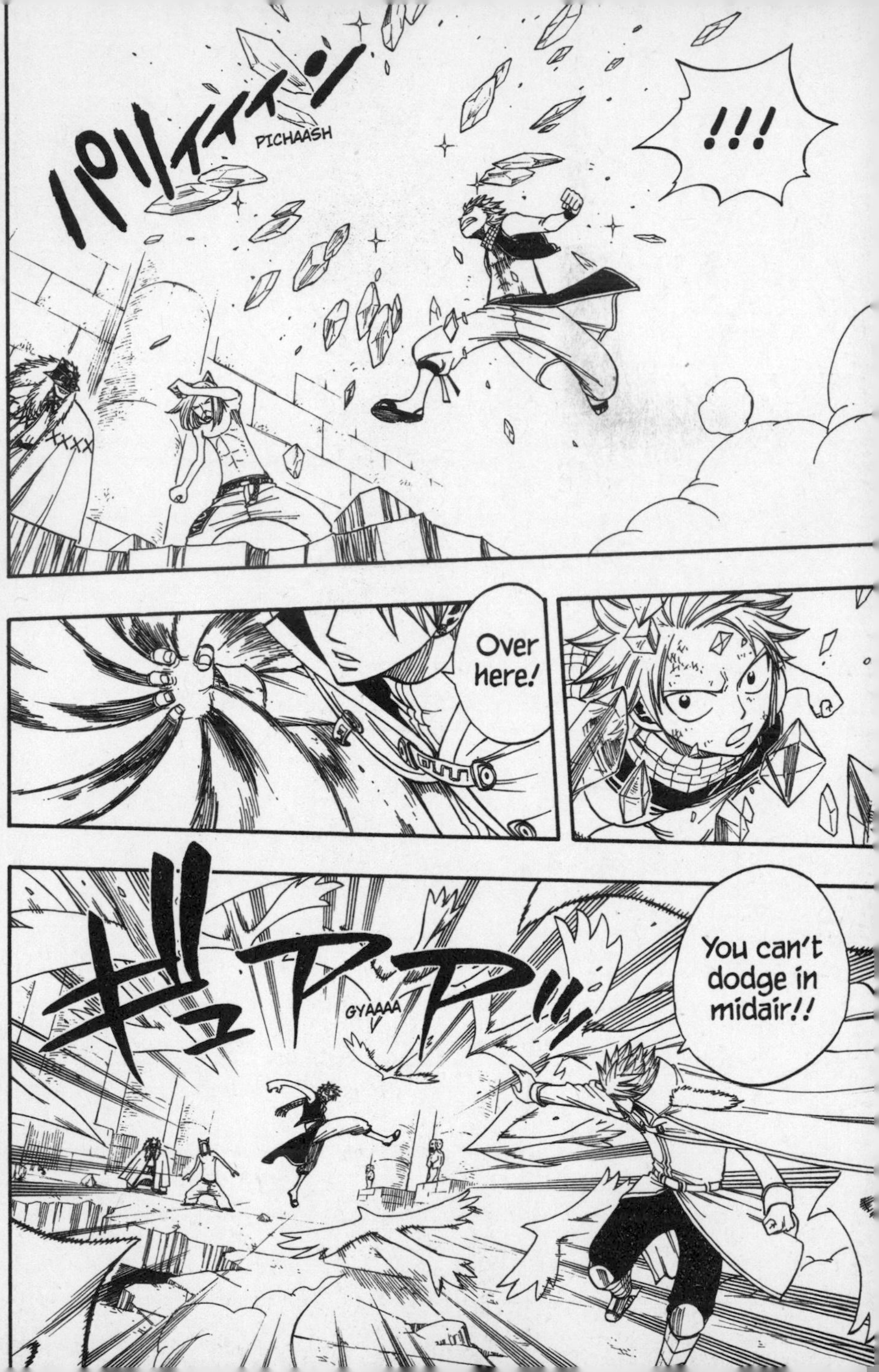
!!!
パリイイイン
PICHAASH
Over here!
You can't dodge in midair!!
ギュアアッ
GYAAAA

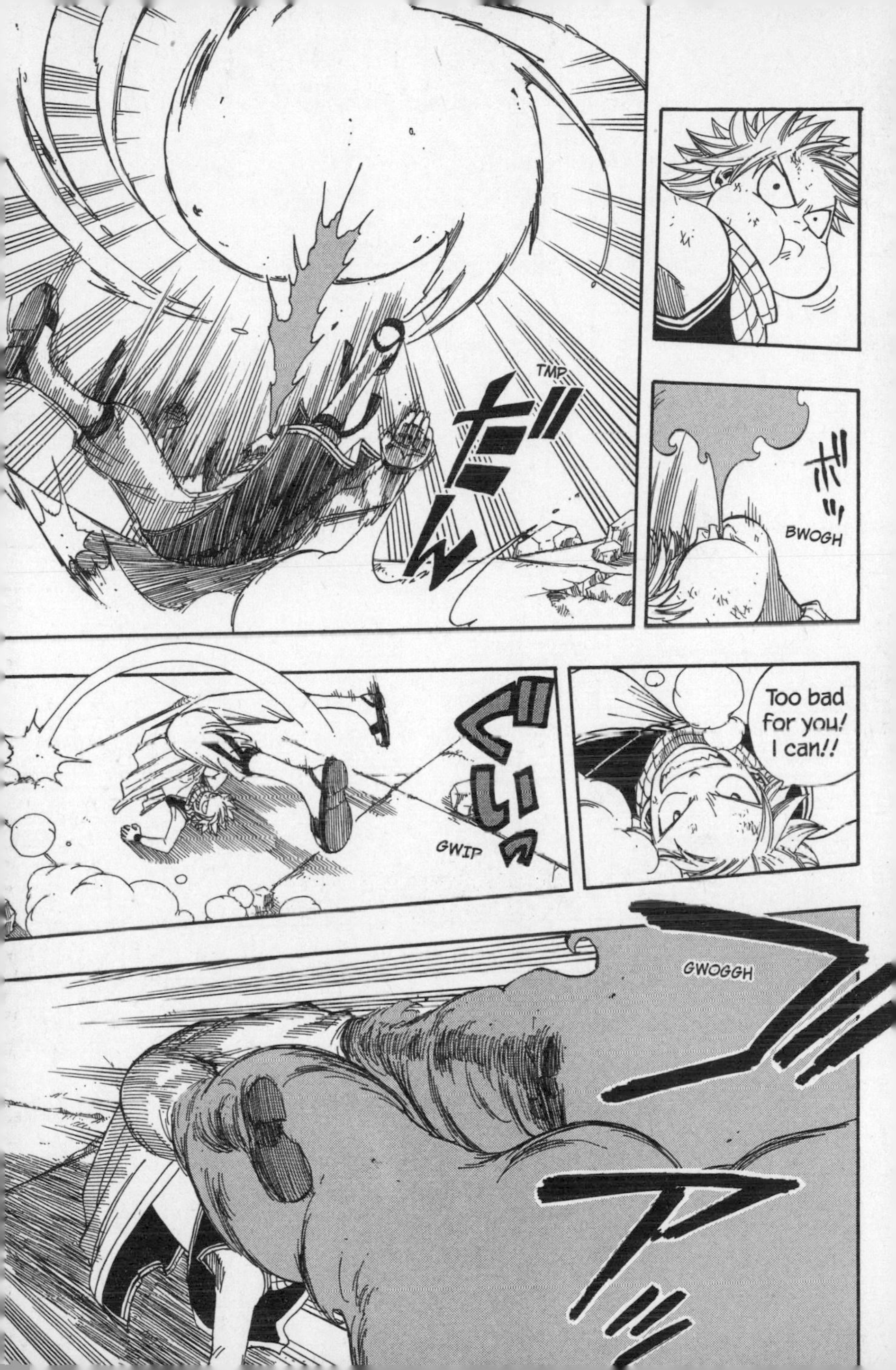
BWOGH
TMP
Too bad for you! I can!!
GWIP
GWOGGH

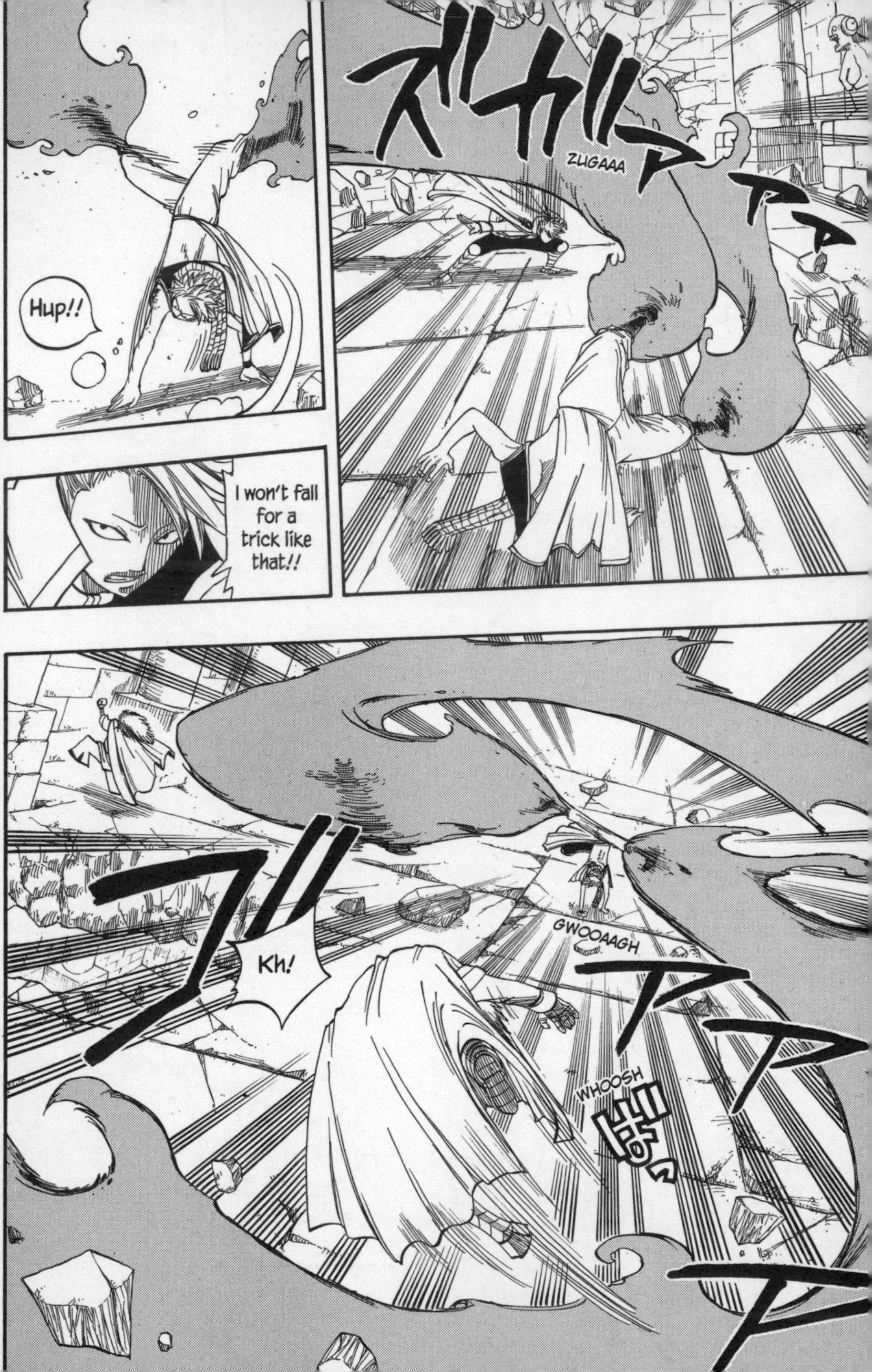
ZUGAAA
Hup!!
I won't fall for a trick like that!!
GWOOAAGH
Kh!
WHOOSH

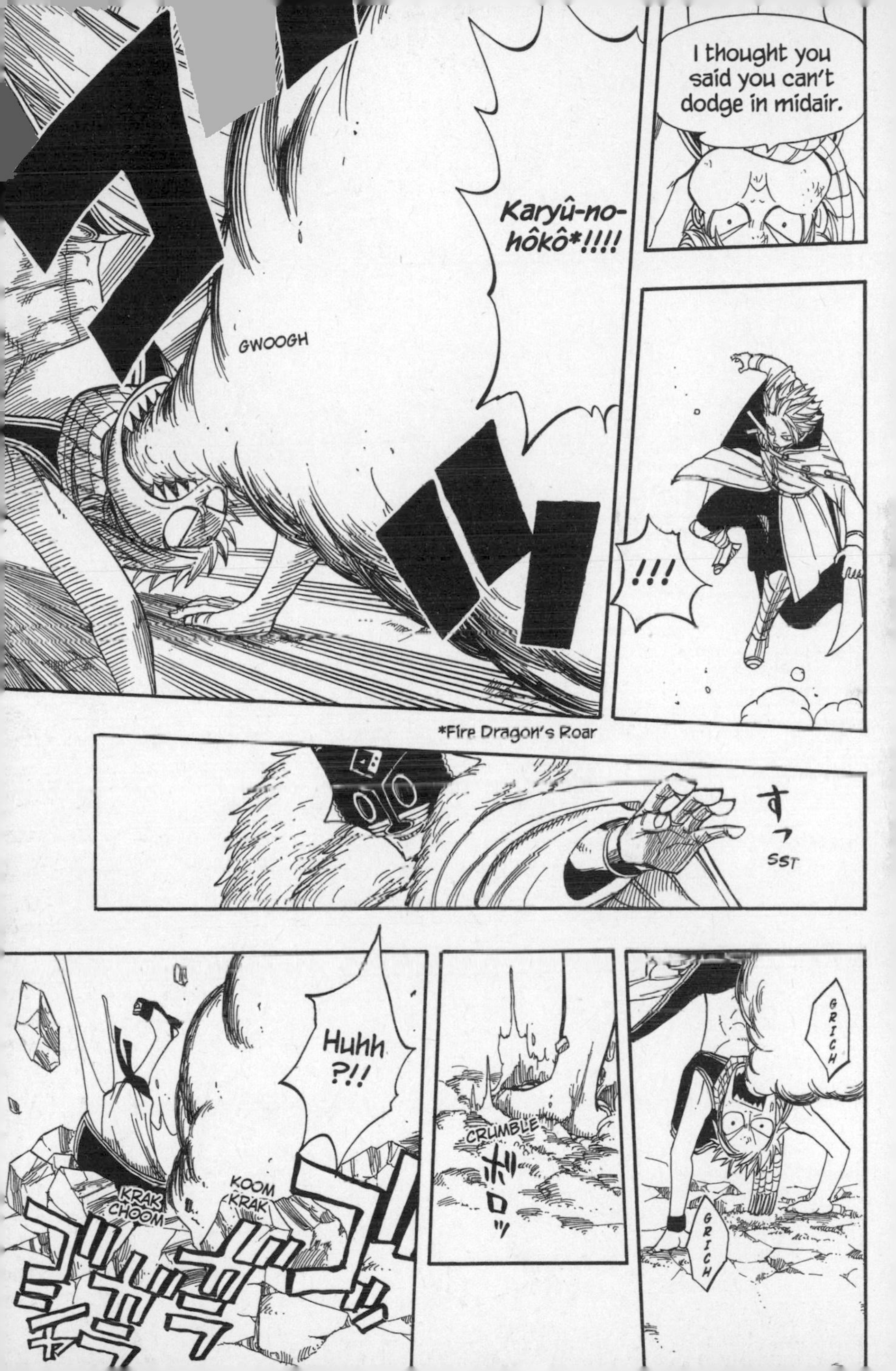
I thought you said you can't dodge in midair.
!!!
Karyû-no-hôkô*!!!!
GWOOGH
*Fire Dragon's Roar
すっ
SST
GRICH
GRICH
CRUMBLE
ボロッ
Huhh ?!!
KRAK CHOOM
KOOM KRAK

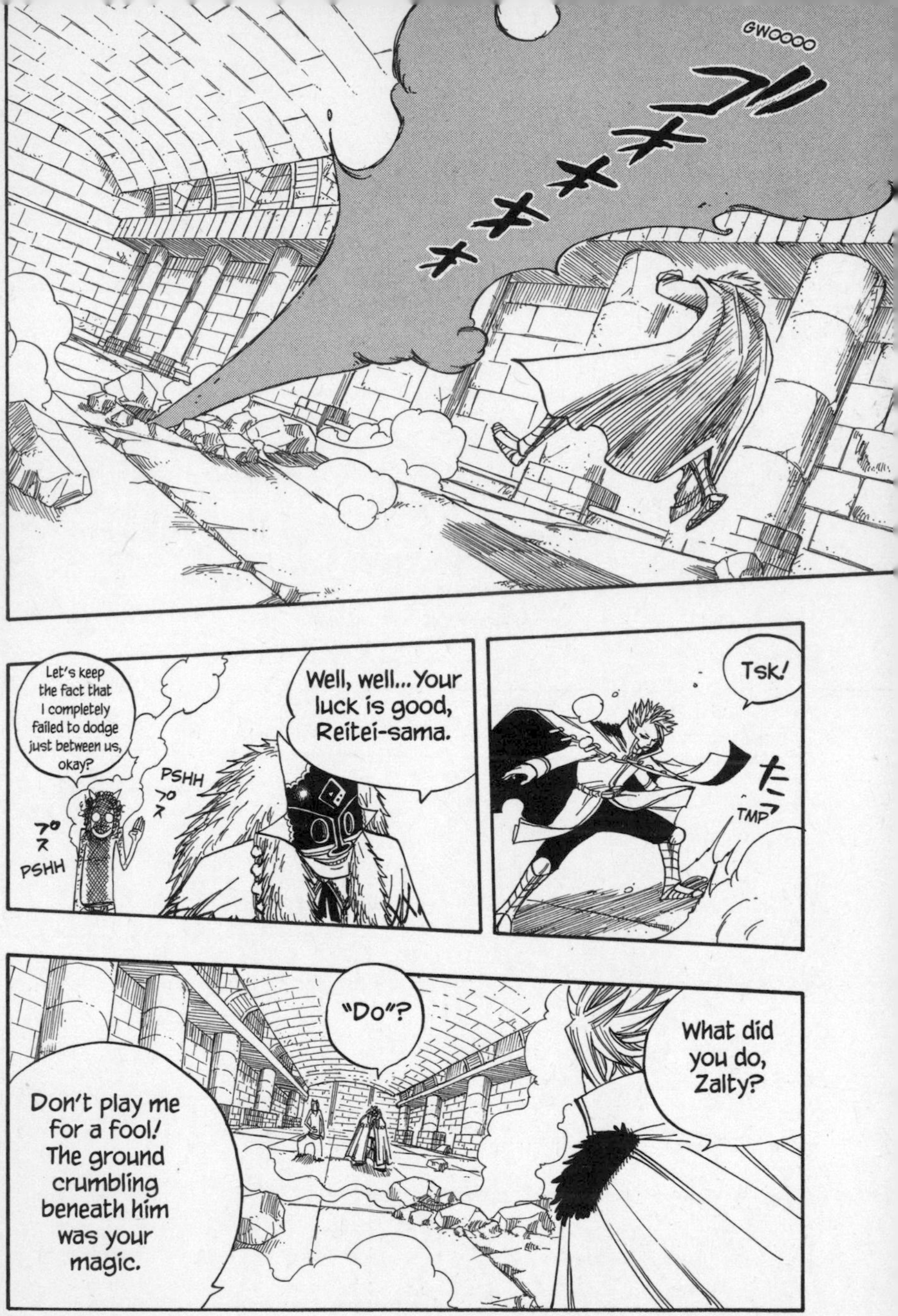
GWOOOO
Tsk!
TMP
Well, well... Your luck is good, Reitei-sama.
Let's keep the fact that I completely failed to dodge just between us, okay?
PSHH
PSHH
What did you do, Zalty?
"Do"?
Don't play me for a fool! The ground crumbling beneath him was your magic.

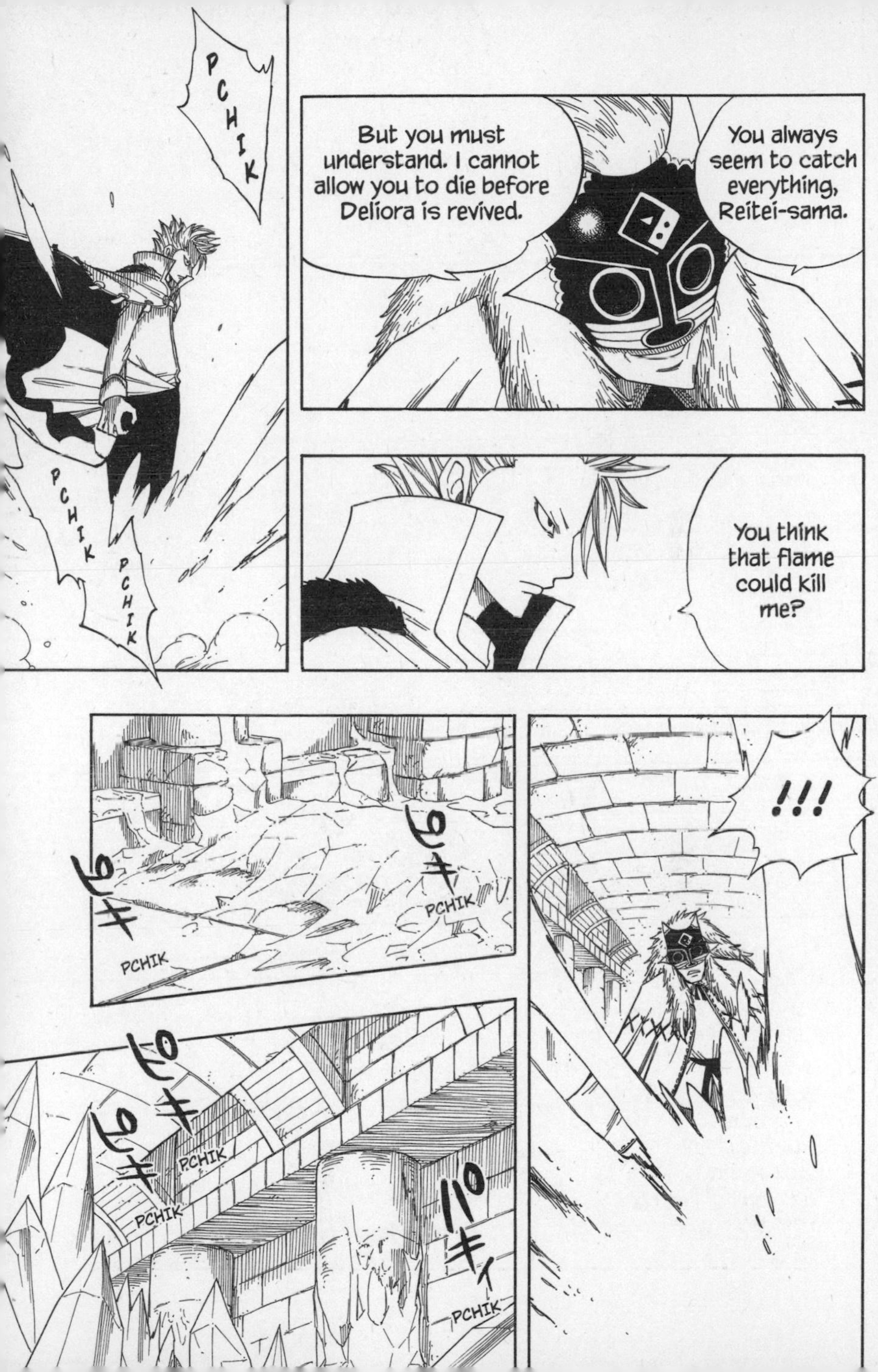
You always seem to catch everything, Reitei-sama.
But you must understand. I cannot allow you to die before Deliora is revived.
You think that flame could kill me?
PCHIK
PCHIK
PCHIK
!!!
PCHIK
PCHIK
PCHIK
PCHIK
PCHIK

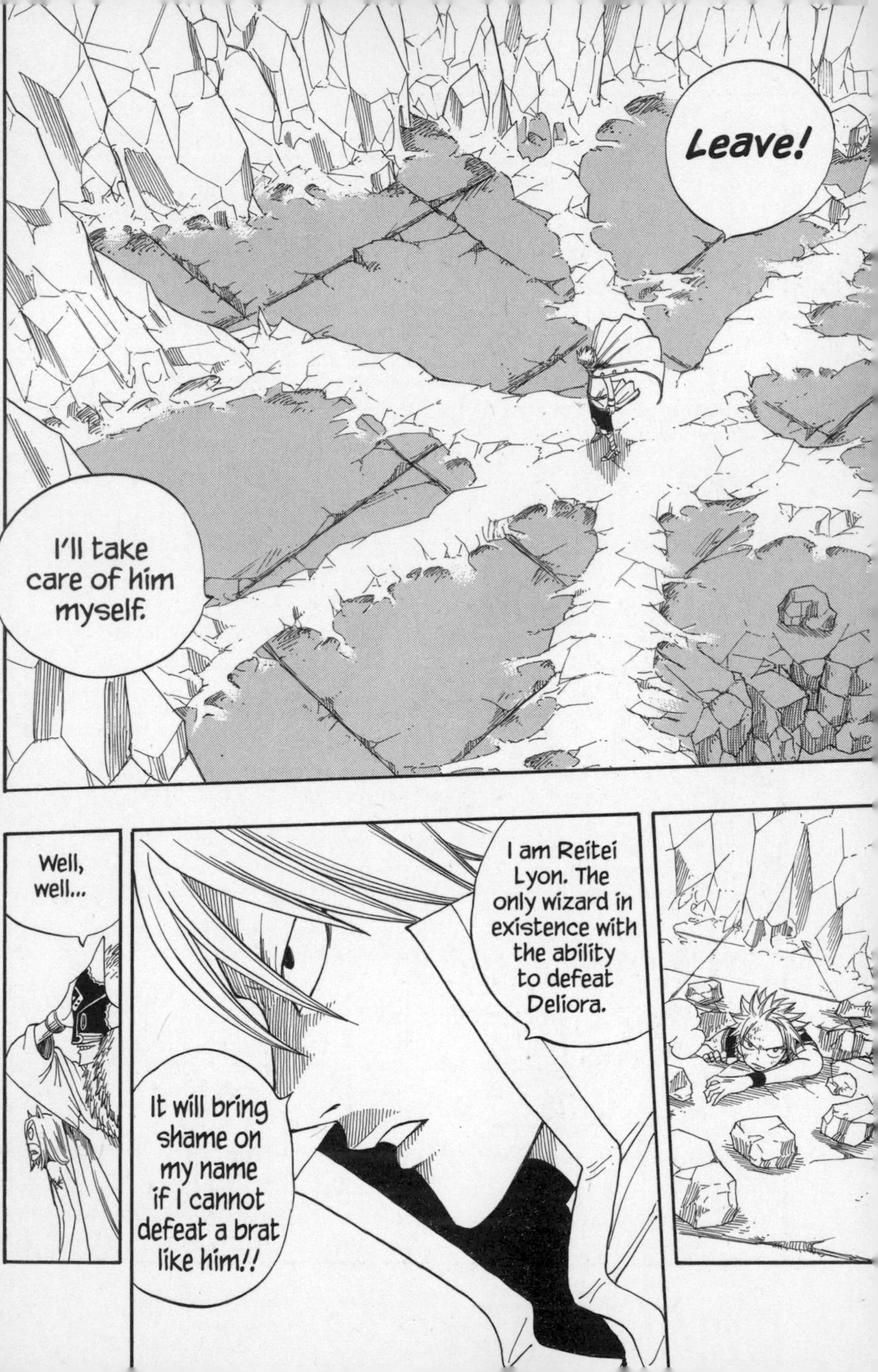
Leave!
I'll take care of him myself.
I am Reitei Lyon. The only wizard in existence with the ability to defeat Deliora.
It will bring shame on my name if I cannot defeat a brat like him!!
Well, well...

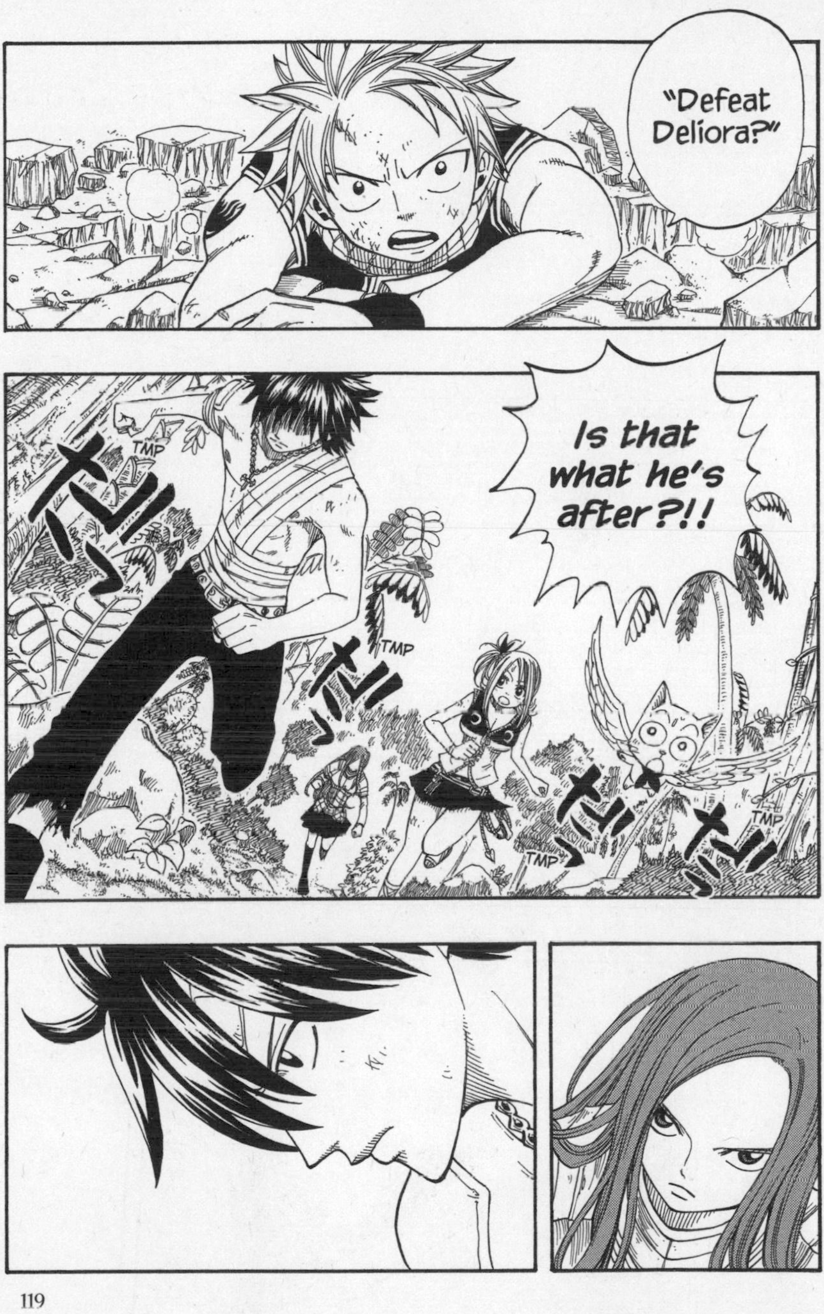
"Defeat Delíora?"
Is that what he's after?!!
TMP
TMP
TMP
TMP

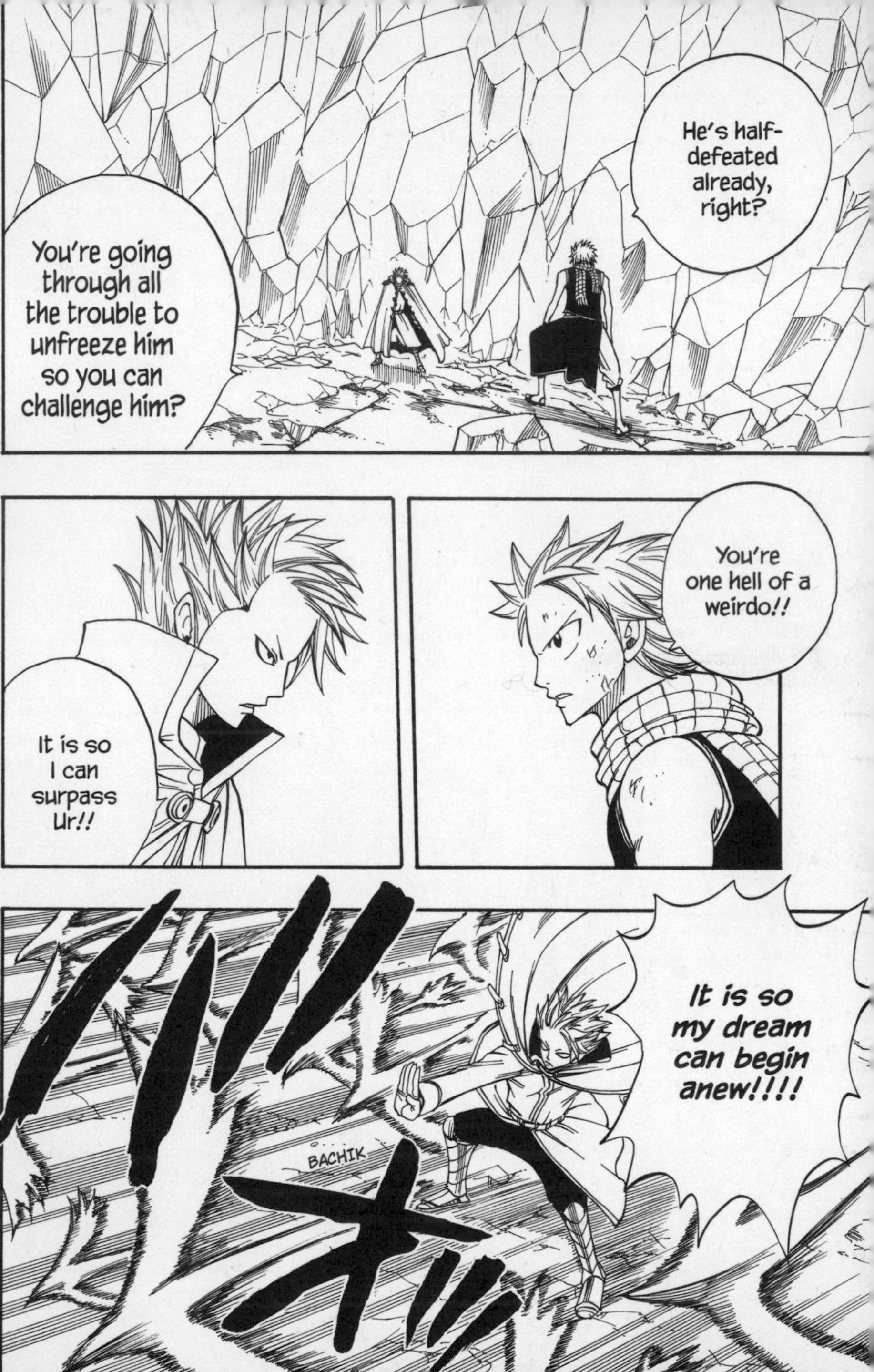
He's half-defeated already, right?
You're going through all the trouble to unfreeze him so you can challenge him?
You're one hell of a weirdo!!
It is so I can surpass Ur!!
It is so my dream can begin anew!!!!
BACHIK

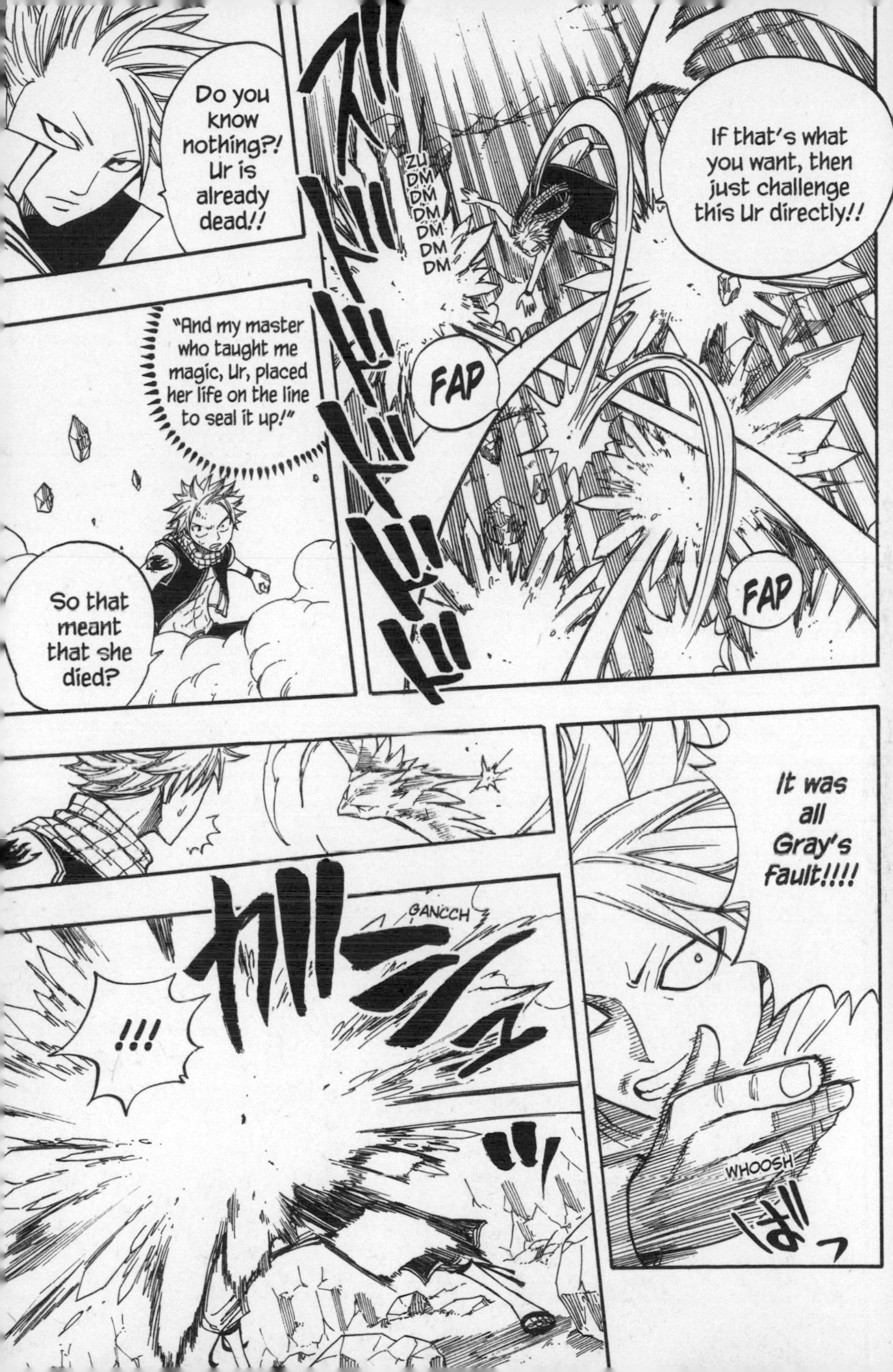

If that's what you want, then just challenge this Ur directly!!
ZU DM DM DM DM DM DM
FAP
FAP
Do you know nothing?! Ur is already dead!!
"And my master who taught me magic, Ur, placed her life on the line to seal it up!"
So that meant that she died?
It was all Gray's fault!!!!
WHOOSH
GANCCH
!!!

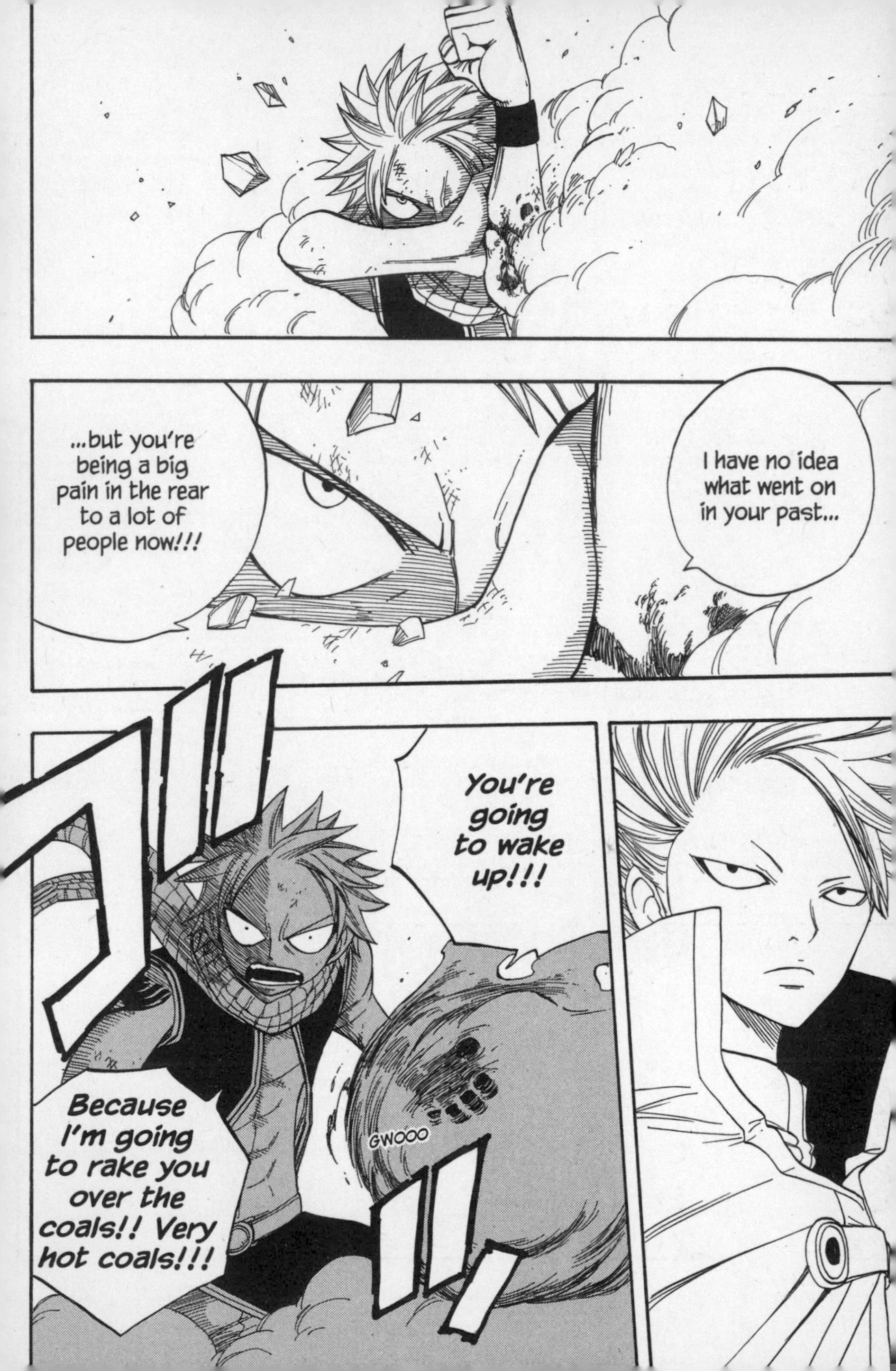
I have no idea what went on in your past...
...but you're being a big pain in the rear to a lot of people now!!!
You're going to wake up!!!
GWOOO
Because I'm going to rake you over the coals!! Very hot coals!!!

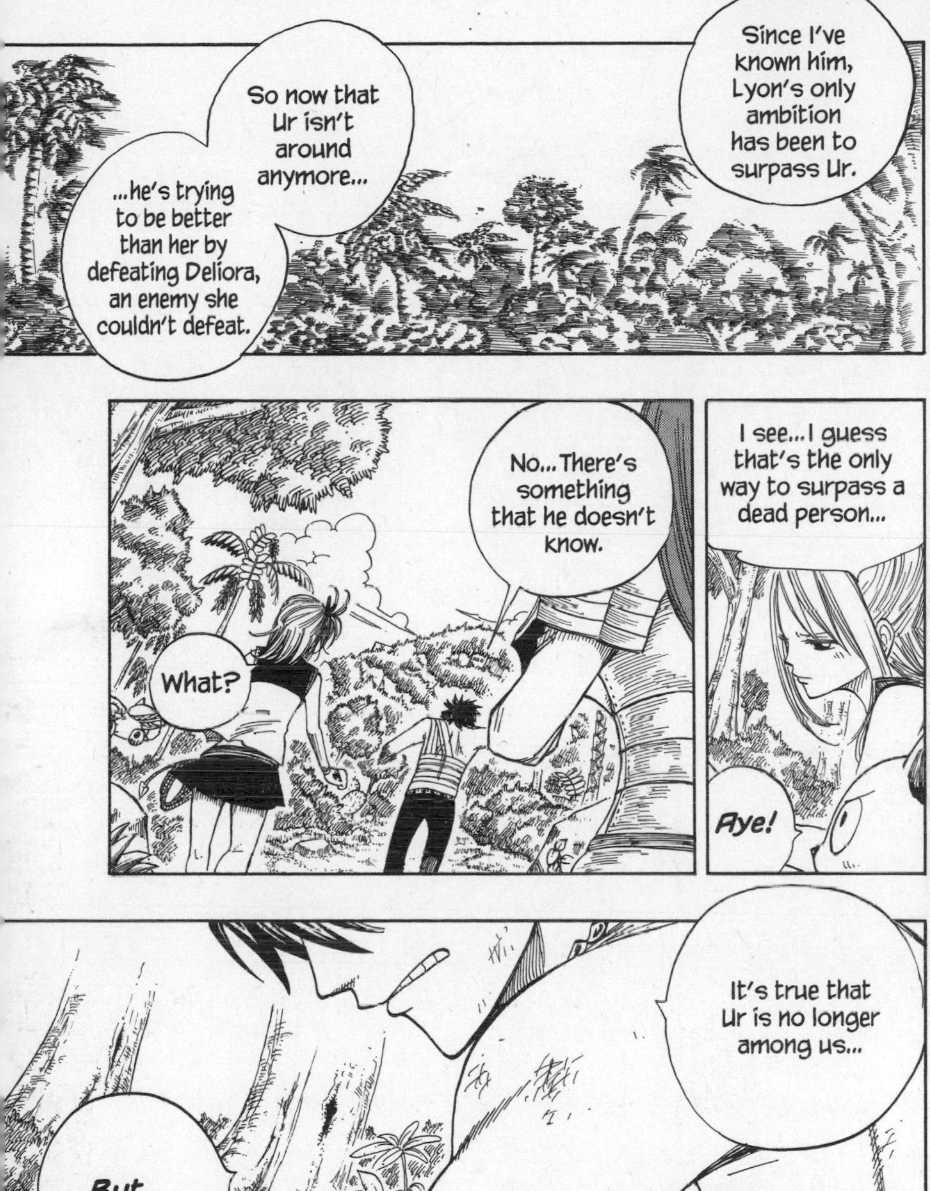

Since I've known him, Lyon's only ambition has been to surpass Ur.
So now that Ur isn't around anymore...
...he's trying to be better than her by defeating Deliora, an enemy she couldn't defeat.
I see...I guess that's the only way to surpass a dead person...
Aye!
No...There's something that he doesn't know.
What?
It's true that Ur is no longer among us...
But...

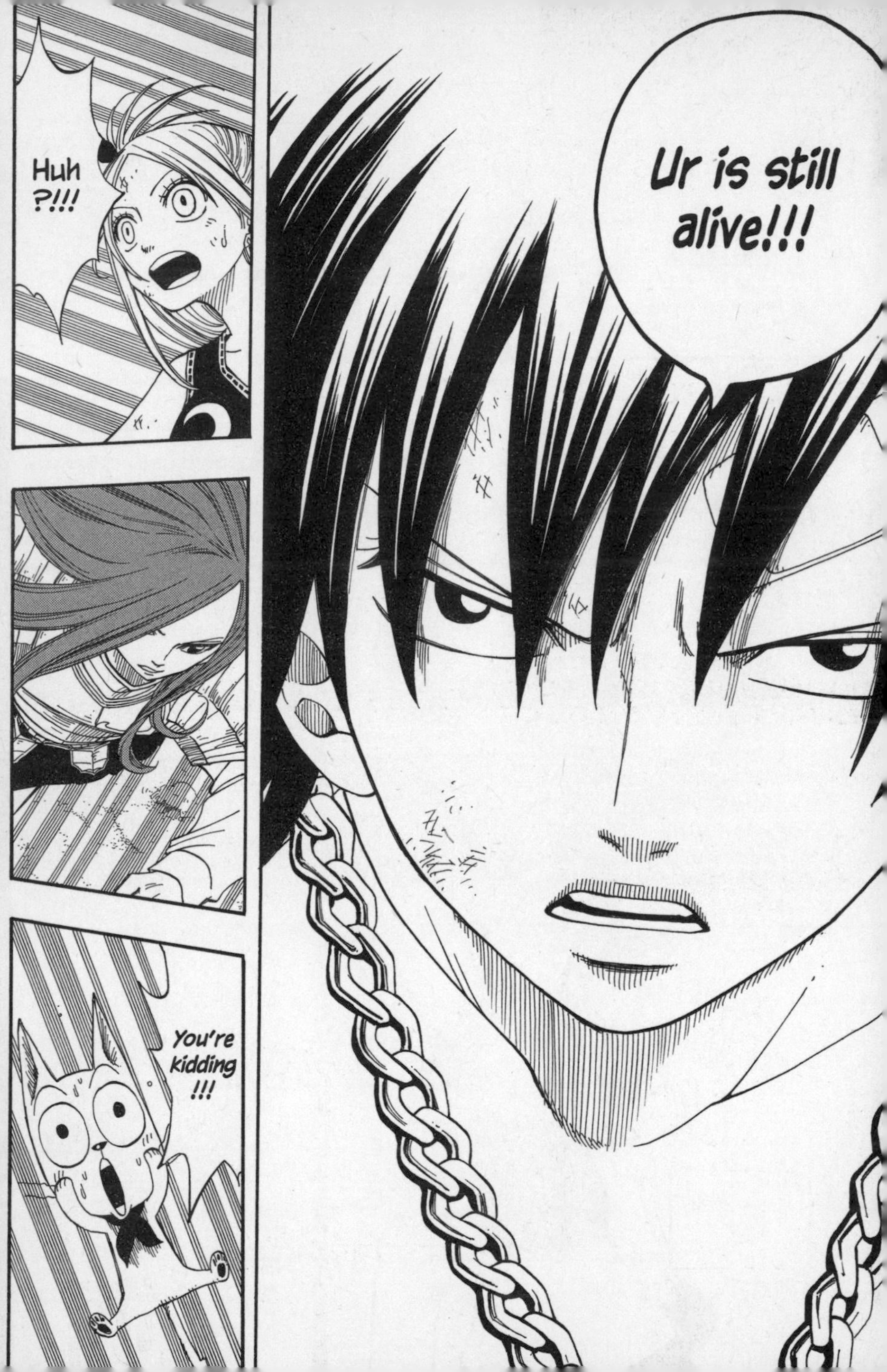
Ur is still alive!!!
Huh ?!!!
You're kidding !!!

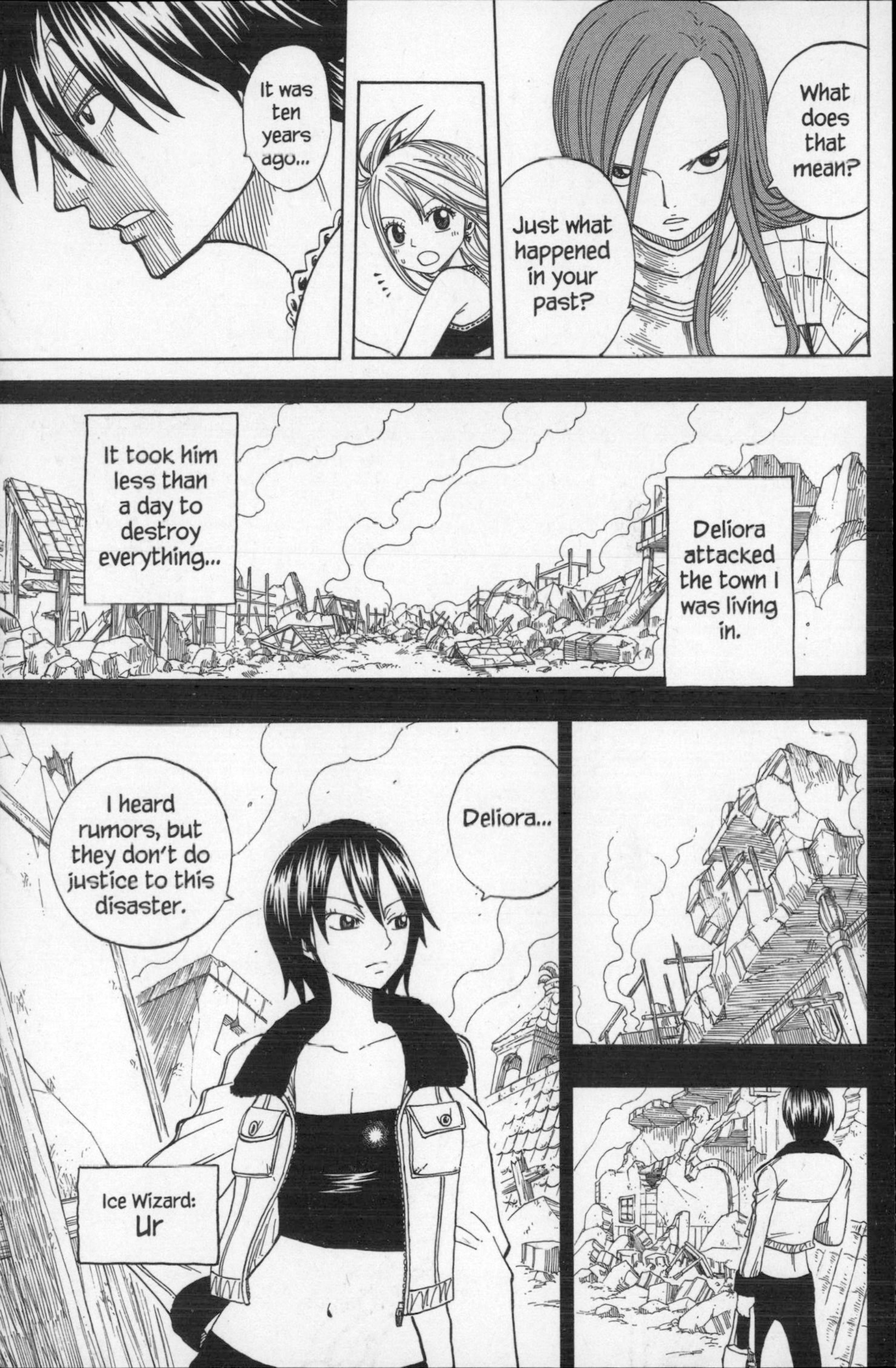
What does that mean?
Just what happened in your past?
It was ten years ago...
Deliora attacked the town I was living in.
It took him less than a day to destroy everything...
Deliora...
I heard rumors, but they don't do justice to this disaster.
Ice Wizard: Ur

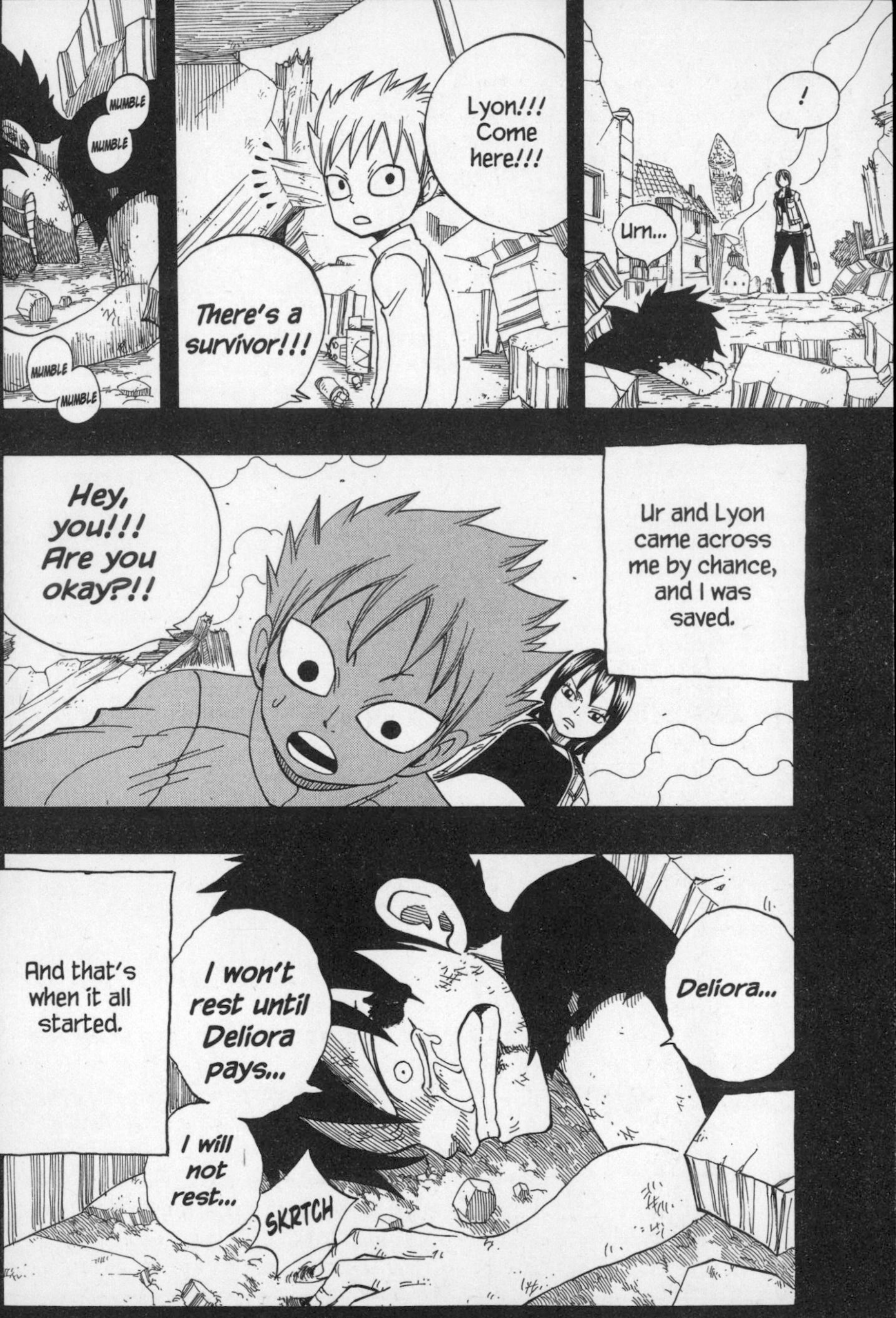
!
Urn...
Lyon!!! Come here!!!
There's a survivor!!!
MUMBLE
MUMBLE
MUMBLE
MUMBLE
Ur and Lyon came across me by chance, and I was saved.
Hey, you!!! Are you okay?!!
Deliora...
I won't rest until Deliora pays...
I will not rest...
SKRTCH
And that's when it all started.

FAIRY TAIL

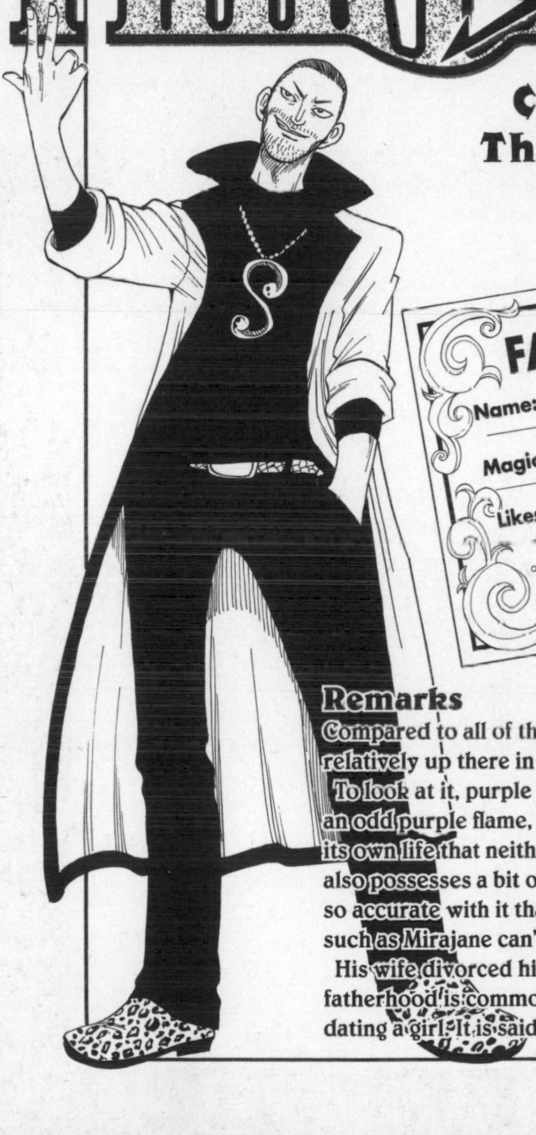

Chapter 37: The Blue Bird

FAIRY TAIL

Name: Macao Conbolt

Age: 36 yrs.

Magic: Purple Fire

Likes: His Son (Romeo)

Dislikes: His Loan

WIZARD GUILD X633

Remarks

Compared to all of the young people in Fairy Tail, he's relatively up there in years.

To look at it, purple fire magic is the manipulation of an odd purple flame, but it is a unique fire invested with its own life that neither wind nor water can put out. He also possesses a bit of transformation magic, and he is so accurate with it that even a transformation specialist such as Mirajane can't see through it.

His wife divorced him three years ago. Single fatherhood is common, but he hates it. So he has started dating a girl. It is said that she's very ordinary-looking.

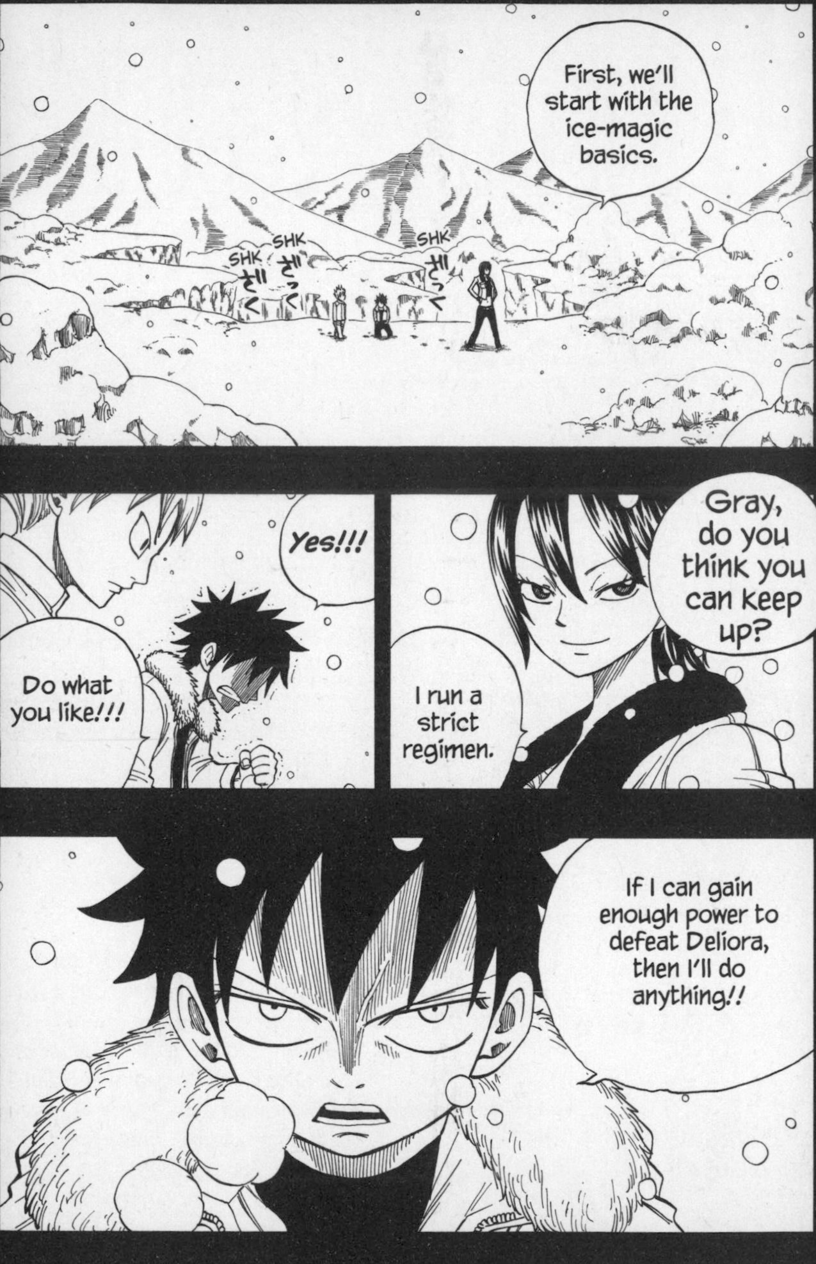
First, we'll start with the ice-magic basics.
SHK
SHK
SHK
Gray, do you think you can keep up?
I run a strict regimen.
Yes!!!
Do what you like!!!
If I can gain enough power to defeat Deliora, then I'll do anything!!

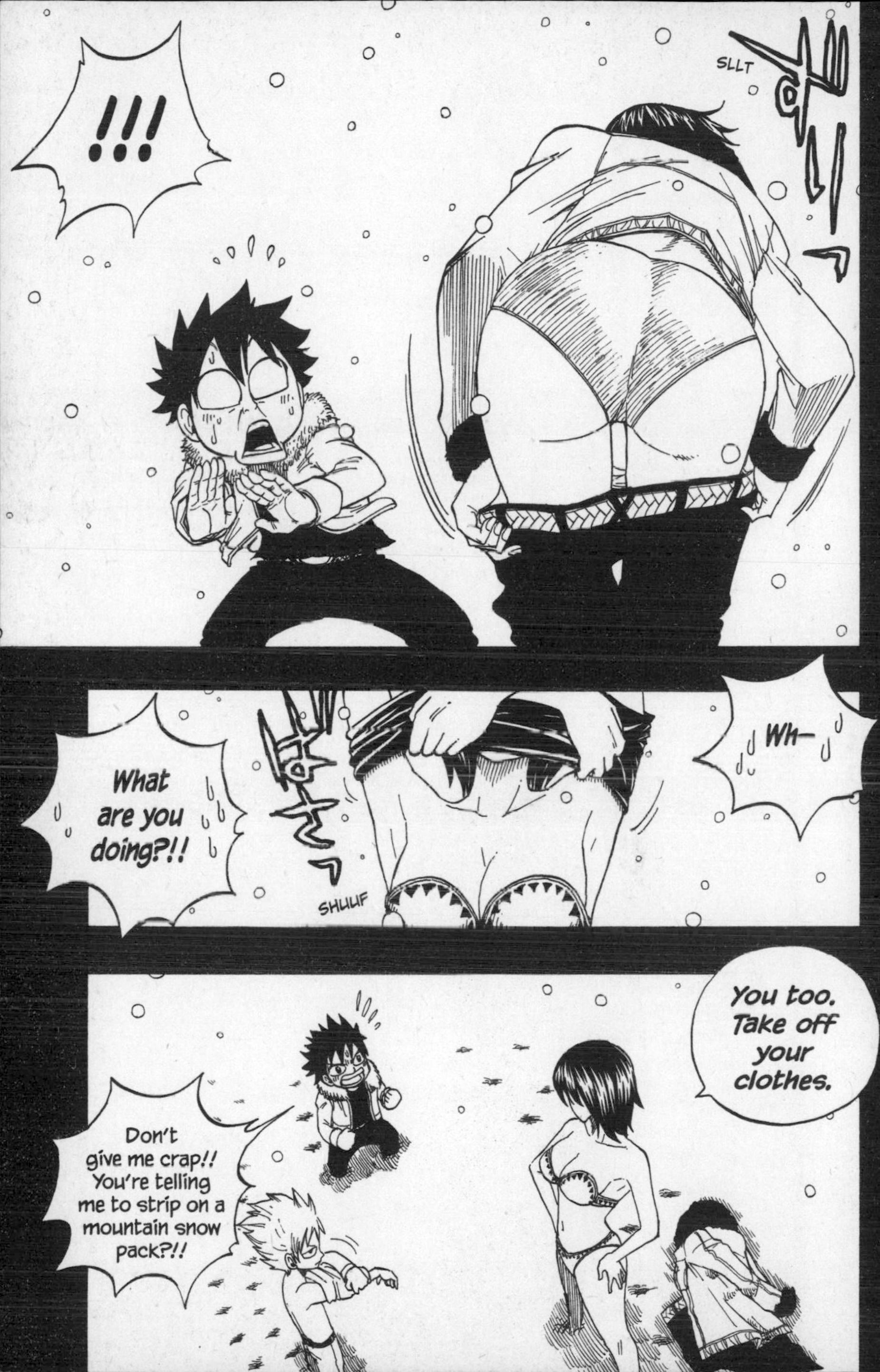
SLLT
!!!
Wh—
SHUUF
What are you doing?!!
You too. Take off your clothes.
Don't give me crap!! You're telling me to strip on a mountain snow pack?!!

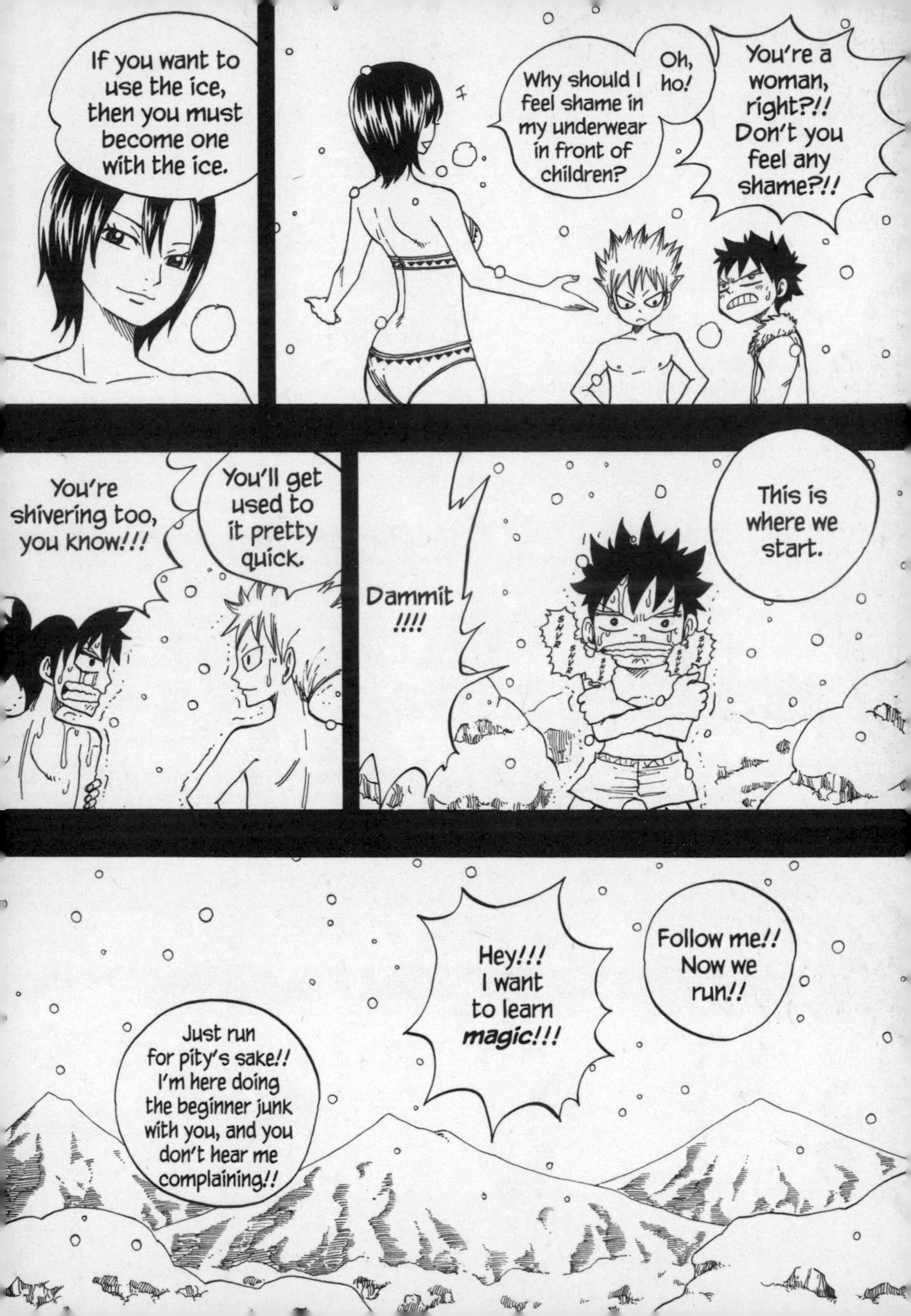
You're a woman, right?!! Don't you feel any shame?!!
Oh, ho!
Why should I feel shame in my underwear in front of children?
If you want to use the ice, then you must become one with the ice.
This is where we start.
SHVR SHVR
SHVR SHVR
Dammit!!!!
You'll get used to it pretty quick.
You're shivering too, you know!!!
Follow me!! Now we run!!
Hey!!! I want to learn *magic*!!!
Just run for pity's sake!! I'm here doing the beginner junk with you, and you don't hear me complaining!!

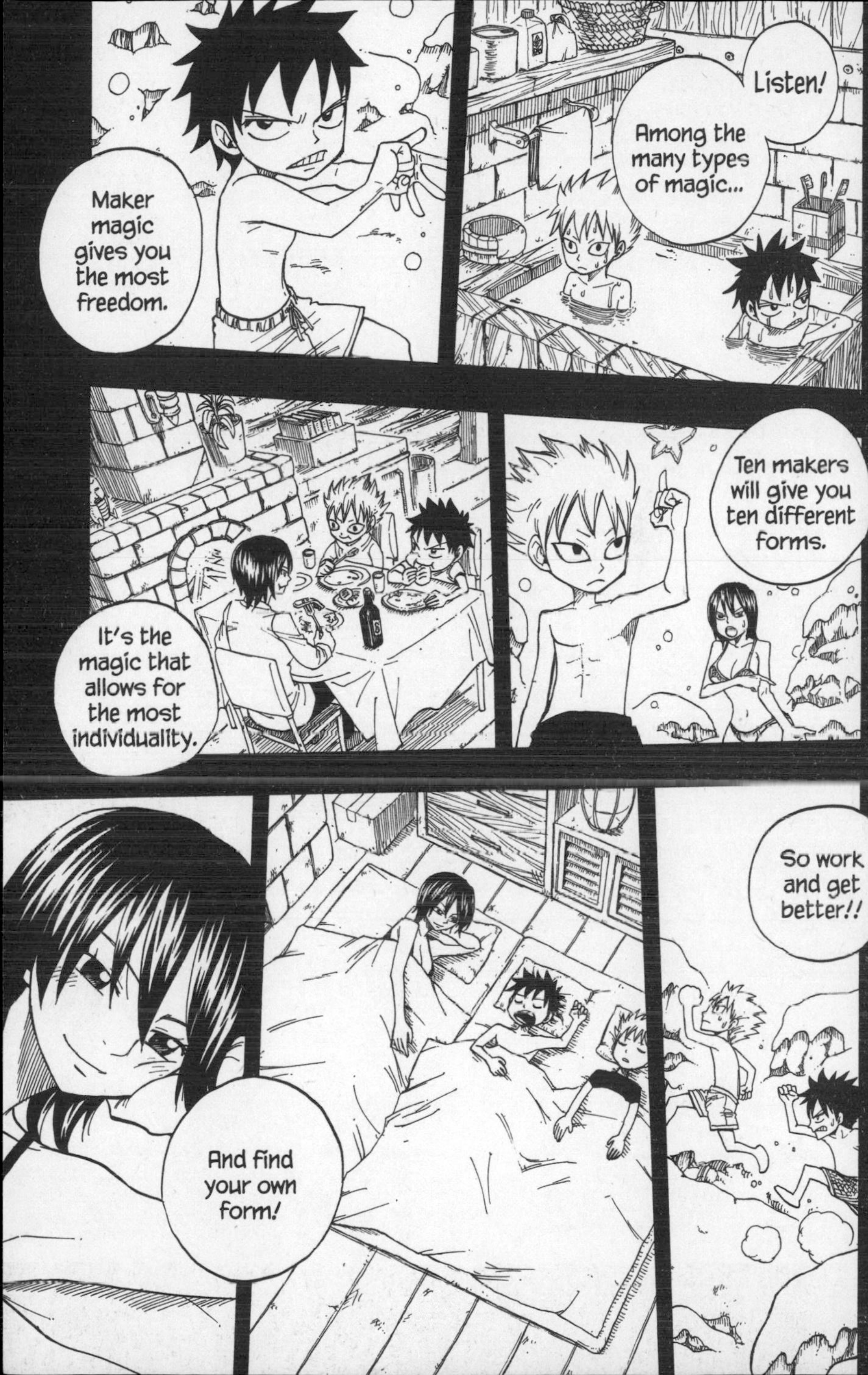
Listen!
Among the many types of magic...
Maker magic gives you the most freedom.
Ten makers will give you ten different forms.
It's the magic that allows for the most individuality.
So work and get better!!
And find your own form!

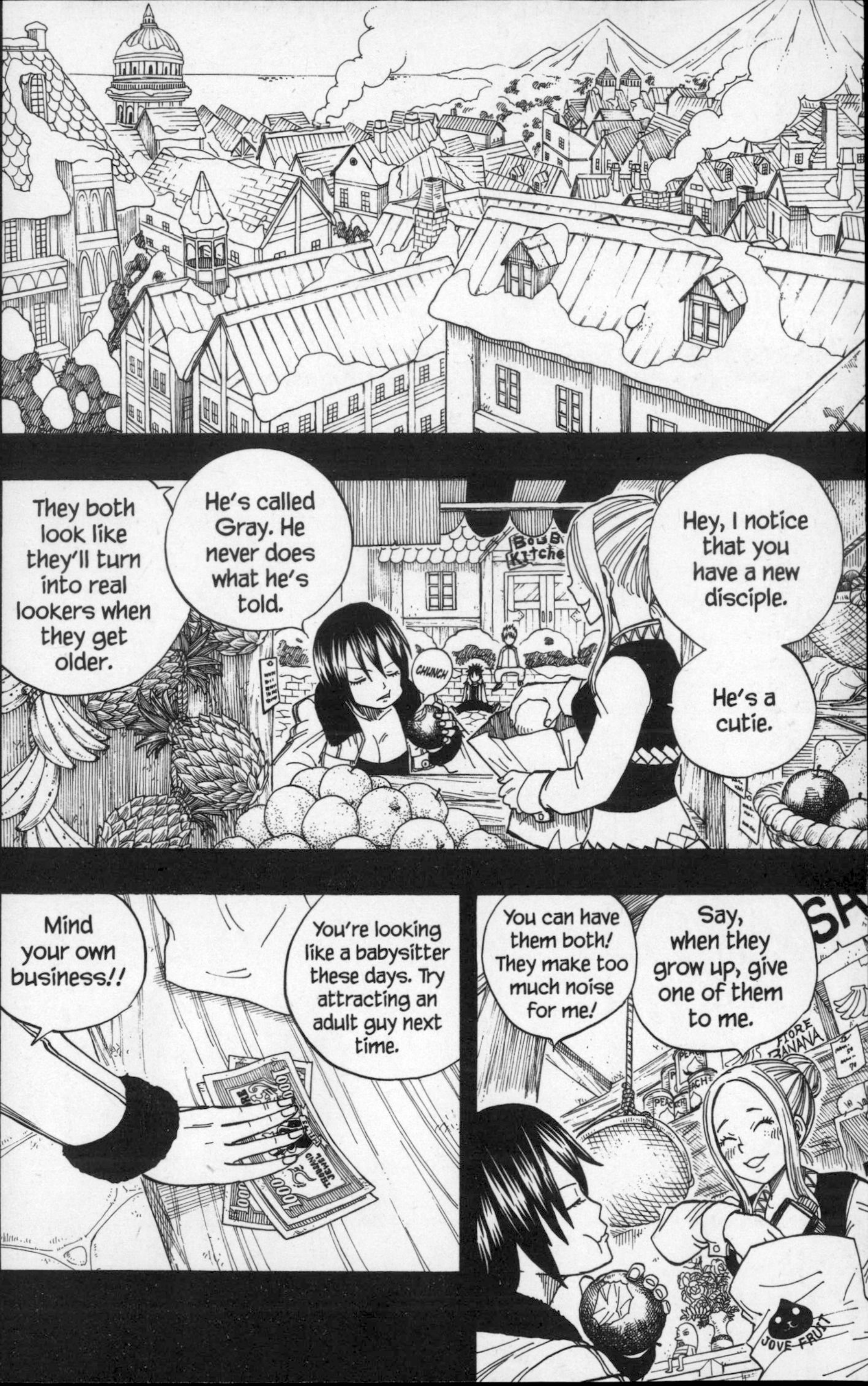
Hey, I notice that you have a new disciple.
He's a cutie.
CHUNCH
He's called Gray. He never does what he's told.
They both look like they'll turn into real lookers when they get older.
Say, when they grow up, give one of them to me.
FIORE BANANA
You can have them both! They make too much noise for me!
You're looking like a babysitter these days. Try attracting an adult guy next time.
Mind your own business!!

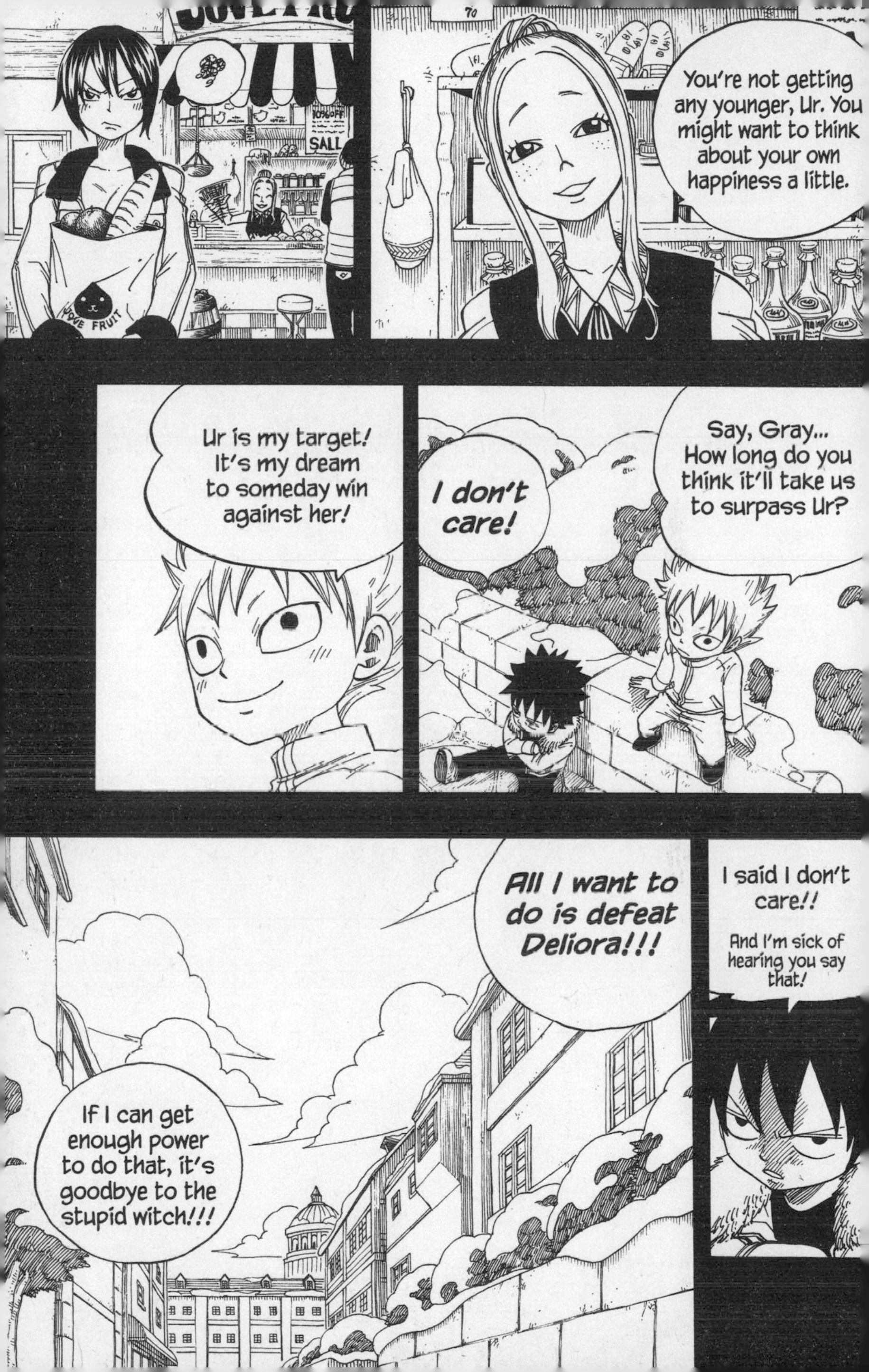
You're not getting any younger, Ur. You might want to think about your own happiness a little.
Say, Gray... How long do you think it'll take us to surpass Ur?
I don't care!
Ur is my target! It's my dream to someday win against her!
I said I don't care!!
And I'm sick of hearing you say that!
All I want to do is defeat Deliora!!!
If I can get enough power to do that, it's goodbye to the stupid witch!!!

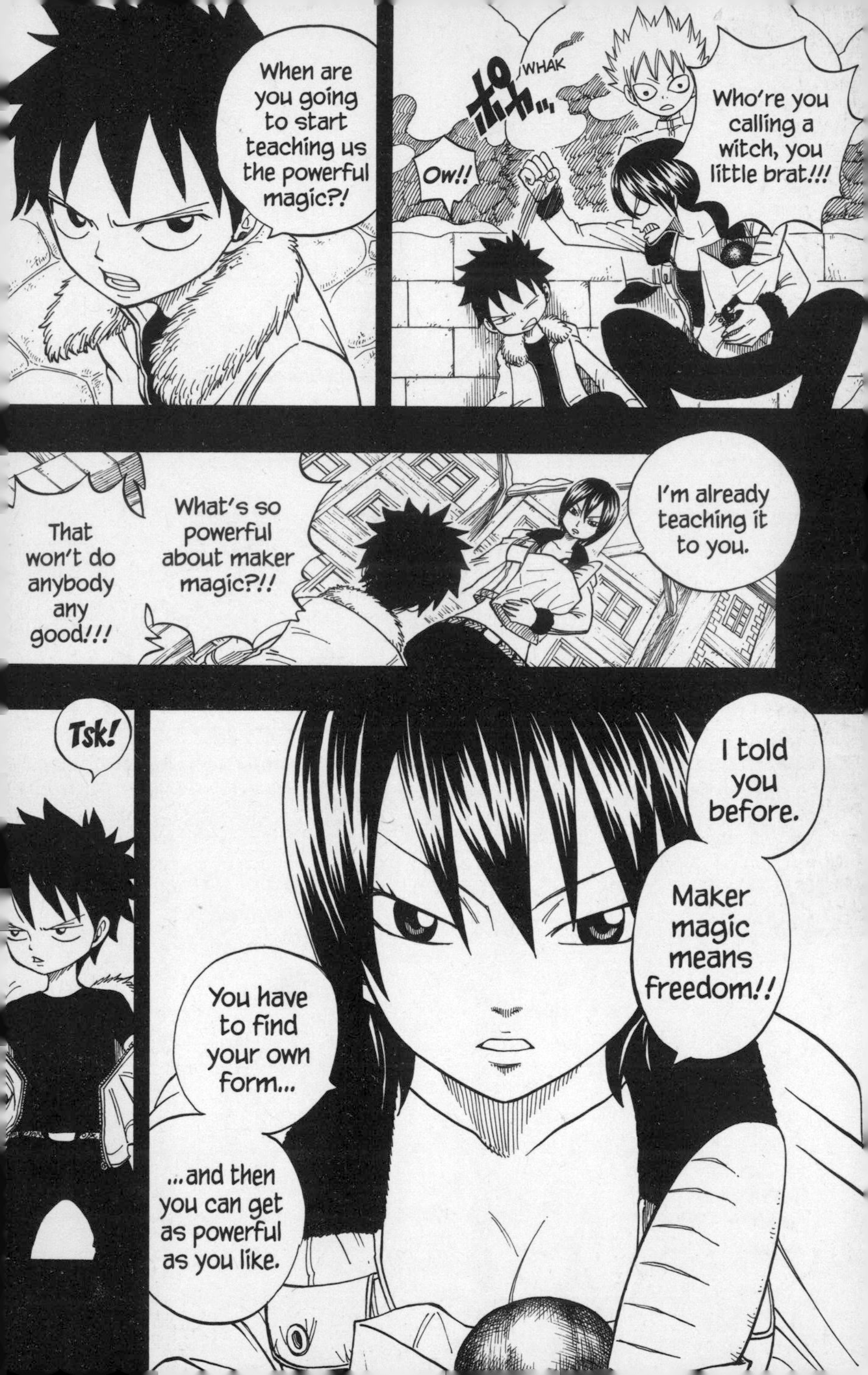

Who're you calling a witch, you little brat!!!
WHAK
Ow!!
When are you going to start teaching us the powerful magic?!
I'm already teaching it to you.
What's so powerful about maker magic?!!
That won't do anybody any good!!!
I told you before.
Maker magic means freedom!!
You have to find your own form...
...and then you can get as powerful as you like.
Tsk!

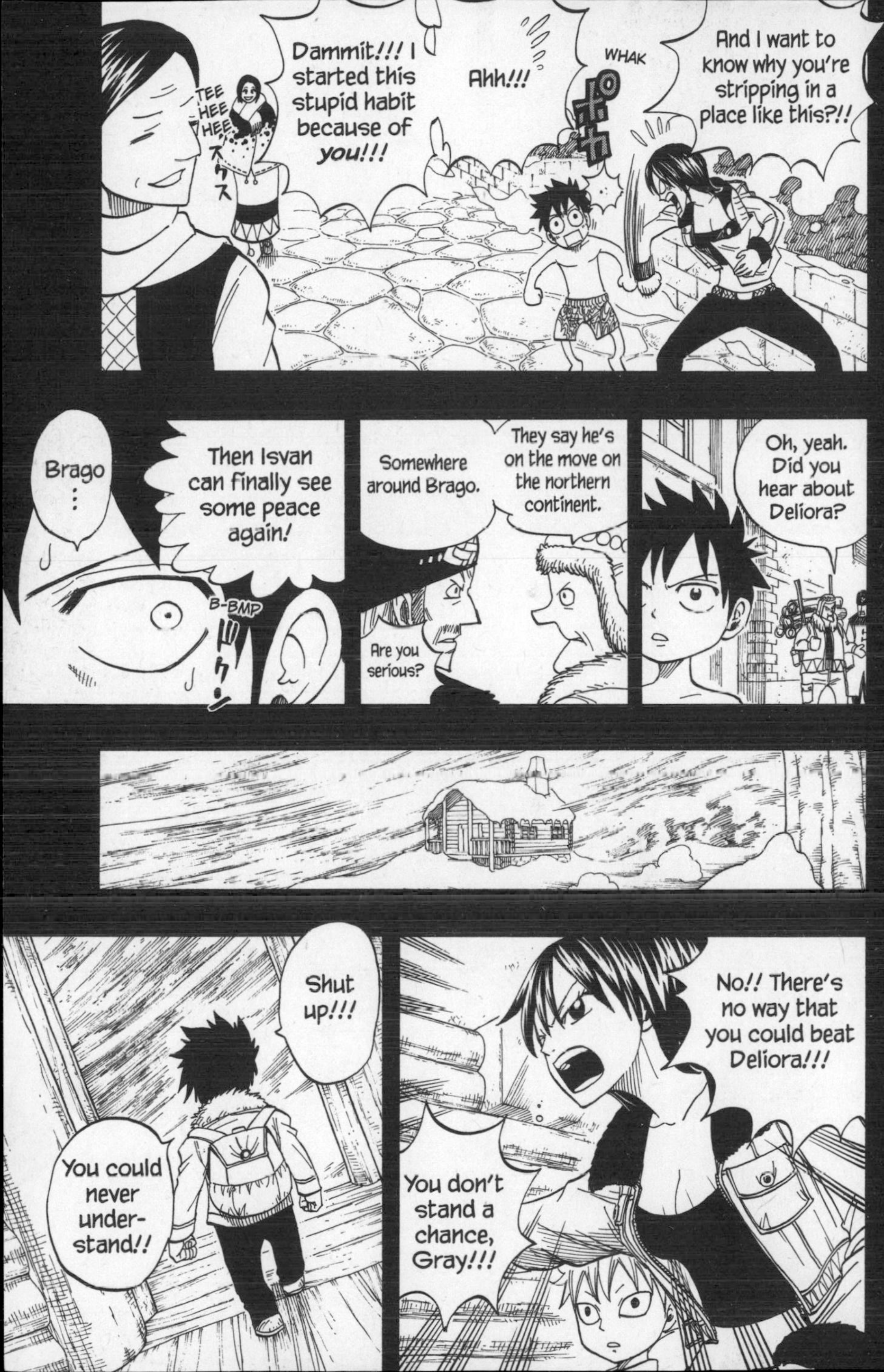
And I want to know why you're stripping in a place like this?!!
WHAK
Ahh!!!
Dammit!!! I started this stupid habit because of *you*!!!
TEE HEE HEE
Oh, yeah. Did you hear about Deliora?
They say he's on the move on the northern continent.
Somewhere around Brago.
Are you serious?
Then Isvan can finally see some peace again!
Brago ...
B-BMP
No!! There's no way that you could beat Deliora!!!
You don't stand a chance, Gray!!!
Shut up!!!
You could never under-stand!!

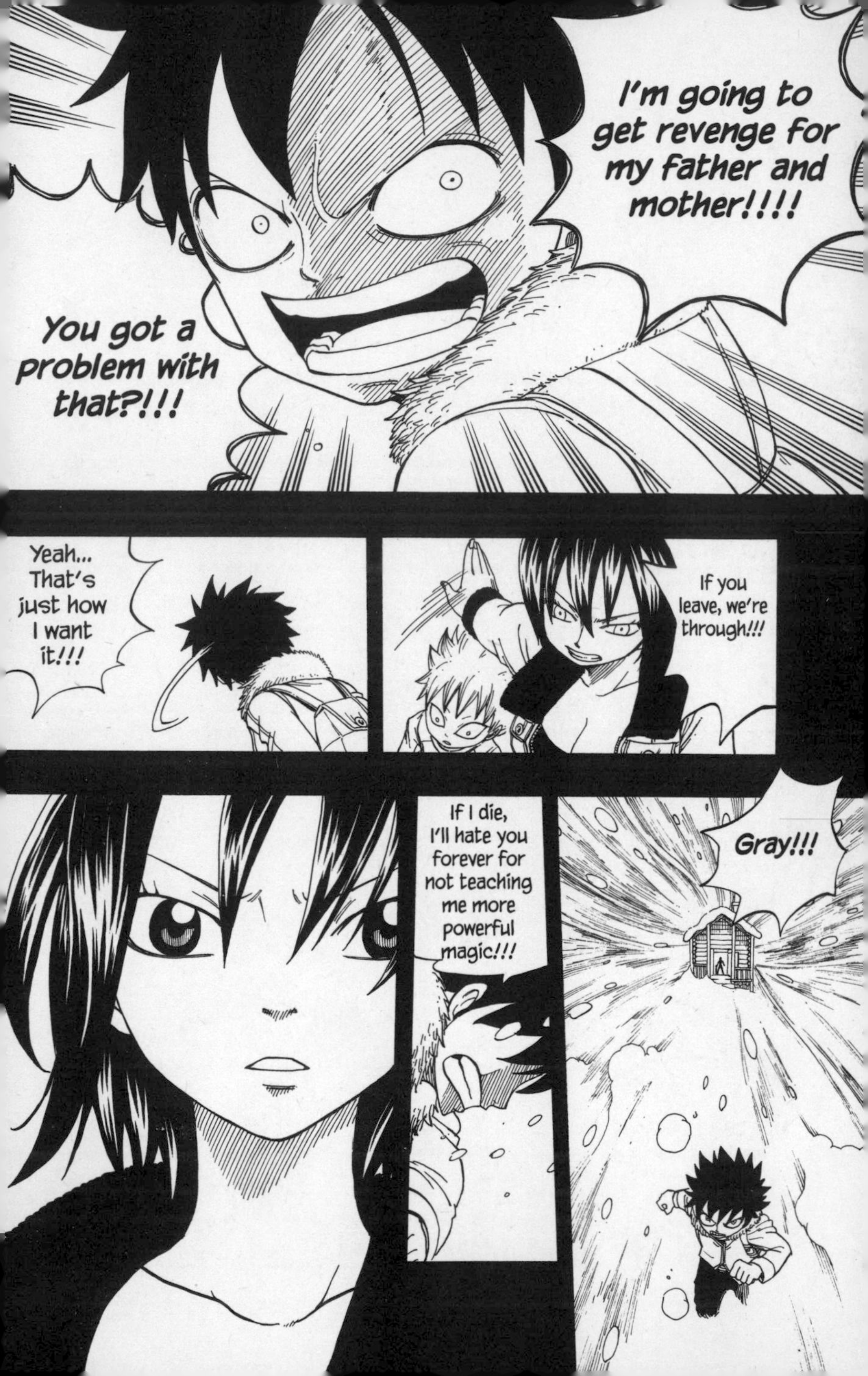
I'm going to get revenge for my father and mother!!!!
You got a problem with that?!!!
If you leave, we're through!!!
Yeah... That's just how I want it!!!
Gray!!!
If I die, I'll hate you forever for not teaching me more powerful magic!!!

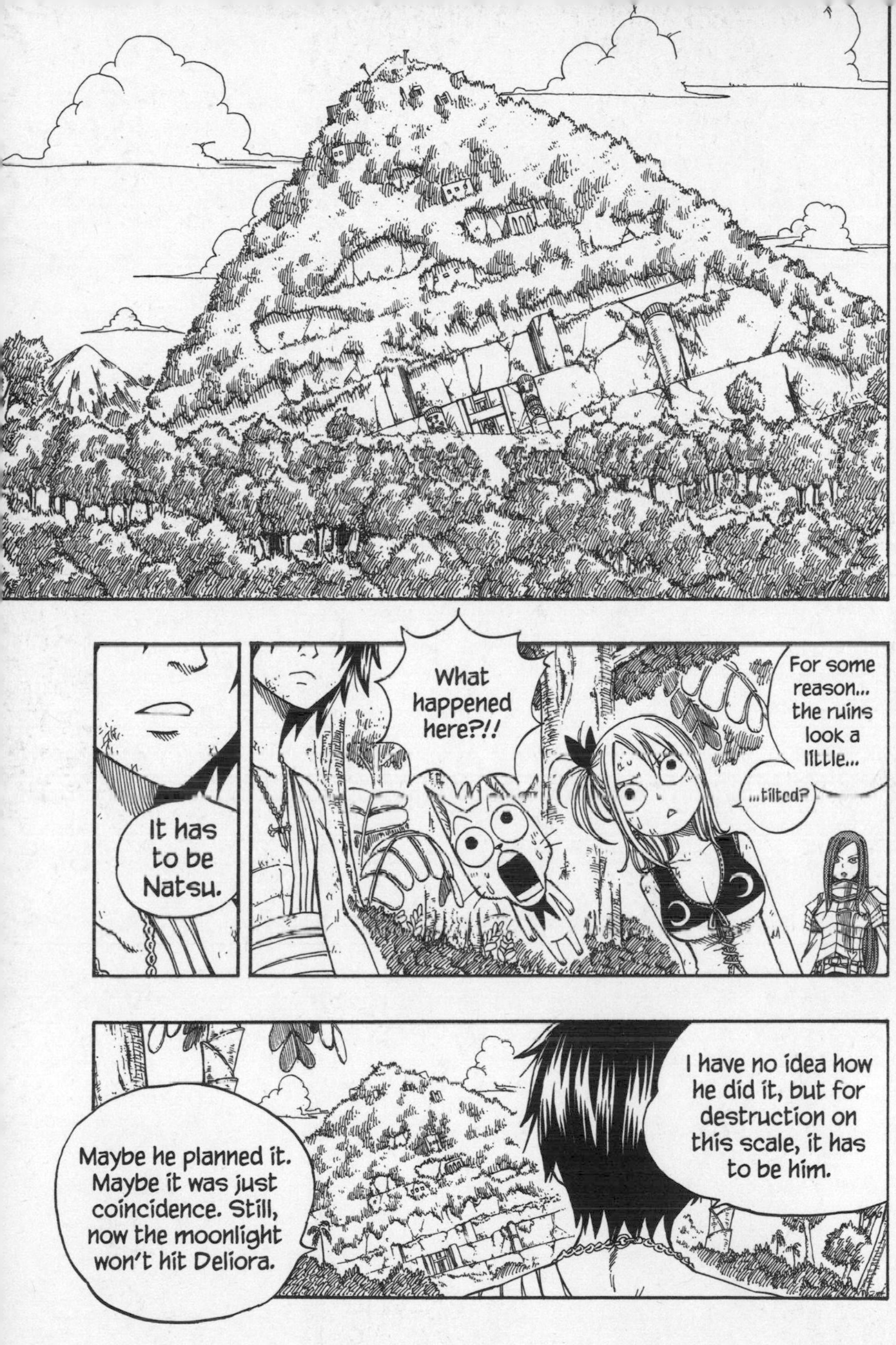
For some reason... the ruins look a little...
...tilted?
What happened here?!!
It has to be Natsu.
I have no idea how he did it, but for destruction on this scale, it has to be him.
Maybe he planned it. Maybe it was just coincidence. Still, now the moonlight won't hit Deliora.

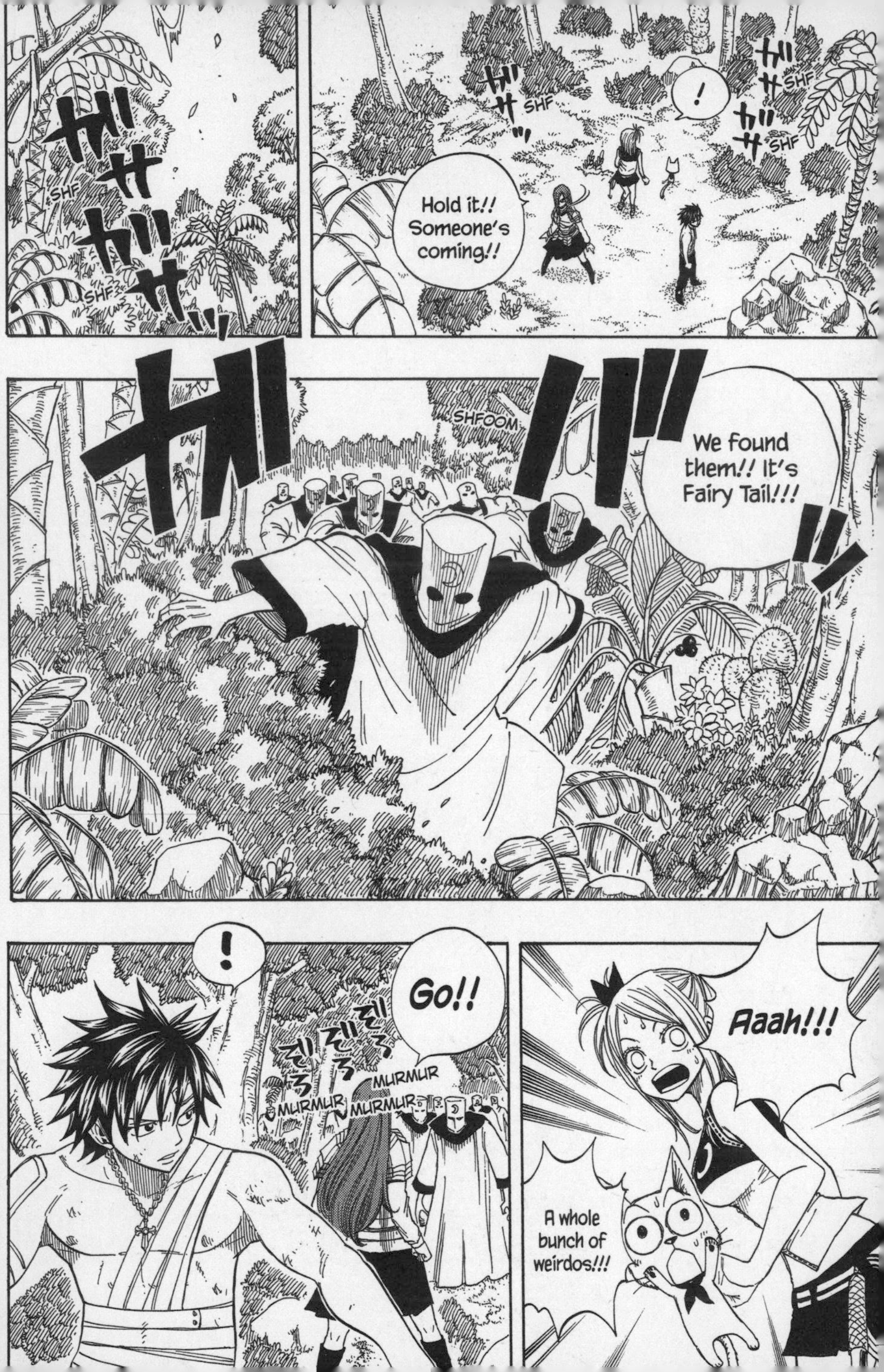
SHF
!
SHF
SHF
Hold it!! Someone's coming!!
SHF
SHF
SHFOOM
We found them!! It's Fairy Tail!!!
Aaah!!!
A whole bunch of weirdos!!!
!
Go!!
MURMUR
MURMUR
MURMUR

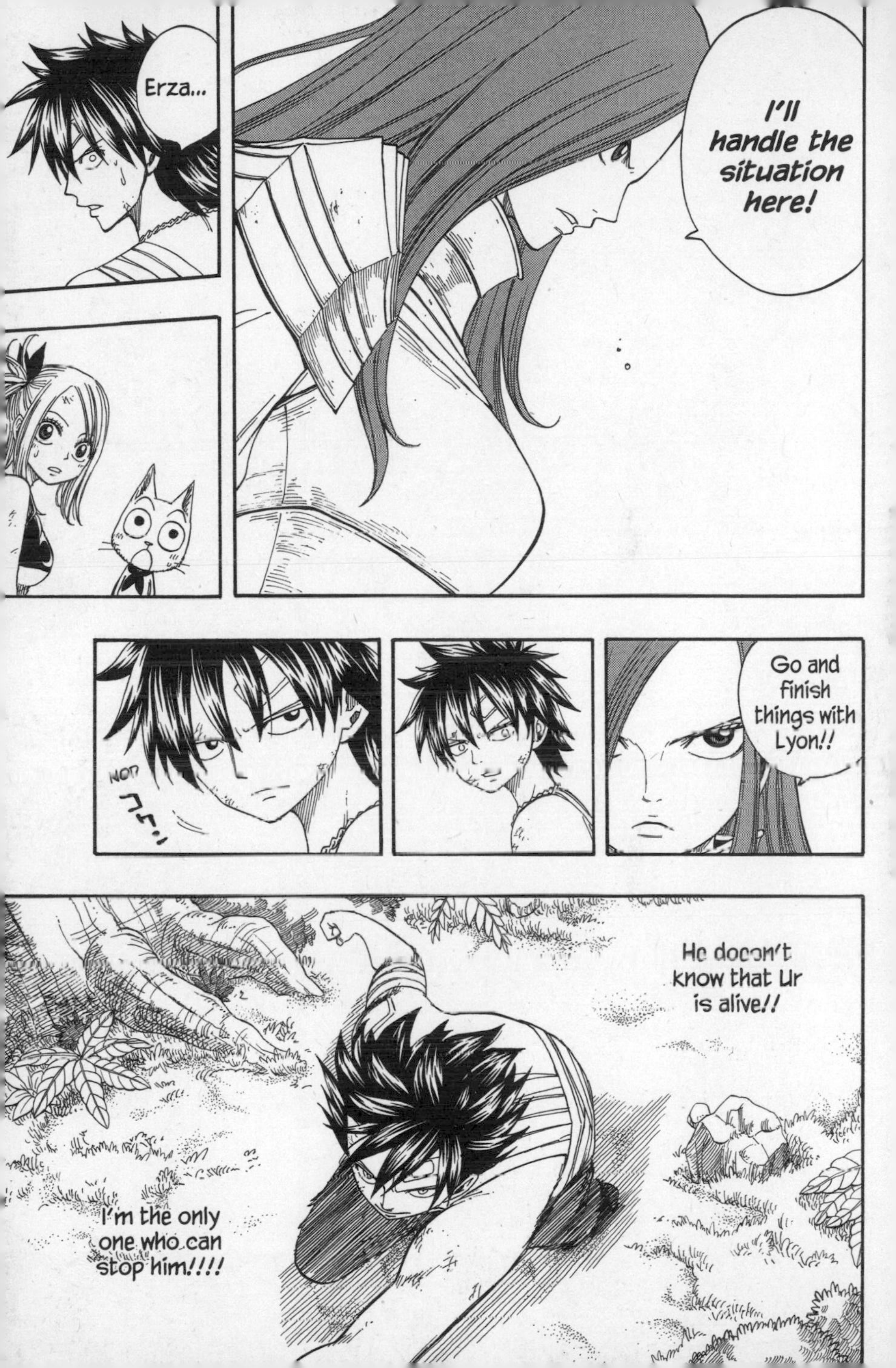
I'll handle the situation here!
Erza...
Go and finish things with Lyon!!
NOD
He doesn't know that Ur is alive!!
I'm the only one who can stop him!!!!

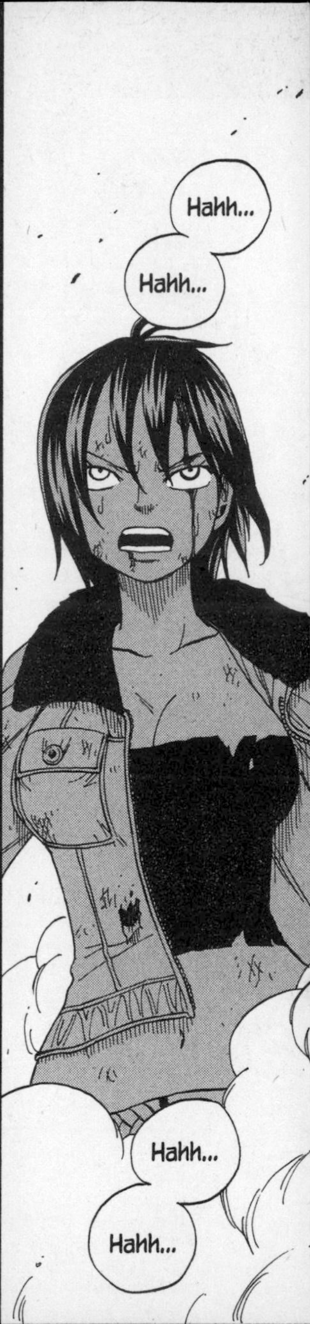
Hahh...
Hahh...
Hahh...
Hahh...
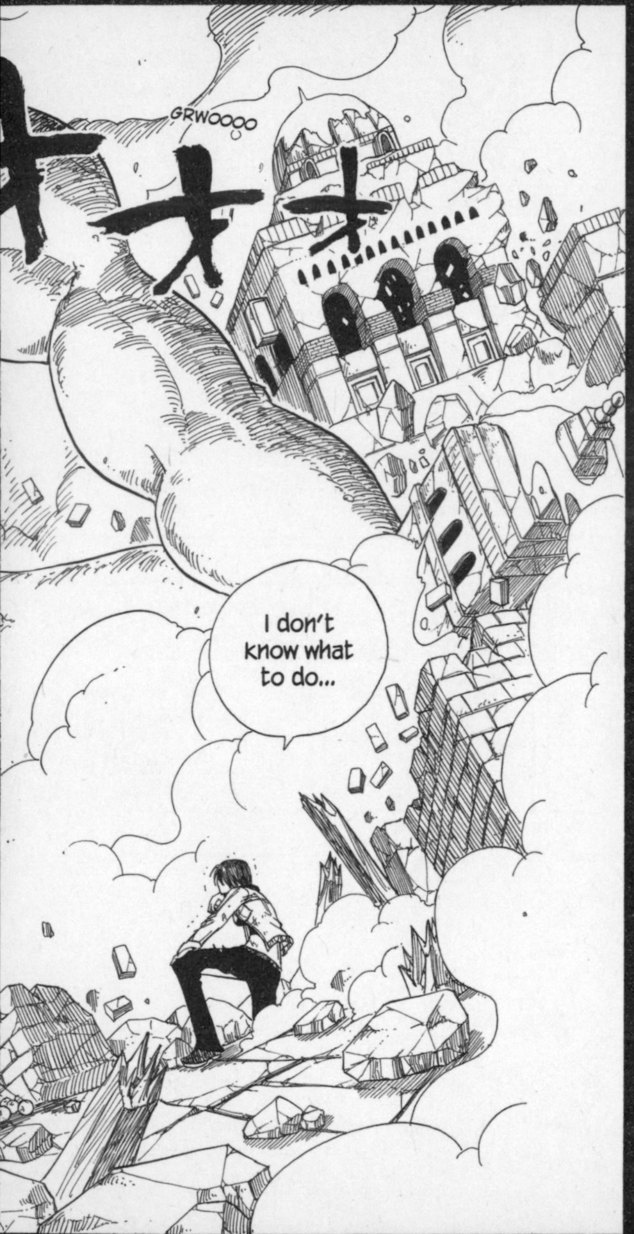
GRWOOOO
I don't know what to do...

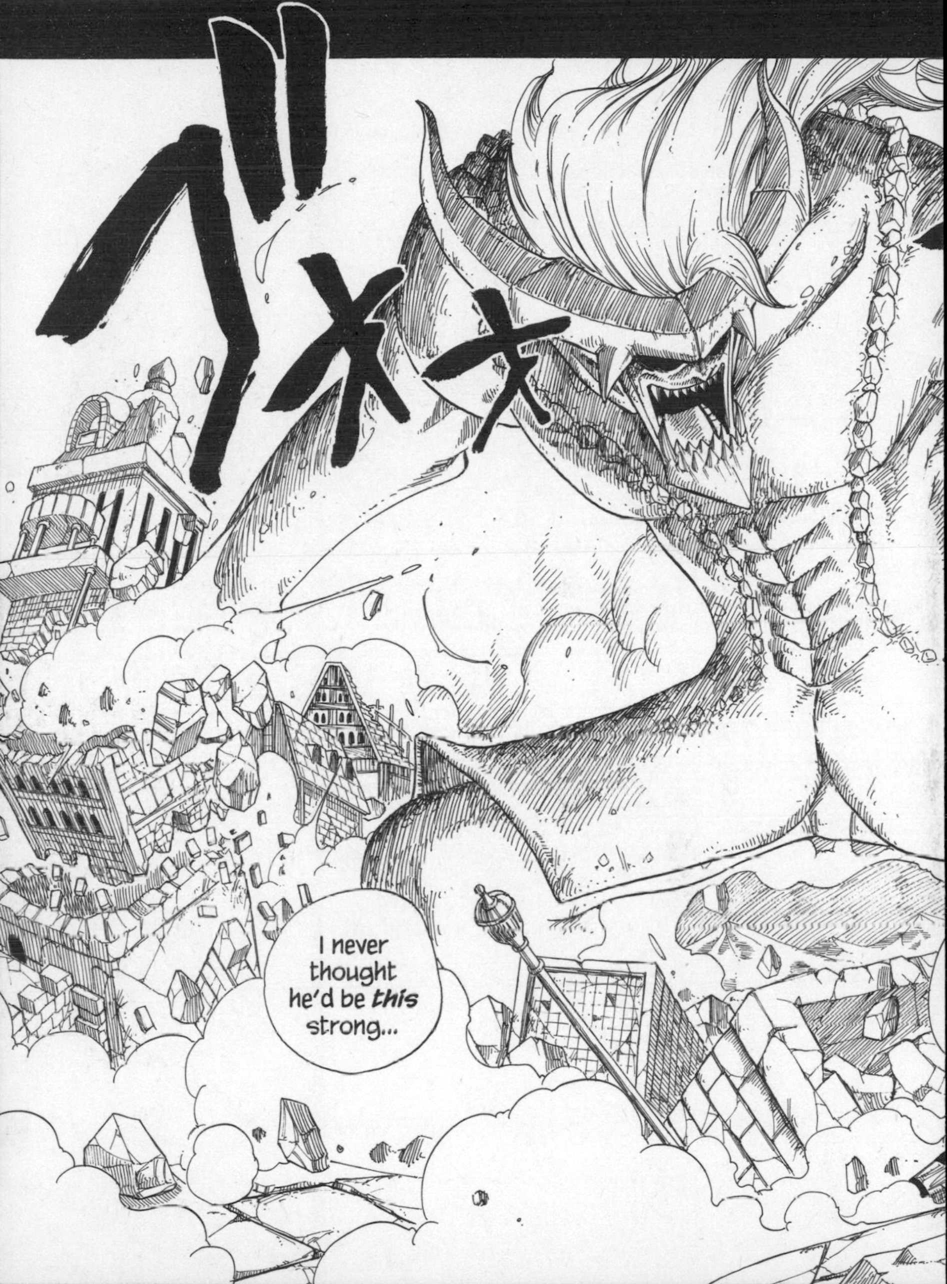
ゴオオ
I never thought he'd be *this* strong...

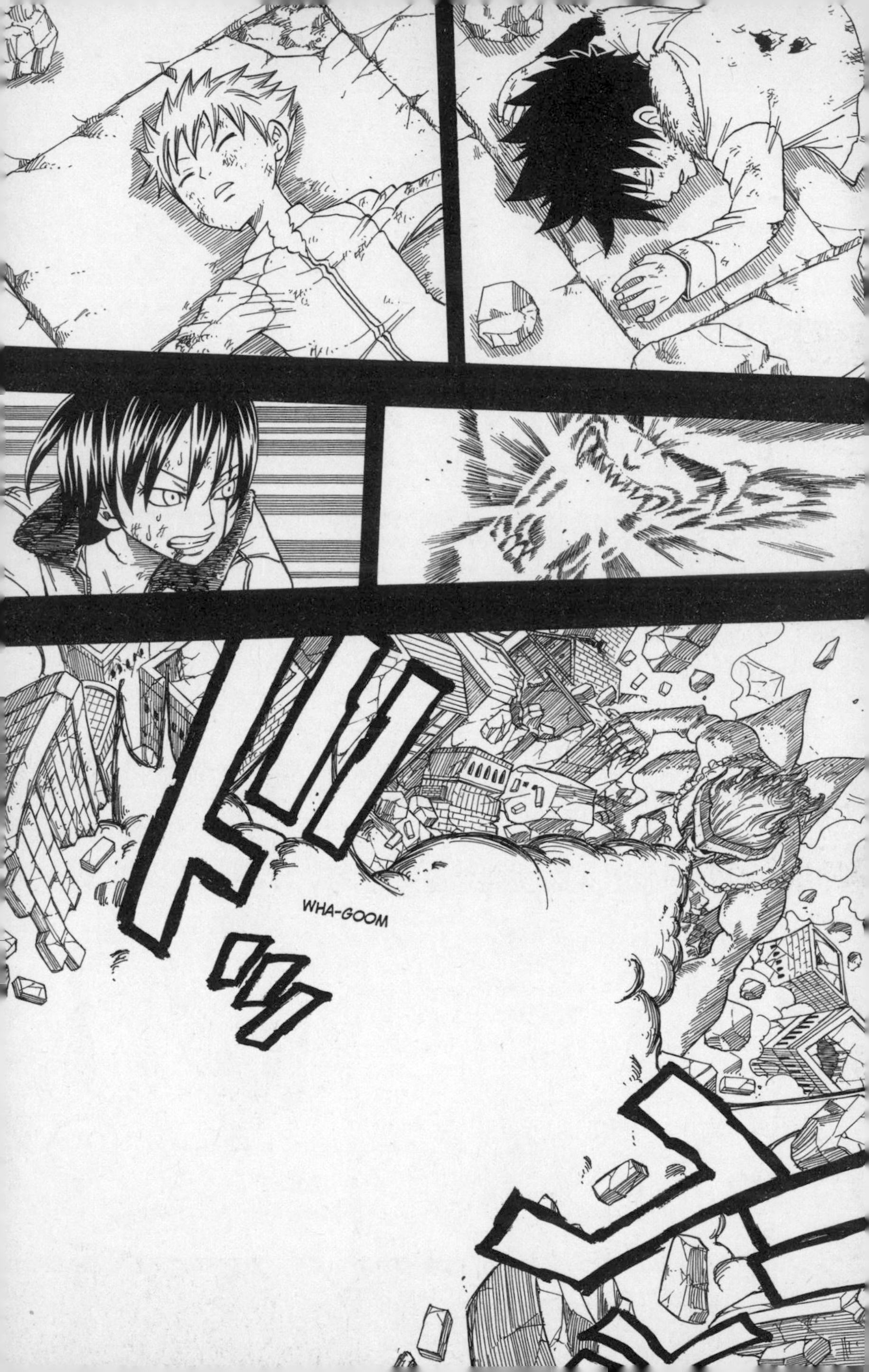
WHA-GOOM

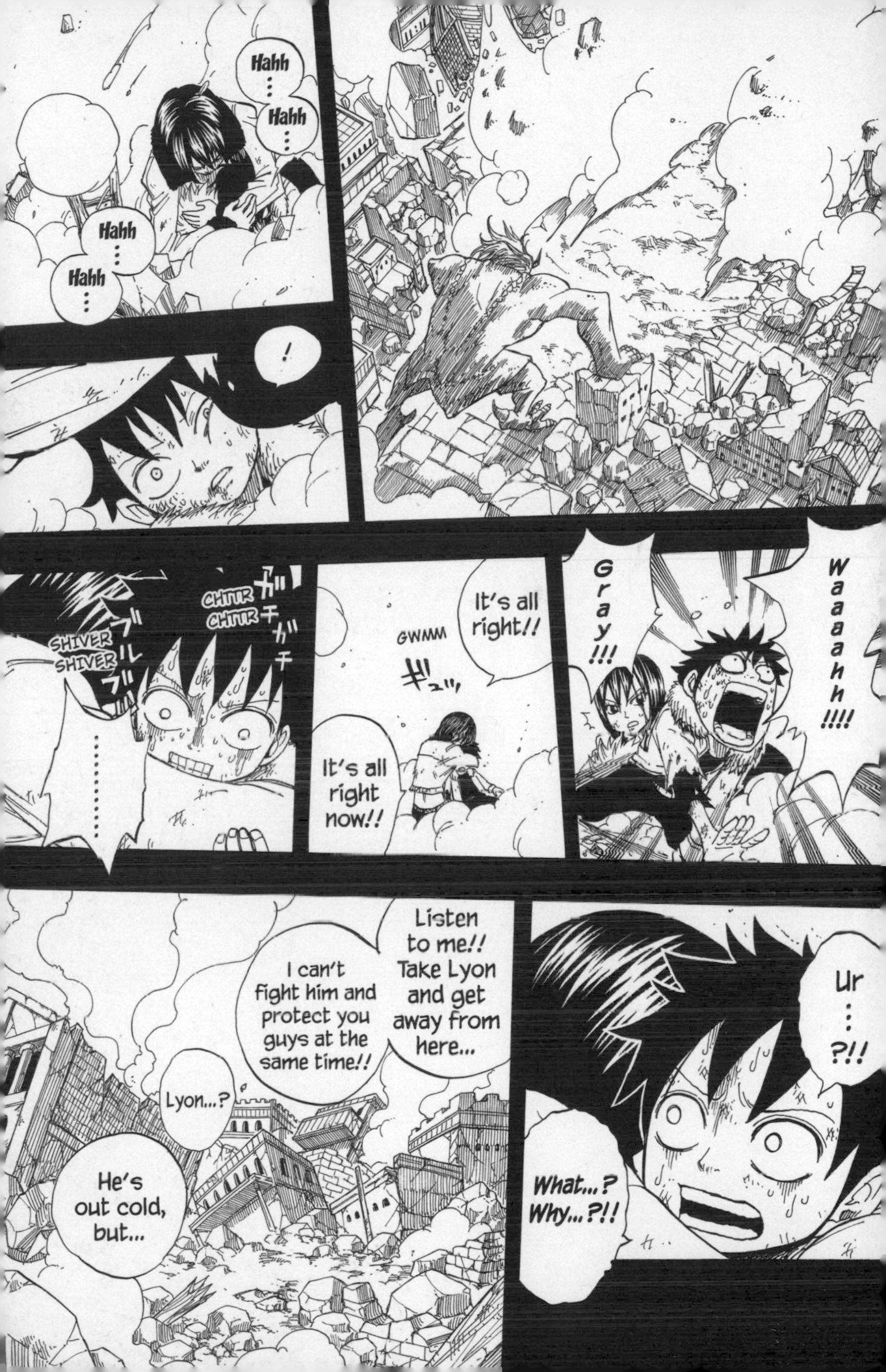
Hahh... Hahh...
Hahh... Hahh...
!
Waaaaahh!!!!
Gray!!!
It's all right!!
GWMM
It's all right now!!
CHTTR CHTTR
SHIVER SHIVER
....
Ur...?!!
What...? Why...?!!
Listen to me!! Take Lyon and get away from here...
I can't fight him and protect you guys at the same time!!
Lyon...?
He's out cold, but...

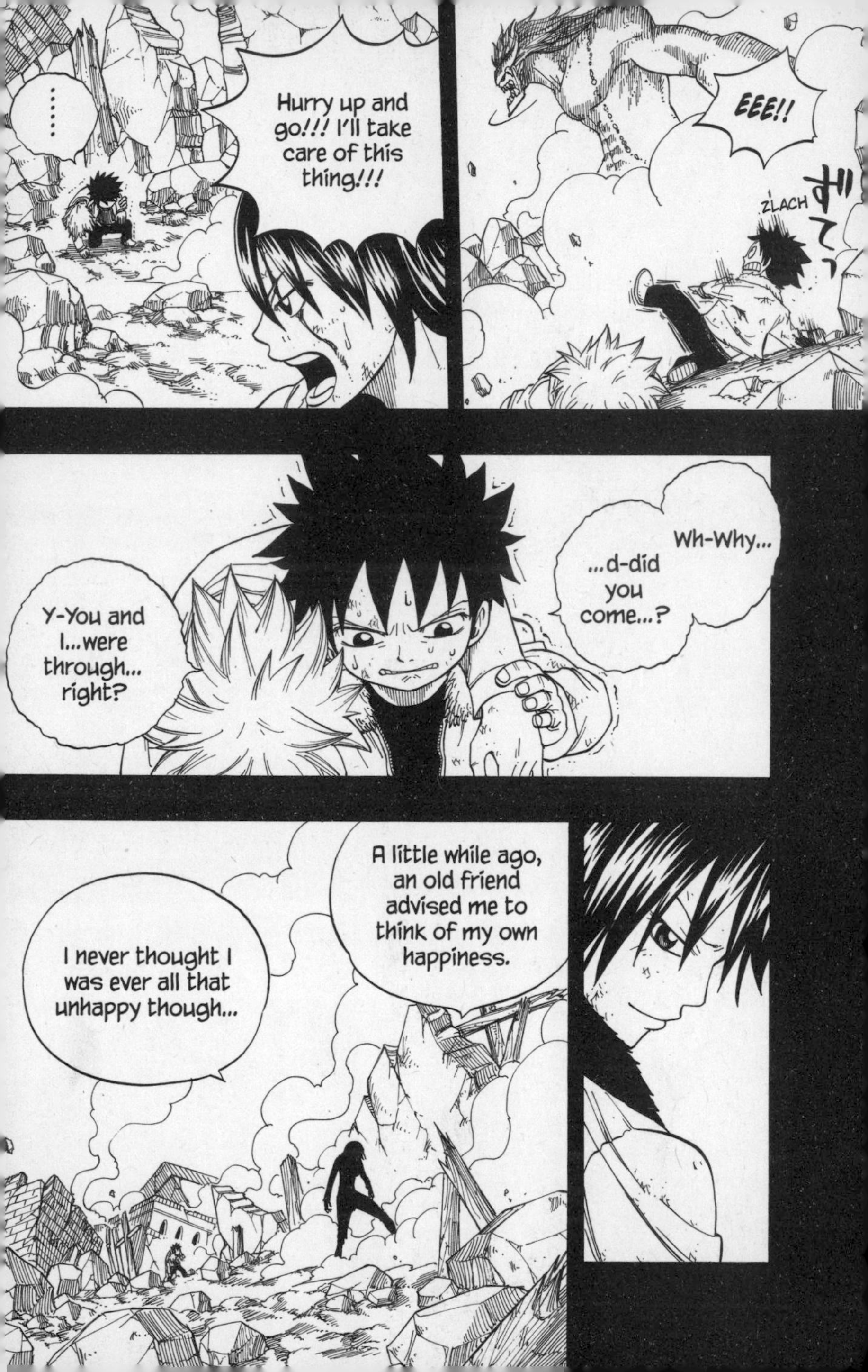
EEE!!
ZLACH
ずてっ
Hurry up and go!!! I'll take care of this thing!!!
......
Wh-Why... ...d-did you come...?
Y-You and I...were through... right?
A little while ago, an old friend advised me to think of my own happiness.
I never thought I was ever all that unhappy though...

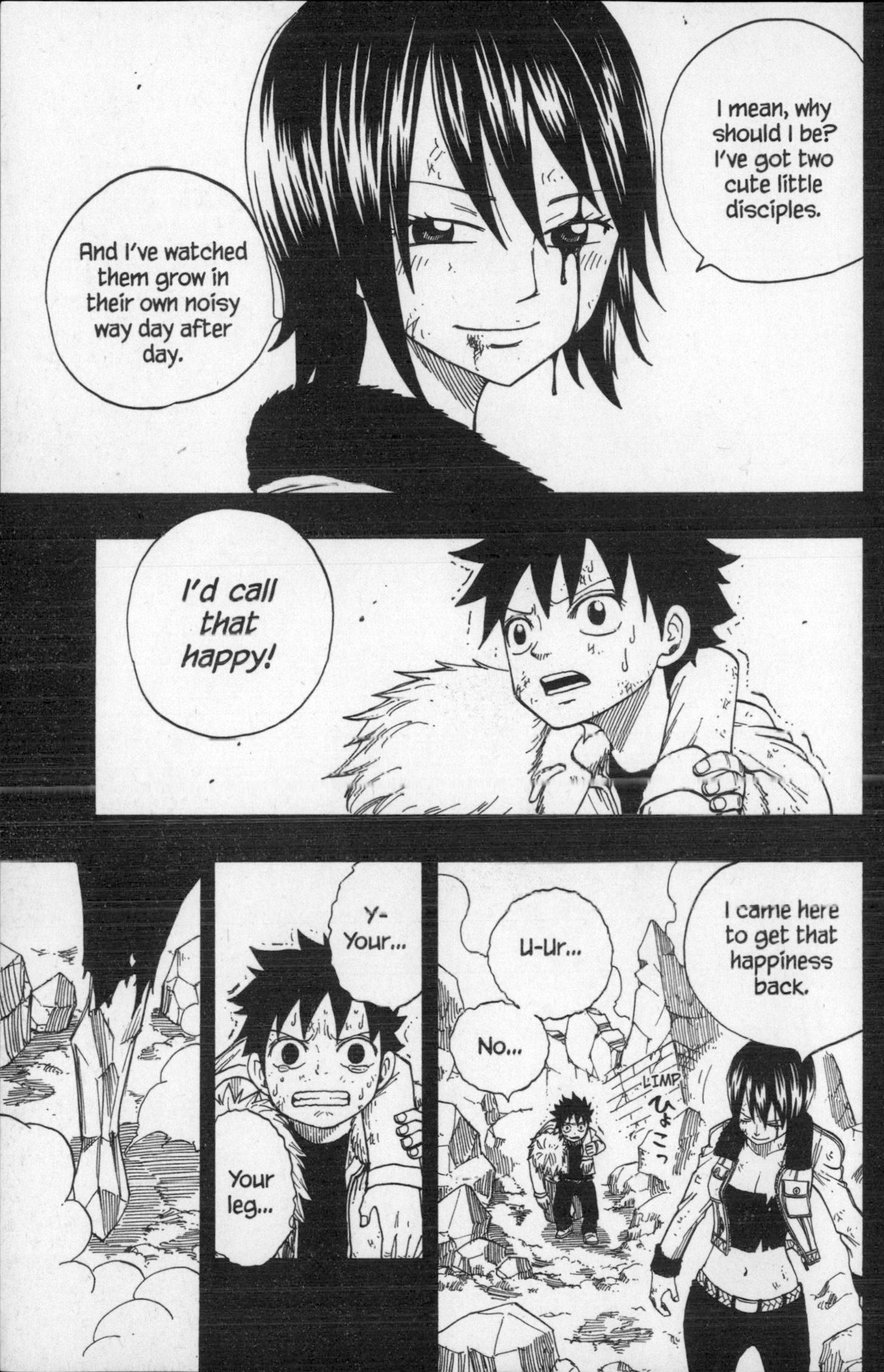
I mean, why should I be? I've got two cute little disciples.
And I've watched them grow in their own noisy way day after day.
I'd call that happy!
I came here to get that happiness back.
U-Ur...
No...
LIMP
Y- Your...
Your leg...

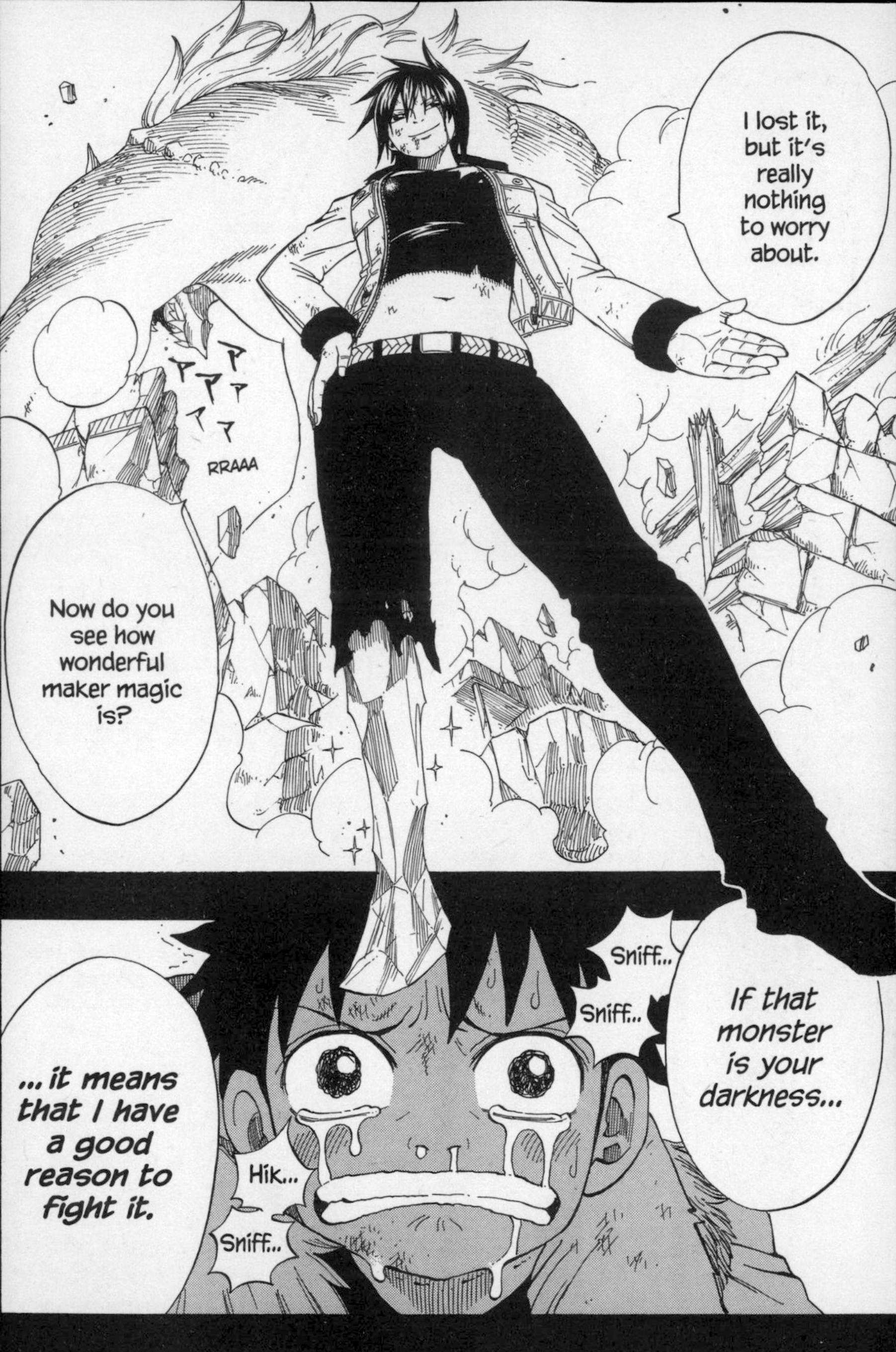
I lost it, but it's really nothing to worry about.
RRAAA
Now do you see how wonderful maker magic is?
If that monster is your darkness...
Sniff...
Sniff...
...it means that I have a good reason to fight it.
Hik...
Sniff...

FAIRY TAIL

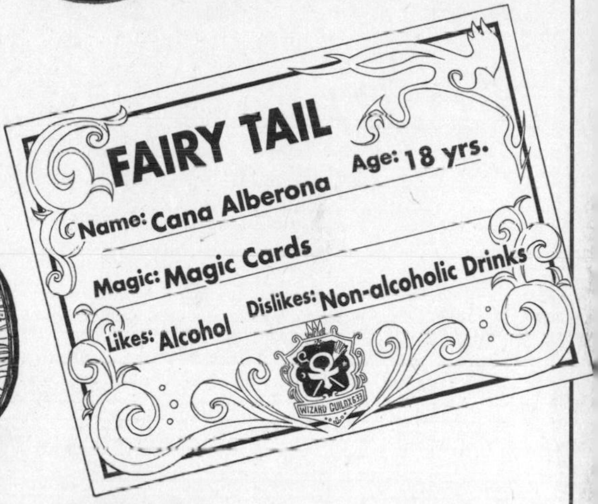
FAIRY TAIL
Age: 18 yrs.
Name: Cana Alberona
Magic: Magic Cards
Likes: Alcohol
Dislikes: Non-alcoholic Drinks
WIZARD GUILD X633

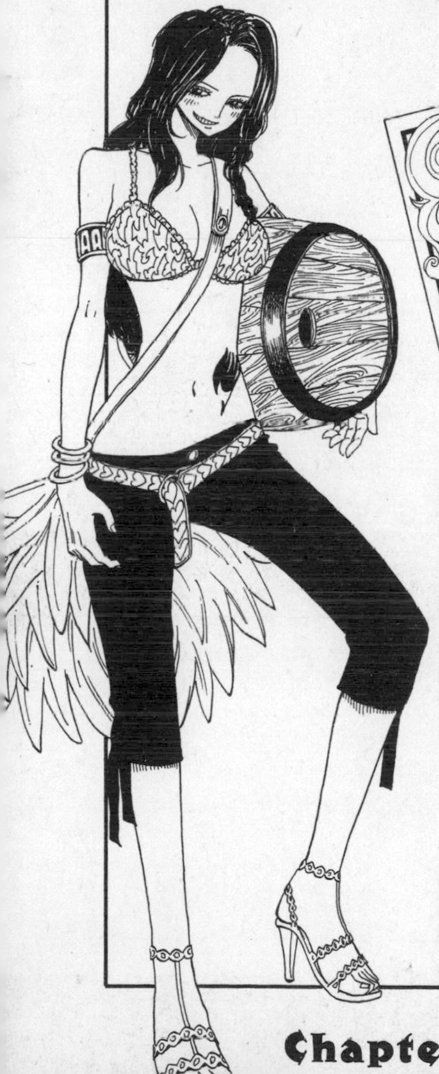

Remarks

First, we should say that the country in which the story takes place has a drinking age of fifteen years old, but Cana started drinking at thirteen. Thirty percent of Fairy Tail's liquor budget goes down her throat. She uses cards for her magic. Sometimes she just throws them, and at other times, she expertly combines them for many different effects making for an all-purpose fighting style.

She's a rather close friend to Macao, who is a drinking buddy. At one point, he suggested that she cut back a little, and she did (a little), but recently she realized that Macao's been seeing a new girlfriend, and she has redoubled her drinking.

Chapter 38: Eternal Magic

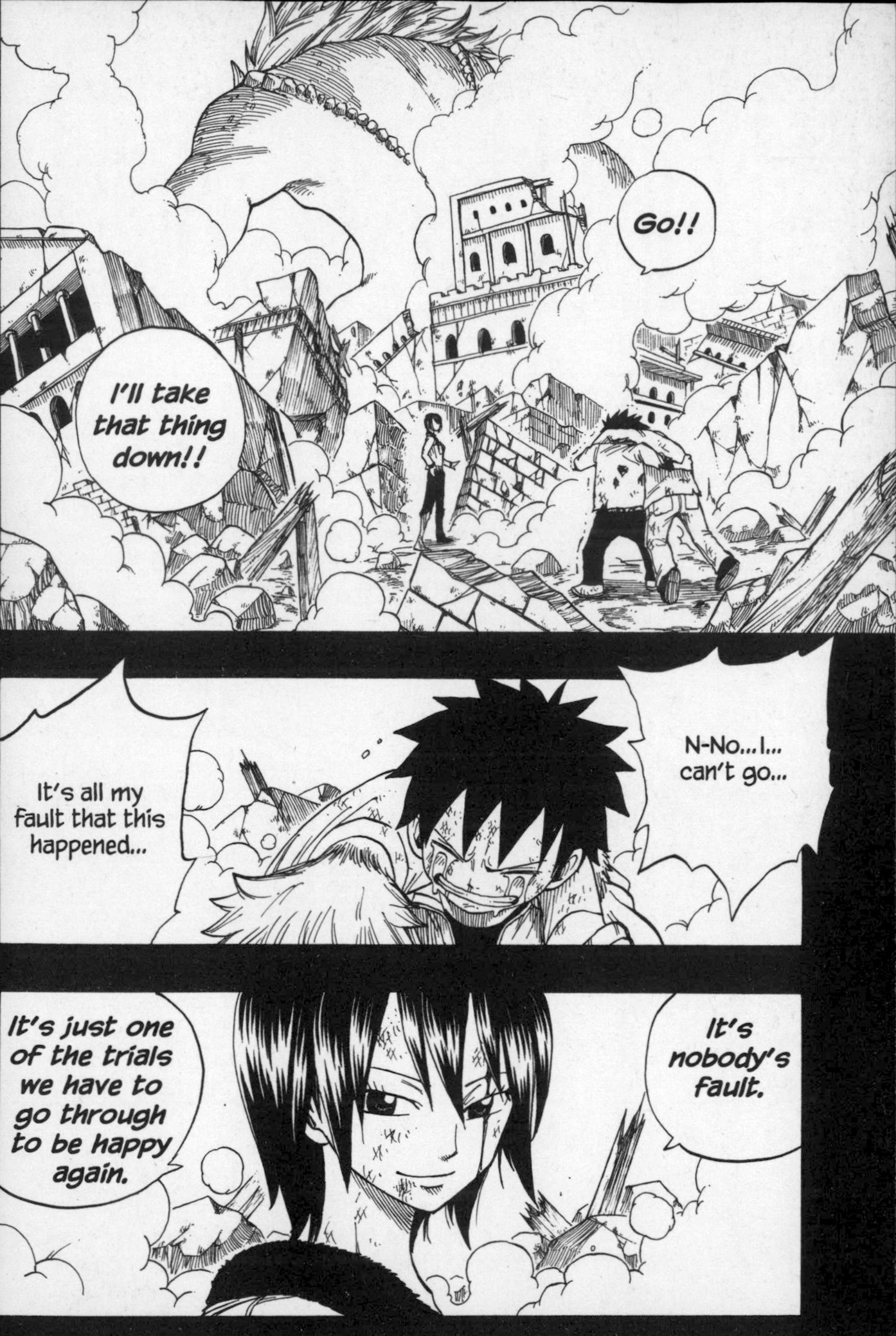
Go!!
I'll take that thing down!!
N-No...I... can't go...
It's all my fault that this happened...
It's nobody's fault.
It's just one of the trials we have to go through to be happy again.

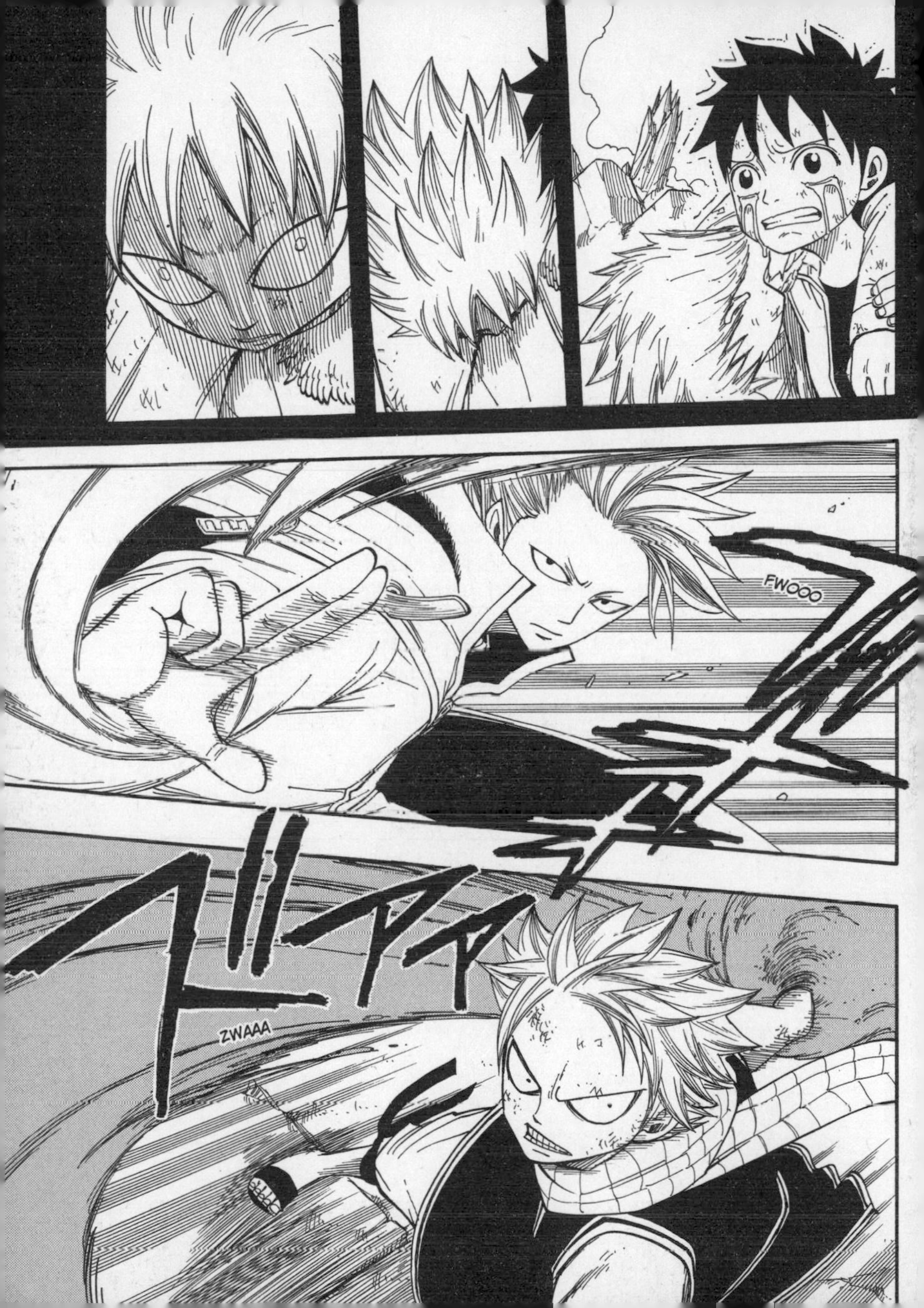
FWOOO
ZWAAA

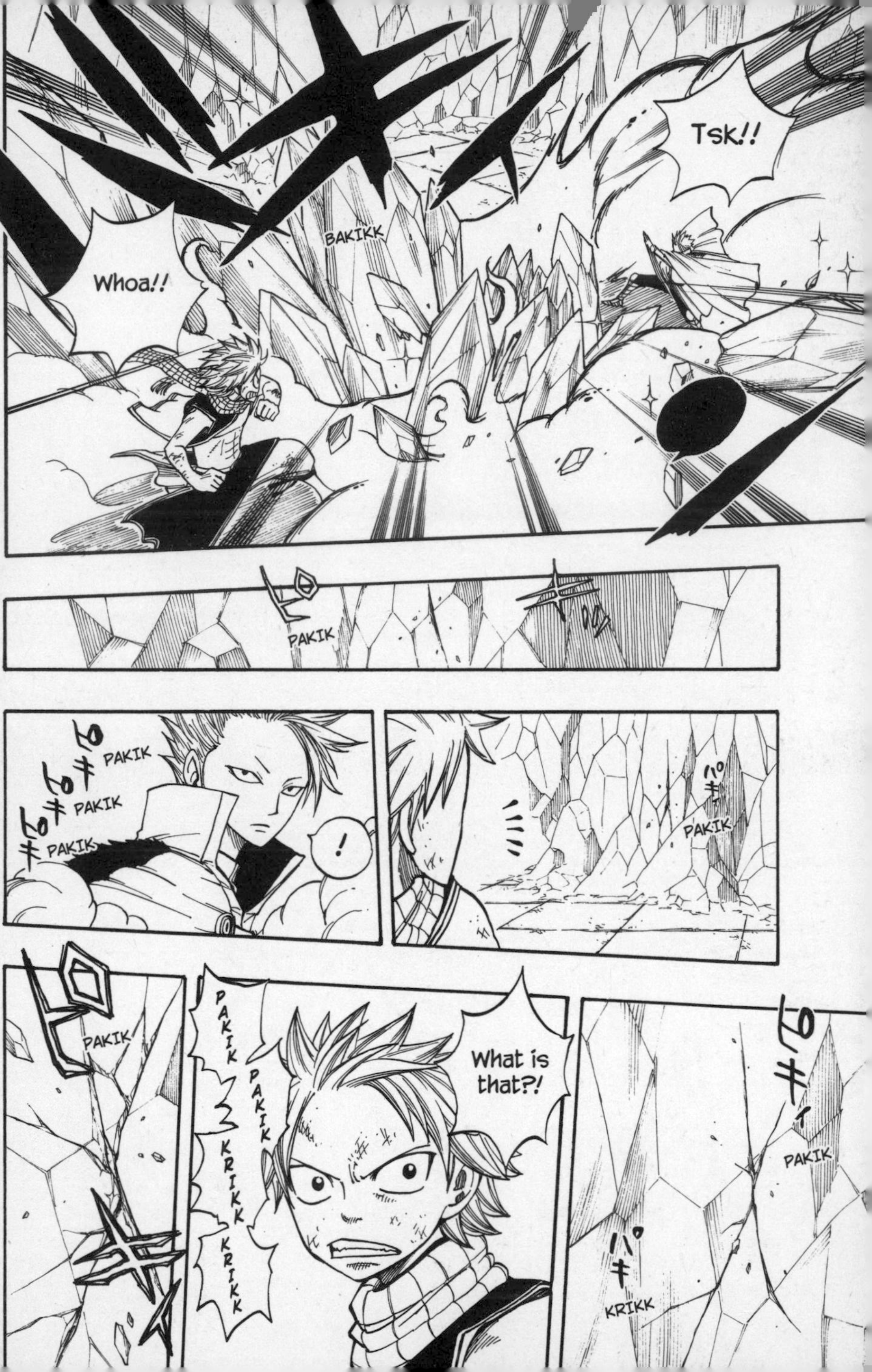
Tsk!!
BAKIKK
Whoa!!
PAKIK
PAKIK
PAKIK
PAKIK
PAKIK
!
PAKIK
KRIKK
What is that?!
PAKIK
PAKIK
KRIKK
KRIKK
PAKIK

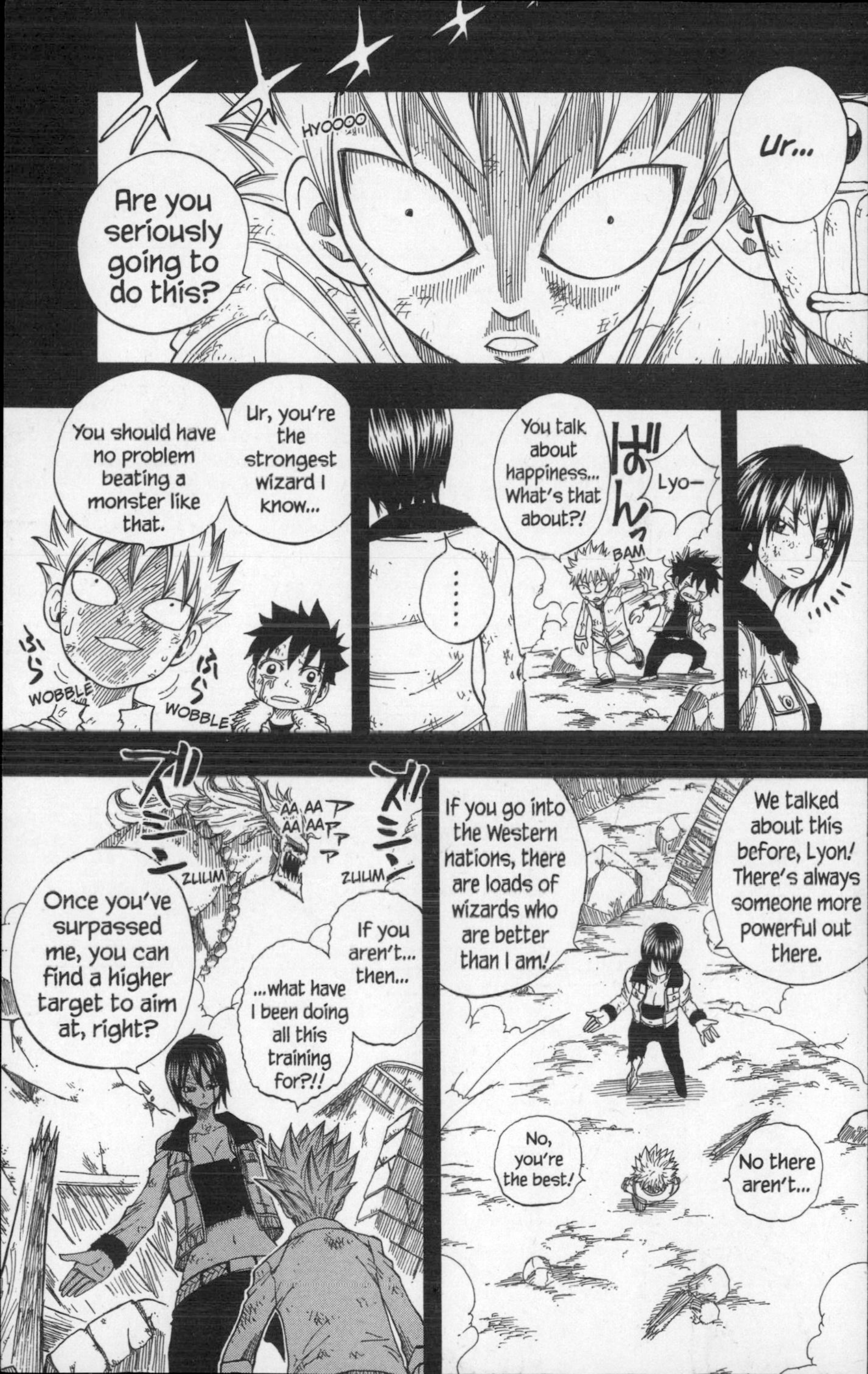
Ur...
HYOOOO
Are you seriously going to do this?
You talk about happiness... What's that about?!
Lyo—
ばんっ
BAM
......
Ur, you're the strongest wizard I know...
You should have no problem beating a monster like that.
ふら
WOBBLE
ふら
WOBBLE
We talked about this before, Lyon! There's always someone more powerful out there.
If you go into the Western nations, there are loads of wizards who are better than I am!
No there aren't...
No, you're the best!
ZUUM
AAAA
ZUUM
If you aren't... then...
...what have I been doing all this training for?!!
Once you've surpassed me, you can find a higher target to aim at, right?

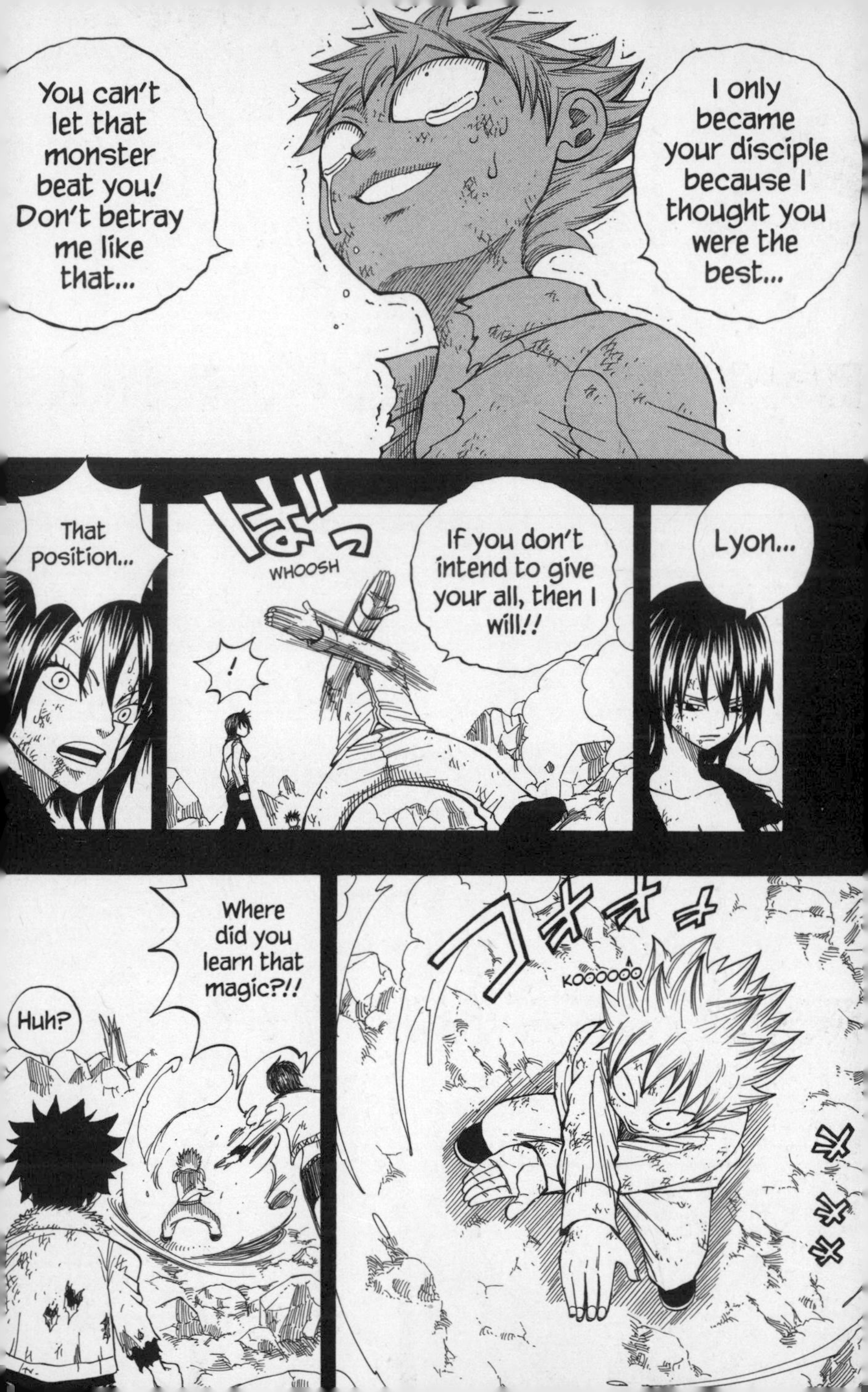
I only became your disciple because I thought you were the best...
You can't let that monster beat you! Don't betray me like that...
Lyon...
If you don't intend to give your all, then I will!!
WHOOSH
!
That position...
KOOOOOO
Where did you learn that magic?!!
Huh?

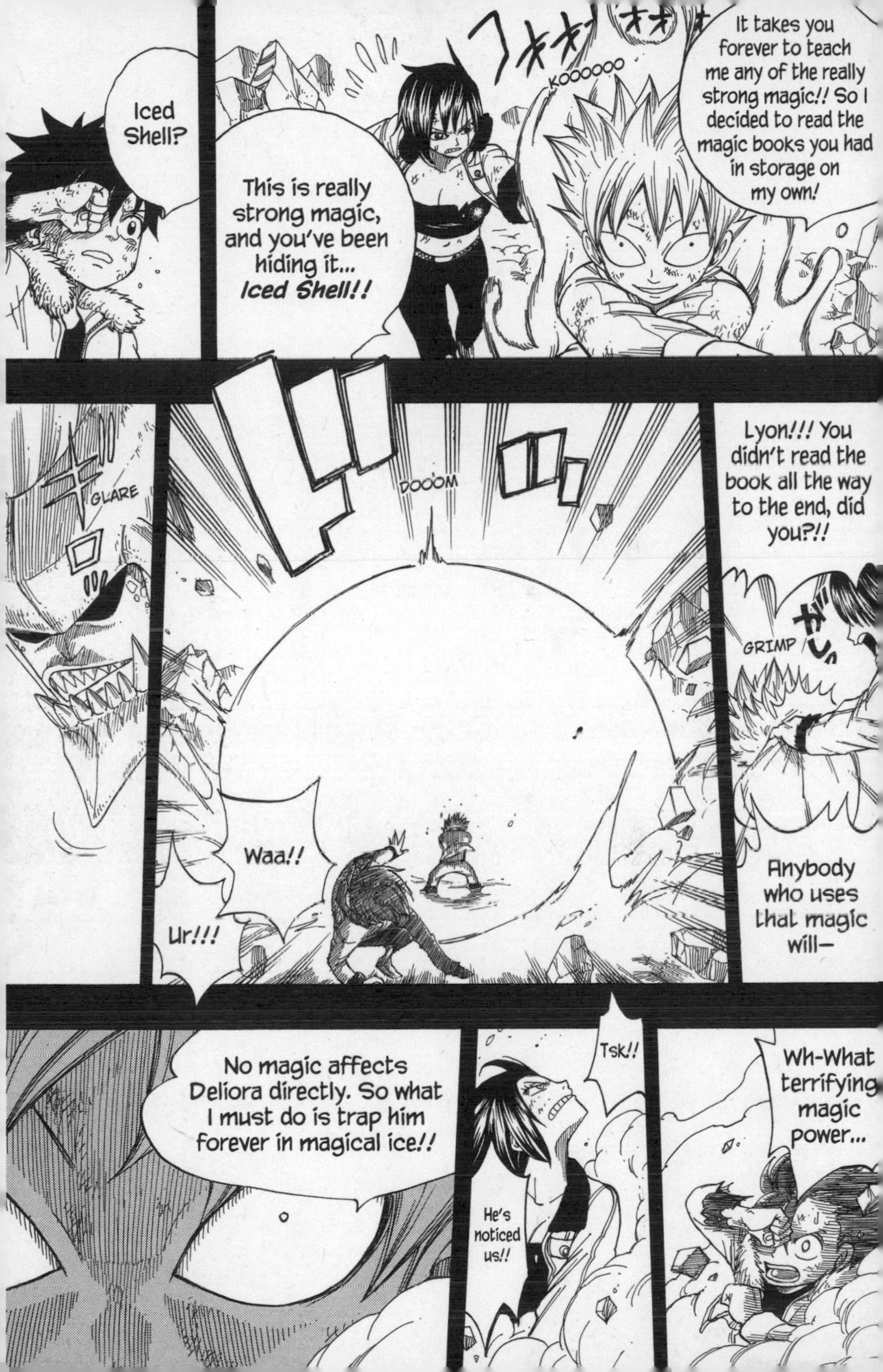
KOOOOOO
It takes you forever to teach me any of the really strong magic!! So I decided to read the magic books you had in storage on my own!
This is really strong magic, and you've been hiding it... *Iced Shell!!*
Iced Shell?
Lyon!!! You didn't read the book all the way to the end, did you?!!
GRIMP
Anybody who uses that magic will—
DOOOM
Waa!!
Ur!!!
GLARE
Wh-What terrifying magic power...
Tsk!!
He's noticed us!!
No magic affects Deliora directly. So what I must do is trap him forever in magical ice!!

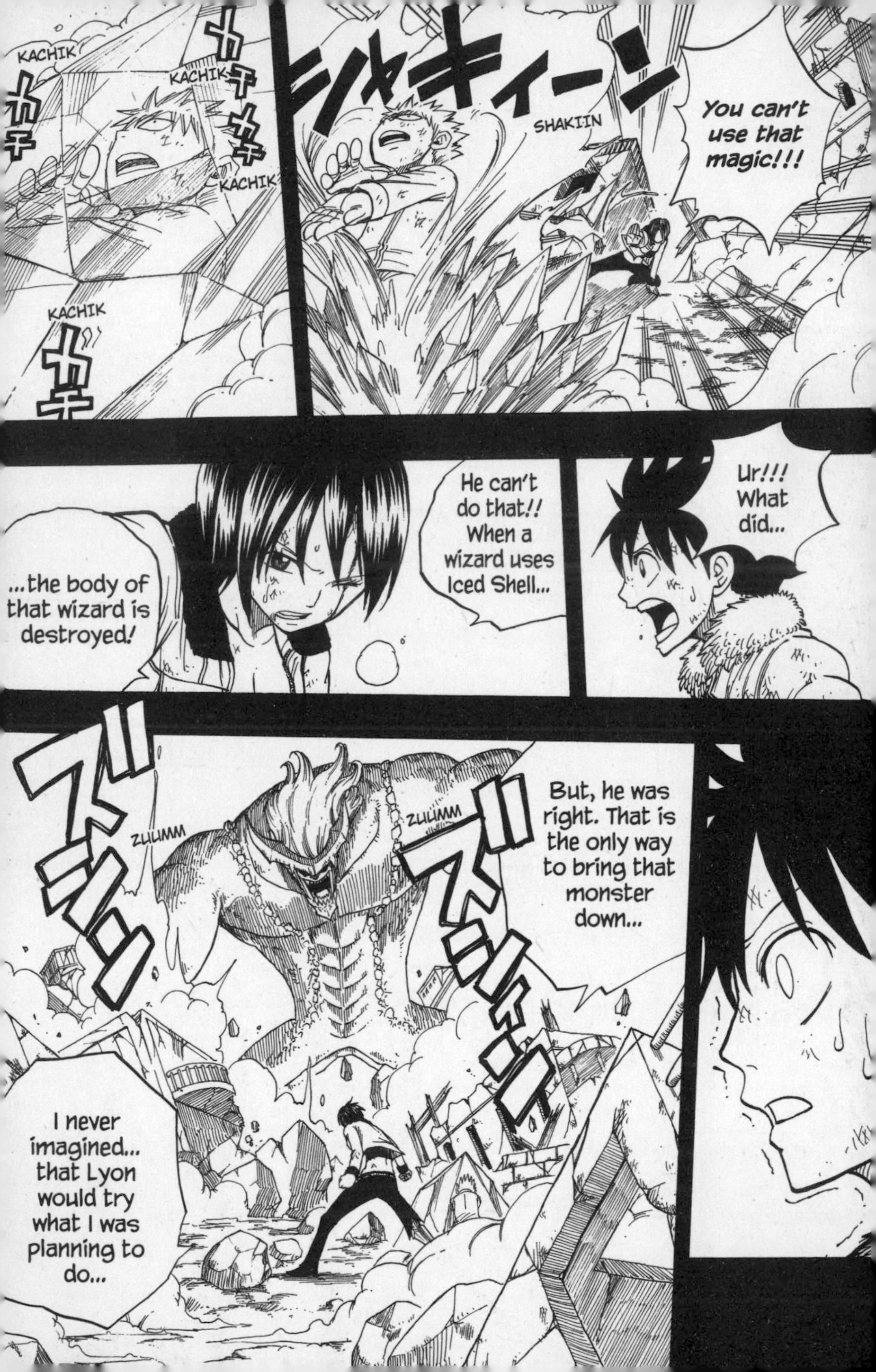
SHAKIIN
You can't use that magic!!!
KACHIK
KACHIK
KACHIK
KACHIK
Ur!!! What did...
He can't do that!! When a wizard uses Iced Shell...
...the body of that wizard is destroyed!
ZUUMM
ZUUMM
But, he was right. That is the only way to bring that monster down...
I never imagined... that Lyon would try what I was planning to do...

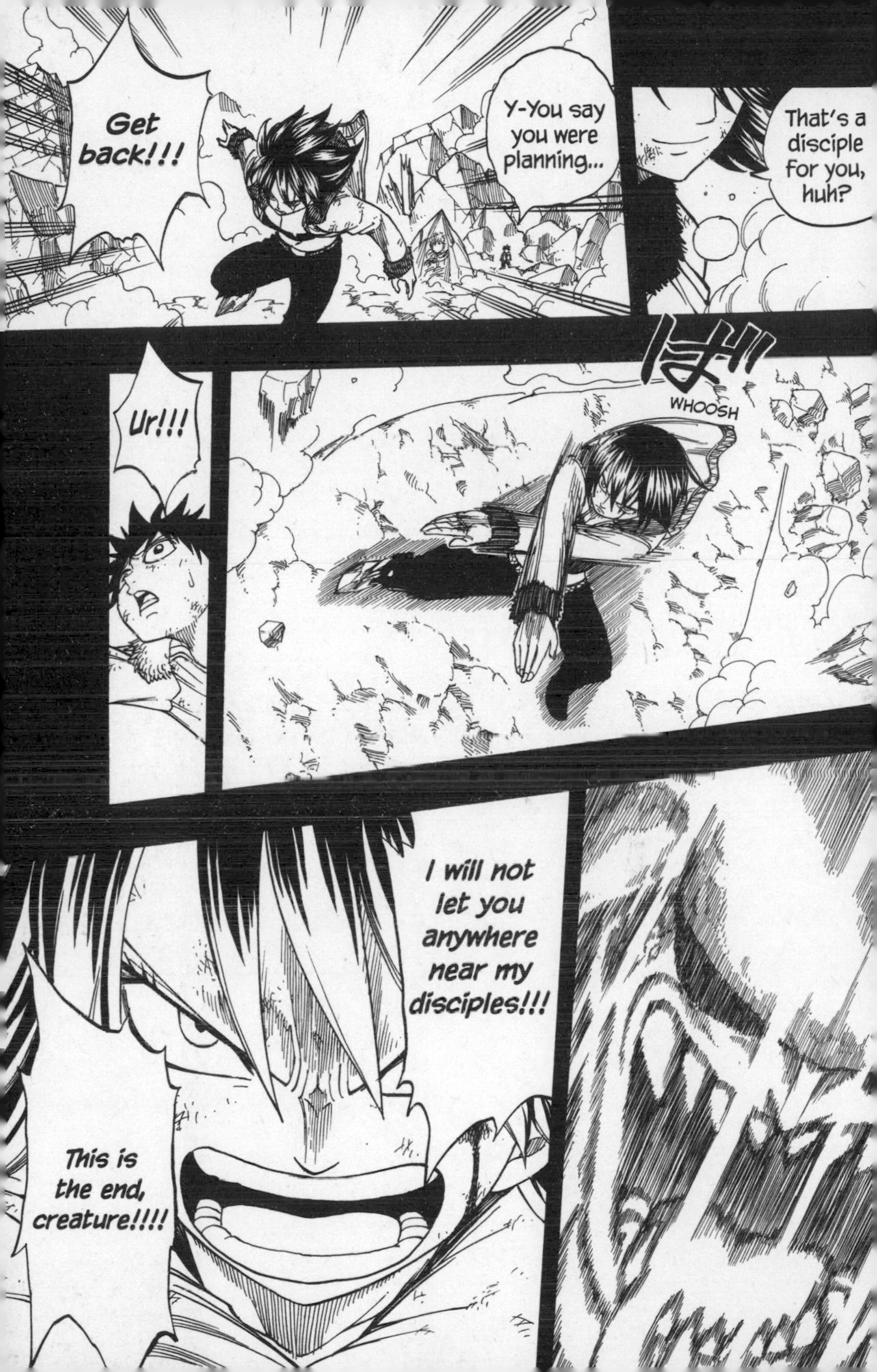
That's a disciple for you, huh?
Y-You say you were planning...
Get back!!!
ばっ
WHOOSH
Ur!!!
I will not let you anywhere near my disciples!!!
This is the end, creature!!!!

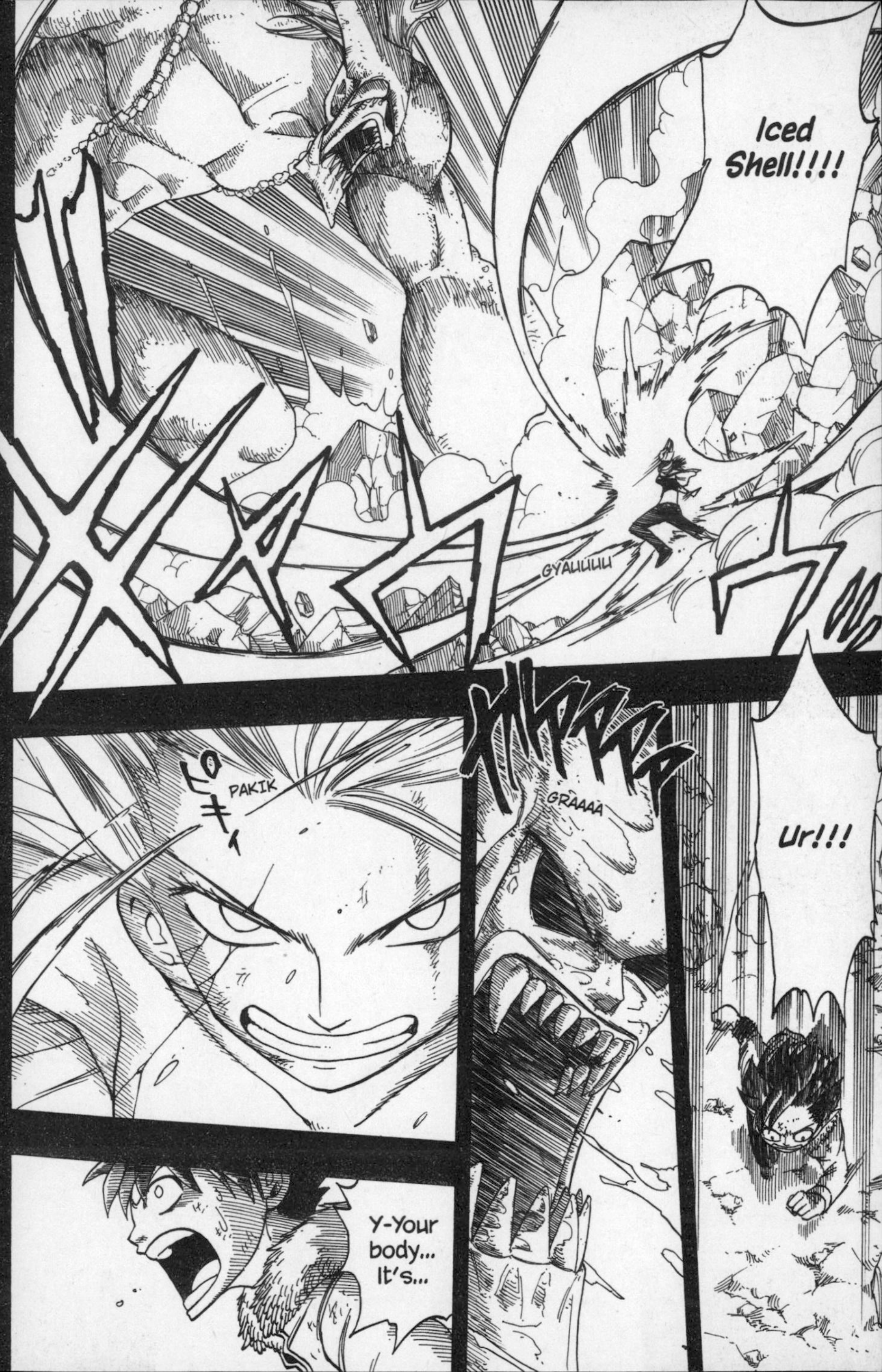
Iced Shell!!!!
GYAUUUU
Ur!!!
GRAAAA
ピキィ
PAKIK
Y-Your body... It's...

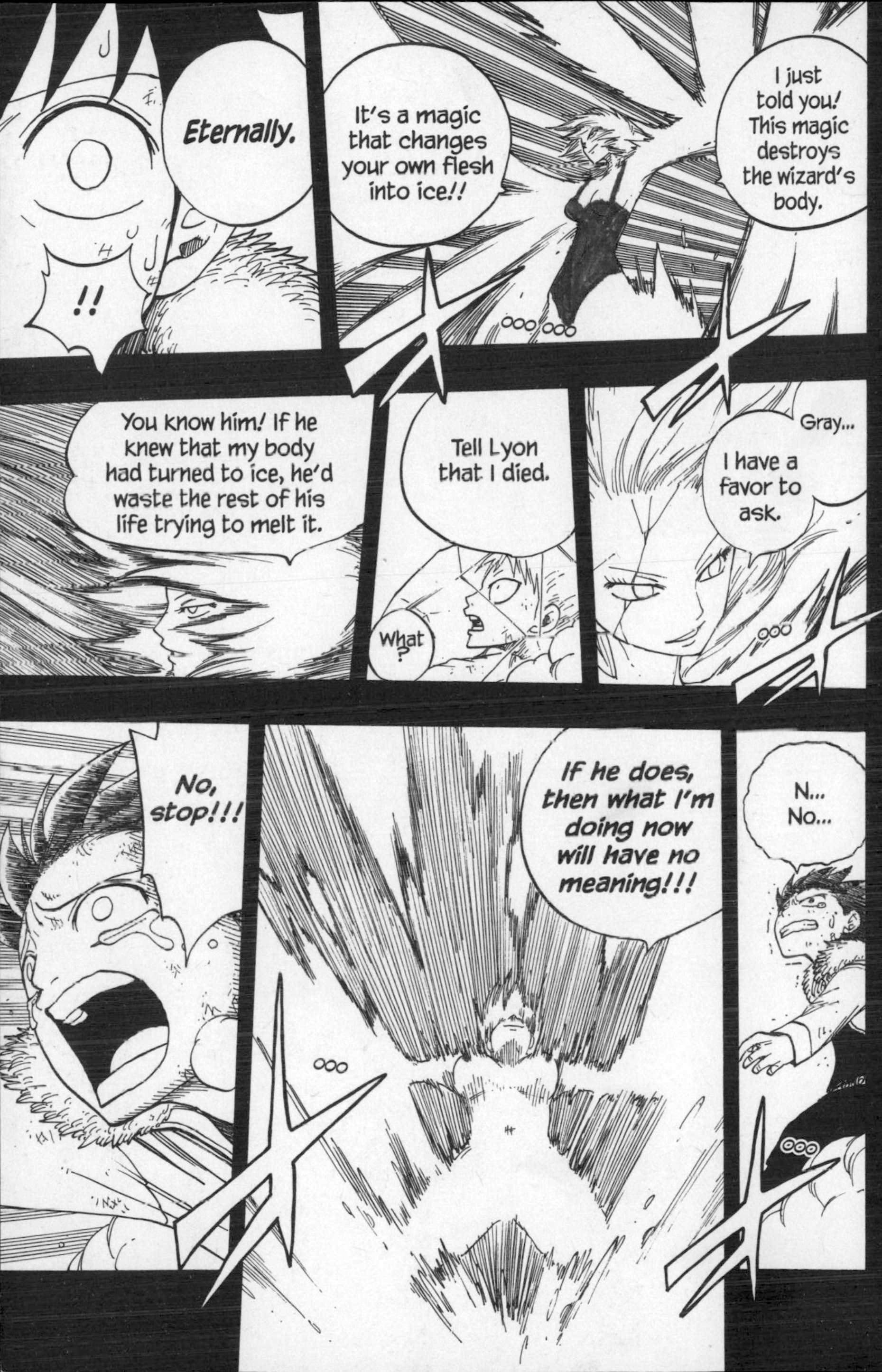
I just told you! This magic destroys the wizard's body.
It's a magic that changes your own flesh into ice!!
Eternally.
!!
Gray...
I have a favor to ask.
Tell Lyon that I died.
What?
You know him! If he knew that my body had turned to ice, he'd waste the rest of his life trying to melt it.
N... No...
If he does, then what I'm doing now will have no meaning!!!
No, stop!!!

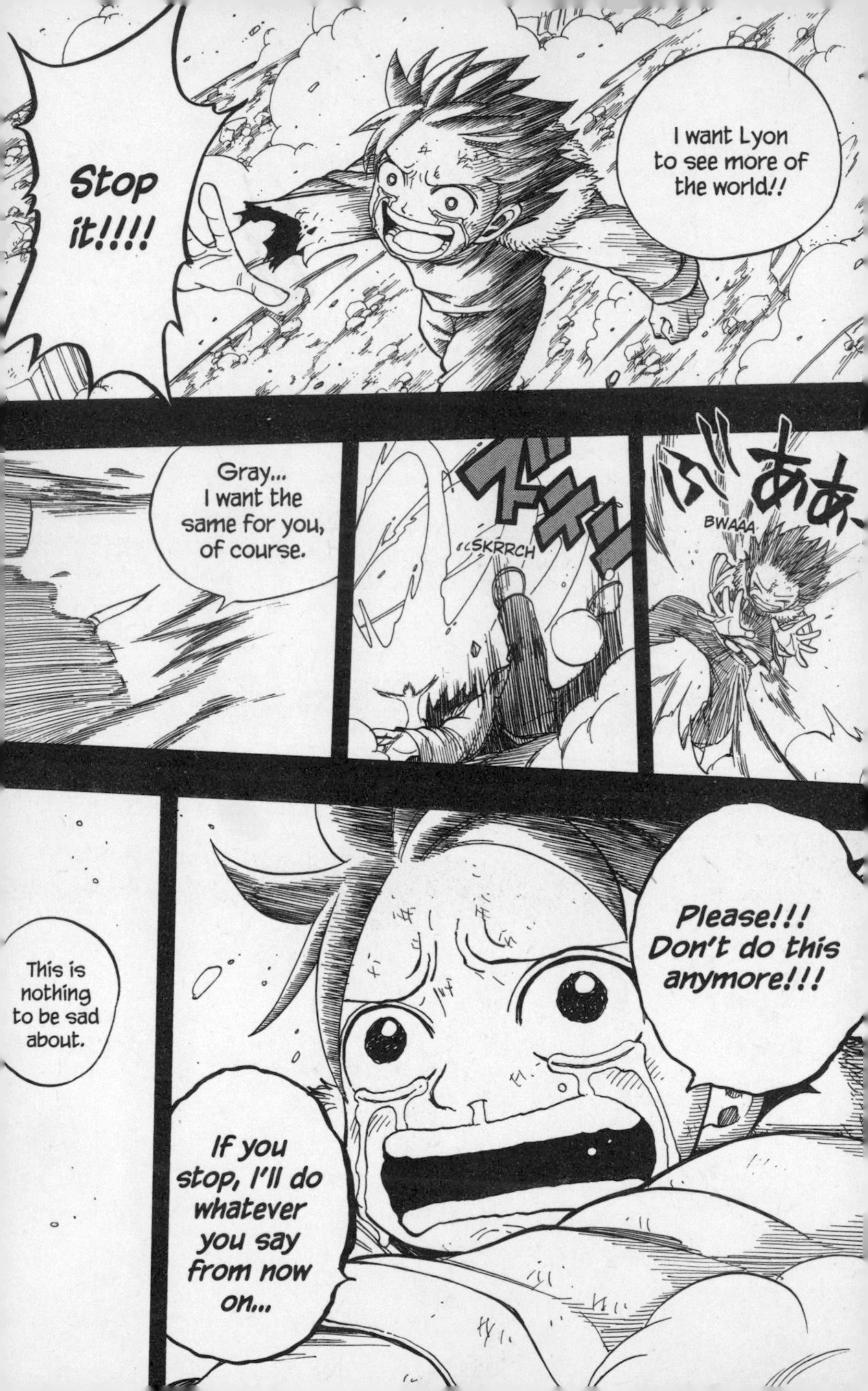
I want Lyon to see more of the world!!
Stop it!!!!
BWAAA
SKRRCH
Gray... I want the same for you, of course.
Please!!! Don't do this anymore!!!
If you stop, I'll do whatever you say from now on...
This is nothing to be sad about.

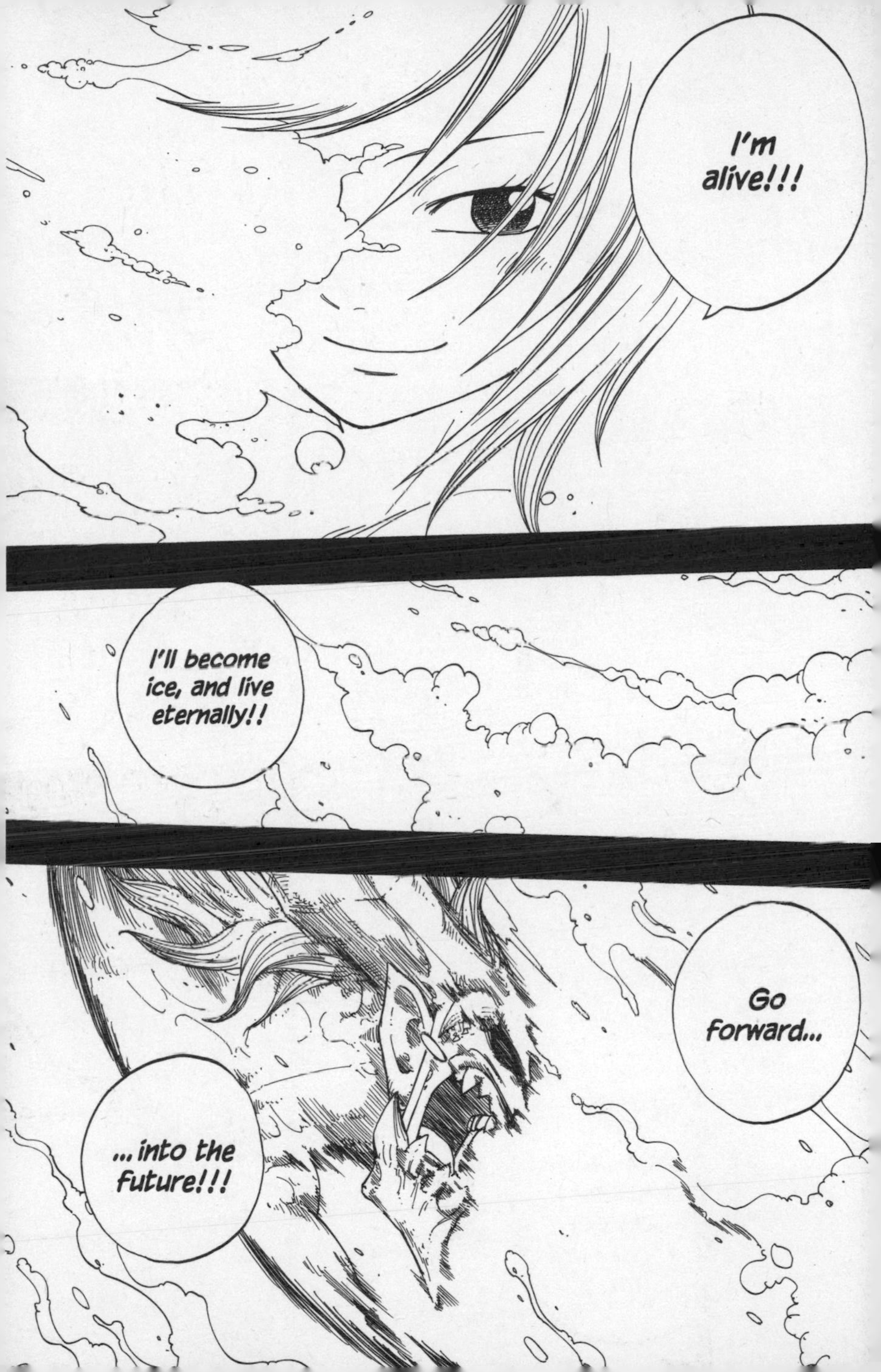
I'm alive!!!
I'll become ice, and live eternally!!
Go forward...
...into the future!!!

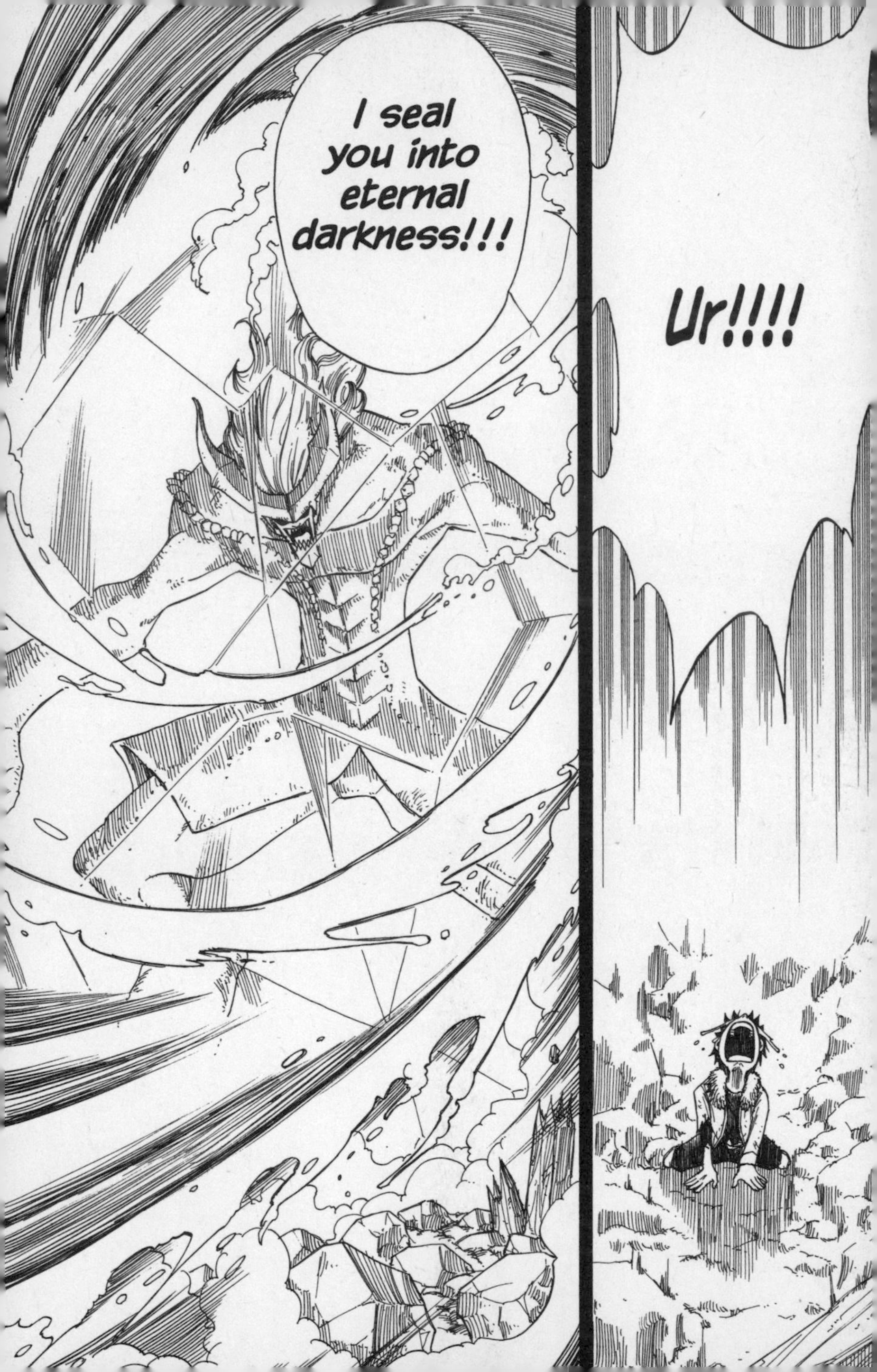
Ur!!!!
I seal you into eternal darkness!!!

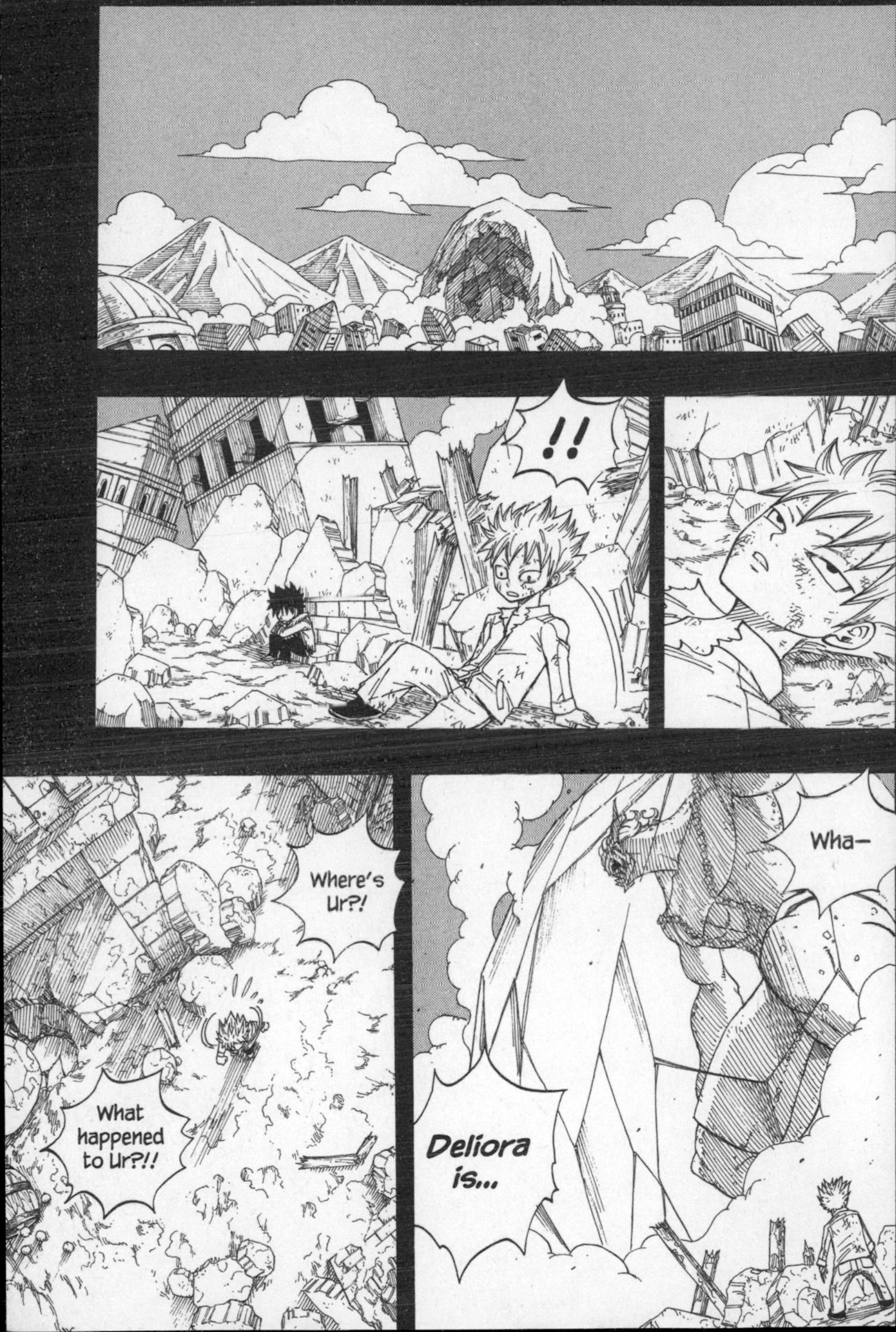
!!
Wha-
Deliora is...
Where's Ur?!
What happened to Ur?!!

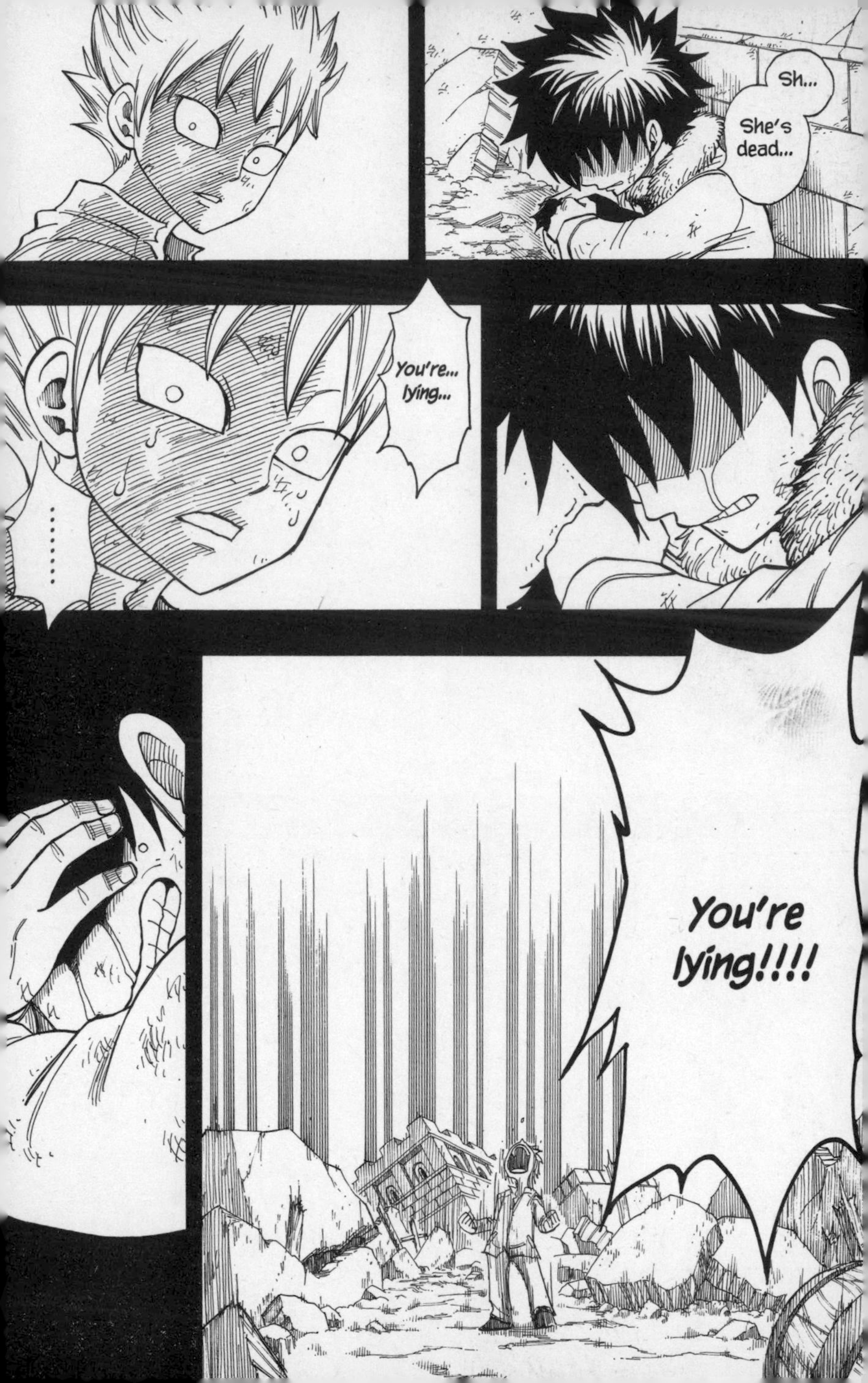
Sh...
She's dead...
You're... lying...
......
You're lying!!!!

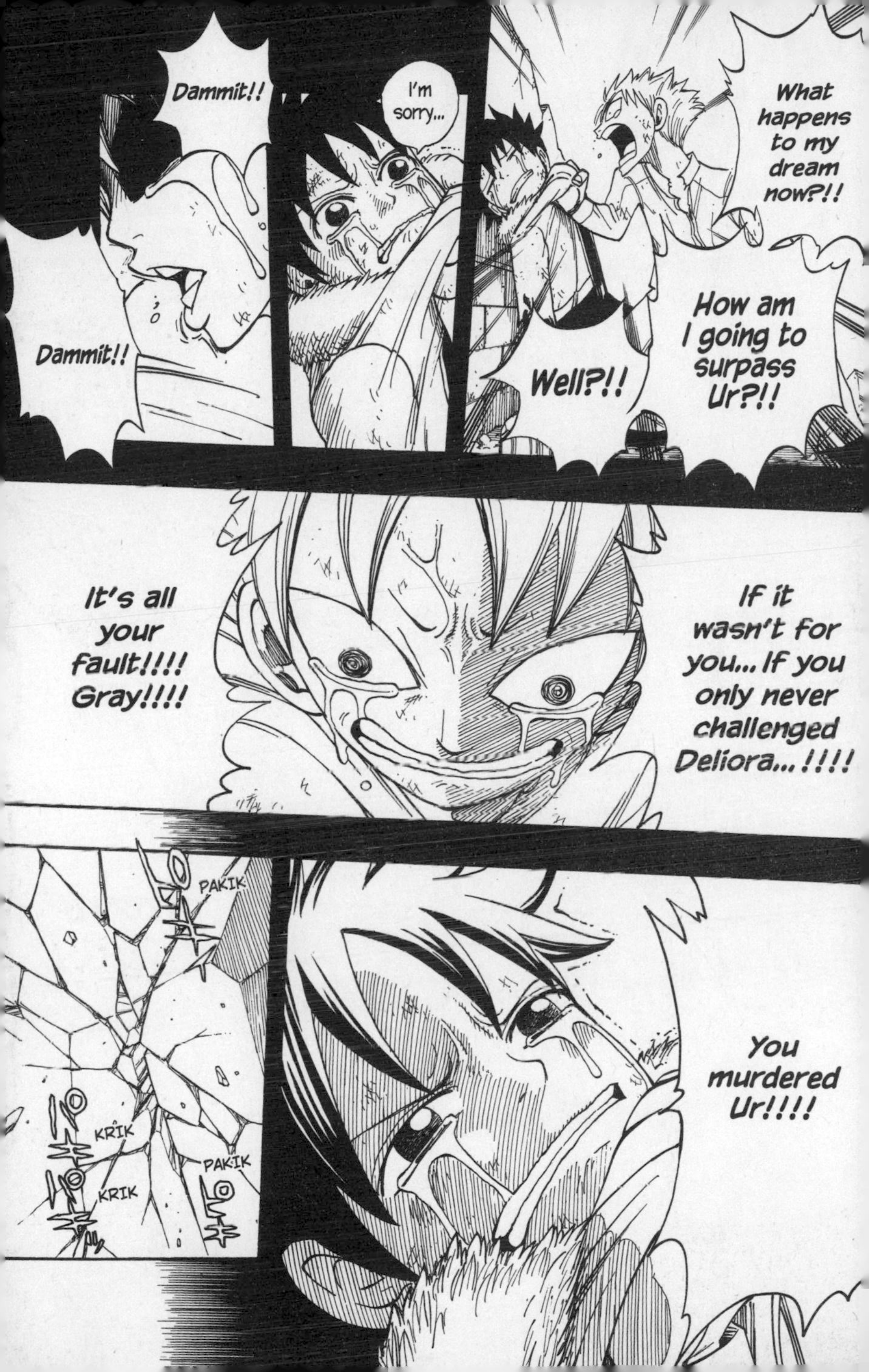
What happens to my dream now?!!
How am I going to surpass Ur?!!
Well?!!
I'm sorry...
Dammit!!
Dammit!!
If it wasn't for you... If you only never challenged Deliora...!!!!
It's all your fault!!!! Gray!!!!
You murdered Ur!!!!
PAKIK
KRIK
PAKIK
KRIK

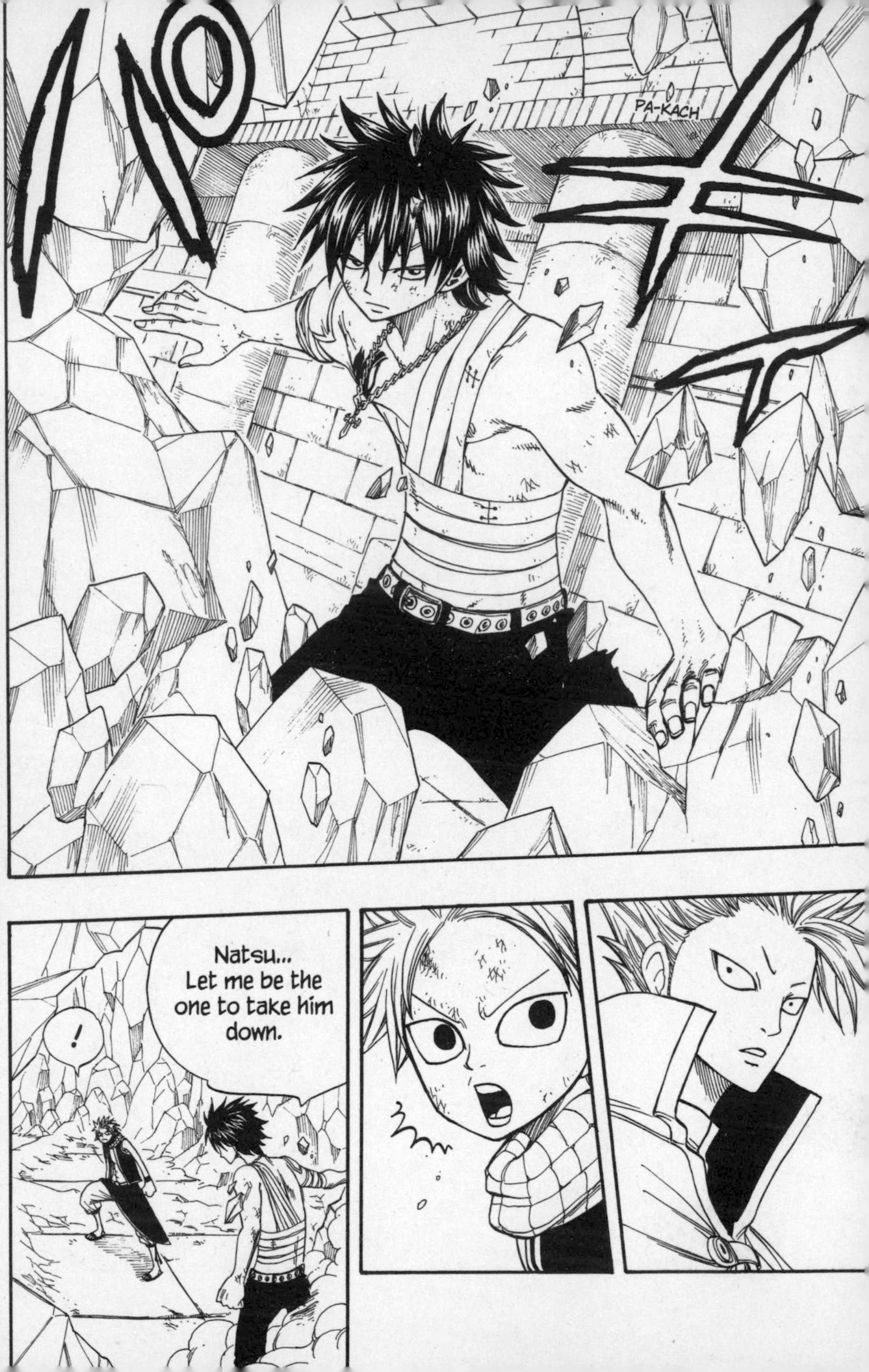
PA-KACH
Natsu... Let me be the one to take him down.
!

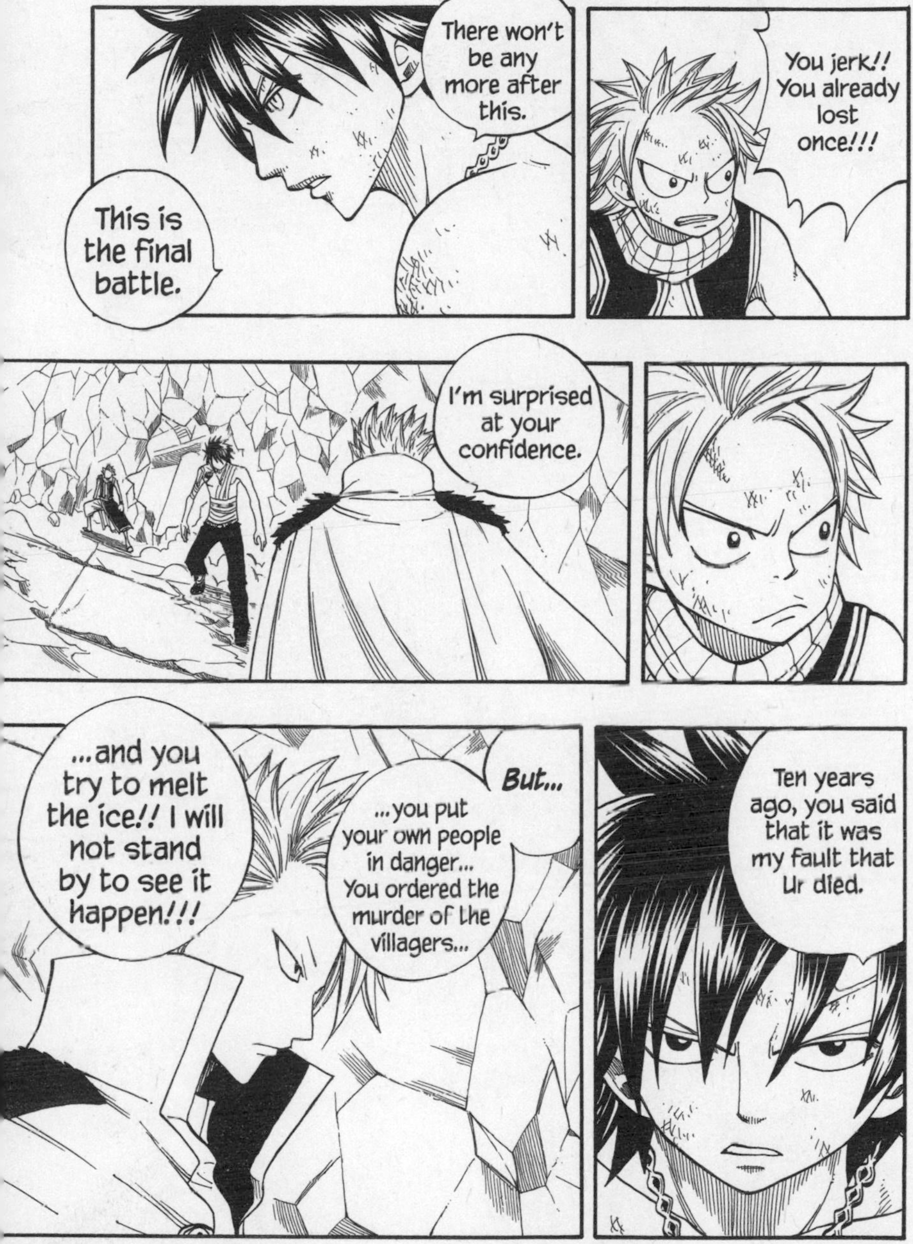

You jerk!! You already lost once!!!
There won't be any more after this.
This is the final battle.
I'm surprised at your confidence.
Ten years ago, you said that it was my fault that Ur died.
But...
...you put your own people in danger... You ordered the murder of the villagers...
...and you try to melt the ice!! I will not stand by to see it happen!!!

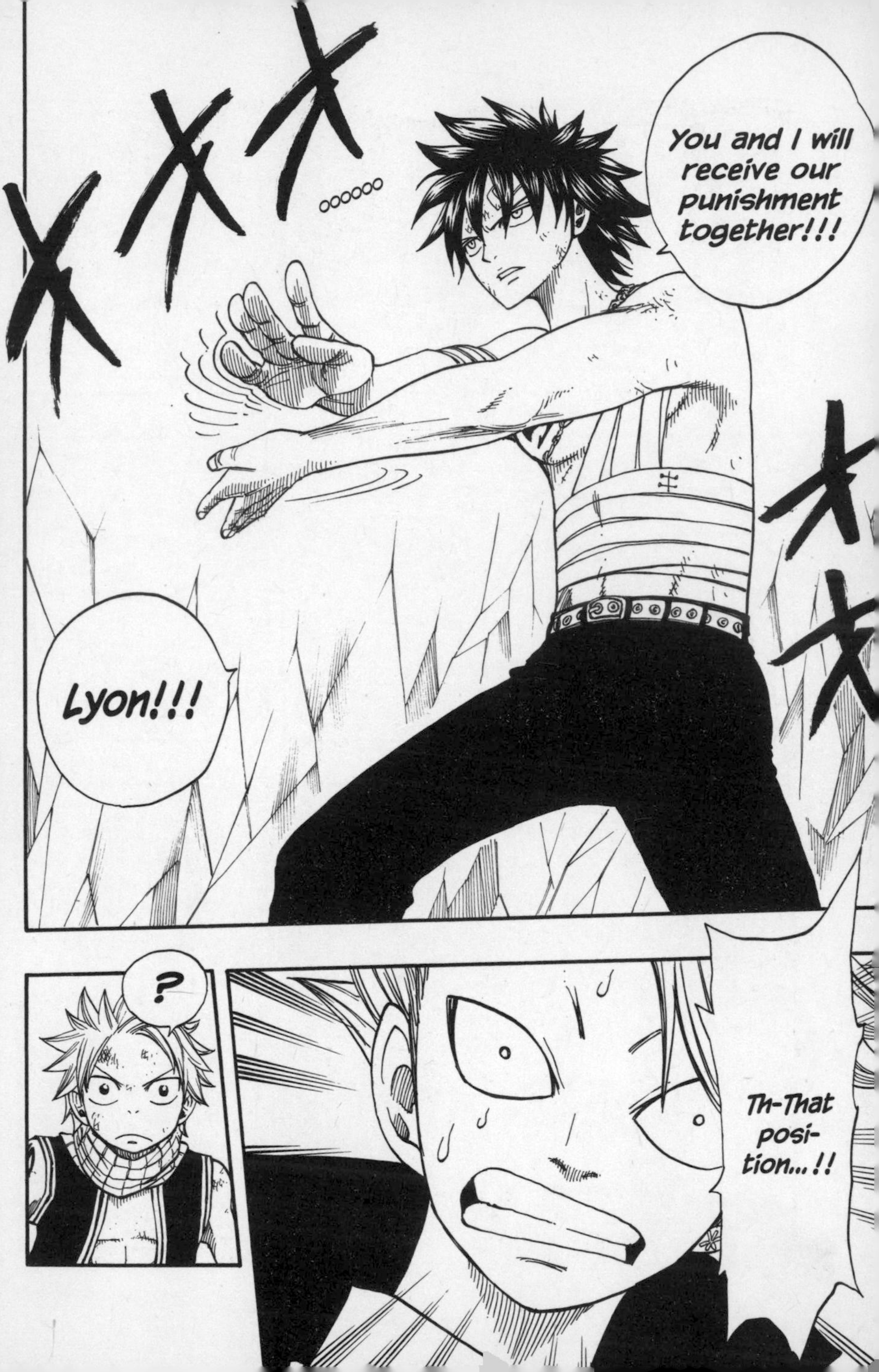
You and I will receive our punishment together!!!
oooooo
Lyon!!!
Th-That posi-tion...!!
?

Chapter 39: The Ice Blade of Tragic Reality

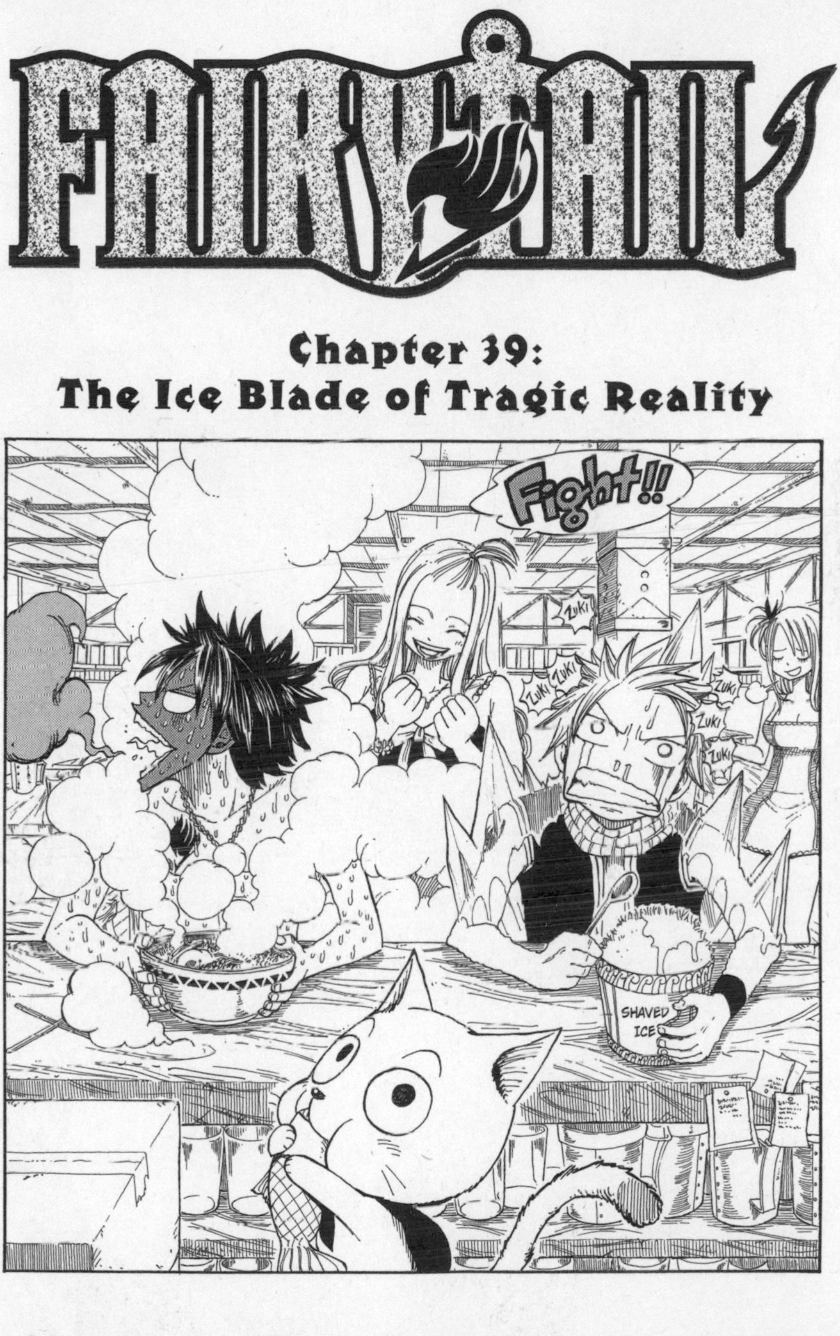
Fight!!
ZUKI
ZUKI
ZUKI
ZUKI
ZUKI
ZUKI
SHAVED ICE

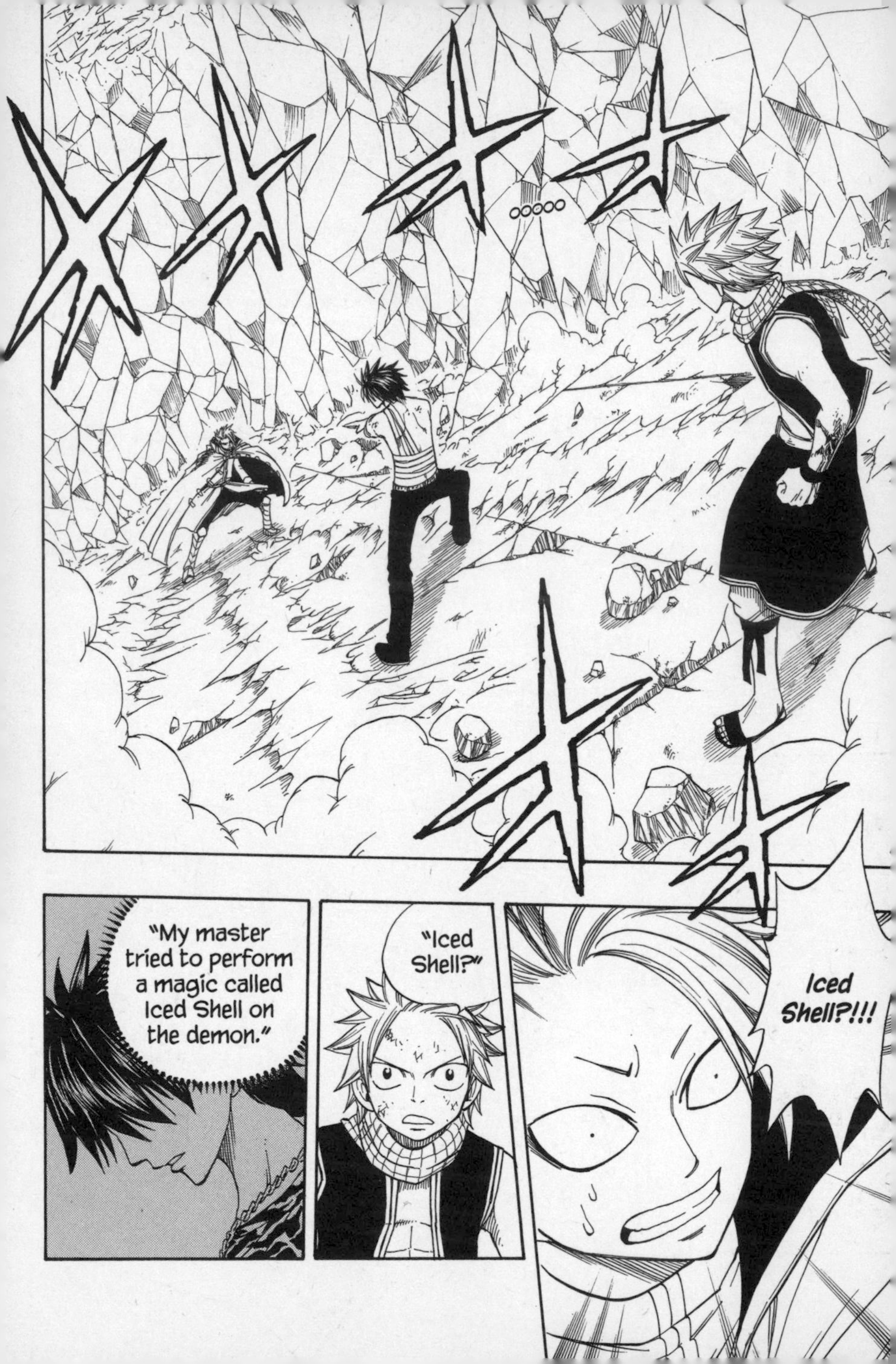
ooooo
Iced Shell?!!!
"Iced Shell?"
"My master tried to perform a magic called Iced Shell on the demon."

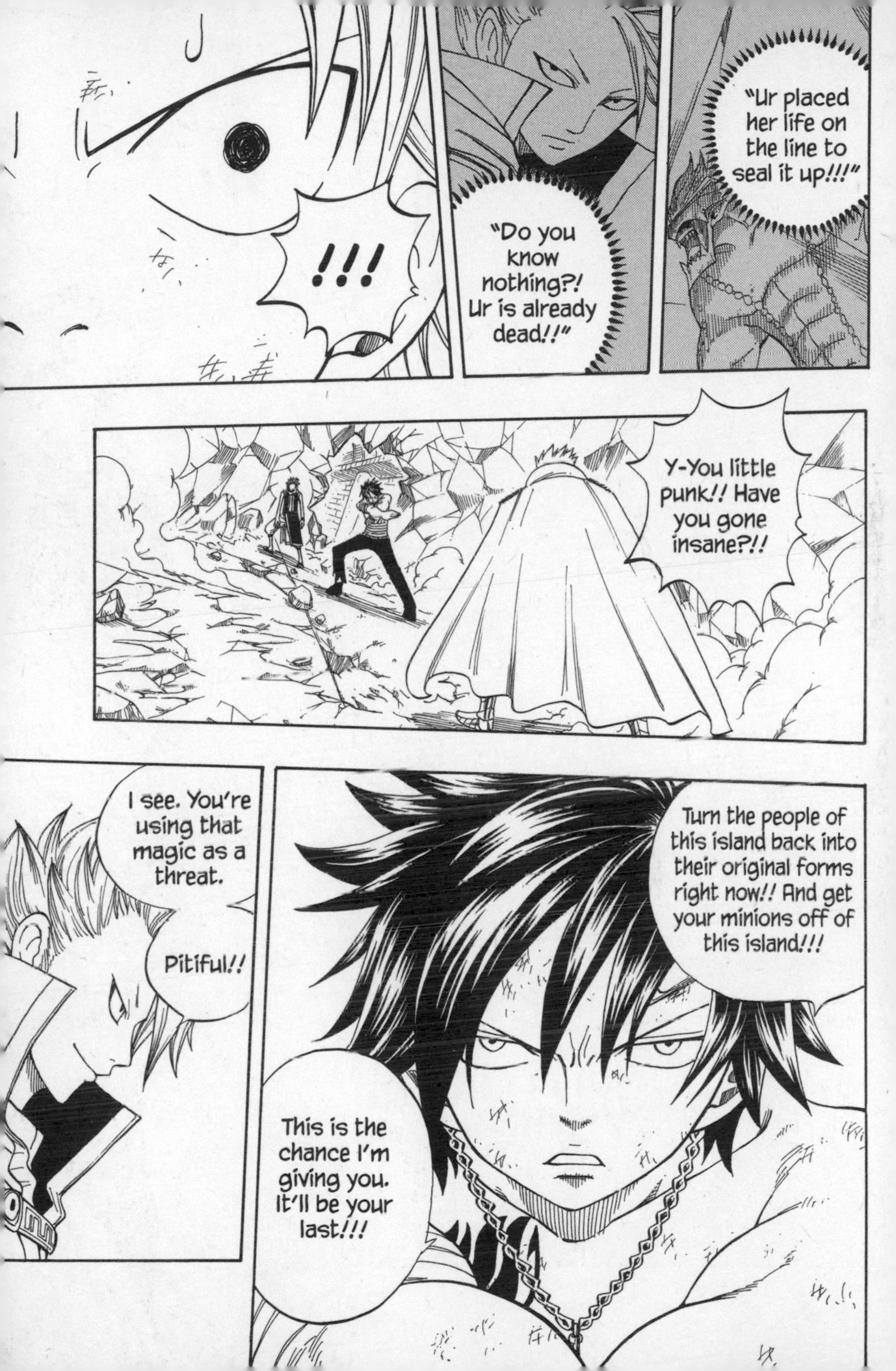
"Ur placed her life on the line to seal it up!!!"
"Do you know nothing?! Ur is already dead!!"
!!!
Y-You little punk!! Have you gone insane?!!
Turn the people of this island back into their original forms right now!! And get your minions off of this island!!!
This is the chance I'm giving you. It'll be your last!!!
I see. You're using that magic as a threat.
Pitiful!!

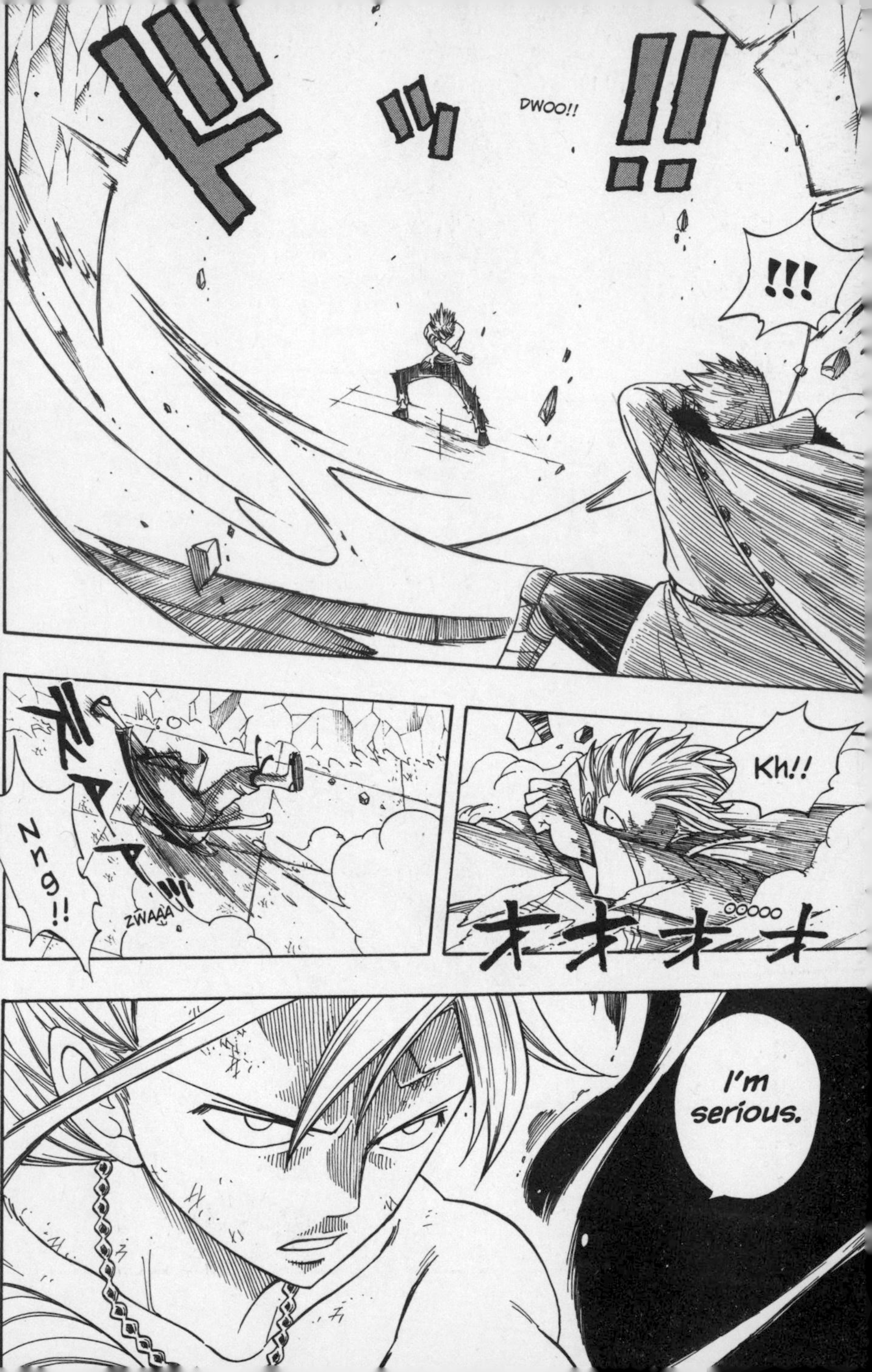
DWOO!!
!!!
Kh!!
ooooo
Nng!!
ZWAAA
I'm serious.

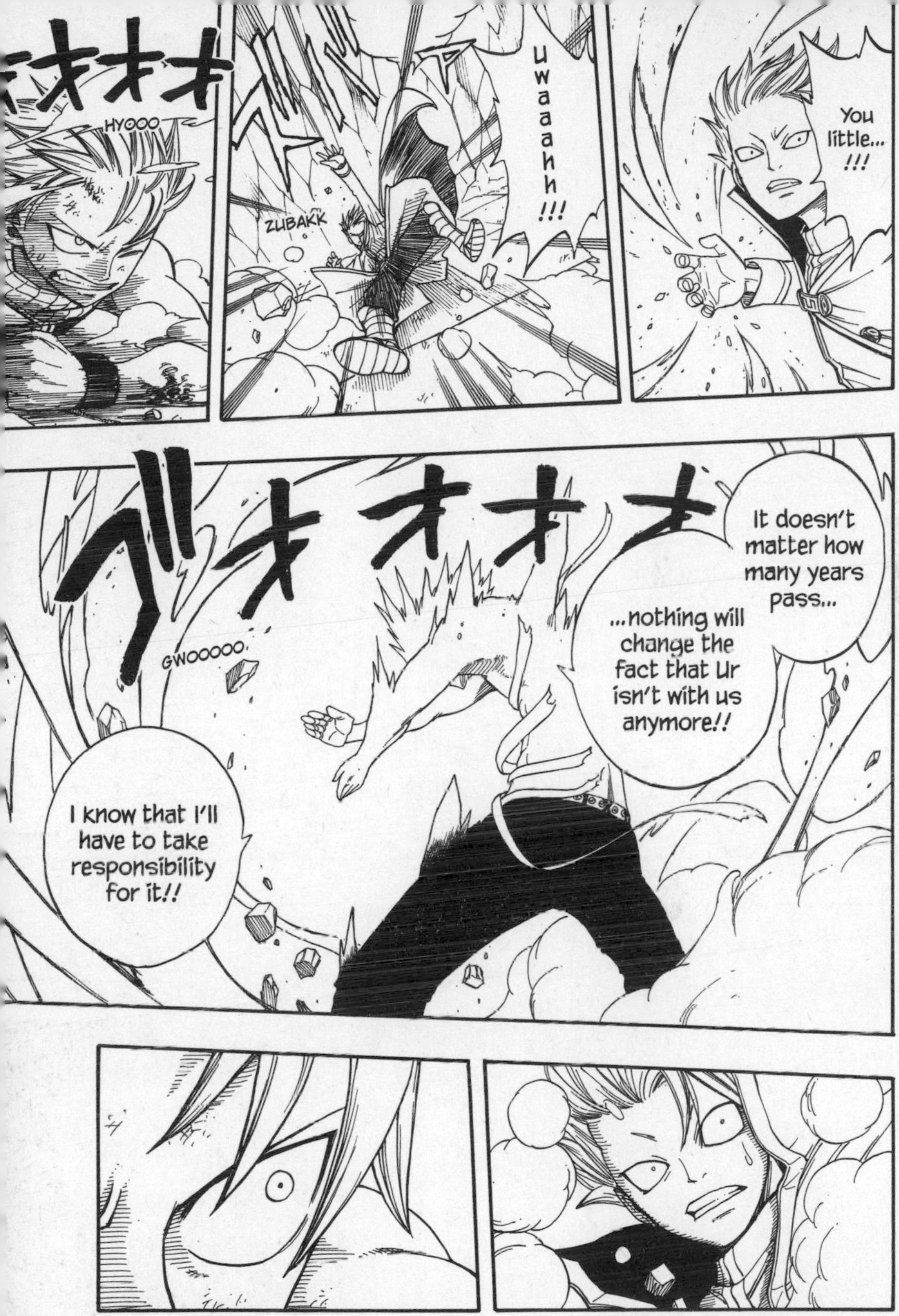
You little... !!!
Uwaaahh !!!
ZUBAKK
HYOOO
It doesn't matter how many years pass...
...nothing will change the fact that Ur isn't with us anymore!!
GWOOOOO
I know that I'll have to take responsibility for it!!

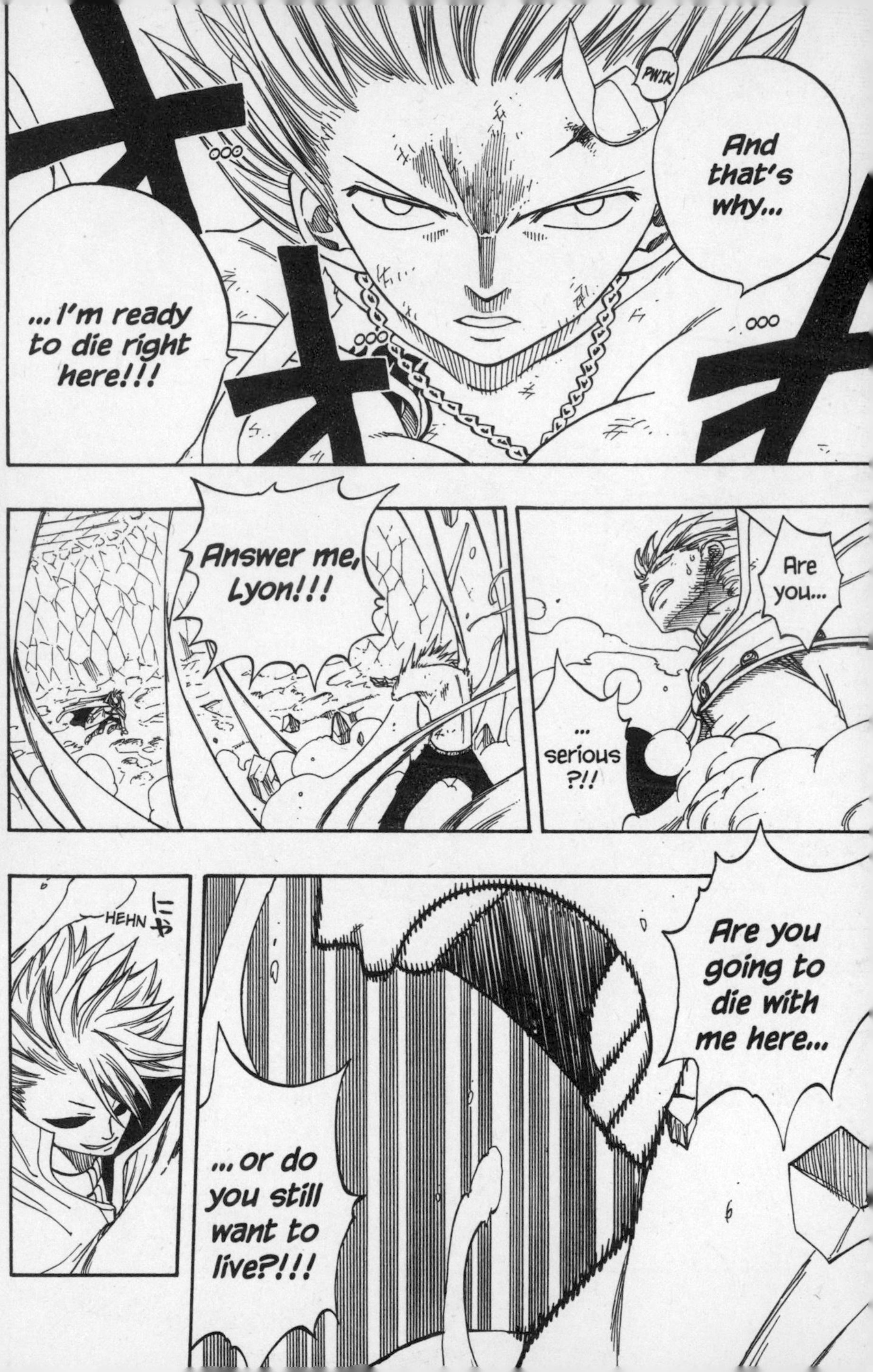
PWIK
And that's why...
...I'm ready to die right here!!!
Are you...
...serious?!!
Answer me, Lyon!!!
Are you going to die with me here...
...or do you still want to live?!!!
HEHN
にや

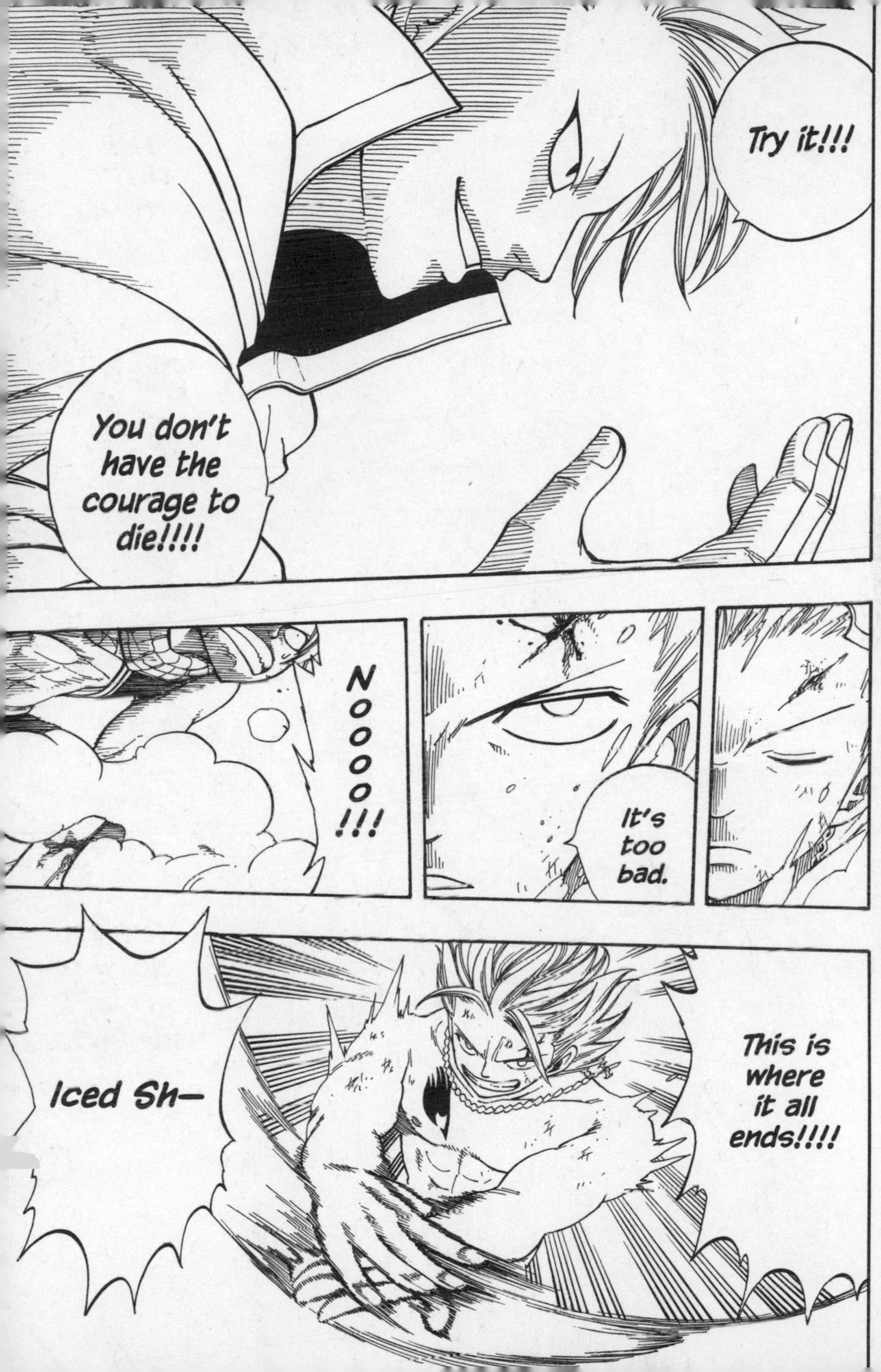
Try it!!!
You don't have the courage to die!!!!
It's too bad.
Noooo!!!
This is where it all ends!!!!
Iced Sh—

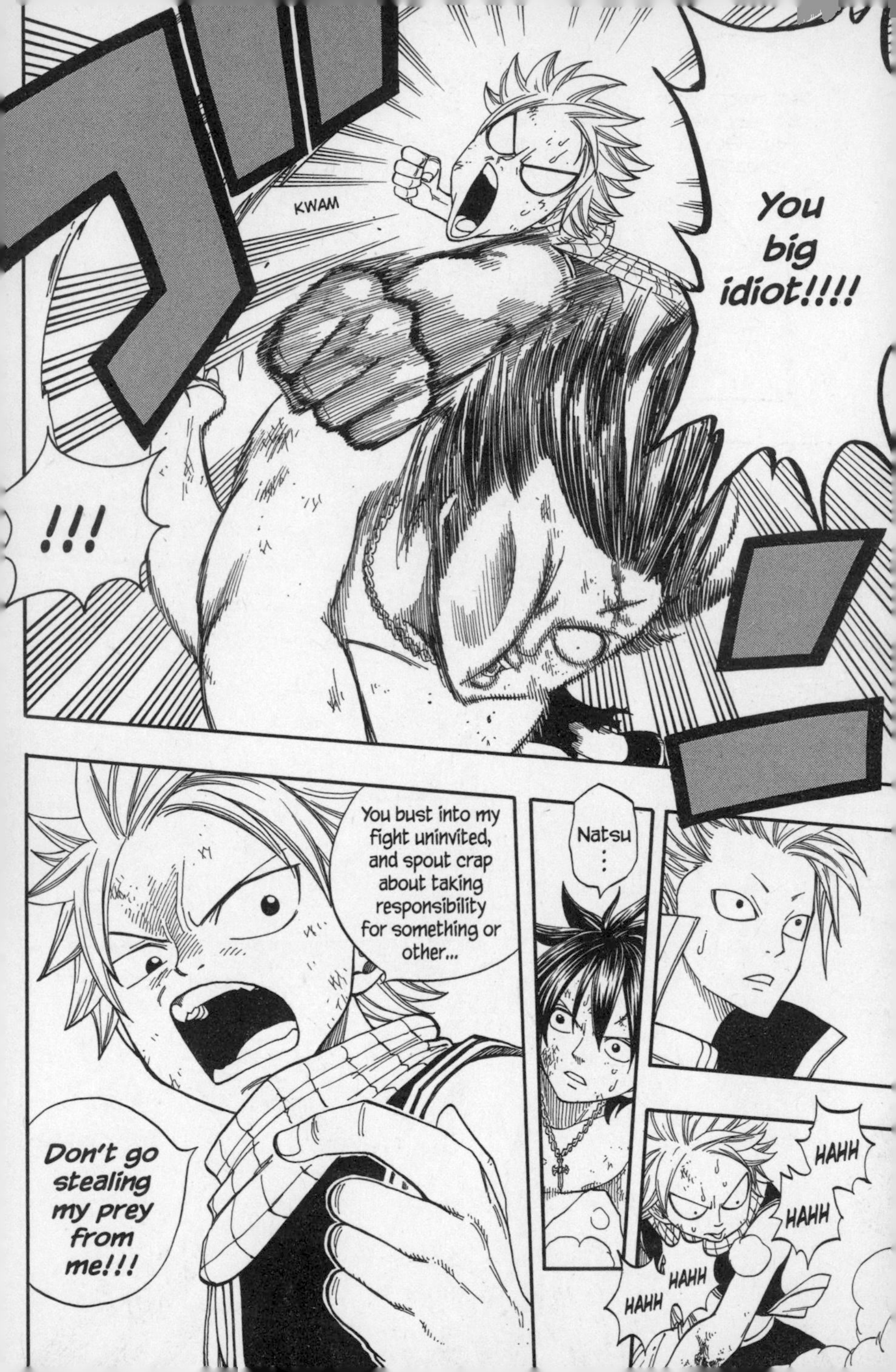
You big idiot!!!!
KWAM
!!!
HAHH
HAHH
HAHH
HAHH
Natsu...
You bust into my fight uninvited, and spout crap about taking responsibility for something or other...
Don't go stealing my prey from me!!!

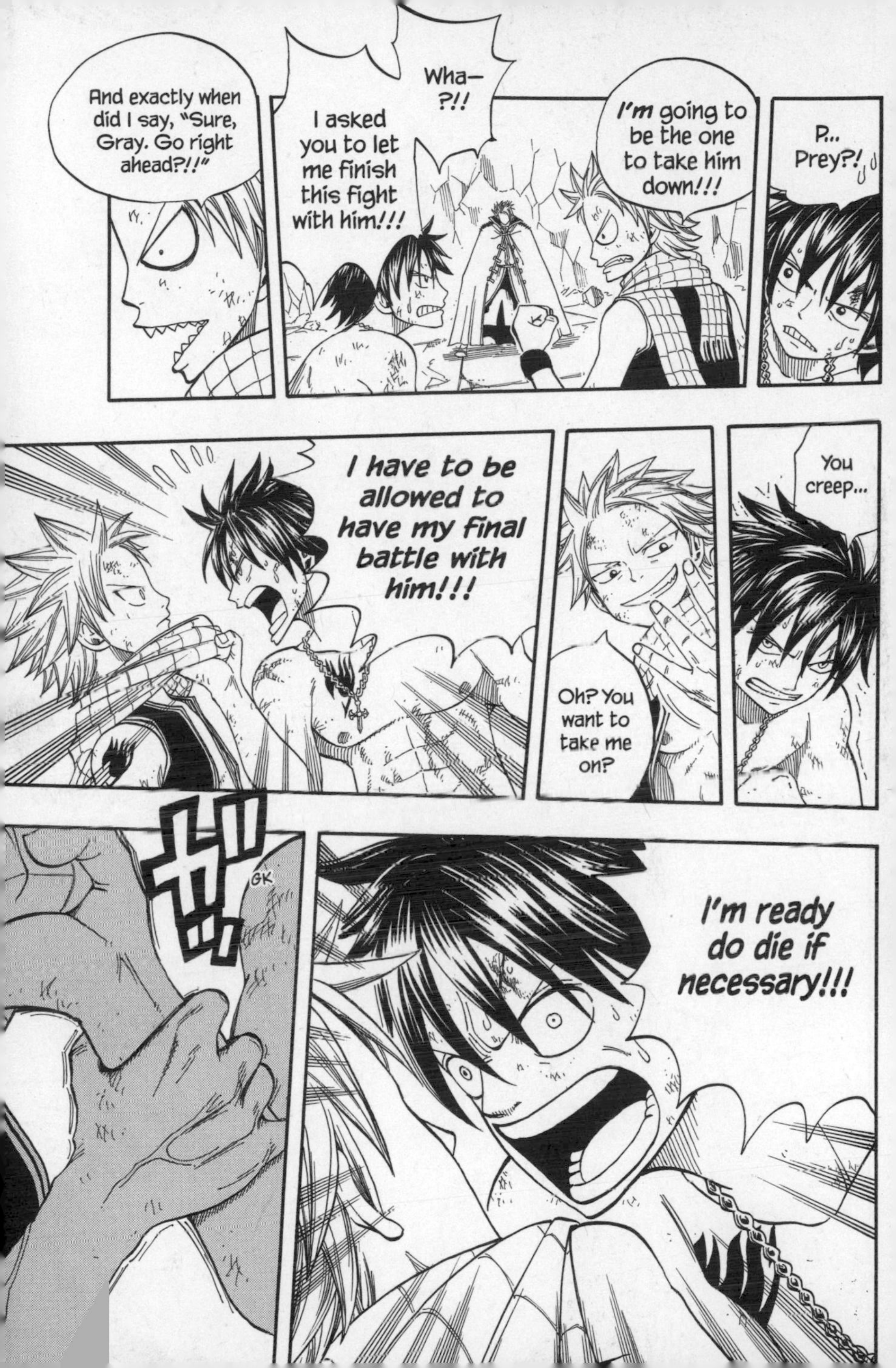

P... Prey?!
I'm going to be the one to take him down!!!
Wha—?!!
I asked you to let me finish this fight with him!!!
And exactly when did I say, "Sure, Gray. Go right ahead?!!"
You creep...
Oh? You want to take me on?
I have to be allowed to have my final battle with him!!!
I'm ready do die if necessary!!!
GK

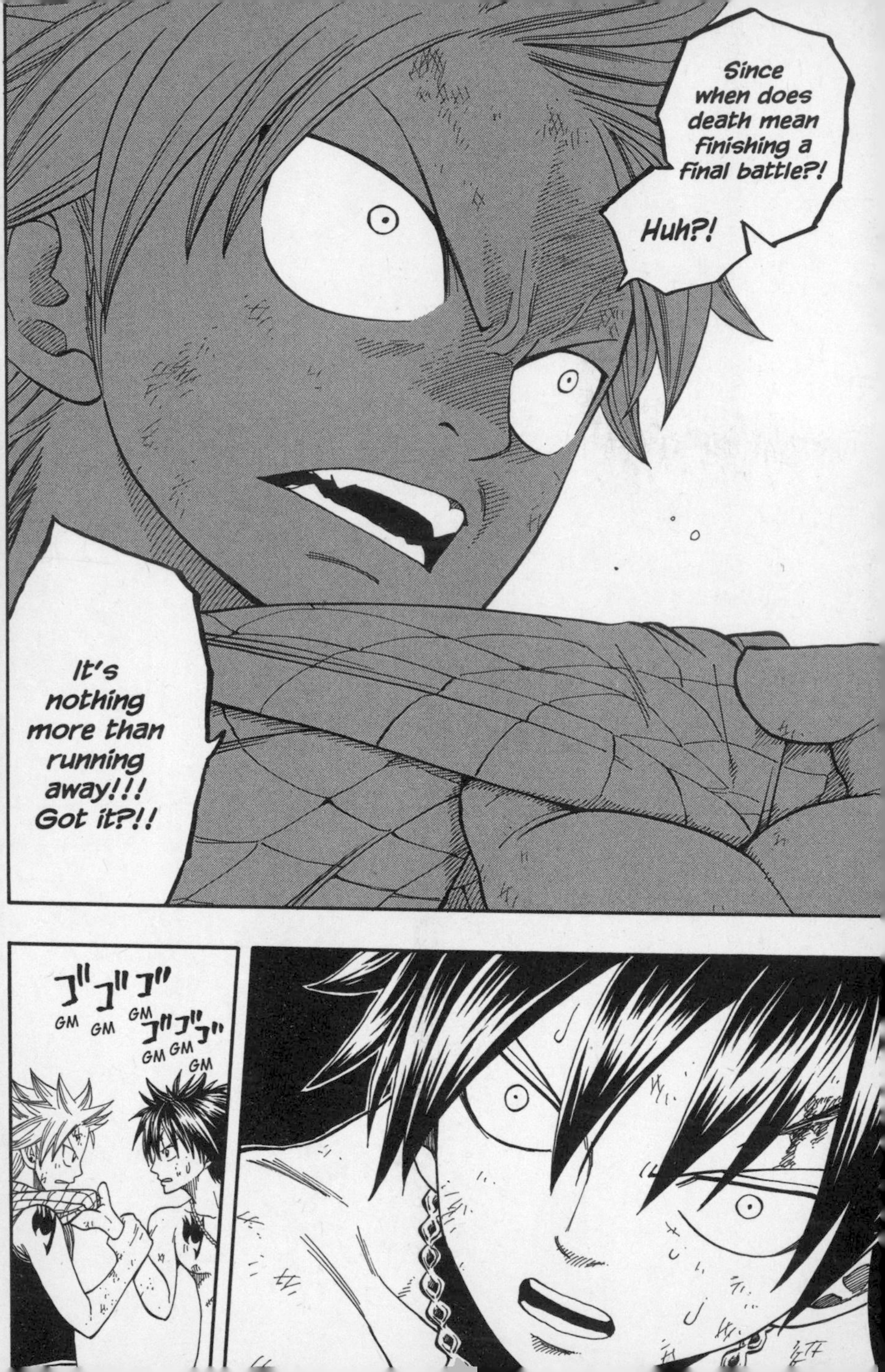
Since when does death mean finishing a final battle?!
Huh?!
It's nothing more than running away!!! Got it?!!
ゴゴゴ
GM GM GM
ゴゴゴ
GM GM GM

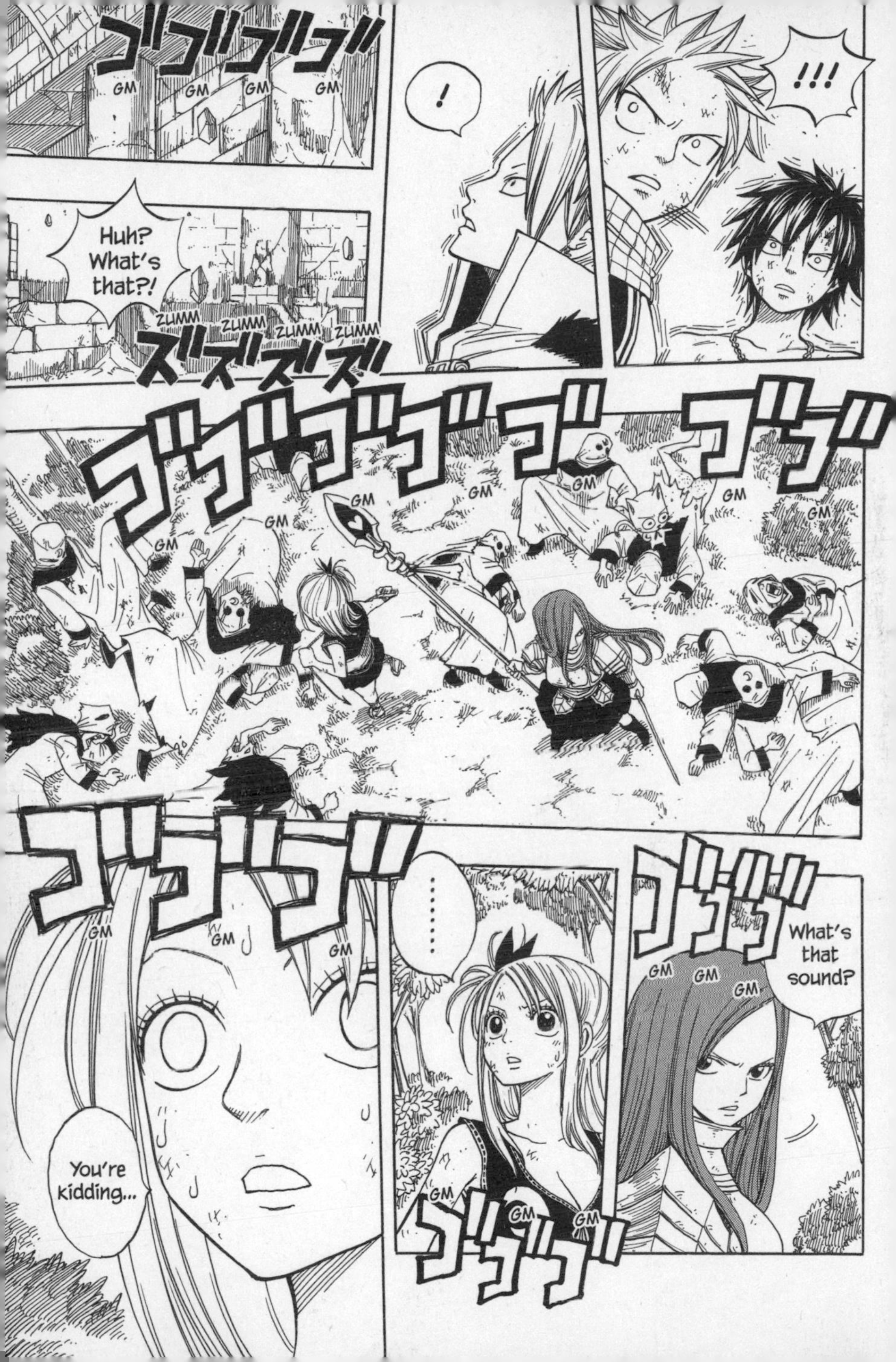

!!!
!
GM GM GM GM
Huh? What's that?!
ZUMM ZUMM ZUMM ZUMM
GM GM GM GM GM GM GM
What's that sound?
GM GM GM
......
GM GM GM
GM GM GM
You're kidding...

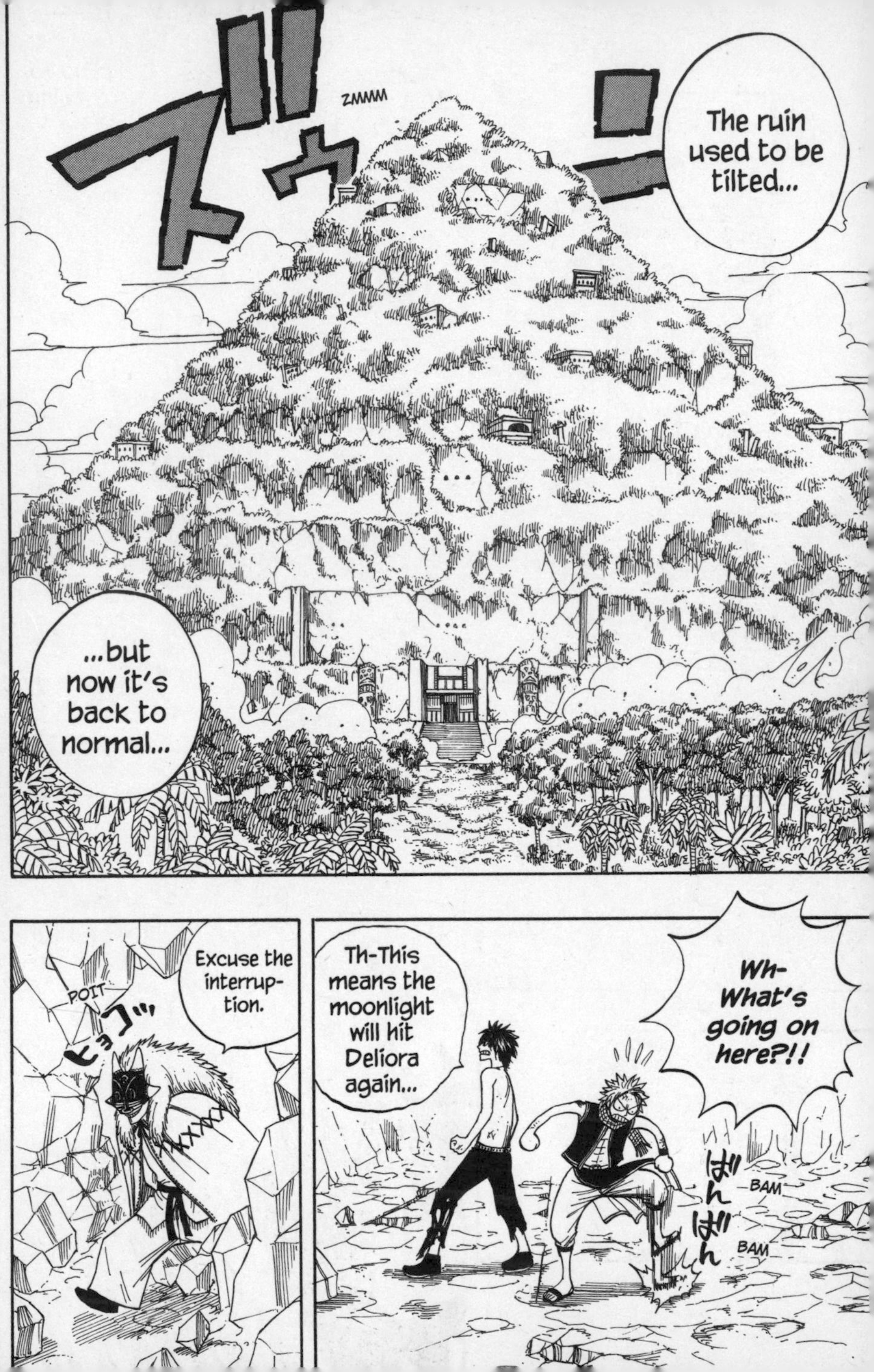
ズゥー
ZMMM
The ruin used to be tilted...
...but now it's back to normal...
Wh- What's going on here?!!
Th-This means the moonlight will hit Deliora again...
ばんばん
BAM
BAM
Excuse the interruption.
POIT

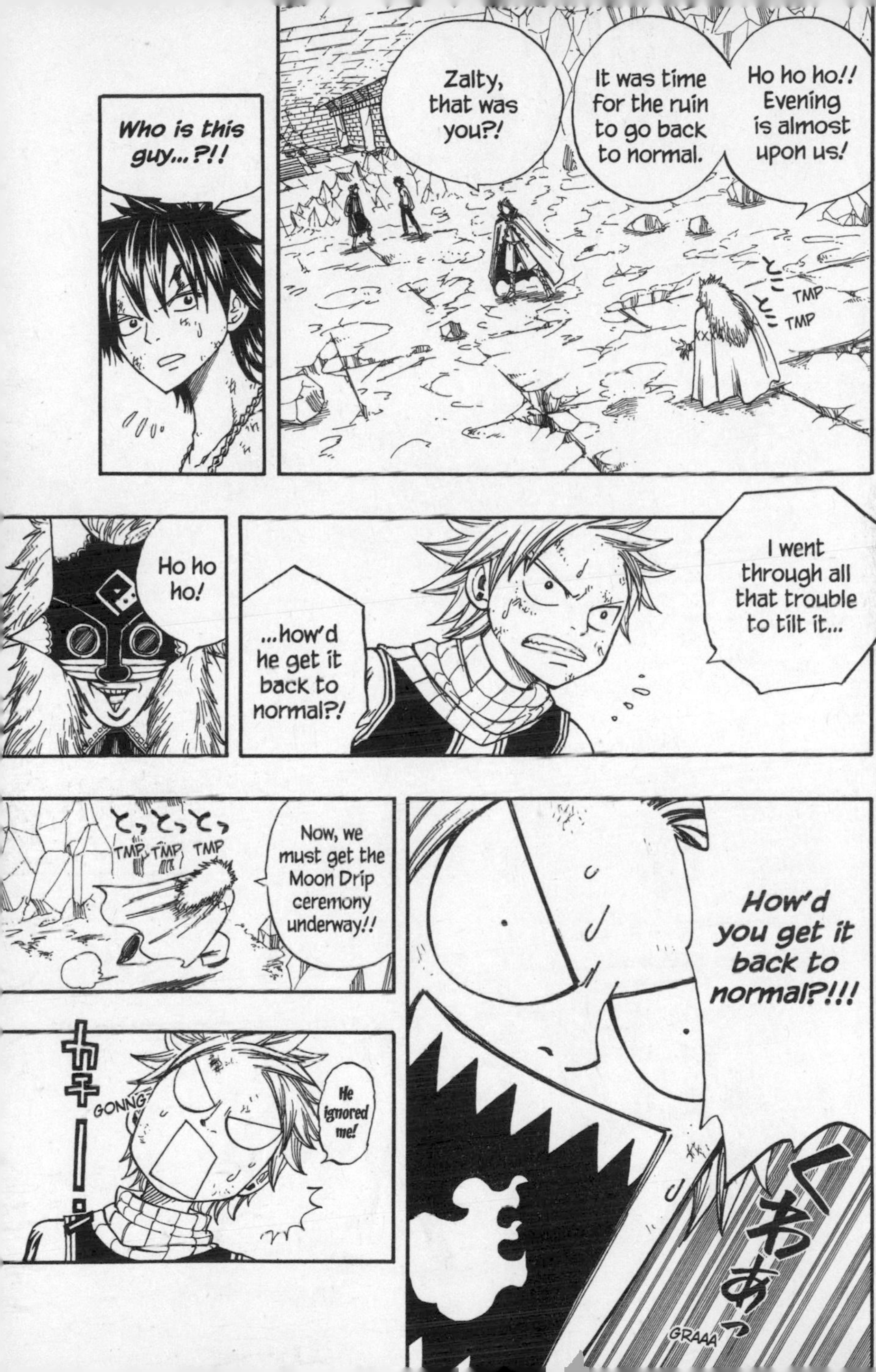
Ho ho ho!! Evening is almost upon us!
It was time for the ruin to go back to normal.
Zalty, that was you?!
TMP TMP
Who is this guy...?!!
I went through all that trouble to tilt it...
...how'd he get it back to normal?!
Ho ho ho!
How'd you get it back to normal?!!!
GRAAA
Now, we must get the Moon Drip ceremony underway!!
TMP TMP TMP
GONNG
He ignored me!

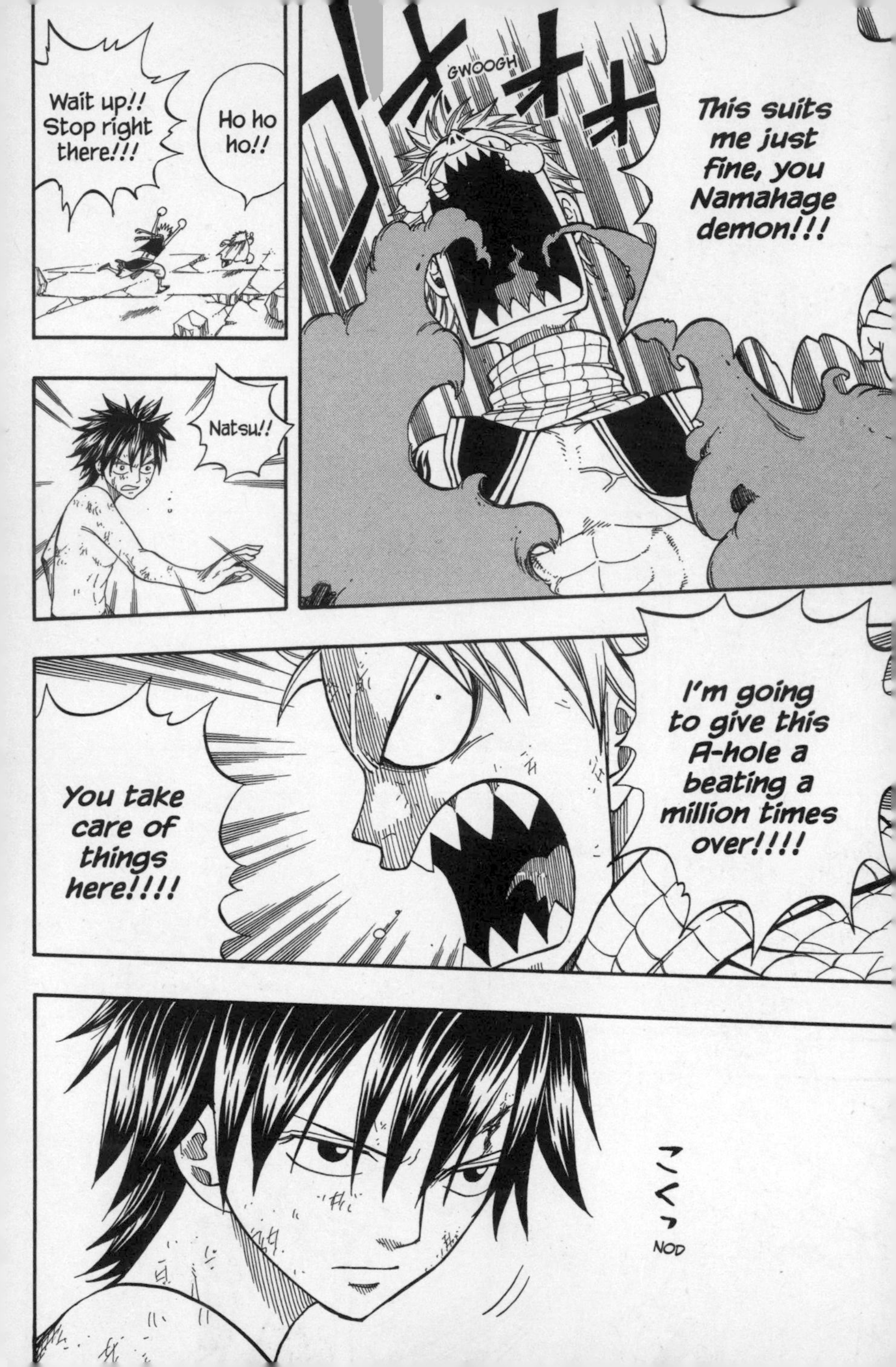
GWOOGH
This suits me just fine, you Namahage demon!!!
Ho ho ho!!
Wait up!! Stop right there!!!
Natsu!!
I'm going to give this A-hole a beating a million times over!!!!
You take care of things here!!!!
こくっ
NOD

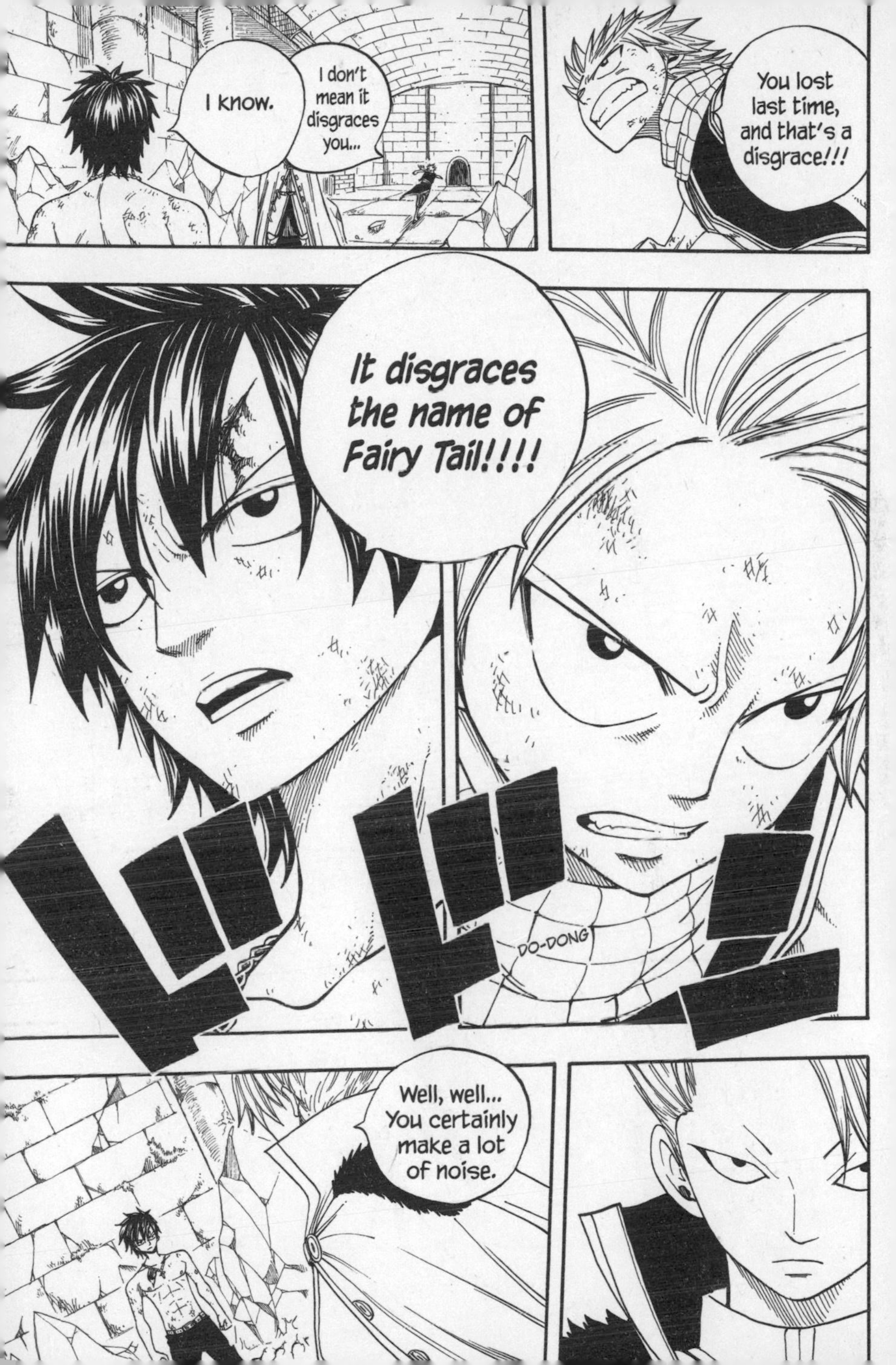
You lost last time, and that's a disgrace!!!
I don't mean it disgraces you...
I know.
It disgraces the name of Fairy Tail!!!!
DO-DONG
Well, well... You certainly make a lot of noise.

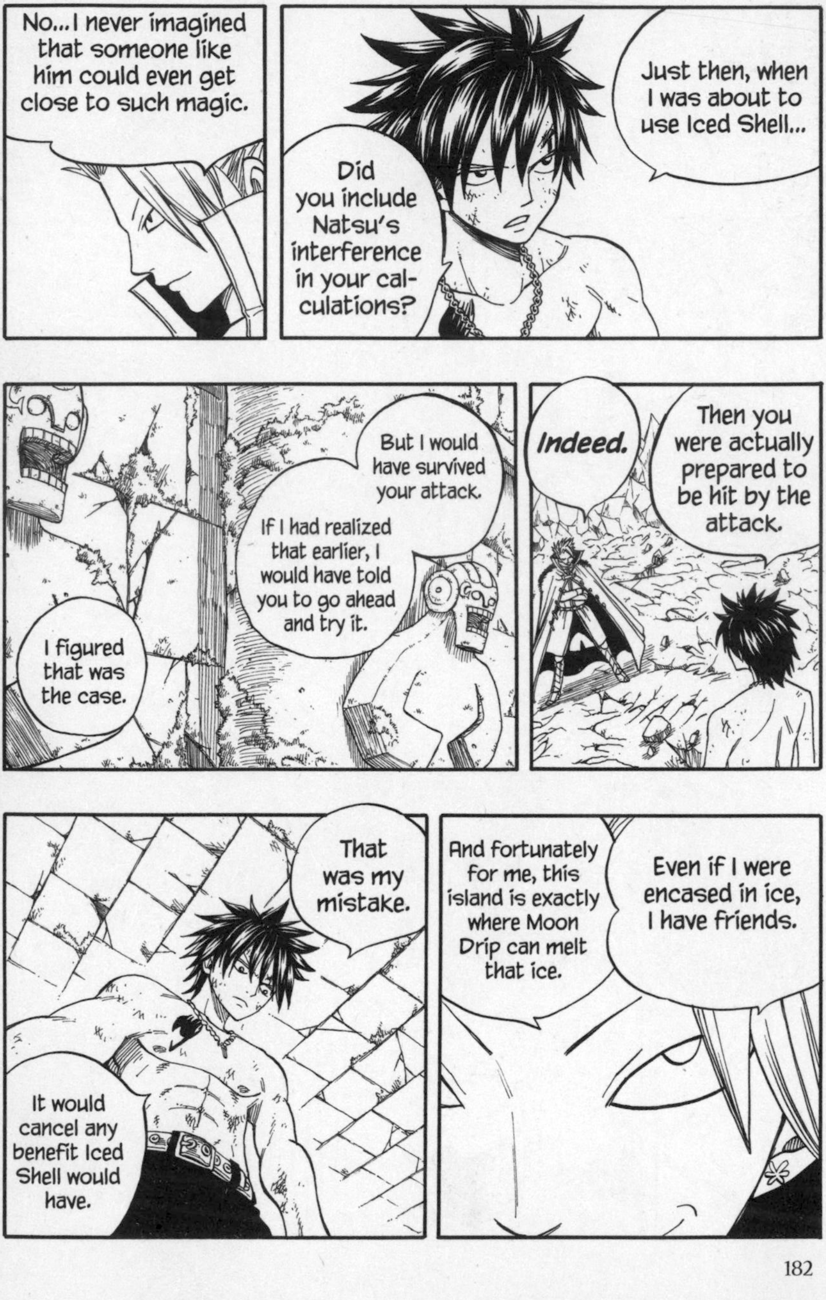
Just then, when I was about to use Iced Shell...
Did you include Natsu's interference in your calculations?
No...I never imagined that someone like him could even get close to such magic.
Then you were actually prepared to be hit by the attack.
Indeed.
But I would have survived your attack.
If I had realized that earlier, I would have told you to go ahead and try it.
I figured that was the case.
Even if I were encased in ice, I have friends.
And fortunately for me, this island is exactly where Moon Drip can melt that ice.
That was my mistake.
It would cancel any benefit Iced Shell would have.

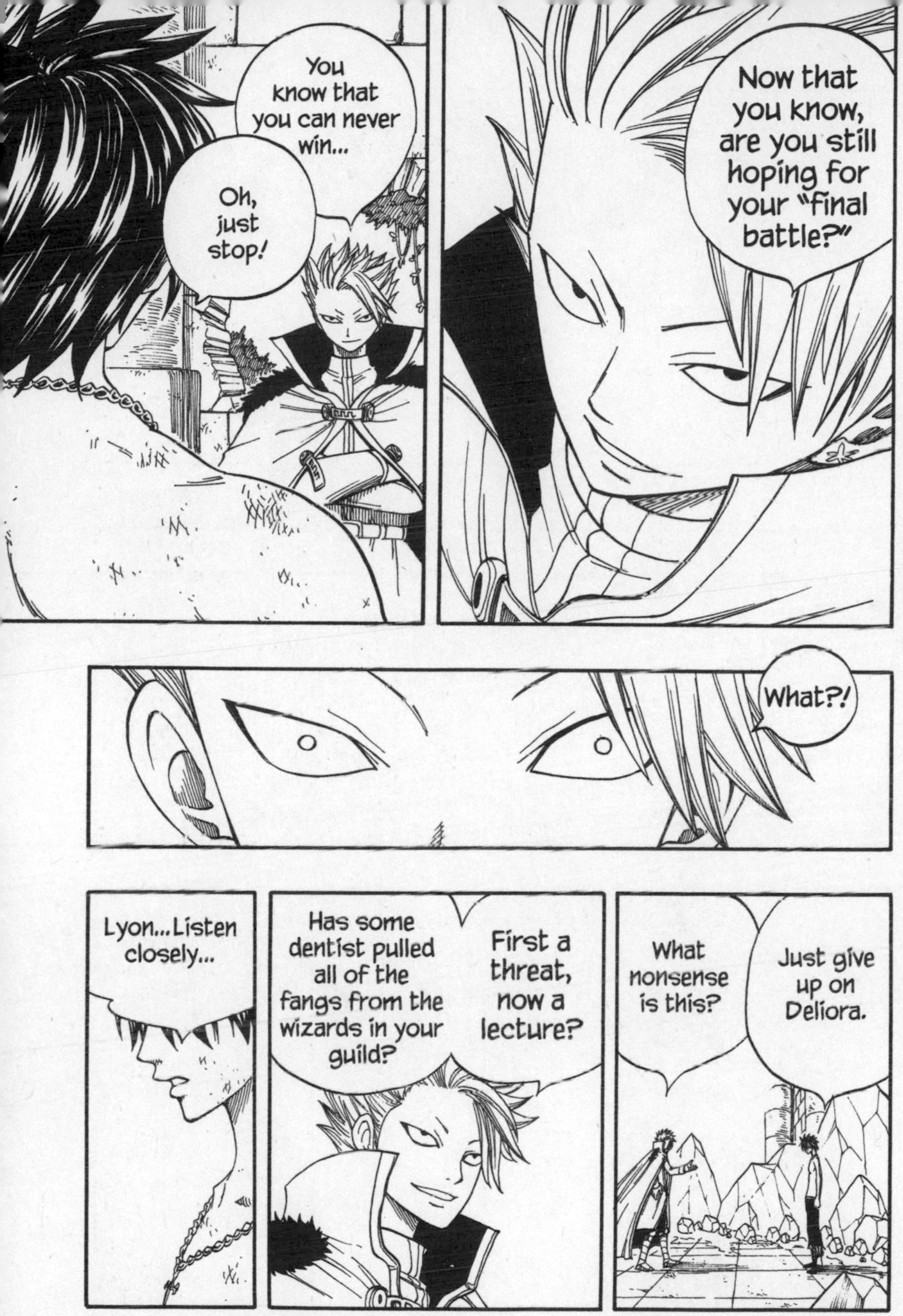
Now that you know, are you still hoping for your "final battle?"
You know that you can never win...
Oh, just stop!
What?!
Just give up on Deliora.
What nonsense is this?
First a threat, now a lecture?
Has some dentist pulled all of the fangs from the wizards in your guild?
Lyon...Listen closely...

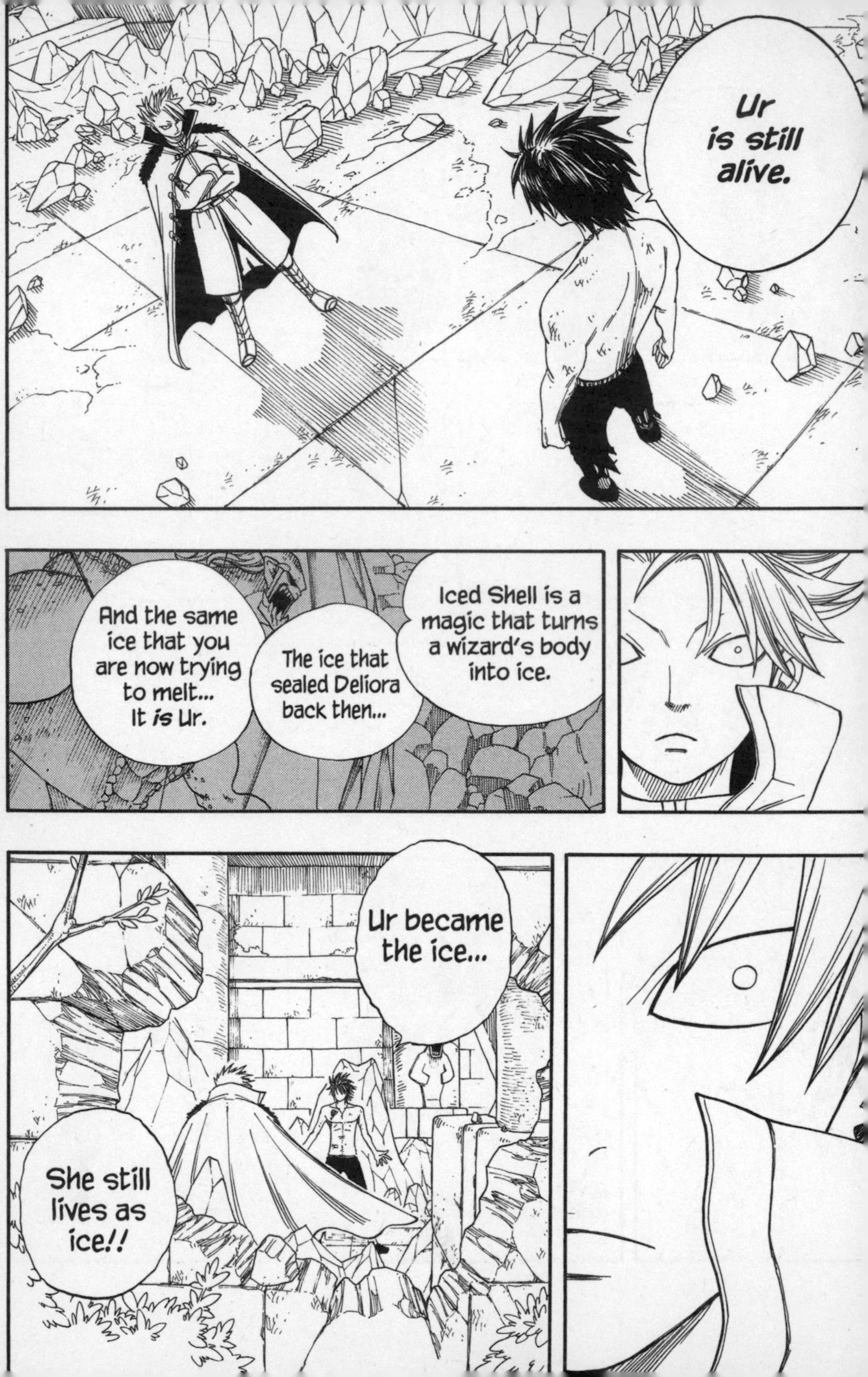
Ur is still alive.
Iced Shell is a magic that turns a wizard's body into ice.
The ice that sealed Deliora back then...
And the same ice that you are now trying to melt... It *is* Ur.
Ur became the ice...
She still lives as ice!!

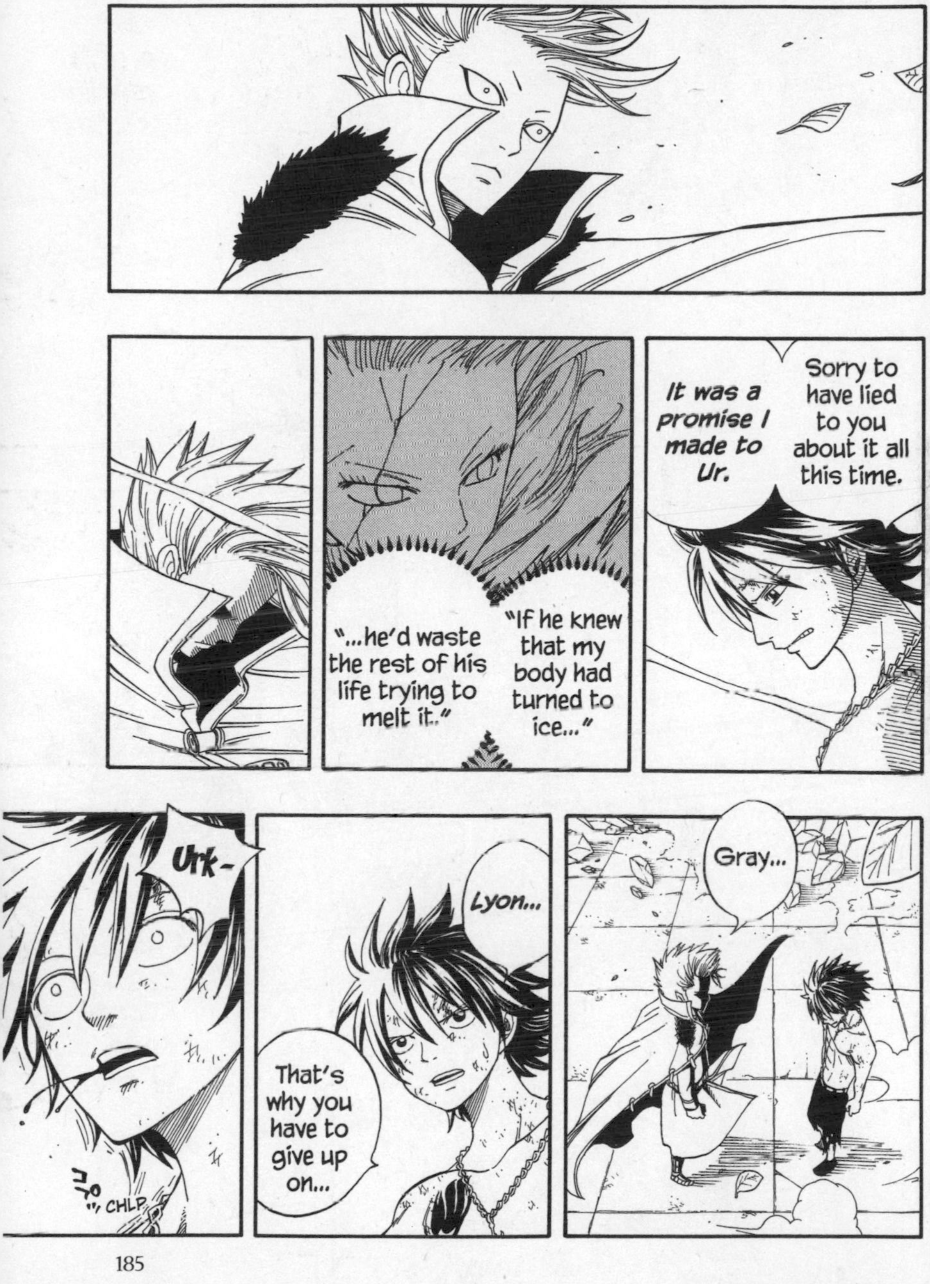
Sorry to have lied to you about it all this time.
It was a promise I made to Ur.
"If he knew that my body had turned to ice..."
"...he'd waste the rest of his life trying to melt it."
Gray...
Lyon...
That's why you have to give up on...
Urk-
CHLP

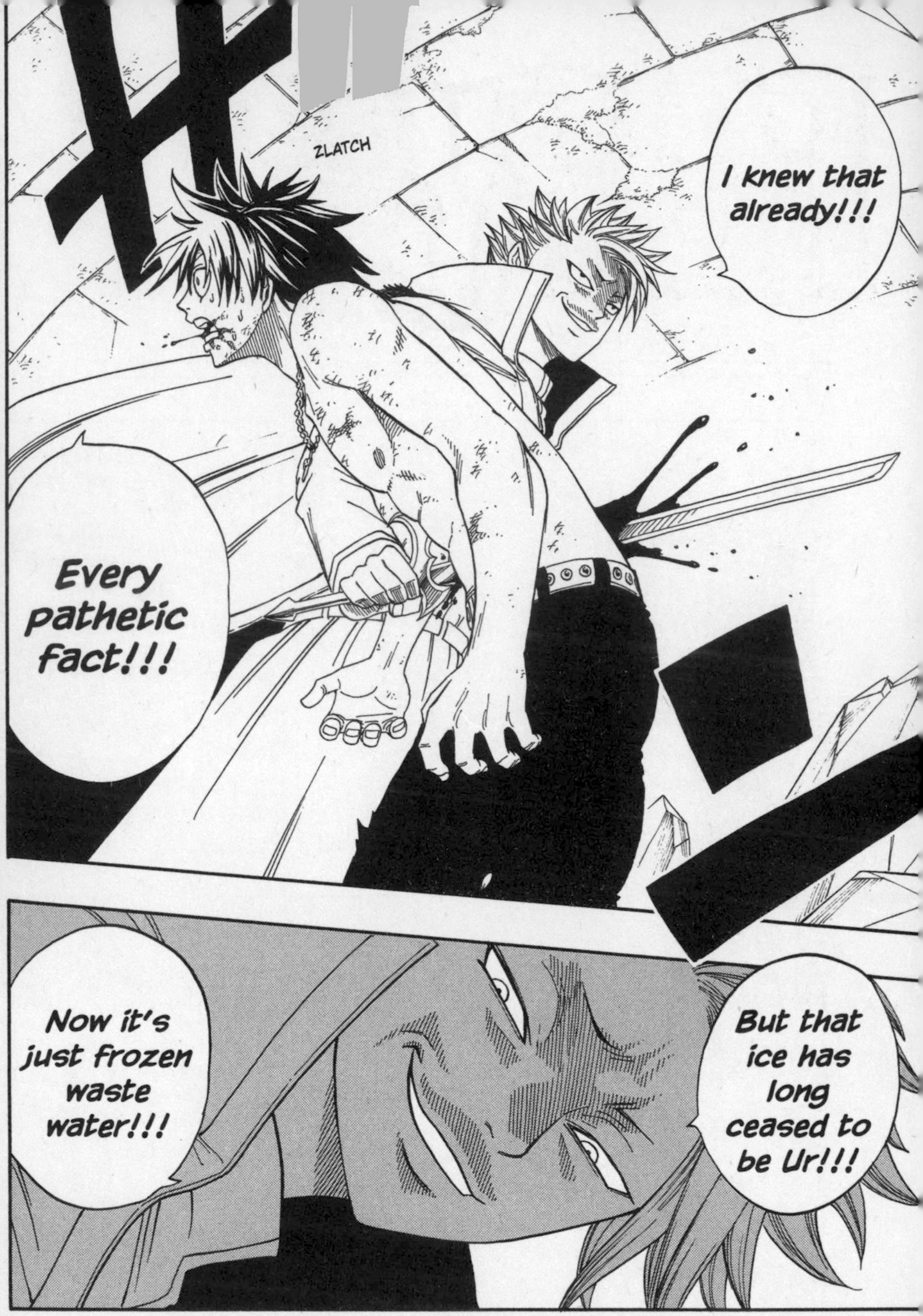
I knew that already!!!
ZLATCH
Every pathetic fact!!!
But that ice has long ceased to be Ur!!!
Now it's just frozen waste water!!!

TO BE CONTINUED

FAIRY TAIL

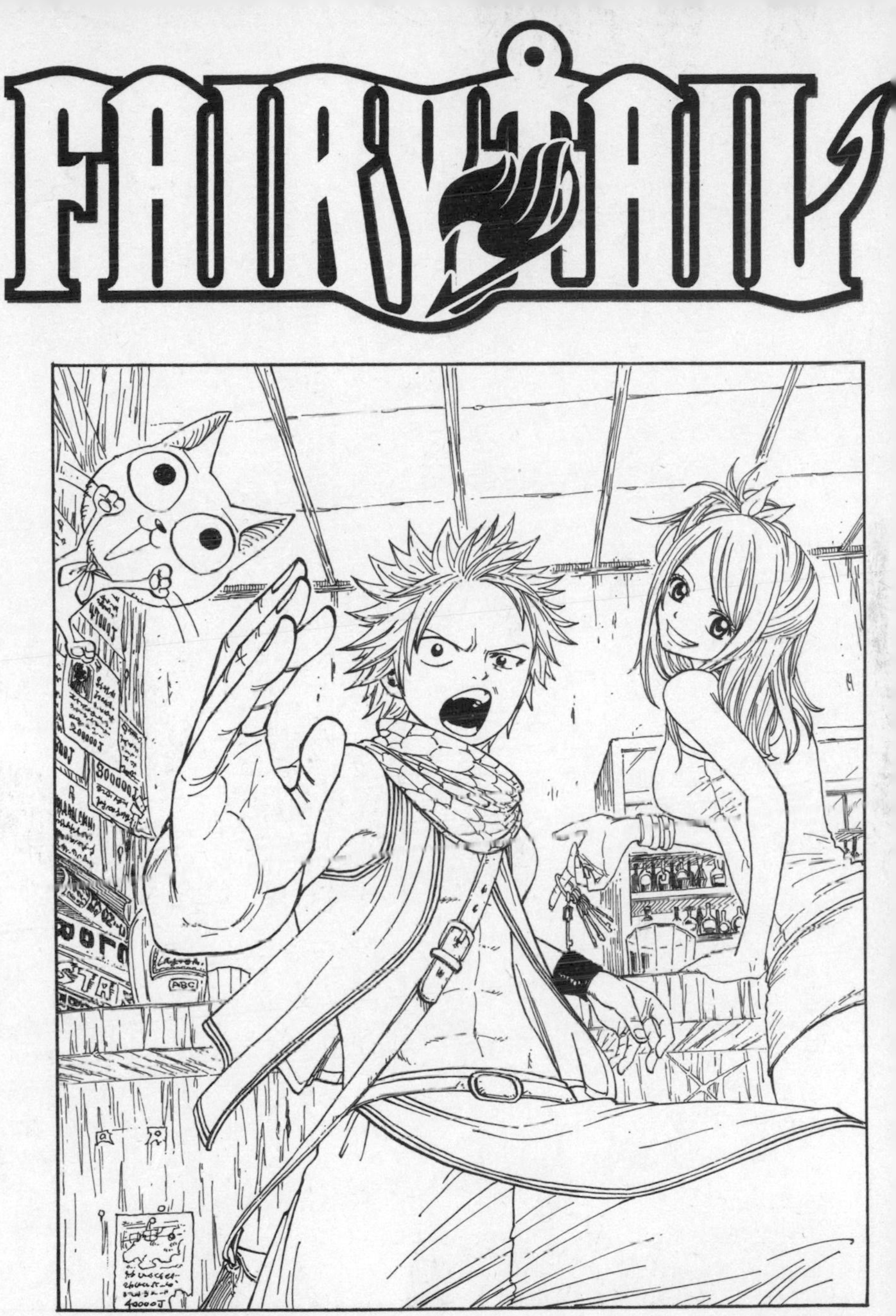

A Coloring Book Page for Good Kids!

TAIL d'ART

The *Fairy Tail* Guild d'Art is an explosion of fan art! Please send in more black-and-white art on large postcard stock!! Those chosen to be published will get a signed mini-poster! ♪ Make sure you write your real name and address on the back of your postcard!

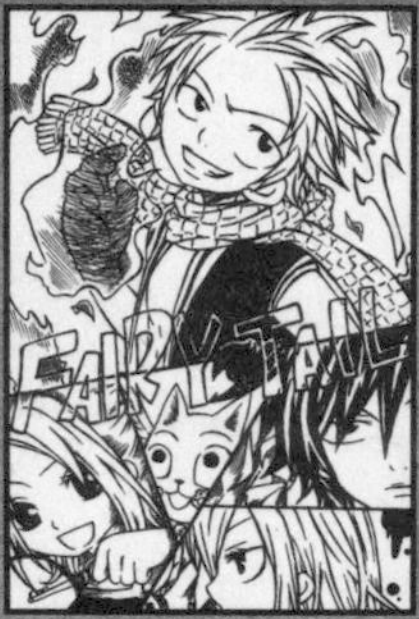
FAIRY TAIL

▼ A cut-in collage of battle scenes. Cool!

Hyogo Prefecture, Mihoko Nii

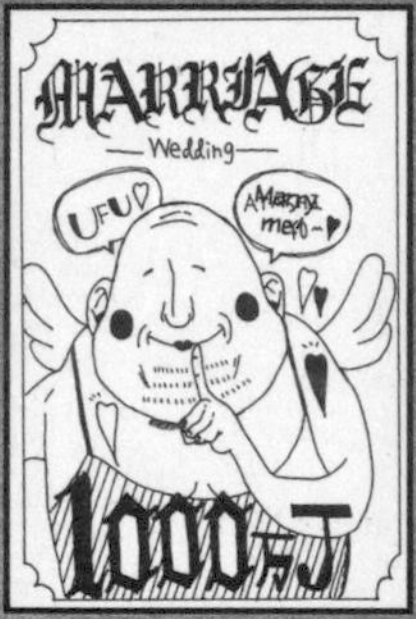
MARRIAGE
Wedding
UFU
1000万J

▼ If somebody marries him, they get 10,000,000J? S-Sorry...

Yamagata Prefecture, Misaki

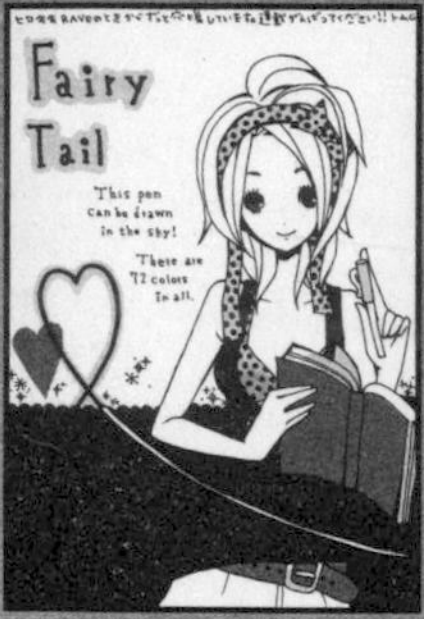
Fairy Tail
This pen can be drawn in the sky!
There are 72 colors in all.

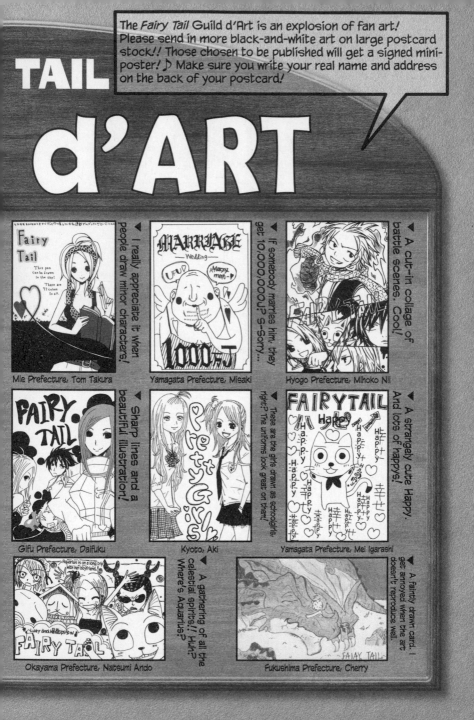

▼ I really appreciate it when people draw minor characters!

Mie Prefecture, Tom Takura

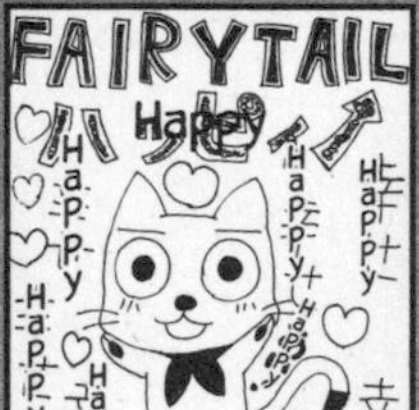
FAIRYTAIL
Happy

▼ A strangely cute Happy. And lots of happys!

Yamagata Prefecture, Mei Igarashi

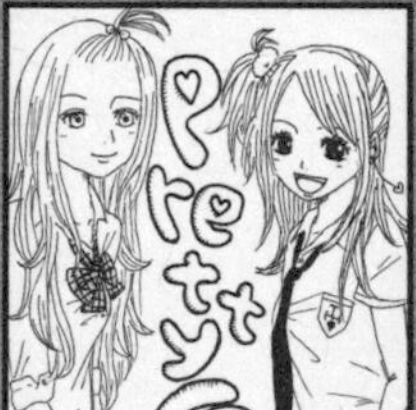
Pretty Girls

▼ These are the girls drawn as schoolgirls, right? The uniforms look great on them!

Kyoto, Aki

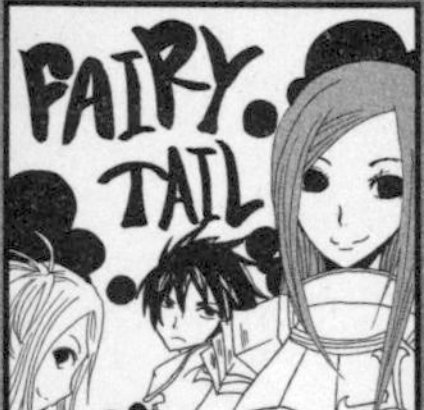
FAIRY. TAIL

▼ Sharp lines and a beautiful illustration!

Gifu Prefecture, Daifuku

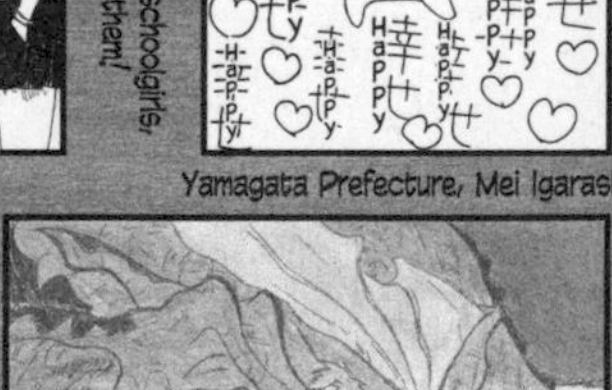

▼ A faintly drawn card. I get annoyed when the art doesn't reproduce well.

Fukushima Prefecture, Cherry

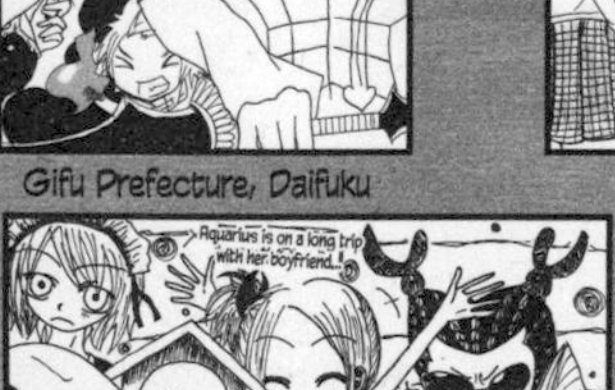
Aquarius is on a long trip with her boyfriend...
FAIRY TAIL

▼ A gathering of all the celestial spirits!! Huh? Where's Aquarius?

Okayama Prefecture, Natsumi Ando

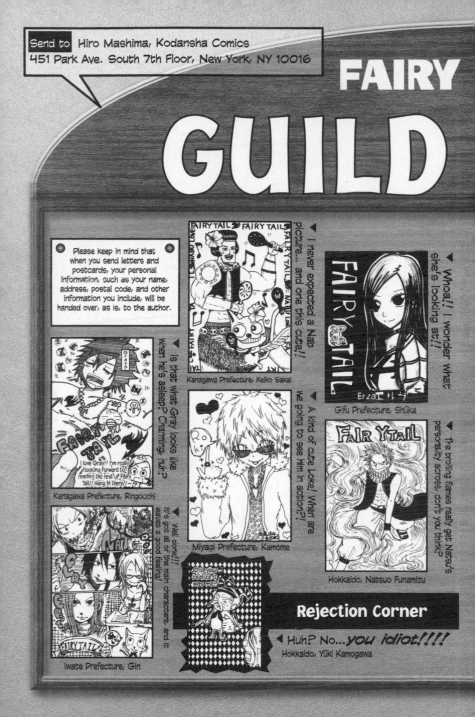

Send to Hiro Mashima, Kodansha Comics
451 Park Ave. South 7th Floor, New York, NY 10016

FAIRY GUILD

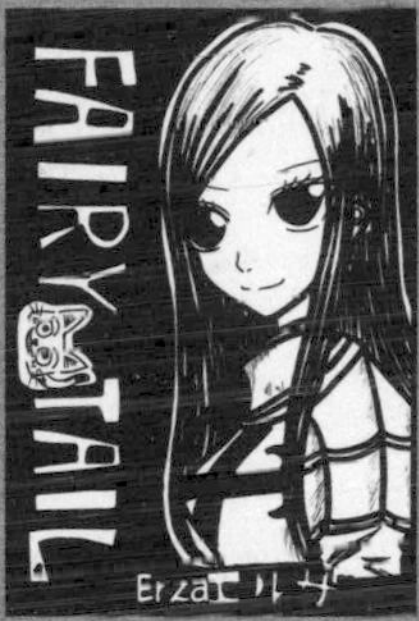
FAIRY TAIL
Erza

◀ Whoa!! I wonder what she's looking at!!

Gifu Prefecture, Shûka

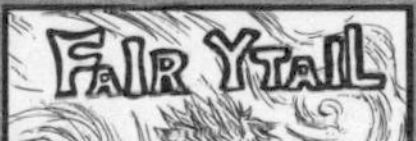
FAIR YTAIL

◀ The broiling flames really get Natsu's personality across, don't you think?

Hokkaido, Natsuo Funamizu

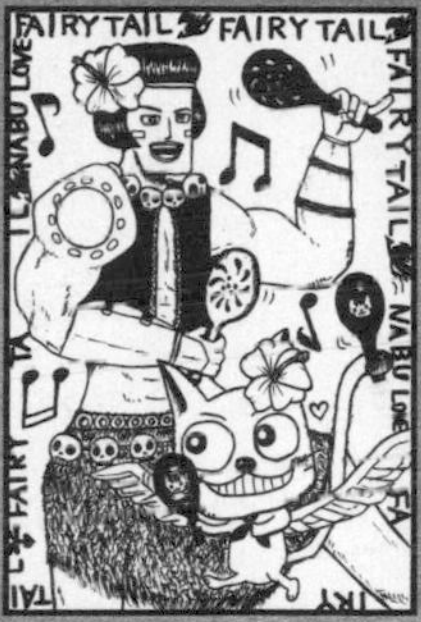
FAIRY TAIL
FAIRY TAIL

◀ I never expected a Nab picture... and one this cute!!

Kanagawa Prefecture, Keiko Sakai

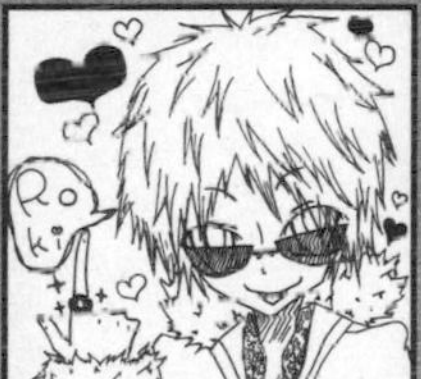

◀ A kind of cute Loke! When are we going to see him in action?!

Miyagi Prefecture, Kamome

Please keep in mind that when you send letters and postcards, your personal information, such as your name, address, postal code, and other information you include, will be handed over, as is, to the author.

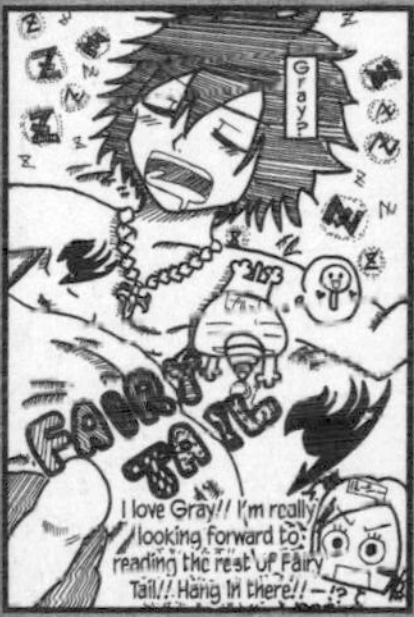
Gray
I love Gray!! I'm really looking forward to reading the rest of Fairy Tail!! Hang in there!!

◀ Is that what Gray looks like when he's asleep? Charming, huh?

Kanagawa Prefecture, Ringocchi

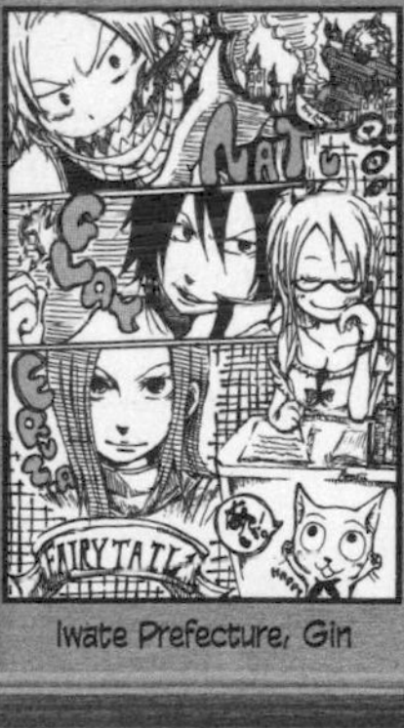
FAIRYTAIL

◀ Well done!!! It's got all of the main characters, and it leaves a good feeling!

Iwate Prefecture, Gin

Rejection Corner

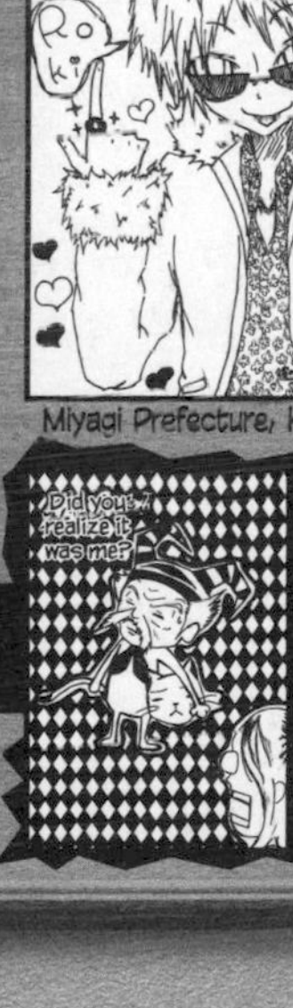
Did you realize it was me?

◀ Huh? No...*you idiot!!!!*

Hokkaido, Yûki Kamogawa

Special Request: "Explain the Mysteries of Fairy Tail!"

From the Fairy Tail Bar

Lucy: Mira-san!! Come look at this for a second!!

Mira: Wow! ♡ Look at all the letters! You've got a lot of fans, Lucy!

Lucy: They aren't my fans! These are letters from our readers! And a whole lot of them say that there are so many mysteries that they're lost!

Mira: I don't think that the author knows the answers either. Can't we just forget we ever saw them?

Lucy: I-I'd rather you didn't say things like that in front of me...

Mira: Well, let's take a look at them. Wow! ♡ This fan artist is good!! ♡

Lucy: That's a postcard for Guild d'Art.

〜〜 Shuffle, shuffle 〜〜 Rip 〜〜

Lucy: For example, this one has a question.

What's the meaning of "ability magic" and "holder magic" that the Vanish Brothers were talking about?

Lucy: Ah! I want to know the answer to that too!!

Mira: Hm...I don't think it's really all that big a deal...

Lucy: They said that Natsu had ability magic and I had holder magic.

Mira: That's right. As the name suggests, ability magic is a kind of magic that, once learned, is connected to one's body.

On the other hand, if you use magic items for your magic, you've got holder magic.

Lucy: Really? When I don't have my keys, I can't use magic, so I have holder magic, huh?

Mira: Erza is too. It wasn't until she got her weapons and defenses that she first started doing magic. That's holder magic.

Lucy: So the magic that Natsu and Gray learned is ability magic, hm?

Mira: Most of the magic you can purchase in shops is holder magic. Even the magic in books. You can read it and remember it, but without the book, you can't do the magic.

Lucy: But it seems like anybody can do holder magic...

Mira: Of course, nobody can do the high-speed requip like Erza without long training.

Lucy: And I finally managed to do a forced closure!!

Mira: Oh? Did you really, Lucy?!

Lucy: I sure did! When I was attacked by a weird woman on Galuna Island!

Mira: Oh, then maybe I can ask a favor!

Lucy: What favor...?

Mira: The bar. I was hoping you could force the bar to close and send everybody home...

Lucy: That isn't the kind of "closure" I'm talking about!!!

We're collecting questions about *Fairy Tail!* Send them to the address below!

↓

Kodansha Comics
751 Park Ave. South, 7th Floor
New York, NY 10016
publicity@kodansha-usa.com

AFTERWORD

One year!! It's been one year since *Fairy Tail* first appeared in the magazine!! Time sure flies, huh? This is my second continuing series in a weekly magazine, so I figured that I'd be able to go for at least a year.... Still, I never thought too hard about it, but it's actually been one whole year. "Ah, this is great," I say with a sense of relief straight from the heart.

What was the hardest thing I had to do this year? Making sure my staff knew exactly what their jobs were. About the time that *Fairy Tail* began, nearly all of my staff from the previous series had gone on to other things. Some made their own debuts. Some went on long trips. I had sad partings and happy partings. The only one left from the previous team was the newest guy of the old group, Bôzu-kun. So on *FT*, I promoted him to interim chief, and I placed the three new people under him. It was a real chore! Nearly everybody was new!! At the time, it was an awful lot of work, but recently everybody's finally gotten a rough idea of their jobs, and now they really help me out! Also, they're a great bunch! They're all such good workers that I've decided I'd rather work with a nice new guy over a talented annoying guy any day. I know that idea isn't very professional, but we spend a lot of time face-to-face, so it's better to be with people you can have fun with!

And so, even though we have a lot of fun on the job, I want to say that I really appreciate each and every person on my staff! Good job, everybody, and I'm hoping we can keep working together for a long time to come!! And to all of you readers, thank you so much for all of your encouragement! FT still has a long way to go!! We'll go for at least three years!!!

About the Creator

HIRO MASHIMA was born May 3, 1977, in Nagano Prefecture. His series *Rave Master* has made him one of the most popular manga artists in America. *Fairy Tail*, currently being serialized in *Weekly Shonen Magazine*, is his latest creation.

Translation Notes

Japanese is a tricky language for most Westerners, and translation is often more art than science. For your edification and reading pleasure, here are notes on some of the places where we could have gone in a different direction in our translation of the work, or where a Japanese cultural reference is used.

General Notes:
Wizard

In the original Japanese version of *Fairy Tail*, you'll find panels in which the English word "wizard" is part of the original illustration. So this translation has taken that as its inspiration and translates the word *madôshi* as "wizard." But *madôshi*'s meaning is similar to certain Japanese words that have been borrowed by the English language, such as judo ("the soft way") and kendo ("the way of the sword"). *Madô* is "the way of magic," and *madôshi* are those who follow the way of magic. So although the word "wizard" is used in the original dialogue, a Japanese reader would be likely to think not of traditional Western wizards such as Merlin or Gandalf, but of martial artists.

Names

Hiro Mashima has graciously agreed to provide official English spellings for just about all of the characters in *Fairy Tail*. Because this version of *Fairy Tail* is the first publication of most of these spellings, there will inevitably be differences between these spellings and some of the fan interpretations that may have spread throughout the Web or in other fan circles. Rest assured that the spellings contained in this book are the spellings that Mashima-sensei wanted for *Fairy Tail*.

Wave-Motion Yûka, page 23

Old-school anime fans may remember a TV series called *Star Blazers*, which was a late-seventies U.S. adaptation of the classic anime *Space Cruiser Yamato* (*Uchû Senkan Yamato*). The title spaceship's ultimate weapon was a huge cannon called the Wave-Motion Gun. The title of this chapter, Wave-Motion Yûka, uses the very same kanji used in the name of the gun, so I translated it the same way.

Toby's arm tattoos, page 34

Just in case you were wondering, the tattoo on Toby's left arm seems to be the Lamia Scale guild symbol. On Toby's right arm the tattoo says "Sashimi," the Japanese raw-fish (or raw anything, really) dish. By the way, most Westerners think that sushi is Japan's raw-fish dish, but that's a misconception. The base to sushi is rice, and many different kinds of foods, raw and cooked, go on top (or rolled within) the rice to make sushi. Sashimi, on the other hand, is a dish consisting of raw foods that are usually dipped in a soy-based dipping sauce before eating.

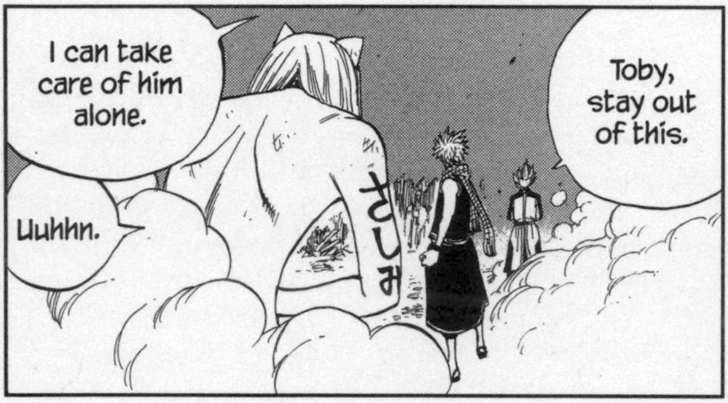
Toby, stay out of this.
I can take care of him alone.
さしみ
Uuhhn.

Erza…san, page 83

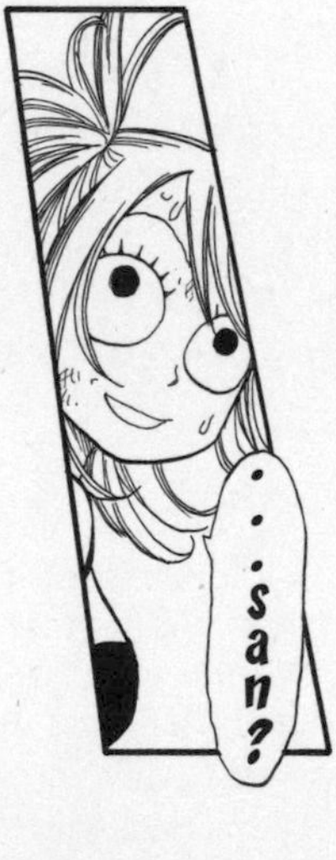
...san?

This is a perfect example of honorifics (described at the end of these notes) in action. One can only call close friends and colleagues by name without any honorifics. To do so without permission is presumptuous and can anger the addressee. In this example, Lucy thinks Erza is being her friend when she takes down the giant rat, but she suddenly realizes that Erza isn't being a friend at all, and the intimacy isn't welcome. It's then that Lucy adds the *-san* honorific onto Erza's name as a sign of respect (or, at least, fear).

Erza-sama?!! page 96

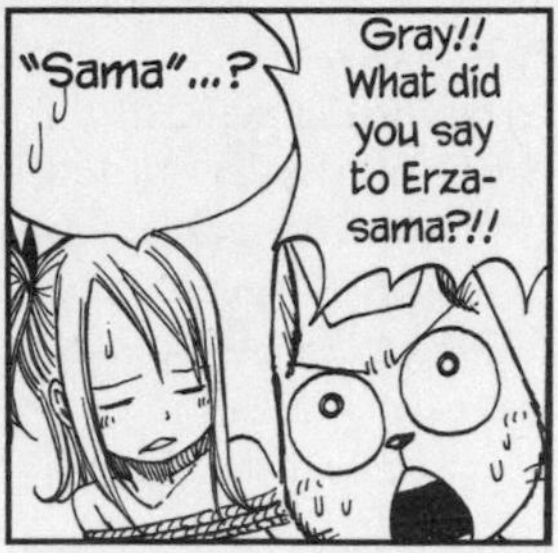
Gray!! What did you say to Erza-sama?!!
"Sama"...?

And this is a case of Happy using an inflated honorific as a way to suck-up to Erza. Using an honorific that is too exalted is much like Western "yes-men," who agree with anything a person in power says in order to stay on their good side.

Loan, page 127

One of the indicators of being grown-up for a man in Japanese society is to take on a home loan for the house in which one's family resides. Housing is scarce and expensive, and unlike in the West, houses lose value as the years go by. When a person buys land in Japan, the first thing they usually do is knock down the old house and build a new one. This all takes a lot of money, and even though Japan has better savings rates than most Western nations, nearly anyone who needs a home must accept a home loan to go along with it. Japanese businessmen hate their loans, but most are dutifully paying theirs off.

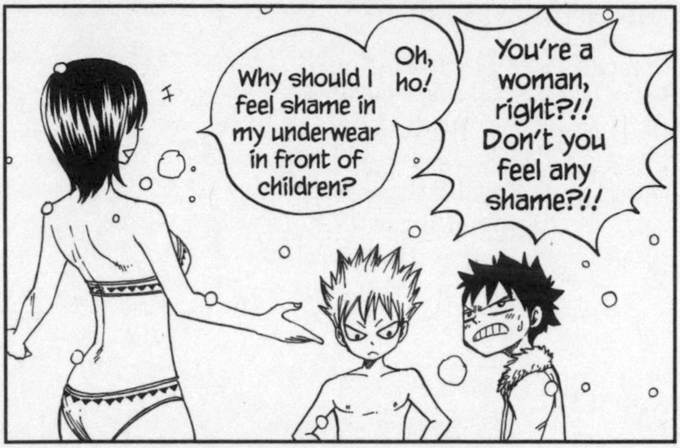
You're a woman, right?!! Don't you feel any shame?!!
Oh, ho!
Why should I feel shame in my underwear in front of children?

Shame in front of children, page 130

Although Japan is not as open with nudity as many of the rumors would have one believe, one common custom is to take baths with one's children. Some bathtubs are even made specifically so that a parent and child can easily fit in the bath together. The master-disciple relationship is similar to parent-child, and although the prevailing attitude is changing, there are a lot of Japanese who would feel no shame being nude in front of a child disciple if the situation warranted it. (The changing attitude is reflected in Gray's assumption that Ur should be ashamed and Ur feeling no shame at all.)

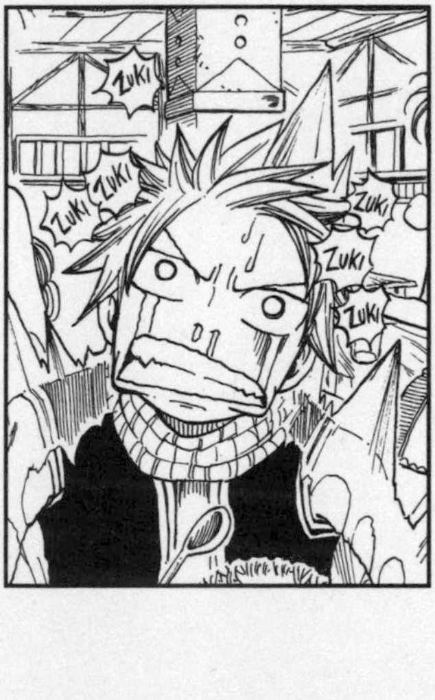
ZUKI
ZUKI
ZUKI
ZUKI
ZUKI
ZUKI

Zuki zuki, page 167

The sound effect *zuki zuki,* which is written around Natsu's head in this splash page, is one of the standard sound effects for stabbing pain. It's indicating that Natsu is having a bad case of a headache called "brain freeze" by some, where one eats ice or ice cream too fast and gets a sharp headache.

Namahage demon, page 180

At the beginning of each year in Akita Prefecture in northern Japan, the Namahage demons come down from the mountain and enter the local homes looking for unruly children and new residents who are lazy or disrespect their elders. Fortunately for the children and newcomers, the adults and locals defend these people from the Namahage demons. Actually, this is a long tradition, where local young men dress in demon masks and grass clothing for the New Year's rite. There is also a Namahage festival in February for tourists, featuring the demons in a ritual march.

It's been a year!!!
At about the same time this book
will be coming out, *Fairy Tail* will
have been published for a year.
A reason to celebrate!!! And it's
all thanks to you readers, the
editorial department, and my
staff! Thank you, everybody!!
And from now on, we're going to
do this at a full-out run!! Even if
we tumble down the cliff, we'll
run to climb back up again. We'll
keep running, even if somebody
says, "You're going the wrong
way!" We're going to do this!!

—Hiro Mashima

Honorifics Explained

Throughout the Kodansha Comics books, you will find Japanese honorifics left intact in the translations. For those not familiar with how the Japanese use honorifics and, more important, how they differ from American honorifics, we present this brief overview.

Politeness has always been a critical facet of Japanese culture. Ever since the feudal era, when Japan was a highly stratified society, use of honorifics—which can be defined as polite speech that indicates relationship or status—has played an essential role in the Japanese language. When addressing someone in Japanese, an honorific usually takes the form of a suffix attached to one's name (example: "Asuna-san"), is used as a title at the end of one's name, or appears in place of the name itself (example: "Negi-sensei," or simply "Sensei!").

Honorifics can be expressions of respect or endearment. In the context of manga and anime, honorifics give insight into the nature of the relationship between characters. Many English translations leave out these important honorifics and therefore distort the feel of the original Japanese. Because Japanese honorifics contain nuances that English honorifics lack, it is our policy at Kodansha not to translate them. Here, instead, is a guide to some of the honorifics you may encounter in Kodansha Comics.

-san: This is the most common honorific and is equivalent to Mr., Miss, Ms., or Mrs. It is the all-purpose honorific and can be used in any situation where politeness is required.

-sama: This is one level higher than "-san" and is used to confer great respect.

-dono: This comes from the word "tono," which means "lord." It is an even higher level than "-sama" and confers utmost respect.

-kun: This suffix is used at the end of boys' names to express familiarity or endearment. It is also sometimes used by men among friends, or when addressing someone younger or of a lower station.

-chan: This is used to express endearment, mostly toward girls. It is also used for little boys, pets, and even between lovers. It gives a sense of childish cuteness.

Bozu: This is an informal way to refer to a boy, similar to the English terms "kid" and "squirt."

Sempai/
Senpai: This title suggests that the addressee is one's senior in a group or organization. It is most often used in a school setting, where underclassmen refer to their upperclassmen as "sempai." It can also be used in the workplace, such as when a newer employee addresses an employee who has seniority in the company.

Kohai: This is the opposite of "sempai" and is used toward under-classmen in school or newcomers in the workplace. It connotes that the addressee is of a lower station.

Sensei: Literally meaning "one who has come before," this title is used for teachers, doctors, or masters of any profession or art.

-[blank]: This is usually forgotten in these lists, but it is perhaps the most significant difference between Japanese and English. The lack of honorific means that the speaker has permission to address the person in a very intimate way. Usually, only family, spouses, or very close friends have this kind of permission. Known as *yobisute*, it can be gratifying when someone who has earned the intimacy starts to call one by one's name without an honorific. But when that intimacy hasn't been earned, it can be very insulting.

Preview of Volume 6

We're pleased to present you with a preview from volume 6, now available from Kodansha Comics. Check out our Web site (www.kodanshacomics.com) for more details!

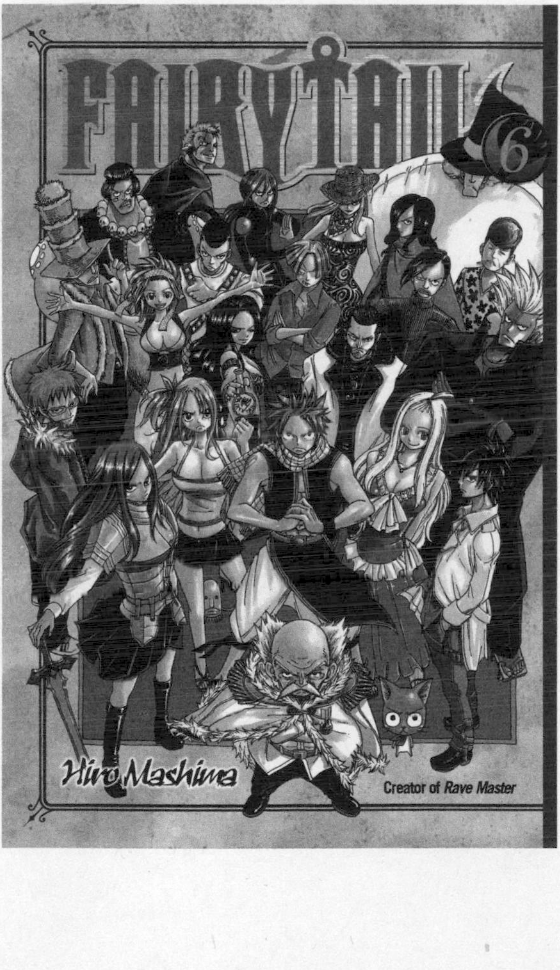
FAIRY TAIL
6
Hiro Mashima
Creator of Rave Master

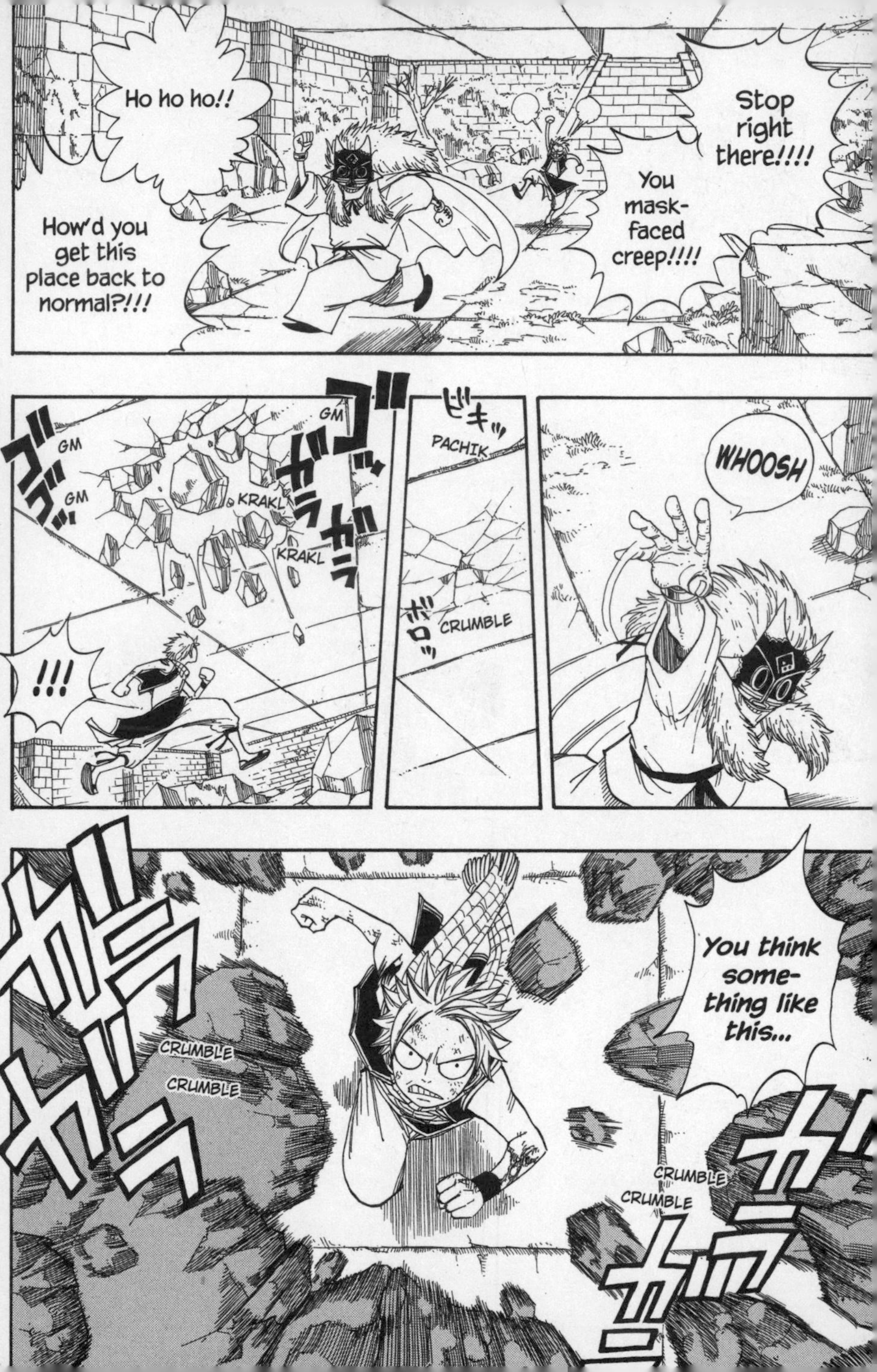
Stop right there!!!!
You mask-faced creep!!!!
Ho ho ho!!
How'd you get this place back to normal?!!!
WHOOSH
ビキッ
PACHIK
ボロッ
CRUMBLE
ゴッ
GM
ガラ
ガラ
KRAKL
KRAKL
ゴゴゴ
GM
GM
!!!
You think something like this...
ガラガラ
CRUMBLE
CRUMBLE
ガラガラ
CRUMBLE
CRUMBLE

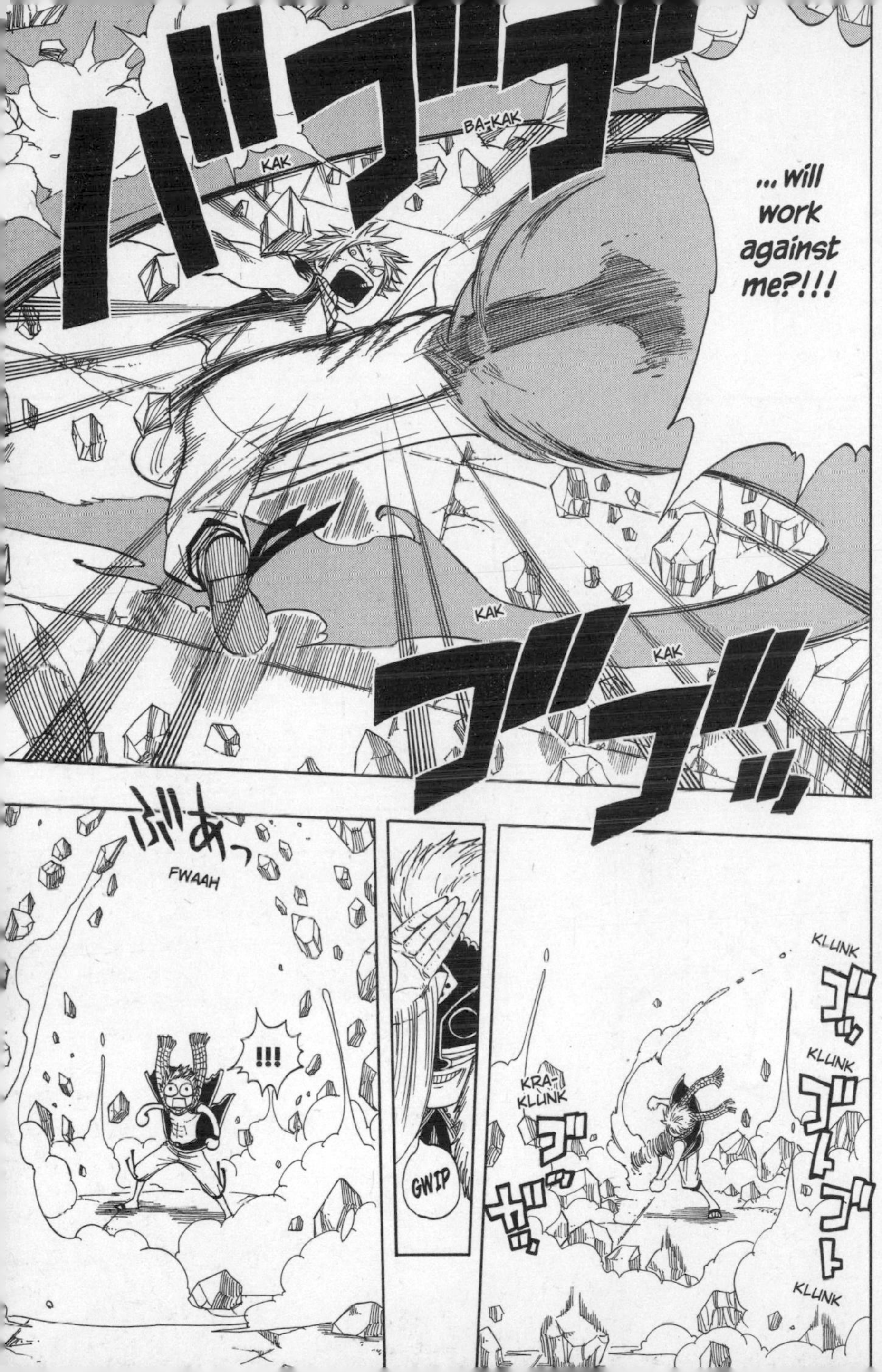

... will work against me?!!!
BA-KAK
KAK
KAK
KAK
KLUNK
KLUNK
KRA-KLUNK
KLUNK
GWIP
ぶあっ
FWAAH
!!!

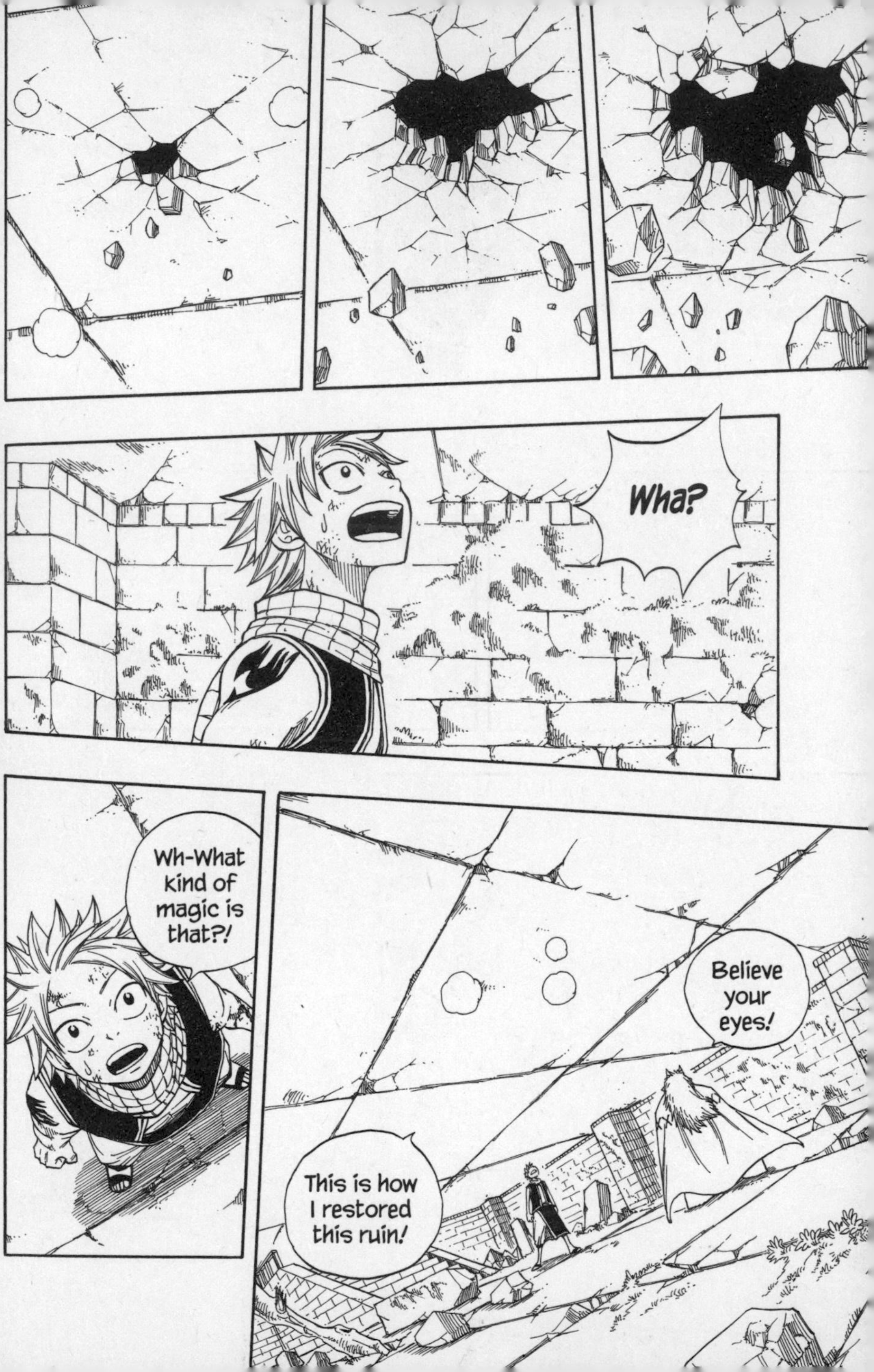
Wha?
Believe your eyes!
This is how I restored this ruin!
Wh-What kind of magic is that?!

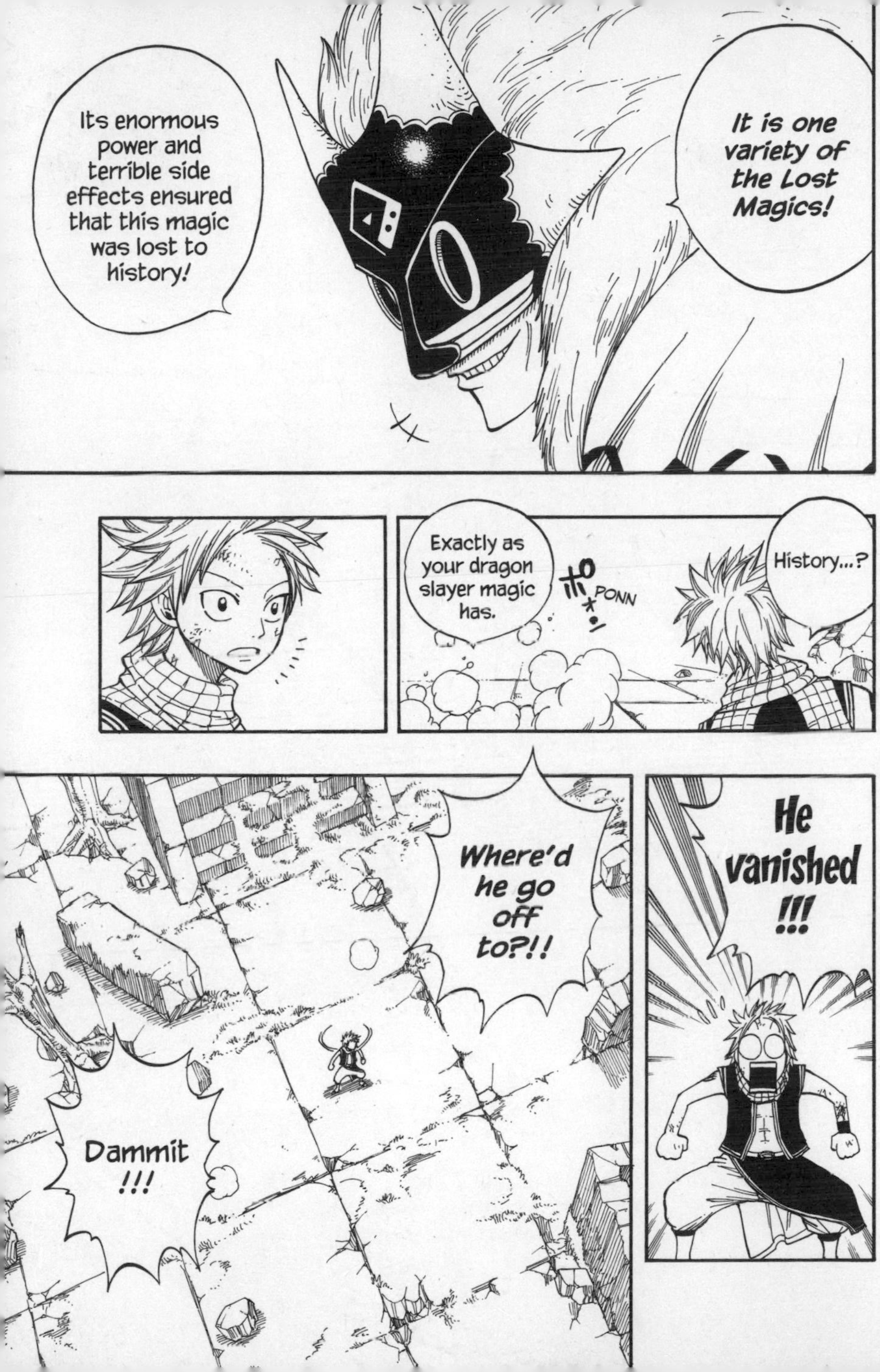
It is one variety of the Lost Magics!
Its enormous power and terrible side effects ensured that this magic was lost to history!
History...?
Exactly as your dragon slayer magic has.
PONN
He vanished!!!
Where'd he go off to?!!
Dammit!!!

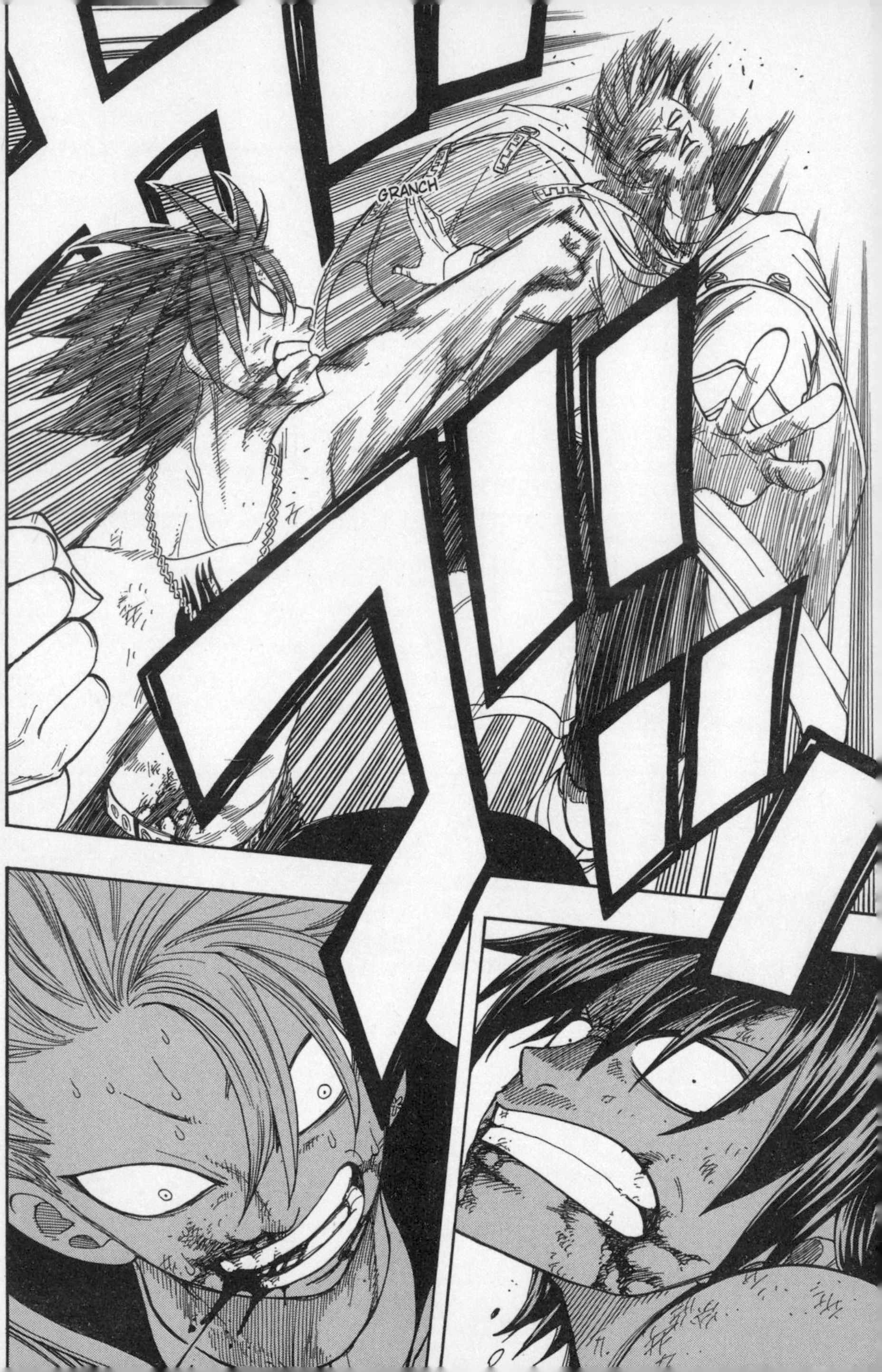
GRANCH

Fairy Tail volume 5 is a work of fiction. Names, characters, places, and incidents are the products of the author's imagination or are used fictitiously. Any resemblance to actual events, locales, or persons, living or dead, is entirely coincidental.

A Kodansha Comics trade Paperback Original

Published in the United States by Kodansha Comics, an imprint of Kodansha USA Publishing, LLC., New York.

Publication rights for this English edition arranged through Kodansha Ltd., Tokyo.

First published in Japan in 2007 by Kodansha Ltd., Tokyo

ISBN 978-1-61262-098-5

Printed in the United States of America

www.kodanshacomics.com

18 17 16 15 14 13 12 11 10

Translator/Adapter—William Flanagan
Lettering—North Market Street Graphics

TOMARE!

止まれ

[STOP!]

You're going the wrong way!

Manga is a completely different type of reading experience.

To start at the *beginning*,
go to the *end*!

That's right! Authentic manga is read the traditional Japanese way—from right to left, exactly the opposite of how American books are read. It's easy to follow: Just go to the other end of the book and read each page—and each panel—from right side to left side, starting at the top right. Now you're experiencing manga as it was meant to be!